Praying
with
Saint Paul

Daily Reflections on the Letters of the Apostle Paul

Edited by Father Peter John Cameron, O.P.

MAGNIFICAT®

Scripture selections are taken from the *New American Bible with Revised New Testament and Psalms*, Copyright © 1991, 1986, 1970 by the Confraternity of Christian Doctrine, Inc., Washington, DC. Used with permission. All rights reserved. No portion of the *New American Bible* may be reprinted without permission in writings from the copyright holder.

Edition number: MGN08010. August 2008.

ISBN: 978-0-9798086-2-3

F o r e w o r d

Father Peter John Cameron, O.P.

I BEGAN TO DEVELOP A SPECIAL LOVE for Saint Paul in the years when I was studying for the priesthood. Saint Paul had helped me get through college. Very often I would begin my day by praying a passage from the Letter to the Romans where the counsel of the Apostle was a constant source of solace: offer your body as a living sacrifice holy and acceptable to God; do not conform yourself to this age but be transformed by the renewal of your mind; then you will be able to judge what is God's will, what is good, pleasing, and perfect (see Rom 12: 1-2). For me, college was a real struggle, challenging and difficult. Making these words of Saint Paul the heart of my morning prayer gave me a new heart to meet each day with hope.

But it was in a Scripture class on the Acts of the Apostles taught by a saintly Franciscan friar that my appreciation for Saint Paul really blossomed. I was assigned to give a class presentation on Saint Paul's speech to the elders at Miletus. In the course of my research, I discovered the fact that several biblical scholars hold the opinion that there is a definite parallel between this farewell address of Paul and the Last Supper discourse of Jesus. The comparisons are amazing.

Paul as Jesus

Try looking at Saint Paul's speech (Acts 20: 17-38), and then compare it to, for example, the Last Supper discourse of the Gospel of John (chapters 14-17). Among the many parallels, Saint Paul attests to how he served the Lord in humility, despite the sorrows and trials that came his way from enemies. And Jesus says in all humility: "The words that I speak to you I do not speak on my own... The Father is greater than I... The world [has] hated me" (Jn 14: 10, 28; 15: 18). Paul testifies that he never shrank from telling the people what was for their good – he taught them constantly in public and in private. Jesus declares, "Father, I revealed your name... The words you gave to me I have given to them" (Jn 17: 6, 8). Saint Paul states that he insisted solemnly on faith in our Lord Jesus Christ. Likewise, Jesus says to his disciples, "You have faith in God; have faith also in me" (Jn 14: 1). Paul claims that he will put value on his own life only if he can finish his race and complete his service of witnessing to the Gospel. In the same spirit, Jesus prays, "Father, [...] I glorified you on earth by accomplishing the work you gave me to do" (Jn 17: 4). Then Saint Paul says that none of those listening to him will ever see his face again. And Jesus says, "In a little while the world will no longer see me" (Jn 14: 19). Paul warns that when he is gone, savage wolves will come to ravage the flock. Jesus warns that his disciples will be persecuted: not only will they be expelled from the synagogue – they will be put to death by people who claim to be serving God (see Jn 16: 2). Paul then commends his people to the Lord and to God's gracious Word which can enlarge them. And Jesus prays to his Father for his followers: "Consecrate them in the truth. Your word is truth" (Jn 17: 17).

After this speech, the Bible says that Paul knelt down and prayed with the people. They all began to weep without restraint, throwing their arms around him and kissing him, so upset were they to hear that they would never see his face again. And Jesus told his disciples: "You will weep and mourn...; you will grieve, but your grief will become joy" (Jn 16: 20).

I was struck at the deliberate manner in which the portrait of Saint Paul on the way to his martyrdom is modeled on Jesus as he approaches his passion. And when I saw how moved the people were at Paul's farewell, I realized that this was a man I needed to get to know better. I wanted to be like him who was so much like Christ.

Ourselves as Paul

When it comes to the spiritual life, we so easily come up with pretexts for discounting the possibility of ever becoming holy. But the great genius of Saint Paul is the way he strips us of every alibi – there is no excuse for not pursuing sanctity. With an authority like no other, Saint Paul attests that "God chose the lowly and despised of the world, those who count for nothing, to reduce to nothing those who are something" (1 Cor 1: 28). This means that no matter how inadequate, deficient, or unworthy I may think I am, the fact is that God has chosen *precisely* people like me. The Father's consummate mercy is expressed in the fact that God "calls into being what does not exist" (Rom 4: 17)… especially what does not yet exist *in my person* that God purposefully calls into being so that I will become fulfilled and happy. When I verify the fact that God acts this way in the world, I get filled with an irrepressible hope, and "hope does not disappoint, because the love of God has been poured out into our hearts" (Rom 5: 5). What is more, my experience of personal inability and anguish becomes a tool for sanctifying others, for God "encourages us in our every affliction, so that we may be able to encourage those who are in any affliction with the encouragement with which we ourselves are encouraged by God" (2 Cor 1: 4).

In order to bless us with unfailing certainty and to protect us from the presumption that would tempt us to take all this for granted, God does something that, on the surface, may seem strangely contradictory. Saint Paul explains how, at a certain point in his life, he and his companions were left to feel like men condemned to death so "that we might trust not in ourselves but in God who raises the dead" (2 Cor 1: 9). God's extreme tenderness extends to providing safeguards that prevent us from falling into self-destructive self-reliance. In this blessed relationship of holy dependence, our freedom is set free (see Gal 5: 1). And even though it may look to the world as if we have nothing, as followers of Jesus Christ we in fact possess everything (see 2 Cor 6: 10). To insure our fidelity and growth in this priceless way of living, God has given us an infallible method: we are "always carrying about in the body the dying of Jesus, so that the life of Jesus may also be manifested in our body" (2 Cor 4: 10). In another place, Saint Paul says it even more emphatically: "I have been crucified with Christ; yet I live, no longer I, but Christ lives in me... For to me life is Christ" (Gal 2: 19-20; Phil 1: 21). This is what prompts Paul to declare: "I even consider everything as a loss because of the supreme good of knowing Christ Jesus my Lord. For his sake I have accepted the loss of all things and I consider them so much rubbish, that I may gain Christ" (Phil 3: 8).

All because of God's goodness – and not because of our own – Jesus Christ has loved us, and that undeserved, indescribable love has utterly transformed us. It has become *who* we are. For "what will separate us from the love of Christ? Will anguish, or distress, or persecution, or famine, or nakedness, or peril, or the sword?" (Rom 8: 35). Paul knows from personal experience that none of these sufferings can ever sever us from the love of Christ because Paul himself personally *went through every one of them* in the course of his life. Christ's love consistently conquered! Which leads Saint Paul to proclaim that "in all these things we conquer overwhelmingly through him who loved us" (Rom 8: 37).

Saint Paul concludes that all that really matters is that one become a new creation (see Gal 6: 15 and 2 Cor 5: 17). And how does this come about? All "depends on faith" (Rom 4: 16). "You have had yourselves washed, you were sanctified, you were justified in the name of the Lord Jesus Christ" (1 Cor 6: 11). In the light of all this, Paul's claim that, as Christians, we even boast of our afflictions (see Rom 5: 3) no longer seems strange but rather perfectly reasonable. As Saint Paul explains, "I will rather boast most gladly of my weaknesses, in order that the power of Christ may dwell with me. Therefore, I am content with weaknesses, insults, hardships, persecutions, and constraints, for the sake of Christ; for when I am weak, then I am strong" (2 Cor 12: 9-10). Even Paul's command, that otherwise would strike us as arrogantly egoistic, comes across in crystal clarity: "Be imitators of me, as I am of Christ" (1 Cor 11: 1). We imitate Paul in the way that he abandons himself totally to the mercy of Jesus Christ. It is the historical fact of his example that dares us to do the same with our life.

How this book came about

The inspiration for the publication of *Praying with Saint Paul* came with the Holy Father's announcement that the Church would celebrate a special Jubilee Year to the Apostle Paul from June 28, 2008 to June 29, 2009 on the occasion of the bimillennium of Saint Paul's birth. When Pope Benedict XVI first announced this Pauline Jubilee Year, he stressed the fact that Saint Paul "lived and worked for Christ, for him he suffered and died. How timely his example is today!" As a way of commemorating the special Jubilee Year, the Holy Father indicated that "special publications on Pauline texts will also be promoted in order to make ever more widely known the immense wealth of the teaching they contain, a true patrimony of humanity redeemed by Christ." MAGNIFICAT'S response to this wish of the Pope is the book you now hold in your hands.

Why *Praying with Saint Paul*?

Since Saint Paul's words express his own profound relationship with Jesus Christ, they remain an indispensable aid for perfecting our prayer life and for deepening our union with the Lord. It is the apostle Paul who enjoins us time and again in his letters to "persevere in prayer" (Rom 12: 12; Col 4: 2) and to "pray without ceasing" (1 Thes 5: 17). "In everything," he says, "by prayer and petition, with thanksgiving, make your requests known to God" (Phil 4: 6). Rather than being an academic study guide, *Praying with Saint Paul* is a handbook to assist you in doing *lectio divina* with the letters of Saint Paul – that is, to engage in the age-old prayer form of sacred reading, specially attuned to the Spirit, that enables the reader to appropriate the wisdom of the texts and thereby come to greater spiritual maturity.

It makes sense to call on the many writings of Saint Paul for this purpose since Paul's letters comprise such a prominent place in the lectionary for Mass. How often during the Liturgy of the Word do we hear the lector proclaim, "A reading from the Letter of Saint Paul to the…?" Yet, it is not often that we get the chance to delve deeply into Paul's words, to meditate on them, and to plumb the meaning of his insights. *Praying with Saint Paul* takes you to the heart of Saint Paul so that, by praying his words, you can take Saint Paul's love for Christ to heart. The newfound appreciation gained for the wisdom of Saint Paul hopefully will move you to want to pray more and will serve to enhance your participation in Sunday Mass week by week.

How do we use *Praying with Saint Paul*? The best way to begin is by setting aside a definite time each day, such as the morning with your other prayers, or maybe at lunchtime, to pray with the book. You might want to start by singing the hymn to Saint Paul found on the inside cover. Then slowly and prayerfully pray the brief excerpt from the letter of Saint Paul given for that day. After a few moments of prayerful silence, read the reflection by the writer for the day. Ask yourself how what the author proposes in that reflection is verified in your own life experience – how does what Saint Paul say apply to my life? Spend some more moments in silence, meditating on what the Lord has shown you. Then conclude by praying the prayer on the bottom of each page. By the end of one year, you will have reflected systematically on some of the most significant passages from the corpus of Saint Paul, from the Letter to the Romans to the Letter to Philemon.

May Saint Paul's timeless example, wisdom, inspiration, and intercession enlighten, encourage, and generate you every day of the year.

Saint Paul:
The Apostle of Christ Crucified

James Monti

It was on a dusty road leading to Damascus that Saul, until then a passionate enemy of the cross of Christ (see Phil 3: 18), met at noon in a blaze of light the very One who was nailed to the cross at noon on Good Friday (see Acts 9: 3-9; 22: 6-11; 26: 12-18). Stricken blind, the sightless Saul could only see Christ, just as on Good Friday the sky turned dark round about Christ crucified (see Mt 27: 45). And the very first words that Saul was to hear from the Lord were about the cross, the cross that his disciples were bearing in union with their Savior: "Saul, Saul, why are you persecuting me?" (Acts 9: 4). Saul's blindness lasted three days, during which he neither ate nor drank (see Acts 9: 9), not unlike the Savior's three days in the dark of the tomb. And just as on the third day the stone before the Lord's tomb was rolled back when he rose from the dead (see Mt 28: 2), so with Saul his triduum of blindness ended when the scale-like coverings over his eyes fell away (see Acts 9: 18). How fitting it was that Saul's conversion, from Saul the persecutor to Paul the Apostle of the Gentiles, should bear a resemblance to the triduum of the Lord, for he was to become the great apostle of the cross and the resurrection, preaching both unceasingly in his epistles.

Paul and the Paschal Mystery

It is clear from the writings of Saint Paul that he is among the greatest of the Church's contemplatives of the passion. Defining his mission as that of preaching "Christ crucified" (1 Cor 1: 23), he declared his one glory to be "the cross of our Lord Jesus Christ" (Gal 6: 14). He sees discipleship as union with Christ crucified: "I have been crucified with Christ" (Gal 2: 19). Certainly it is in large part through the teaching of Paul that the crucifix has become the pre-eminent symbol of our faith. Moreover, in his writings Paul adds to what we know from the Gospels about Holy Week and Easter. He gives us his own account of the Holy Thursday institution of the Eucharist (see 1 Cor 11: 23-26), the details of which he would have learned from the other apostles. And it is only from Paul that we know of two further appearances of Christ after his resurrection not mentioned in the Gospels: those of Christ to the apostle Saint James the Less (the son of Alphaeus) and to over five hundred disciples at one time (see 1 Cor 15: 6-7). Paul has also imparted to the Church a perfect summation of the Paschal Mystery: "If we have died with him, we shall also live with him" (2 Tm 2: 11).

Paul's deep love

Although Paul never saw Christ during his public ministry, his contemplation of the Lord's words and actions as recounted to him by the other apostles and disciples wrought in him a deep love of the Lord that pervades his writings: "For the love of Christ impels us" (2 Cor 5: 14); "For to me life is Christ, and death is gain... I long to depart this life and be with Christ" (Phil 1: 21, 23). This hallmark of Paul's thought bears witness to the first of the two great commandments of Christ, that we should love the Lord with all our hearts, with all our souls, with all our minds, and with all our strength (see Mk 12: 29-30). There has been an unfortunate tendency in recent times to emphasize the second great commandment, the love of neighbor (see Mk 12: 31), to the point of virtually excluding the first. Paul's life and words attest that genuine love of neighbor draws its inspiration from the depth of our love for God.

Paul the convert

Paul's love of Christ impelled him to action, action he describes repeatedly in terms of a holy battle in which we "put on the armor of God" (Eph 6: 11) to fight the good fight of the faith (see 1 Tm 6: 12). It is at one and the same time a battle for personal holiness and for the salvation of mankind, according to the will of God, who wishes all people to be saved (see 1 Tm 2: 3-4). Stressing that "Christ Jesus came into the world to save sinners," Paul considers his own conversion to be wrought by the mercy of God as an example to encourage others to conversion (1 Tm 1: 15-16). The seventeenth-century Jesuit Scripture scholar Father Cornelius a Lapide († 1637) observes that the Church annually celebrates the conversion of Saint Paul on January 25 in order to propose the apostle as an example of penitence to all sinners, and to invoke Paul the convert, that "from heaven he may convert sinners, for still, although transported into heaven, he converts very many by his example, his prayers, and his epistles."

The remarkable event of Paul's conversion has so changed the world that the expression "Damascus conversion" has become commonplace. And throughout the Church's history, humanly inexplicable conversions have continued to occur in a myriad of ways. One night, the Italian Jesuit priest Saint Francis de Geronimo († 1716) experienced an inspiration urging him to go to a particular street corner of Naples and preach there. Upon arriving at the site, he found it to be a windswept and deserted place. With not a soul in sight, he preached to an empty street in the dead of night. The following day, as Father de Geronimo sat in his confessional, a woman penitent arrived, telling him in a flood of tears how she had lived in sin until in the night she heard through her open window his street-corner sermon, moving her to repentance. Now in heaven with the "King of kings... who dwells in unapproachable light" (1 Tm 6: 15-16), Saint Paul continues to intercede that all men and women may become "children of the light" (1 Thes 5: 5) as he did on that road to Damascus.

Praying
with
Saint Paul

Daily Reflections on the Letters of the Apostle Paul

No Slave Is above His Master

Father Romanus Cessario, O.P.

"Paul, a slave of Christ Jesus, called to be an apostle and set apart for the gospel of God, […] the gospel about his Son, descended from David according to the flesh, but established as Son of God in power according to the spirit of holiness through resurrection from the dead, Jesus Christ our Lord." (Rom 1: 1-4)

When pilgrims travel today to Rome, they witness the evidence of two thousand years of Catholic life. Churches, monasteries, and colleges testify to the eventual success of Saint Paul's Letter to the Romans. Pilgrims at the same time encounter the remains of another Rome – ancient Rome, with its Colosseum, its circuses, and its assorted reminders of pagan imperial power. There is a difference between these two Romes greater than one may gather from a well-conducted tour of the Eternal City. Whatever there is to admire in the artifacts of ancient Rome, the truth is that her empire collapsed under the weight of its own inability to sustain the reasonable human good. Within this culture of top-down expansionist power, no lower social position existed than that of the slave. So when Saint Paul announces himself a slave of Christ Jesus, he reverses the established expectations of the most powerful political authority of the day. Who would want to be the slave of anyone? Remember too that it was under the authority of the Roman procurator of Judea that Christ was crucified (see Mk 15: 15). Now Paul presents himself as the slave of a man that had been executed as a malefactor. Further, he tells both the Romans and us that the same Christ now brings to all peoples holiness of life and the bright promise of immortality. No wonder Christian authors speak about the Great Reversal. The incarnation inaugurates a turnabout in human history that no political power can match. True enough, salvation comes from the Jews. The apostle Paul announces that whatever God promised to the people of Israel now belongs by divine right even to the inhabitants of pagan Rome. Saint Paul, then, is the Apostle to the Gentiles. We know that after several centuries of bloody martyrdoms, at the head of which stand the apostles of Rome, Peter and Paul, these very same inhabitants accepted Saint Paul's Good News – the Gospel of God.

Blessed apostle Paul, obtain for us the grace to read your letters with spiritual profit. God chose you to announce the power of his Son Jesus Christ over sin and death. May we grow daily in your spirit of holiness.

A New Way of Living

Father Romanus Cessario, O.P.

"We have received the grace of apostleship, to bring about the obedience of faith, for the sake of [Jesus'] name." (Rom 1: 5)

The urgency that attaches to the Letter to the Romans is felt today as much as it was in the first century when Saint Paul composed it. Consider, for instance, the chief ways that the secular media proposes to make human life better. We find ourselves encouraged either to promote political changes or to rearrange the material dimensions of things. We hear over again the rhetoric of political campaigns or theories of economic development. Whatever successes these enterprises may deliver, they do not fulfill the deep-down desires of the human heart. Indeed, to reflect seriously for a moment, one might conclude that contemporary culture has not surpassed the practices of ancient Rome with its bloody political maneuvers and its enforced slave labor. Saint Paul instead announces another way to change the world. He wants to "bring about the obedience of faith." Both nouns are important: obedience means that the change comes about as a result of human freedom. Only the free are obedient. Faith in this context points to the definitive body of truths that Christ teaches to the apostles and which they in turn hand on to us. Only these truths deeply satisfy the human person made in God's image. The pagan world was capable of achieving moments of excellence, such as aqueducts, which in some parts of the world were not surpassed until the latter half of the twentieth century. But pagan antiquity was incapable of providing for men and women the truth about overall human excellence. Saint Paul, however, does: we are made for union in faith with God. Faith here refers to the assurance by which we cling to God. Saint Paul identifies himself by the grace of apostleship that he has received. Today, we need contemporary apostles who are ready to preach the obedience of faith. The task is urgent. For each human person on the planet must surrender to the obedience of faith, for the sake of Christ's name.

Lord Jesus Christ, your yoke is easy and your burden is light. Give me the grace both to desire and embrace the obedience of faith for the sake of your Holy Name. You died to save me from eternal death; make me love everything that comes to us from the apostles.

An Unfamiliar Gift

Father Romanus Cessario, O.P.

"I long to see you, that I may share with you some spiritual gift so that you may be strengthened, that is, that you and I may be mutually encouraged by one another's faith, yours and mine."
(Rom 1: 11-12)

The exchange of gifts is a cherished activity in which friends engage. The saints accept the classical notion of the friend as the other half of one's soul. They further teach that when we reveal something to a friend it is as if the revealing friend has not taken it out of his own heart. From this mutual exchange follows the effective sharing of goods. Since the friend is looked upon as another self, the sharing of material goods serves to succor the friend. In other words, the exchange of gifts reveals something about what it means to be a friend to another. No wonder Catholics complain about the crass commercialism that surrounds "holiday giving." It appears that giving the traditional Christmas presents fulfills a social obligation. Saint Paul on the other hand longs to give his fellow Christians in Rome "some spiritual gift." What is a spiritual gift? And what is more important, why should we become excited about receiving one? A spiritual gift is one that fortifies or comforts the human soul. Take the primordial spiritual gift, the Eucharist. When we receive Holy Communion, Christ strengthens and forgives us. Spiritual gifts also include instruction about spiritual things. One needs to learn about the Eucharist. There is no way to gain immediate access to the mystery of the Eucharist other than by knowing the truth about the Eucharist. Other spiritual gifts teach us how to act morally and for spiritual benefit. Not every Christian moral value is self-evident. Some we need to be taught. That's why the saints form an important part of our Catholic life. We discover in the details of their lives how to recognize spiritual gifts. In the saints, we see the spiritual gifts in action, and in turn our desire to receive the same gifts grows. To show our desire for the spiritual gifts, we should frequently ask God, through the intercession of Saint Paul, to bestow them on us.

Heavenly Father, with the Son, you send the Holy Spirit so that we can grow in the love of spiritual things. Through the prayers of Saint Paul, give us the graces that we need to grow in appreciation for the spiritual gifts that you lavish on the members of your Church.

The Just Man Lives by Faith

Father Romanus Cessario, O.P.

"I am not ashamed of the gospel. It is the power of God for the salvation of everyone who believes… For in it is revealed the righteousness of God from faith to faith." (Rom 1: 16, 17)

It is remarkable to ponder that the world is saved by a first-century Jewish man, one moreover who was crucified. Still, Saint Paul is not ashamed of this man's Gospel. God gave the Apostle to the Gentiles a penetrating glance into the divine plan for the world's salvation. We discover in his writings, especially in the Letter to the Romans, how God today is saving the world. There are secular and religious writings to which people ascribe authority and by which they live their lives. None ranks with the New Testament. The Gospel that Paul is not ashamed to preach contains a divine truth. What else explains the fact that the New Testament, a text written by first-century men of uneven intellectual abilities to describe their personal relationship with a man called Jesus, continues to exert influence throughout the world? The Gospel that Saint Paul preaches carries with it until the end of time a power to transform individual human lives. The lives of the saints, those who have done the will of God throughout the ages, supply the evidence for the truthfulness of what Saint Paul preaches. There is a catch, however. Saint Paul limits the power of the Gospel to those who believe. For some persons, this qualification may cause alarm. People today find believing a challenge. But Saint Paul accepts this challenge. He speaks about the Gospel revealing the righteousness of God. He means God's own goodness and love. It is from this goodness and love that God acts. When God acts to save us, he creates within us not only faith but also growth in the faith. "From faith to faith." When we come to understand this great mystery of God's plan for our salvation, we like Saint Paul will find no reason to be ashamed or fearful of the Gospel of Jesus Christ. Instead, we will embrace it – in faith. Then we will experience the righteousness of God within ourselves.

Holy Spirit of Truth, your gift of justification makes us righteous and capable of performing the works of righteousness. Teach me to value the life of sanctifying grace, and to seek frequently the sacramental aids that ensure that this share in your divine life grows from faith to faith.

The Heavens Proclaim the Glory of God

Father Romanus Cessario, O.P.

"The wrath of God is indeed being revealed from heaven against every impiety and wickedness of those who suppress the truth by their wickedness. For what can be known about God is evident to them, because God made it evident to them." (Rom 1: 18, 19)

Hardly a person in the world has looked up into the starry sky and not wondered where God makes his dwelling. This inclination is not an illusion, even when we realize that God is not encompassed by the boundaries of space and time. The magnitude of the universe and the patterned movement that stars and moon and sun observe (however much subject they may be to change and mutation) point to Someone who stands above the magnitude and behind the ordered movement. In any case, this is what Saint Paul taught his readers. He gave no quarter to the modern error: if there is no God, then everything is allowed. On the contrary, he argued that there exists a law of nature that displays the foundational norms for human living, that is, for achieving the good of the human person. This law of nature lies open even to those who have not been taught the law of Moses. This assertion is not a merely academic one. Saint Paul makes the law of nature the basis for his claim that God can legitimately punish those who violate its precepts and inclinations. He especially condemns the pagan practice of idol worship – of making God into the image of mortals, birds, and snakes. Saint Paul is not referring to people who find themselves ignorant about the true God. He addresses those whose personal wickedness compels them to reduce God to a craven idol. The warning is a perennial one. Whenever we start to rationalize sinful practices, we can expect to find ourselves redefining God. In the end, we will try to make God look like our own distorted image of what it means to be human. The warning that Saint Paul places at the beginning of the Letter to the Romans is pertinent today. The deformations of culture that dominate the contemporary landscape are not much different than what Saint Paul himself witnessed among the inhabitants of ancient Rome.

Lord Jesus Christ, you are the true image of the living God and the perfect refulgence of the Father's glory. Draw us close to you. Keep us from the deformity of sin so that we will be ready to meet God face to face.

What Wonders Your Hands Have Made

Father Romanus Cessario, O.P.

"Ever since the creation of the world, [God's] invisible attributes of eternal power and divinity have been able to be understood and perceived in what he has made." (Rom 1: 20)

Think about the last thing you made. It may be something artistic like a drawing or a flower arrangement, or something useful like a back porch or a model airplane. When you reflect with satisfaction on your artifact, you come to the realization that something of yourself is reflected in the work of your hands. The more you develop your artistic or other skills, the more you can identify with your handiwork. If this happens with us poor mortals, who are bound to work with already existing materials, think of what it is like for God who creates everything out of nothing. The Latin phrase is *ex nihilo*, out of nothing. When we make something, we search to discover a model or pattern to use as the basis for our designs. When God creates out of nothing, there is no already existing pattern on which he relies. Instead, the divine wisdom itself serves as the exemplar or model or pattern for what comes into being. That is why Saint Paul is able to remind everyone, not only Christian believers, that there is no excuse for forgetting God or for refashioning God into the image of a creature. Each human being can discover in creation a perception of God's invisible attributes, his eternal power and his divinity. In many quarters today, we witness the return of old-fashioned materialist atheism. Scientific types look around the world and declare that creation, instead of proclaiming the invisible attributes of God, persuades us that there is no God. Matter needs no explanation, they allege. Saint Paul refused this simplistic and reductionist account of the created world. On the contrary, he told the people of his day that they could find no excuse for failing to worship the God who made heaven and earth. And then he held out the terrible display of immorality that characterized the moral landscape of the first century. The lesson: forget God, and the creature disappears.

Heavenly Father, you created all things to reflect the glory of your name. Grant to all peoples the grace to recognize your ownership of all that exists, and to treat all creation with a respect that will lead them back to you and your Son, Jesus Christ.

Don't Wait for Tomorrow

Father Romanus Cessario, O.P.

*"Do you hold [God's] priceless kindness, forbearance,
and patience in low esteem, unaware that the kindness of God
would lead you to repentance?" (Rom 2: 4)*

The Letter to the Romans begins by making a case for the
divine judgment. During long periods of Christian history,
it was commonly held that the reality of divine judgment is
something that can be known by reason. In other words, one does
not have to rely on faith to know that God will come to judge the
living and the dead. There is an advantage in this way of thinking.
Awareness of judgment prompts people to believe in God and to
seek his forbearance. Saint Paul seems to have this argument in
mind when he warns his readers that they will not escape the judgment of God. Is it reasonable to think about divine judgment outside the context of revealed faith? The answer is yes. Judgment is a
corollary of freedom. If I recognize the reality of my human freedom, then it follows that I should accept personal accountability
for my actions. The Church urges us to act on the basis of a moral
conscience. She wants us to acknowledge that our actions lead to
consequences, to states of being that either conform or not to a
standard of moral truth that is accessible to every human creature.
The sobriety of Saint Paul's warning should not be dismissed as
overly dour. We need reminders to keep our moral bearings. The
Apostle to the Gentiles instructs best on the reality of original sin.
He understands the disorders that the sin of Adam has introduced
into the world. Saint Paul forces upon us a realistic account of the
human predicament so that we will be disposed to receive the free
gift of salvation. It is difficult to read the Letter to the Romans and
to come away with the view that, since in the end everyone will be
saved, it does not matter how one acts. Instead, Saint Paul inter-
prets the divine forbearance as an invitation to repentance. Be aware
of the patient kindness of God!

*Almighty Father, you are the just judge who calls us to repentance.
Trusting in your forbearance, we return to you with confidence. Give
us the grace to remain fully united with your Son so that we will never
fear the severe judgment that our sins deserve.*

Sin Is Ugly

Father Romanus Cessario, O.P.

*"There will be glory, honor, and peace for everyone
who does good."* (Rom 2: 10)

When you read or hear news reports about what human beings do, it is easy to come away with the impression that moral norms depend largely on what individuals or groups judge to be right or wrong. Sometimes the sinful receives public approval, whereas at other times the honorable meets with scorn. Relativism remains a deadly threat not only to everyday right thinking but also to our embracing the highest Good. Saint Paul is not a relativist. He announces plainly and without qualification that "there will be glory, honor, and peace for everyone who does good." Saint Paul is able to express this confidence about the triumph of the good in the world for a reason. That reason is the exalted Lord. When Christ met Saul on the road to Damascus, the future Apostle of the Gentiles encountered the primordial source of goodness in the world. This experience of conversion transformed Saul of Tarsus' way of thinking about God. So Saint Paul now assures the Romans that "there is no partiality with God." In other words, there exists a foundation for goodness in the world that is not tied to a specific religious tradition, even to the authentic and divine revelation made to Israel. The existence of the highest Good explains why Saint Paul can address the same message about human conduct to both Jews and Gentiles. Whether one sins outside the law or under the law, judgment follows for the sinner. The technical name for the norm of human conduct that is written into the structure of creation, especially the human creature, is "natural law." Glory, honor, and peace are qualities that surround the good and the beautiful. Christian virtue draws us to the moral good. Virtuous actions in turn exhibit the beauty that brings honor and peace. What is broken is ugly. Saint Paul warns not only Christian believers but the whole world to avoid moral relativism. He knows that sin is ugly.

Holy Spirit of Truth, illumine our minds and guide our actions. You lead all men to the fullness of divine life that brings glory, honor, and peace to the world. Make us always reflect the beauty of the divine goodness.

Truth in the Heart

Father Romanus Cessario, O.P.

*"When the Gentiles who do not have the law by nature observe
the prescriptions of the law, they are a law for themselves even
though they do not have the law. They show that the demands
of the law are written in their hearts." (Rom 2: 14, 15)*

One often hears the complaint that Christians, especially
Catholics, try to impose their religious views on everybody.
This argument is made especially when the Church urges
those who bear the burden of civil governance to adopt provisions
that enable the institutions of marriage, family, and health care to
safeguard and promote important natural law goods such as pro-
creative love, the education of children, and human life itself. For
a variety of reasons, many modern people hold that religion is an
exclusively private engagement that should be kept out of the way
of public affairs. This typically modern outlook would have astonished Saint Paul. The opening chapters of the Letter to the Romans
not only indict the moral confusions generated by pagan antiquity
but also stipulate the place that God enjoys in the public square.
Saint Paul affirms that when those without the benefits of divine
revelation observed the prescriptions of the law, they became a law
for themselves. So it would never have occurred to him that political authorities are free to ignore or deny these same prescriptions.
Saint Paul goes on to explain that the demands of the law are written in the hearts of all men and women. Later theologians would
explain that the law given to Moses on Mount Sinai – what Saint
Paul calls simply "the law" – communicates by way of divine revelation what is already inscribed in the structure of the human being.
Catholics, then, should never try to isolate the orders of creation
and salvation, or the orders of nature and grace. Granted that legitimate political authority enjoys its own subsidiary position in governing secular affairs, God remains the creator of heaven and earth.
It is the divine law that governs all things sweetly. Saint Paul also
reminds us that when we act against the prescriptions of natural
and divine law, we act against the inclinations of our own hearts.
In a word, when we commit sin, we act against ourselves.

*Heavenly Father, we stand before you with reverence and gratitude.
You have shown us the path to true wisdom. Grant us what we need
always to fulfill the prescriptions of your law with ease, promptness,
and joy.*

O Saving Grace

Father Romanus Cessario, O.P.

"But now the righteousness of God has been manifested [...],
the righteousness of God through faith in Jesus Christ
for all who believe." (Rom 3: 21, 22)

During the Paschal Vigil, the priest sings a hymn that includes this arresting phrase: "O truly necessary sin of Adam that merited for us so great a Redeemer." As she prepares to celebrate Easter, the Church reminds Christian believers that nothing surpasses their enjoying friendship with Christ. Indeed, if we were unable to enjoy this friendship, it would have been better not to have been born. Of course, the celebration of Easter confirms that we can enjoy Christ's friendship. It is a gift offered to all who believe in him. Saint Paul calls friendship with Christ "the righteousness of God." He emphasizes that this friendship entails communion or fellowship with God. Because the basis for communion with God is the gift of his love, the divine friendship changes us. We are no longer aliens and strangers in God's household; instead we are made his own sons and daughters. This is the preferred analogy that Saint Paul employs to describe what it means to be transformed by the righteousness of God. The filial image indicates that those whom God has made righteous start to look like Christ, the one beloved Son of the Father. The righteousness that comes through faith in Jesus Christ is salvation. God so loved us that he redeemed us by sending one like ourselves, though free from sin, so that he could see and love in us what he sees and loves in Christ. No wonder the Church is able to call the sin of Adam, the original sin, something "necessary." She expresses the paradox of the divine goodness that makes the occasion of a creature's rebellion the motive for the incarnation. This provision of the divine goodness affords us both consolation and a warning. We are reassured that sin is never an obstacle to our returning to Christ, and at the same time we recognize the inestimable gift that is friendship with Christ. We must cherish this friendship above all things.

Lord Jesus Christ, your paschal victory over sin and death restores us to friendship with God. Make us confident of the new life and righteousness that is ours through faith in you. Never let us be separated from your love.

Saved by His Blood

Father Romanus Cessario, O.P.

"They are justified freely by his grace through the redemption in Christ Jesus, whom God set forth as an expiation, through faith, by his blood, to prove his righteousness because of the forgiveness of sins previously committed, through the forbearance of God."
(Rom 3: 24-26)

We are very accustomed to look at our lives from our own perspectives. We think about our plans, our friends, our finances, and many other things that make up a happy life. It is easy to forget that we also should think once and a while about our lives from God's perspective. When we do, we should remember the forbearance of God. What does it mean to say that God forebears us. In a word, it means that God puts up lovingly with us. Because we frequently fail to do the good that we should or, more often, commit the sins that we should not, we need to rely on the divine forbearance. Many people find this invitation to trust the forbearance of God something difficult to embrace. Sin finds a way of blackmailing us. The Evil One stands ready to accuse us, arguing that God has had enough of our foolishness. The devil urges us to accept our fallen state as a given about which nothing can be done. Even people who appear complacent about sin or steeped in sinful dispositions suffer from this devil's blackmail. They cannot bring themselves to believe what Saint Paul announces with full confidence and joyous thanksgiving: we are redeemed in Christ Jesus. This redemption comes and can only come as a free gift of God's grace. There is more. Redemption does not come as a divine exoneration. God does not wipe the tally board of our sins clean. God knows the burden that sin puts upon us. So it is not enough to say to us, "Oh, forget about it." Instead, he sent his Son. And the Son so loved us that he made of himself an expiation for our sins. This expiation comes, not at the price of pronouncements, but of blood. The forbearance of God is ordered toward our believing in the redemption that, by his grace, is ours in the blood of Jesus Christ.

Holy Spirit of Truth, strip away every illusion that attaches to my sinful way of life. Illumine my mind and strengthen my resolve so that I may always turn to Christ as the source of my redemption. Draw me again and again to the covenant of Christ's blood.

A Promise without Limits

Father Romanus Cessario, O.P.

"It was not through the law that the promise was made to Abraham and his descendants that he would inherit the world, but through the righteousness that comes from faith." (Rom 4: 13)

The Church calls the patriarch Abraham "our father in faith." She does this to underscore the continuity that exists between the old and the new covenants. The promise made to Abraham entails progeny: "Look up at the sky," God told Abraham, "and count the stars, if you can. Just so… shall your descendants be" (Gn 15: 5). In other words, God makes Abraham a promise without limits. This promise without limits passes over to the Church of Christ that reveres the law and the prophets. It would have been easy for Abraham to trust his own human estimate of things. He was after all a smart man, a business man, a man accustomed to facing the problems of everyday life. Instead, Abraham accepted as true God's limitless promise. The Book of Genesis states this plainly of Abraham: "[He] put his faith in the Lord, who credited it to him as an act of righteousness" (Gn 15: 6). Not only the promise made to Abraham but the faith of Abraham reaches fulfillment in the Church of Christ. The righteousness bestowed upon Abraham achieves its definitive exposition in the supreme holiness of Jesus Christ. Because of Christ's holiness, the Church is constituted as the "universal sacrament of salvation." Her mission given by God is to proclaim the Gospel to every member of the human race. All are saved through the righteousness that comes from faith. As the Church advances throughout the nations, she recognizes in her growth the fulfillment of what was promised to Abraham, namely, "that he would inherit the world." God acts continuously to save the world. He acts both through his promises and their fulfillment. Because he is the first to set aside human judgments and to accept as true what God promised to him, Abraham remains the father in faith for every Christian. At the same time, salvation comes from the Jewish people, who were the first to place their hope and their faith in God.

Almighty and everlasting God, source of all goodness and righteousness in the world, hear our prayer. Grant to your people the gift of salvation by renewing in them the gift of divine faith. Let not those who hope in you ever be put to shame.

Everybody Needs a Father

Father Romanus Cessario, O.P.

"[Abraham] is our father in the sight of God, in whom
he believed, who gives life to the dead and calls into being
what does not exist." (Rom 4: 17)

Saint Paul says that Abraham "is our father in the sight of God." We should observe the emphasis that Saint Paul puts on paternity, both spiritual and carnal. Abraham and his wife Sarah were very old when God promised to make Abraham the father of many nations. The birth of their son Isaac confirmed the confidence that Abraham reposed in the divine promise. Abraham generates in a spiritual order as well. He shows us the right way to relate to God. There is all the difference in the world between thinking of God as a detached ruler of the universe and thinking of God as one "who gives life to the dead and calls into being what does not exist." The difference lies in a personal relationship. But this relationship of faith is not something that one could arrive at without help. God made Abraham a model of the new way of thinking about oneself. Faith is not self-starting. The human family needs a father in faith, "our father in the sight of God." God provided one in Abraham. God initiated Abraham into the new personal way of faith. From that moment on, it is fair to say that spiritual paternity becomes part of a spiritual way of life. We have to be taught how to believe in God and in the righteousness that comes to us from God. The history of Christian spirituality is marked by the works of little Abrahams, spiritual fathers who begot people in the faith. Each needs a father in faith. Why is spiritual paternity indispensable in the Christian life? We need someone to show us how to overcome our native indisposition to trust that another will provide good things for us. We also need someone to reassure us that we are not obliged to provide for ourselves. This reassurance is best communicated when we see a "father in the sight of God" already living by faith, and happily so.

Lord Jesus Christ, you draw those who believe in you into God's own righteousness. Help us to grow strong in the virtue of faith. Make us eager to teach others about the life of faith and the new life that it brings in your name.

Promise

Father Joseph T. Lienhard, S.J.

"[Abraham] did not doubt God's promise in unbelief; rather, he was empowered by faith and gave glory to God and was fully convinced that what he had promised he was also able to do."
(Rom 4: 20-21)

We have often heard the phrase, "Promises, promises." Inevitably, it implies "Promises, yes; but no delivery." In the Bible, however, the word "promise" has a different sense, because the promises come from God. In fact, it is an essential article of Old Testament faith that God can and does keep his promises. "Promised Land" is a familiar biblical phrase. Saint Paul meditates on God's promises to Abraham, which were promises of land and posterity. Both promises seemed preposterous, for Abraham and his wife Sarah had never had children, and Abraham was a wandering stranger in Canaan who even had to buy a small plot of land so he could bury his wife. In his meditation, Paul ponders the relation of law and promise. Promise must be superior to law, for a promise is absolute. If God is faithful to his promises, Israel should be faithful to God's commandments; but even if Israel fails, God will keep his promise. The New Testament expands the field of vision and sees the entire Old Testament as one great promise, which has been definitively fulfilled in Christ. To Abraham, Isaac, and Jacob, and to their posterity, God had promised the land. Moses led the people to the Promised Land. But, centuries later, the land was conquered and the Israelites sent into exile. Was God's promise broken? No, his promise was to be fulfilled in a higher way, in Christ; not in one kingdom on one shore of the sea, but in a kingdom of truth and life, a kingdom of holiness and grace, a kingdom of justice, love, and peace, as we hear in the Preface of Christ the King. In another passage, Paul draws out the implications of our faith when he writes these beautiful words about Christ: "All the promises of God find their Yes in him." God's final word to us is "Yes," a word incarnate in Christ our Lord.

All-powerful and eternal God, whose promises to Abraham, Isaac, and Jacob have come to fulfillment in Christ, grant us, we beseech you, the courage to receive your promises in faith and joy.

27

His Holy and Glorious Wounds

Father Joseph T. Lienhard, S.J.

"Believe in the one who raised Jesus our Lord from the dead, who was handed over for our transgressions and was raised for our justification." (Rom 4: 24-25)

The Christian faith is a matter of life and death – or rather, a matter of life and death and life. We see the crucifix everywhere: over the altars in our churches, on the walls of our bedrooms, in the classrooms of Catholic schools, even in our pockets, on the rosary. We can forget how surprising, even shocking, the crucifix is: the image of a man who has been executed as a criminal, a corpse hanging on a wooden frame. The crucifix makes sense – is beautiful – deserves honor – for only one reason: the death of Jesus Christ was not the end but a new beginning, the beginning of a new and glorious life. Saint Paul urges us to believe in God, the one who raised Jesus our Lord from the dead. For that battered, broken body was taken down from the cross and laid in a tomb. But God the Father raised Jesus up and gave him, not just the life he had had, but a higher, fuller sort of life. Yet Christ's suffering and death were not simply put behind him. In a beautiful if mysterious passage in the Gospels, the apostle Thomas does not see the risen Lord on the first Easter night. But he knows that, if he does see him, Jesus' wounds will still be there. Thomas says, "Unless I… place my finger in the mark of the nails, and place my hand in his side, I will not believe." During the Easter Vigil, the priest inserts five grains of incense, which is a sign of worship, into the paschal candle. As he does so, he says a prayer that sums up the whole mystery of the cross and what it did for us: "By his holy and glorious wounds may Christ our Lord guide us and keep us. Amen." "His holy and glorious wounds" – a perfect summary of this mystery.

Almighty, ever-living God, who raised Jesus our Lord from the dead, come to the aid of those you have justified, and who pray: "We adore you, O Christ, and we bless you, because by your holy cross you have redeemed the world."

Peace

Father Joseph T. Lienhard, S.J.

"Since we have been justified by faith, we have peace with God through our Lord Jesus Christ, through whom we have gained access [by faith] to this grace in which we stand."
(*Rom 5: 1-2*)

In one of the most famous paragraphs he ever set down, Saint Augustine of Hippo wrote of peace as the result of good order. There is, he wrote, a peace of the body, a peace of the irrational soul, a peace of the rational soul, and a peace of body and soul together. Peace between mortal men and God is an ordered obedience in faith. Peace among men is an ordered agreement of mind. The peace of a home is an ordered agreement about commanding and obeying. The peace of the heavenly city is harmonious fellowship in the enjoyment of God. And the peace of the whole universe is the tranquility of order. Perhaps we think of peace too exclusively in merely political terms, as peace between nations, or even simply as the absence of war. But, in fact, we also speak of inner peace. Most of us know families that are peaceful, and others that seem to be in a constant state of guerilla warfare; it's easy to know which we'd prefer. It is worth meditating on the beauty and the merits of peace. A state of inner peace is the time when we can most be ourselves, when we are most fully human. At Mass we offer each other a sign of peace. That moment can be a valuable one, if we have the chance to make it more than a quick handshake and a smile, if we seek out someone with whom we are not at peace and bring peace into that person's life and into our own. Peace is no trivial thing, and it does not come about cheaply or automatically. Perhaps peace should be an important part of our next examination of conscience, with two questions: Do I cultivate and savor inner peace, the peace of my own heart? And, do I bring peace to others?

Lord Jesus Christ, you have reconciled us to the Father by the blood of the cross. Fill our hearts with the grace of your peace and, through us your unworthy servants, let your peace reign in all the world.

Hope

Father Joseph T. Lienhard, s.j.

"We boast in hope of the glory of God." (Rom 5: 2)

What is hope? You may have heard of the Optimists' Club, people who devote themselves to telling each other that the future is going to be better than the past, that everything is going to turn out well. There's nothing wrong with optimism, of course, and a better future is an attractive idea. But optimists don't know the future; they simply act as if they did. Christians don't need optimism, because they have hope. For Christians do know the future; they know how the Great Story is going to end. It's going to end with the reign of Christ the King over the whole universe. This fact, this knowledge, is what we celebrate each year on the last Sunday of the Church's calendar. By the virtue of hope we affirm that God, from all eternity, has had a plan for the world. The God who created us will not abandon us, and he proved that his plan is effective when he sent his only-begotten Son to take on flesh for our sake. Hope is also the response by which we graciously accept our place in God's plan. Saint Paul wrote of faith, hope, and charity, and the Church calls these the three theological virtues. "Theological" here means that God himself infuses these virtues into the soul. Every human being desires happiness; even the ancient philosophers taught us that. The Christian virtue of hope fills up the vessel that is happiness and shows us in what our happiness will consist. Hope orders all our activities toward the kingdom of heaven; it keeps us from discouragement; it opens our hearts to a sure and certain expectation of eternal beatitude. Thus Saint Paul rightly says, "We boast in hope of the glory of God." "Boast" is one of Saint Paul's favorite words. But his boast is not about himself, but about the hope that God has given him; and that makes all the difference.

Almighty God and Father, you have graciously promised us every blessing through Jesus Christ our hope. Grant us, we beg, forgiveness of our sins, fidelity to your commandments, and a peaceful, trusting heart.

Character

Father Joseph T. Lienhard, s.j.

*"We even boast of our afflictions, knowing that affliction
produces endurance, and endurance, proven character,
and proven character, hope."* (Rom 5: 3-4)

"No pain, no gain" is a motto of those dedicated to exercise,
fitness, and body-building. Normally, affliction or suffering is a bad thing; no one wants to suffer for suffering's
sake. But suffering can be turned to good. Saint Paul liked the image
of an athlete training for competition; in one of his letters he wrote
about foot races and boxing. Perhaps he had competed in sports
when he was a young man. An athlete, he wrote, must exercise self-
control; a boxer will train his body. So too, affliction can lead to
good, and that good is character. We speak of building character,
of strength of character. What do we mean when we say that someone has character? We mean that he has good and clear principles
and lives by those principles, no matter what the price. A man of
character knows himself and what he stands for. Saint Paul, too,
invites us to reflect on what we mean by character, and how to build
character, moral or ethical strength. Those who speak of character
often invoke the image of athletes' training. An athlete uses resistance, like weights, to build muscle, and exertion, like long runs, to
build endurance. So Saint Paul invites his readers to follow his own
example: His afflictions, if he accepts them and uses them rightly,
will build up his character, and good character will give him hope.
But in Christian usage, the word character has another meaning,
too: we speak of a sacramental character, imparted by baptism and
confirmation, for example, which marks a person for ever. Once
received, these sacraments cannot be repeated, because they impart
a permanent character. How are the two sorts of character related?
By the one, we build character by exercise and training; by the other,
God builds up our Christian character by the power of the sacraments. Moral character and sacramental character together build
up the Mystical Body of Christ Jesus our Lord.

*Almighty God and Father, you give us life and strength through our
parents, and the grace of the sacraments through our holy Mother, the
Church. Confirm us in your grace, and give us strength unto life everlasting.*

The Love of God Poured Out

Father Joseph T. Lienhard, S.J.

"Hope does not disappoint, because the love of God has been poured out into our hearts through the holy Spirit that has been given to us." (Rom 5: 5)

Being a Christian is all about accepting a gift. There are people who seem to be unable to accept a gift graciously. As soon as you give them a gift, they begin to think of how they can balance the books, give you something of the same value. They cannot abide being in someone's debt. There is finally something selfish about that attitude, something that says, I will not allow you to be generous to me, because it may suggest that you are somehow superior to me. Perhaps that's what makes being a Christian hard – being able to accept a gift, being able to admit one's need, even being able to acknowledge that, by ourselves, we are helpless. Throughout much of his writing, Saint Augustine had a distinctive interpretation of the verse we are pondering. "The love of God" can mean either our love for God, or God's love for us. Saint Augustine regularly took the second interpretation: even our love for God is a gift from God; by our own effort, we cannot love God, but God graciously enables us to love him. And that gift comes through the Holy Spirit. Saint Augustine had a great deal of fun with biblical numbers. In one place, he deals with the number seventeen. Seventeen, he writes, is made of ten plus seven. Ten stands for the commandments, seven for the gifts of the Holy Spirit. So the number seventeen shows us that we cannot keep the commandments – even love of God and love of neighbor, which sum up the ten commandments – without the grace of the Holy Spirit. Saint Augustine was probably smiling as he wrote that, but his message is profound and true: the Holy Spirit gives us that gift of love that enables us to live the life that God calls us to.

Almighty God and Father, confirm us in your gift of hope. All our trust is in you, and you alone. We humbly pray, do not desert us or abandon us, but bring us to the fullness of life in you.

The Appointed Time

Father Joseph T. Lienhard, S.J.

"Christ, while we were still helpless, yet died at the appointed time for the ungodly." (Rom 5: 6)

Saint Paul had a great and broad vision: he saw God's plan from its beginning to its fulfillment. In one of his resounding sentences he wrote, "But when the time had fully come, God sent forth his Son, born of a woman, born under the law." In the same vein, Paul assures us that Christ died at the appointed time. What do we mean by appointed time? In one sense it can mean holidays and celebrations that recur regularly; and there is something reassuring about such holidays. In the Christian calendar, Christmas and Easter, Ash Wednesday and Good Friday, All Saints' Day and the Immaculate Conception, mark out the year. Each year these days come again; we know what to expect. We know where the Christmas decorations are stored, and whom we will want to send cards to and give presents to. These are appointed times, but they are not the time that has fully come or, as Saint Paul's phrase is sometimes translated, "the fullness of time." The best we can do, as human beings, is to repeat a cycle of feasts, to divide the year into peaks and plains. Only God can establish the fullness of time. No human being could know that, for thousands of years, time had not reached its fullness; only the Lord of history, who sees all of history at once, could fix the appointed time. This truth of our faith should be deeply consoling. We are not adrift on a boundless sea of yesterdays and tomorrows; God has fitted us into his great plan. When the Easter candle is inscribed on Holy Saturday night, the priest says, in part, "Christ yesterday and today, the beginning and the end;… all time belongs to him, and all ages." If Christ is the beginning and the end, then he embraces us and our lives, and our short days are taken up into his endless time.

Almighty, ever-living God and Lord, you appointed the time when Christ your Son offered himself for our redemption; by his glorious resurrection, deliver us from the bonds of time and bring us to the fullness of life in him, Jesus Christ our Lord.

While We Were Still Sinners

Father Joseph T. Lienhard, s.j.

"God proves his love for us in that while we were still sinners Christ died for us." (Rom 5: 8)

At the end of his Spiritual Exercises, Saint Ignatius Loyola placed a meditation called "Contemplation to Attain the Love of God." He began the meditation with two observations. The first, a well-known phrase, is that "love ought to manifest itself in deeds rather than in words." In the second point, Saint Ignatius observes that love consists in mutual sharing of goods; two people in love are eager to give something to each other. He then invites us to ponder the magnificence of creation, God's indwelling in the world, God's activity in the world, and how all blessings descend from above. The conclusion is simple: the retreatant is to ask, how much can I give in return? Saint Paul says the same thing, in far fewer words: "God proves his love for us." Saint Ignatius invites us in his great "Contemplation" to ponder the entire universe, land and sea and sky and all that is in them. Saint Paul invites us to ponder what happened on a small hillside outside Jerusalem on a dark Friday afternoon. Who has more to show us? Saint Paul, I think. Saint Ignatius invites us to ponder creation; Saint Paul turns our gaze to the one "through whom all things were made," through whom the universe came to be, as we confess in the Creed. Jesus Christ, the eternal Son of God, the Second Person of the Blessed Trinity, who for us and for our salvation took flesh of the Virgin Mary and became man, gave his life in sacrifice for us. We were sinners; we had offended God. But God did not reject us. Indeed, he reached out to us. If love manifests itself in deeds rather than in words, there is no greater deed than this one: while we were still sinners Christ died for us. It is fitting to end with Saint Ignatius' prayer from the great "Contemplation."

Take, Lord, and receive all my liberty, my memory, my understanding, and my entire will, all that I have and possess. Thou hast given all to me. To Thee, O Lord, I return it. All is Thine, dispose of it wholly according to Thy will. Give me Thy love and Thy grace, for this is sufficient for me.

Reconciliation

Father Joseph T. Lienhard, S.J.

"Indeed, if, while we were enemies, we were reconciled to God through the death of his Son, how much more, once reconciled, will we be saved by his life. [...] We also boast of God through our Lord Jesus Christ, through whom we have now received reconciliation." (Rom 5: 10-11)

Older Catholics will remember well the phrase "going to confession" and the ritual attached to it. One went to confession on Saturday afternoon, or on the eve of First Friday, as a preparation for receiving communion the next day. The lines were often long, and the confessional was dark. It all took about three or four minutes. Even then, however, the better name for going to confession was the sacrament of penance. In recent decades, confession has more often been called the sacrament of reconciliation. And each successive name – confession, penance, reconciliation – indicates a deeper appreciation of this sacrament. Confession is just one part of the sacrament. Penance, repentance, reparation are surely an important part of the sacrament, but they are still something that we do. Reconciliation is a better name. Reconciliation is an old word in English. Accountants speak of reconciling two accounts, getting them to balance. Feuding parties or enemies are reconciled when they resolve their disagreements and reach concord and harmony. But the word reconciliation is used most often in a religious sense. Reconciliation expresses the new relationship between God and ourselves that this sacrament brings about. And further, the term shows us that individual reception of this sacrament is simply one instance or application of a far greater reconciliation: for God was in Christ, reconciling the world to himself through the blood of the cross. Saint Paul reminds us that, by ourselves, we could not achieve reconciliation with God; but Jesus Christ achieved it for us, by his death on the cross. By that cross, we have been changed from enemies of God to friends of God, and are saved, now, by his life. What a privilege, what a beautiful thing to be a friend of God, as Saint Paul tells us – and that is what we are.

Eternal God and Father, by the blessed and glorious cross of Jesus Christ your Son you have reconciled the world to yourself and forgiven our sins. By the power of that cross make us instruments of your peace in our families, our Church, and our world.

One Person – Two Persons

Father Joseph T. Lienhard, S.J.

*"For if by that one person's transgression the many died,
how much more did the grace of God and the gracious gift of
the one person Jesus Christ overflow for the many."*
(Rom 5: 15)

To contrast Adam and Christ has been a rich source of Christian reflection. Saint Paul introduced the theme, and Saint Irenaeus of Lyons, a great second-century Christian theologian, developed it. The theme was worked out further during the Middle Ages in art and music. Saint Paul calls Christ the last Adam, or the final, perfect man, in contrast to the first Adam. Saint Irenaeus wrote of Christ in terms of recapitulation, meaning not "summing up" but "beginning again." Adam started it all and got it wrong; Christ started it again and got it right. As Christian writers develop the theme, they see further parallels. Just as sin entered the world from the tree in the Garden, so redemption came to the world through the tree of the cross. Just as the woman Eve was taken from the side of the sleeping Adam, so the Church was born from the side of the dead Christ. Adam's disobedience resulted in defeat; Christ's obedience resulted in victory. The virgin (as Irenaeus believed) Eve became the cause of death by her sin; the Virgin Mary is the cause of salvation by her "Yes," her "Let it be done unto me." Eve listened to a serpent; Mary listened to an angel. A medieval tradition even held that the hill of Calvary was the site of Adam's grave. Depictions of the crucifixion sometimes show a skull at the foot of the cross: it was meant to be, not any skull, but the skull of Adam. By the marvelous medieval sense of harmony, the Fall and the Redemption are united in one place. Thus Saint Paul invites us to contemplate the great cosmic drama of our redemption by contrasting two persons, Adam and Christ, and seeing the whole history of the human race summed up in these two, the first Adam and the last Adam.

Eternal Lord of history, you wondrously created the human race and even more wondrously restored it. We beseech you, bring to fulfillment in us what you have promised in Christ.

The Abundance of Grace

Father Joseph T. Lienhard, S.J.

"For if, by the transgression of one person, death came to reign through that one, how much more will those who receive the abundance of grace and of the gift of justification come to reign in life through the one person Jesus Christ." (Rom 5: 17)

One of the most important concepts that Saint Paul has given us is "grace." In its root meaning, the word grace indicates something that delights. A graceful person, such as a dancer or an athlete, is pleasing to the eye and to the sense of beauty. The word grace also came to designate the favor that a ruler might show to his subjects. The Old Testament speaks often of God's graciousness. In the New Testament, Saint Paul uses the word grace to describe the event of salvation, by which he means that God makes us glad by his gifts to us, gifts that he gives freely and that we do not merit. When all this background is summed up, we come to an important insight about grace. We cannot simply make ourselves graceful dancers or skilled athletes by sheer power of will, and we surely cannot make ourselves beautiful or handsome. In the same way, grace comes from God, not from us. God's basic gift to us is saving grace, the grace by which we are delivered from the bondage of sin and made pleasing to God, by no merit of our own. But we also speak of other kinds of grace, like sacramental grace, bestowed by baptism, the Eucharist, reconciliation, and other sacraments. We speak of the grace of vocation, which helps us exercise our responsibilities as Christians. Sanctifying grace is an abiding gift, which enables us to live in God and to act by his love. Actual graces are God's occasional interventions, which help us to do what is right and good at the moment of choice or decision. The verse from Saint Paul that we are pondering finally says it all, and says it best: through one man, Jesus Christ, we receive the abundance of grace unto the fullness of life.

Gracious God, giver of all good gifts, hear us, we ask you: by the power of your grace, deliver us from sin and preserve us in your faithful service.

Condemnation and Acquittal

Father Joseph T. Lienhard, S.J.

"Just as through one transgression condemnation came upon all, so through one righteous act acquittal and life came to all."
(Rom 5: 18)

Courtroom drama has long been a staple of the theater, and of novels, movies, and television. Shakespeare used it effectively in *The Merchant of Venice*. The courtroom novels of John Grisham are best sellers. Films like *The Caine Mutiny Court Martial* are classics. The TV series *Law and Order* is a hugely successful show, but it is only one of dozens of series about trial lawyers, which almost always lead to a dramatic courtroom scene. Of course, the genre is far older. The Book of Daniel in the Old Testament gives us the wonderful story of Susanna, who is accused of a capital crime by two corrupt old men. The young and clever Daniel is the brilliant prosecutor, and he saves Susanna's life. The trial of Jesus in the New Testament is very different; there an innocent man is convicted and condemned in an unjust trial but, in God's mysterious plan, his unjust death brings justification to many sinners. Saint Paul sees the human race, too, in terms of a courtroom drama. Because of sin, the whole human race was rightly condemned. But – and here we see the mystery of God's action, which does not follow the rules of human trials and sentencing – the sentence of condemnation is not the last word. Rather, through the mystery of Christ, we are later acquitted, because Christ's action drew the punishment away from us. The story is told of a judge in traffic court. At the end of a long day, the judge's own son is brought before him. The young man is clearly guilty. What does the judge do? He imposes the highest possible fine on his own son. Then he takes off his black robe, walks with his son to the cashier, and pays the fine himself; and they go home together. Do you see a parallel here?

Lord our God, creator of all things and judge of the world, show us, we implore you, the fullness of your mercy. Forgive us our sins and bring us to our everlasting home, in Christ Jesus our Lord.

Obedience and Righteousness

Father Joseph T. Lienhard, S.J.

"Just as through the disobedience of one person the many were made sinners, so through the obedience of one the many will be made righteous." (Rom 5: 19)

Original sin may not seem like a fit subject for an uplifting meditation, and perhaps it isn't. But the verse from Saint Paul quoted above states, as clearly as any passage in Scripture, that the disobedience of one man made sinners of the many. The Catechism teaches that Adam and Eve, who stood at the head of the human race, sinned and thereby lost for themselves and all their descendants the original grace of holiness. Thus all of us are born in a state of deprivation. But original sin is not like personal sin: it is contracted, not committed; it is a state, not a personal act. This state is transmitted to all human beings (except the Virgin Mary), although how it is transmitted remains a mystery. As a result of original sin, human nature is wounded, but not totally corrupted; even wounded reason can attain some natural knowledge of God. Because of original sin, we are subject to ignorance and suffering, to the dominion of death, and to that strange inclination to sin that is called concupiscence. But the Holy Scriptures, even as they recount Adam's fall, also recount God's promise that evil would finally be conquered, and man, who had fallen, would be raised up, when God's own hand reached down to him. According to a beautiful old tradition, Genesis 3: 15 is called the *Protoevangelium*, the First Gospel; there God promises that the woman's offspring will crush the serpent, the tempter. Even here, we can sense the spiritual message of original sin: that the state we are in is not the one God intended; God did not mean our lives to be marked by sorrow and pain. But even in the midst of sorrow, God offers us hope – not only offers, but promises. Sin may appear to be a strong force in our lives, but God's grace is far stronger, and the power of sin can never stand up to it.

Lord, Creator and Father, look upon us, we ask you. We have fallen far from you. Reach out your saving hand, Jesus Christ our Lord, raise us up in life and joy, and guide us to our everlasting home.

Grace Abounding – But Not on Loan

Anthony Esolen

"Where sin increased, grace overflowed all the more, so that, as sin reigned in death, grace also might reign through justification for eternal life through Jesus Christ our Lord." (Rom 5: 20-21)

Some people think of God's grace as a rich bank account. The more righteous we grow, the more freely we can draw from it. "Oh, it's you?" says the Almighty. "You haven't failed me yet. Take what you like."

Now Jesus does say we'll be rewarded according to our merits – though we'd best not be too hasty to assume we know where true merit lies. Paul can teach us that lesson in both caution and hope. His own life shows us that we cannot know how many terrible sinners are close to God, even closer to him than those who are satisfied with their righteousness. For Paul was such a sinner. There he stood, "serving" the Lord on the streets of Jerusalem by overseeing the first martyrdom, watching the cloaks as an infuriated rabble stoned Stephen to death.

Sin played the tyrant in Paul, to the peril of his soul. But to this sinner came the Lord with his blinding light, calling out, "Saul, Saul, why do you persecute me?" Grace abounded far above the sin, like a flood of healing waters. Isn't it astonishing, isn't it an offense to our sense of decency, that God can mold the most violent sinners into the most fiery saints?

But don't we see that in our own lives? One year from my youth was so dark that almost everything that happened in it seems to have been stripped from my memory. But in this time, my faith gasping on its sickbed, my heart yearning for the very sin that had crushed it and left it for dead, grace abounded beyond the sin. I too turned a corner of the road, and met a Christian gentleman whom God used to return me to light. Were it not for that man, that instrument of grace, I would not be writing this now.

O Father, you that walk beside us in the valley of the shadow of death, grant that we may never despair of your grace, but trust in your abundant mercies.

Come to the Water

Anthony Esolen

"Are you unaware that we who were baptized into Christ Jesus were baptized into his death? We were indeed buried with him through baptism into death, so that, just as Christ was raised from the dead by the glory of the Father, we too might live in newness of life." (Rom 6: 3-4)

What does Paul mean, to be baptized into Christ's death? We know about a man who died with Christ – in one sense, the only man who ever did. The thief whose heart turned to Jesus not only watched his Savior die, but heard words of death and life from Jesus' lips: "This day you shall be with me in paradise." What hope and joy and fear must have swept over him, when he saw the soldiers coming to break his legs and bring on the final agony? That was a baptism like no other.

To die with Christ is to be baptized, to descend to the dead with him, that we may rise with him again. It's true, the Lord permits the Church to baptize little babies, "drowning" them in holy water and anointing their heads with oil, to mark them as his. But we're mistaken if we think baptism is just a pretty ceremony of welcome into the Church, an occasion for photos and feasting. We celebrate it because of the new life to which it invites us. Every Easter we renew our baptismal vows, because that dying-to-rise is the essence of the Christian life. And that's what we fear.

More than we fear death, we fear life. I don't mean the hard-shelled routine that passes for life, but the real thing, fresh and free, foolish in the world's eyes, stripped of the trappings of worldly honor and wealth and power, naked as a little child – or as Christ on the cross, clothed only in obedience and love. We shy away. Who knows whether that other thief, the unrepentant, had a moment when he too could have caught at dying to live again, but feared, and turned away with a jest?

Jesus calls us to save our lives by losing them. In him we are that corn of wheat that falls into the ground and dies, to bring forth much fruit.

Father, you that sent your Spirit upon your well-beloved Son as he was baptized in the Jordan, and upheld him in the Spirit as he died upon the cross: grant us that same Spirit of life that we too may die with Christ and rise with him again.

Let the Old Man Die

Anthony Esolen

*"We know that our old self was crucified with [Christ Jesus],
so that our sinful body might be done away with, that we might
no longer be in slavery to sin." (Rom 6: 6)*

I bear a constant reminder of death. It won't put me in the grave any time soon; it's only a leg with a rare defect in the veins and lymph vessels. The veins have no valves, or only a few, and so the blood will wash backwards, pool up, and leave the leg prone to infections. Such as has struck me today, with a sudden high fever and great pain.

It isn't itself sinful, this infirmity, nor has it kept me from doing pretty much as I please. But it reminds me of the genuine infirmity, the one that stoops me in idleness, or that riddles the joints of my soul in a palsy of anger. It's the infirmity that twists an eye sidelong in the leer of envy. It stiffens the neck, it cramps the knees to make them creak and rattle if you try to bend them in prayer. The infirmity is sin, and it makes us old.

For when Saint Paul speaks of that "old self" crucified with Christ, I don't think we should hear merely "the self I used to have." It is *old*, hobbling and doddering to destruction. Don't we see the fresh glance of youth in the eyes of a grandmother whose life has been full of the cheer of holy works? Don't we see the little child she has become by God's grace, ready to enter the kingdom? Or can't we catch the spiritual age, the soul's frailty and decay, in the pale mask of a "youth" whose sins are so habitual that he no longer derives even illicit pleasure from them?

God grants us seventy years or so. We don't need that many to grow old. It's just that it takes some of us the full seventy to finally put the old self to death on the cross, to be young and whole and free.

Father, you that so loved the world that you gave your only-begotten Son to die for us upon the cross: help us to scale that cross, that our old selves may die, and that we may rise in the freedom of life.

Be Ready for the Wonder

Anthony Esolen

"If [...] we have died with Christ, we believe that
we shall also live with him." (Rom 6: 8)

In my darkest moments, I don't doubt that Christ rose from the dead. Some people say the apostles were simpletons who believed what they wanted to believe. Then they say that these same simpletons perpetrated the subtlest hoax in the history of the world. They had to interpret all of Jewish history and prophecy as summed up and fulfilled in the teaching and the person of Jesus. They had to scramble their accounts a little, just enough to make it *appear* that they were giving independent versions of the same events whereof they or their teachers were eye-witnesses. Then they had to put in Jesus' mouth words of such simplicity and grandeur that they make the world's wisest men, a Socrates or a Confucius, seem like muddleheaded boys.

No, I know Christ rose from the dead. And I believe he will raise up all who have died in the faith. He'll raise my father. He'll raise the saintly monsignor who oversaw my boyhood school, my grandmother who smiled so often that the lines of her goodness were etched upon her brows, and my old friend the lover of Chaucer, who came to the faith as a young man when he saw that the world asked all the wrong questions and could not answer them anyway. Christ will raise them all. But in my darkest moments, I wonder why he would trouble to raise *me*.

Then comes a voice of sanity. "So, you believe somehow that it depends on *you*? That you should be good enough to shake the dust from your shroud? That God may do with you only what *you* think is fitting? That he should be sparing of his gifts, just as you would be if you were God? Quit wallowing in your pride, which you call humility. You will be raised. It's been revealed. Prepare for it, then! Grapple yourself to the One who died, and you shall live with him."

Father, you that raised your Son from the tomb: grant us the faith to
bind ourselves to his death, that he may bind us to him in life.

Free at Last

Anthony Esolen

*"You too must think of yourselves as [being] dead to sin
and living for God in Christ Jesus." (Rom 6: 11)*

"I've got no strings on me!" sings the silly Pinocchio in the movie. He won't obey his kindly maker and father, Geppetto. So he obeys instead the malicious Fox and Cat, though he has a wooden head and believes he is free to follow his own desires, not obeying anybody.

There really are only two choices in this life of ours, and Saint Paul delineates their terms most clearly. You can obey sin, and die, or you can die to sin, and live for God in Christ Jesus. There is no third possibility.

What must it be like to be dead to sin? Imagine Sin as a once-imperious master, calling out to you from afar, "Come back to me! Remember the good things I gave you, remember the fleshpots of Egypt! You can have them again, you can enjoy the few nights remaining to you. Only do my bidding, and they shall be yours." And we, living for God but not yet made perfect, hear that call and are moved by it; though somehow it feels as if Sin were appealing to a dead man, someone in the tomb of the past, a wooden-headed fool jerked about on strings. And we remember that fool's misfortunes, but as if they'd happened in another life, to someone else.

And that's not the half of it. We can't simply die to sin; we must live for God. The reason why we don't heed the old master anymore is that we are too busy attending the new. And as we grow in strength, freely surrendering more and more of our lives to God, and becoming more and more human as we do, that voice of the evil master will grow feeble. It will die, like the last thin scratchings of a gnat on the wrong side of a stained-glass window. Then we will be enfolded in the songs of life and victory.

*Father, whose victorious Son died to take away the sting of the grave
and to put death to death: send forth your Spirit to slay the sin in us,
that we may live in you and for you, our true and only Ruler.*

Shut That Shop's Doors for Good

Anthony Esolen

"Present yourselves to God as raised from the dead to life and the parts of your bodies to God as weapons for righteousness. For sin is not to have any power over you, since you are not under the law but under grace." (Rom 6: 13-14)

Ebenezer Scrooge, that hardhearted, grasping, covetous old sinner, wakes from his journey in the company of the Ghost of Christmas Yet to Come. His last vision in that dream was of his own grave, unmourned, a fit end for a "respectable" life given to the dull slow works of death.

But now he is pierced to the heart. He sees the snow floating down in the morning light. He is alive – he has in fact been *raised from the dead to life*. He is Ebenezer, born anew. "I don't know what day it is!" he laughs, he the master of the counting house, the buyer of bad debts, ever so precise. "I am quite a baby!"

It's a wondrous paradox, his being raised from the dead. He is still Scrooge, and more truly himself than ever. He still has a bit of the wag about him, playing a brilliant trick on his clerk Bob Cratchit, sending him a huge Christmas turkey (anonymously) for his family to feast on, and then pretending impatience when Bob walks in late the next day. But he begs Bob's forgiveness and declares his intent to use his means – his "weapons of righteousness" – to assist the struggling family.

Yet he is *not* the same Scrooge. We miss the point if we suppose he's just become a little freer with his money. He has passed over from the realm of law to the realm of grace. He sees now that there's a Buyer of bad debts infinitely greater than he: the Redeemer, to whom he owes everything. Who among us, his bad debt redeemed for ever, would contract for another, complete with legal instructions as to when it must be paid? Paul exhorts us: we are no longer to dwell in the counting house of the law. Sin must have no more dominion over us.

Father, you that send your Spirit to write in our hearts the new law of charity: scour our hearts and make them shine as burnished weapons, bold and free.

There Are Bonds, and There Are Bonds

Anthony Esolen

"Thanks be to God that, although you were once slaves of sin, you have become obedient from the heart to the pattern of teaching to which you were entrusted. Freed from sin, you have become slaves of righteousness." (Rom 6: 17-18)

The people of Saint Paul's day, as we all know, owned slaves. Sometimes the slaves were women and boys hauled away as plunder from a conquered city. Sometimes they were men, and their families, who had lost everything and had only their hands and their backs to barter for food and a roof over their heads.

To be a slave, among the Greeks and Romans at least, was so great a shame that the son of a man who had been emancipated still lived under a social shadow. Christianity would come to change all that, but not, at first, by decrying the wicked institution itself. If Paul had cried out, "There shall be no more slaves," he would have gotten some puzzled looks, not least from some of the slaves themselves, who might well have said, "Then how am I supposed to feed my children?" or, "But I have served my master faithfully for forty years."

Paul's message was more radical than that. "You are all slaves, all of you!" he declares. "Don't you see? You have bent your backs under the lash of the cruelest master of all. Sin is your lord. Whatever hateful thing Sin commands, you do. You loathe it and grit your teeth, or you do it tamely – such good slaves that even if Sin did not bother to command, you would do his bidding anyway."

And what then does Paul recommend? How are we to escape this slavery? The Gospel is our Underground Railroad, leading us from slavery into Slavery! For man is meant to obey. He longs to lay his will at the feet of a Lord worthy to be obeyed. And when he lays his will at the feet of God, as a slave of righteousness, he shares in the abundant freedom of God. He becomes like Christ, the Way, the Truth, and the Life: and the Truth sets him free.

Father, in whose Spirit we call upon you as sons and daughters, grant us the courage to cleave to the Good News, that we may prove good and faithful servants.

Never Ask What You Will Be Paid

Anthony Esolen

"Now that you have been freed from sin and have become slaves of God, the benefit that you have leads to sanctification, and its end is eternal life. For the wages of sin is death, but the gift of God is eternal life in Christ Jesus our Lord." (Rom 6: 22-23)

The first real job I ever had was to be the all-purpose boy at my uncle's shirt factory. I'd sweep up, pack shirts, haul huge bolts of material upstairs on the conveyor belt, mow the grass, cut slots in flannel for ponchos, and load boxes of finished product on the truck. But when I could, I'd steal out of the top-story window and lie on the roof, basking in the sun. I'd done what we had contracted for. I'd earned my wages.

Notice that though Saint Paul says that the wages of sin is death, he does *not say* that the wages of righteousness is eternal life. Here, as often, is something the secular world cannot understand about Christianity, because even Christians find it hard to understand. As long as I believe that I'll be piling up a jackpot of wages earned by my good and diligent work, my employer will be named Sin, and I will earn death for my pains. For the relationship bound by the wage is not wholly free. If I would be paid, I must do the work, but if I do the work, I must be paid. Then God becomes *my debtor!* I strut before him, saying, "Look here, I cast out demons in your name!" Not every demon, apparently. "Depart from me, you evil-doer," God replies. "I never knew you."

No, we are not meant to be hirelings, punching a Catholic time-card. God wants to give us eternal life, beginning right now with our sanctification. But he can only give it if we accept it as a gift, unearned, free. For there is a grace and humility in receiving a gift: in the blushing confession that it is far more than we've deserved. Demand your wages, and you will receive them. Let go of your pride, and you will hear the Father call, "Come, good and faithful servant, and enter into your Master's joy."

Father, who sent your Son that we might not be hirelings but servants, and, if servants, then also your beloved sons and daughters: grant us the wisdom to seek good gifts from your hands, even the gift of eternal life.

An Arm Alone Is No Arm

Anthony Esolen

"You also were put to death to the law through the body of Christ, so that you might belong to another, to the one who was raised from the dead in order that we might bear fruit for God."
(Rom 7: 4)

Today we are taught that only a fool would "belong to another." Even Catholics who would never dream of a divorce will not say, "I belong to her" or, "My body is his." We are made for independence, aren't we? Doesn't it say that somewhere, in the Letter of Thomas to the Philippians?

Saint Paul reminds us instead that we are put to death to the law "through the body of Christ." What body is he talking about? Certainly the body of Christ that died upon the cross and rose again on Easter Sunday. But it is also the body that Christ gives us in Holy Communion, the sacrament that is the center of the Church's worship, because it is the sacrament that *makes the Church*. We belong to Christ not by asserting our independence, but by grafting ourselves upon the body of believers. Through the Church we have learned of Jesus, through the Church we receive his body.

Independence is an illusion. Before we belonged to Christ, we belonged to the law – a law that we sinners could not fulfill. We were subjects in the kingdom of death. But now we belong to the Body of Christ, the glorified body raised up on Easter, the body present in communion under the accidents of bread and wine, and that mystical Body, the Church, spanning the ages and bridging earth and heaven. So when someone says, "I believe in Jesus, but not in the Church," he shows that he doesn't yet know who Jesus is. He is a severed limb.

We bear no fruit on our own. We are no body, but a heap of dead branches, dry sticks, good for nothing but kindling. There is no Church in the garbage-pit of hell. But graft that limb upon the tree of life, and the fruit will blossom. Christ has given us his Body, that we might do just that.

Father, in whose Spirit we live and move and have our being: grant us the humility to become living members of the Church, that we may yield fruits of faith, hope, and charity, to the glory of your name.

No Sinner Like a Righteous Sinner

Anthony Esolen

"Sin, seizing an opportunity in the commandment, deceived me and through it put me to death." (Rom 7: 11)

Satan likes to appear as an angel of light. Even the serpent whose body he commandeered in Eden was sleek and beautiful. If Satan appeared in his true form, twisted and tarnished, consumed from within by the fires of his envious heart, eyes frozen in the ice of hatred of his Maker, who would listen? But we do listen. "It can't be wrong," we say, "if it feels so good." To translate: "How can that be the Prince of Darkness, when he's so shiny?"

All the wretch can do is to deform: he twists good things to evil ends. So he does, appallingly enough, with our desire to follow the very commandments of God. It is Satan's most dangerous temptation, because it is the hardest to discern. Easy for the drunkard in the ditch or the lecher in the brothel to know he has gone astray; hard for the Pharisee in the temple – or at the communion rail.

So Sin seizes upon God's commandment, and we lose both ways. If we break the commandment, we sin. If we pride ourselves on not breaking it, we deceive ourselves, and we sin all the more. Paul, the erstwhile Pharisee, a scrupulous adherer to the law, swallowed up in pride, knew whereof he spoke. Such sinners are like the walking dead. Do we then wonder why Jesus had to raise his voice so high against them, crying, "Woe to you, scribes and Pharisees, hypocrites!" It's not easy to make yourself heard by the dead.

Then let us not fool ourselves. The law is holy, and we are not. The law is good, and the best thing it does for us is to convict us of our wickedness. Then we must throw ourselves upon God's mercy. To do otherwise is to hand the commandment over to Sin, which has had long practice in wielding it – to kill.

Father, you that on Mount Sinai gave to Moses the law that only your Son would fulfill: protect us from the deceit of both our righteousness and our despair.

I Only Want… I'm Not Sure What I Want

Anthony Esolen

"What I do, I do not understand.
For I do not do what I want, but I do what I hate."
(Rom 7: 15)

Alas, poor man! Not only does he not know what he wants, sometimes he doesn't even "want" what he wants. Saint Paul here describes the muddy ruts of sin. Not any spectacular crime, like murder; just the dull habit of doing the evil you don't want, and failing to do the good you do want. Is this possible? Peer into the crazy passages of man's heart, and you'll see that it's not only possible, it's what life apart from the grace of God inevitably collapses into. How many people put their families on ice to win and keep a job they don't really like, to buy things they don't need, to gain pleasures they don't enjoy? Or sweat themselves to death with ambition to win… what? The chairmanship of a department full of people among whom they've never spent a single unguarded human moment?

The fact is, we far more often sin by choosing what we do not genuinely desire than by pursuing a full-blooded lust. C. S. Lewis' devil Screwtape gives away the secret. First you tempt with pleasure, to elicit the sin. Then slowly you take away the pleasure, all while bolting the man's soul to a sin he has grown to hate, but which he chooses anyway. Keep sinning like that long enough, and you will become one who wouldn't grasp for salvation even if it took no more effort of the will than what you'd need to brush away a fly.

Pause now, reader, and ask, "Do I understand myself?" Outside the window of your soul lies a land of rest, with deep green glades and chattering brooks and fresh mountains rising against the sky. It is a land of peace, and youth renewed, and love; and something in one of the forgotten alleys of your heart cries out for it. Then why turn back to the dim little cell of your sin?

Father, you whose will can never fail of its end: instill in us your Spirit of understanding, that we may know your will, and know it as ours also, and perform it to the best of our strength.

If Only I Might Betray Myself

Anthony Esolen

"The willing is ready at hand, but doing the good is not.
For I do not do the good I want, but I do the evil I do not want.
Now if [I] do what I do not want, it is no longer I who do it,
but sin that dwells in me." (Rom 7: 18-20)

How beautiful our faith is! Each of us is called to be a saint, or rather, to be *this saint here*, wonderfully distinct from that saint over there, yet all one in Christ. Some saints will rule kingdoms, like Louis IX of France, and some saints will walk barefoot upon the mountains, like the little Francis. Grace sharpens us so that we become ourselves, that is, what God has meant us to be. It is sin, like a foul black lump of sludge, that dulls and obscures the core of our beings.

So then, as Saint Paul says, when we sin, it is not we ourselves who do the evil, but that sin – a parody of the Holy Spirit – that dwells within us. Now let us understand him correctly. If John takes Tom's wife, John will be punished for it, because John is sinning. But in another sense it is not John who wills the sin. It's not John as God meant him to be, that true man lying stifled far beneath the encrustations of sin. It's a false John, a thing that has taken him captive.

Most of the time a sinner will not even know that he's not himself. He will so deeply identify himself with his sins that they may come to seem virtuous to him, and to part with them would feel like having his chest opened and that stony thing called a "heart" pried out with red-hot pincers. But sometimes even he will see the truth of the matter. When his will is at cross-purposes to itself, when he knows what is good and desires it but cannot do it, then he sees that he is like a captive city, whose acts are decreed by the governor within. Sin is that usurping governor. And for sin there is no remedy but to fling the gates wide for another Conqueror, Christ the Lord.

Father, you to whom your Son taught us to pray, "Thy will be done":
send your Spirit to drive our sin out and to dwell within us, that
we may be ourselves at last, and yours.

Even This Poor Body Will See the Light

Anthony Esolen

"Miserable one that I am! Who will deliver me from this mortal body? Thanks be to God through Jesus Christ our Lord."
(Rom 7: 24-25)

The problem isn't that it's a body. Saint Paul is clear about that. When he went up to the Hill of Mars to preach to the sophisticated men of Athens, they listened politely enough, till he came to the resurrection of the body. Then most of them laughed, shook their heads, went home for dinner. Who would want this rotting husk of a body back?

We Christians would – but a rotting husk no more. For as Paul says, "What is sown in corruption, is raised in incorruption." Then does he merely yearn for freedom from the *mortality* of the body?

That's part of it, but not the most important part. The body is not just mortal. It is, even while it lives, a "body of death." That is, the body and its members lie in the dead grip of sin. On the day when Adam and Eve ate the forbidden fruit, they died. Yes, they walked about the earth for many years after. They wept in repentance, they prayed; they made love, and raised children, one of whom they would bury, murdered by his brother. They knew grief and consolation. They grew old, their hearts stopped beating, and they returned to the dust whence they came. But from the moment they sinned, they were infected with death.

So are we, apart from Jesus Christ. God is far from us; our wills do not obey us; we fight a losing battle against Sin and Death as they march through the lands of our being, planting their flags on one hill, then another, till we are imprisoned in what is now Death's body, a body of death.

Who then can deliver us? He who was born in the flesh, who suffered and died in the flesh, and who rose in the flesh, gloriously triumphant. Only he can slay this body of death, and raise both soul and body to glory.

Father all-powerful, Author of life and light, you that desire the death of no man: help us to seek our deliverance from your Son, from him who shut the jaws of death, that our bodies too may rise in glory from the grave.

The Spirit Brings Freedom

Father Francis Martin

*"The law of the spirit of life in Christ Jesus has freed you
from the law of sin and death." (Rom 8: 2)*

Just as the phrase "the city of Washington" means "the city which is Washington," so the expression "the law of the spirit of life" means "the law which is the spirit of life," and "the law of sin and death" refers to the law which binds together sin and death. This latter expression is not unlike "the law of gravity." It is inevitable: just as a body released in space is pulled toward the earth, so sin goes toward death; in fact sin already participates in death, the absence of life. We are freed from this "law" by another "law," namely, the Holy Spirit who is life and who replaces the sin that is pulling us into death. When we speak of the forgiveness of sins we are referring to the gift of the Holy Spirit. In the prayer over the gifts for the Saturday before Pentecost, we ask the Father that the Holy Spirit heal our minds with divine sacraments, "because he himself is the remission of sins," and in the formula of sacramental absolution we address the Father by saying, "you sent the Holy Spirit among us for the forgiveness of sins." The Spirit who is life replaces sin which is death. If we continue to reflect further we are surely intrigued by the fact that the Spirit of life is called a law at all. The explanation is that Saint Paul is directing our minds back to a prophecy pronounced by Jeremiah and then developed by Ezekiel. Jeremiah (31: 33) recorded God's promise to put a new law within us and write it on our hearts, and Ezekiel (36: 27) further specifies that this will come about because God will give us his Spirit to dwell in us and be the source of our actions. We are free because of the divine joy and energy that is given to us, moving us out of sin into an eternal life.

Father, we bless you for your gift, your very own Spirit by whom you are bound to your Son. We pray for your whole Church: make us one, lead us to the freedom and enthusiasm for your will that filled the heart of Jesus, your Son, so that all the world will see us and glorify you from whom we have the Spirit of life.

Power to Fulfill the Law

Father Francis Martin

*"For what the law, weakened by the flesh, was powerless to do,
this God has done: by sending his own Son in the likeness of
sinful flesh and for the sake of sin, he condemned sin in the flesh,
so that the righteous decree of the law might be fulfilled in us,
who live not according to the flesh but according to the spirit."*
(Rom 8: 3-4)

In Saint Paul's mind, there is a difference between meeting the demands of the law and fulfilling them. Suppose we are at a dinner party and on the table there is nothing to drink. I get up and volunteer to get something. All at dinner wait for me to bring some water, but I come back with a tray carrying glasses filled with a beautiful wine. I have not "met" your expectations, I have "fulfilled" them; I have gone beyond what you expected. This is what Saint Paul means when he tells us that the Father, by sending his Son in the flesh and condemning Sin right within humanity (the flesh) he has enabled us to "fulfill" the righteous decree of the law, that is, to obey the law by going beyond it. As Paul tells us later in this letter (Rom 13: 8): "Owe nothing to anyone, except to love one another; for the one who loves another has fulfilled the law." You may notice that I wrote that the Father condemned "Sin," not "sin." "Sin" for Saint Paul is a force; it is a combination of many forces: political, economic, military, emotional, mental, volitional, and demonic. Our own sin is our personal appropriation of this force within and around us by which we contribute to the power of Sin. Saint Paul is telling us that God sent his Son among us so that the Sin force, which is present in all of us and ratified by our sin, might be condemned and deprived of its power through the death of Christ in the same flesh as we possess, though sinless. Now we can fulfill the just decree of the law, going beyond its requirements: we can love as Jesus loves, and in the power of the Holy Spirit make him known and loved in this world.

Father, it is only by your Spirit of love that we can bring the law you gave our fathers to the goal you always planned for it and which was supremely fulfilled in Jesus, your Son. Thank you for the power you give us through his passion and resurrection to live for you and answer your desires.

What Is Your Preoccupation?

Father Francis Martin

"For those who live according to the flesh are concerned with the things of the flesh, but those who live according to the spirit with the things of the spirit." (Rom 8: 5)

When Saint Paul contrasts "flesh" and "spirit" as he does here, he is not speaking of "body" and "soul," but rather of a biblical view of a human being. When he speaks of "flesh" in negative terms as here, he is referring to the whole human being in our disordered state with drives that are inimical to the law of God: drives to self-indulgence, self-aggrandizement, self-protection, and a position of enmity to any one or any thing that could thwart these drives. He is speaking as well of our inner experience of these drives with its concomitant shame, defensiveness, and opposition to God. When he speaks of "spirit" on the other hand he is referring to the deepest or highest point of our soul, that aspect of our being that is available to be energized and enlightened by the Holy Spirit who, from this point, can elevate and purify our will, our desires, our mind, as well as our whole physical and emotional being. To live according to the flesh thus means to be concentrated on that whole environment described above, to be concerned, even preoccupied with an individual and social jungle of conflicting and imperious drives: the world portrayed for our emulation by most of the media; that world which is daily decaying through the illusion of desire. On the contrary, those who live under the sway of the Holy Spirit, moving us through our spirit, become more and more captivated by the beauty of Jesus Christ, his life, his truth, his freedom, and peace, his ineffable presence in us and in others. You may remember that at the beginning of this letter (1: 16), Paul said that the Good News, the "reality" carried by the preaching, is "the power of God for the salvation of everyone who believes." He was speaking of the power of the cross imparted by the Spirit.

Father, thank you for your gift of the Holy Spirit who has brought our spirit alive. Blessed Gift, you dwell in us. Move us to overcome our convoluted desires and identify us with the desires in the heart of Jesus Christ.

Standing at the Crossroads

Father Francis Martin

*"The concern of the flesh is death, but the concern
of the spirit is life and peace." (Rom 8: 6)*

In order to enter into Saint Paul's thought, we will have to consider more attentively the words he is using. The Greek word underlying our English "concern" can imply something like "preoccupation" or "drive." Thus, the preoccupation of the flesh, in all the ways just described above, is a drive to death. Death is eternal separation from God. The preoccupation of the Spirit-filled human spirit is a drive to life, a life of intimate union with God here in this life and an existence for ever in which the very self-gift of the Trinity becomes the life-giving eternal existence of our body and soul, an ineffable, intimate joy made greater by being shared with millions of others. Already Psalm 1 had traced out for us the "two ways" that lie before us, urging us to treasure God's instruction and stay away from the way that leads to being blown away like useless chaff. In the light of Christ and of the "new creation" he has made of us, Paul looks to the interior principles that give rise to our actions: the drive of the flesh and the drive of the spirit. The secret of the way to life is an attentive obedience to the movement of the Holy Spirit within us: his voice resounds in many ways saying, "Come to the Father." We can hear him and be encouraged by him if we fight each day for a precious time of prayer. Prayer itself, according to the Catholic Catechism (2564) is "the action of God and of man, springing forth from both the Holy Spirit and ourselves…" Can you see how deeply God wants us to come to "life and peace"? He is the one who moves us in prayer, so that our spirit, yielding to the Holy Spirit, so yearns for God that we go against the drives of the flesh and enter into life.

*Father, you have sent the Spirit of your Son into our hearts crying,
Abba! Thank you for this personal gift. Please stay with us and give
us a knowledge of your Fatherly reality: what a joy to know and
love you even in this life; what must heaven be!*

We Have the Spirit of Christ

Father Francis Martin

"But you are not in the flesh; on the contrary, you are in the spirit, if only the Spirit of God dwells in you. Whoever does not have the Spirit of Christ does not belong to him." (Rom 8: 9)

Saint Paul's thought and language are very compressed. We have to pay attention to every word. Consider the word "in." We are not "in the flesh." Paul surely means more here than when he writes to the Galatians (2: 20) saying of himself, "insofar as I now live in the flesh, I live by faith in the Son of God…" "In the flesh" here means more than "living in this body." It means living dominated by all that the term "flesh" has meant in this context. By telling his audience that they are not in the flesh, Paul means to awaken in them a deeper self-knowledge, calling them to an awareness of what the death and resurrection of Christ, onto which they have been grafted by baptism, has done for them. They (and we) are new creatures. Just compare the icons of sensuality, power, and greed that dominate our daily news with the lives of Mother Teresa, John Paul II, the Amish community who forgave the murderer of their children, and you will see what "in the flesh" and "in the spirit" finally result in. On the basis of our faith and baptism we are "in the spirit" and "in the Spirit" if only the Spirit of God dwells in us. And he does dwell in us unless we reject his intimate presence by serious sin. Saint Paul goes further and states that in order to "belong to" Christ, we must have the "Spirit of Christ." Note how the Spirit of God is also called the Spirit of Christ. In order to belong to Christ, that is, to be actually joined to him and be a living part of his Body, we must "have" the Spirit who comes from Christ. What does this mean? The divine Spirit is a gift to us; that means we "possess" him "freely to use and enjoy," as Thomas Aquinas says, and yet, at every moment he is being given to us by the Father.

Blessed Holy Spirit, because you willingly dwell in us, more intimately than we can imagine, we reverence you. Because you join us to Jesus Christ, the incarnate Word, we are part of his Body. Move in us, guide us so that we learn to love and obey the Father with the heart of Christ.

Dead and Alive

Father Francis Martin

"But if Christ is in you, although the body is dead because of sin, the spirit is alive because of righteousness." (Rom 8: 10)

Saint Paul develops his thought from the previous line by pointing out that to have the Spirit of Christ dwelling in us means that by his action we have Christ dwelling by faith in our hearts (see Eph 3: 17). Before we go any further, let each person stop and ask himself: "Am I aware of Christ dwelling in my heart?" One might say, "I am not aware of serious sin in my life and so I am allowed to conclude that Christ so dwells." Surely Paul means more than this. Pope Benedict challenges us in a similar way when he tells us that Christ "is in need of witnesses who have encountered him, who have known him intimately through the force of the Holy Spirit, men and women who, having touched him with their hand, so to speak, can attest to him" (May 9, 2005). The result of our Lord's indwelling is that, although the body is dead in that it still remains subject for a time longer to the realm of death and sin, the Spirit is (literally) "Life." Our spirit shares this quality and is already in the realm of Life because we share in the righteousness of Christ and are being beckoned to the fullness of that righteousness which is a transforming union with the Trinity and ultimately an eternal life in which our body shares. Why is Paul telling us this? Surely because he wants us to live in reality and to interpret realistically our experience of death and Life. Christ is in us. Pray every day, seek his presence, listen to his invitation to help you break with sin and darkness: he is leading you to an awareness of his nearness to you, his love for you. When you pray he says to you, "You have my undivided attention." Rejoice in this and let the Holy Spirit show you its truth.

Jesus, risen and glorious, your Holy Spirit brings you to dwell in my heart. Lead me out of my darkness, strengthen me so that I die to sin and live to you, help me to yield to the action of your Spirit as he conforms my heart to be like yours, loving the Father and his will, and being your instrument in this world.

Eternal Life for Our Bodies

Father Francis Martin

"If the Spirit of the one who raised Jesus from the dead dwells in you, the one who raised Christ from the dead will give life to your mortal bodies also, through his Spirit that dwells in you."
(Rom 8: 11)

Once when I, as a priest, was beside the coffin of a young man as he was being lowered into the ground, I felt this prayer of the Holy Spirit well up in me (remember he comes to our aid by praying in us). I addressed the ground and I said: "Thank you, earth, for providing a resting place for this young man's body, but remember, he loved Jesus Christ and tried hard to follow him. The very Spirit of the Father who raised Jesus from the dead dwelt in him and moved him in his heart and actions, and will return to take this body to glory. His body is dead now, but it will rise again when the Spirit comes seeking his own, those in whom he had delighted to dwell. And you, earth, you yourself are now eagerly awaiting the revelation of the sons of God. How proud you will be to have welcomed this young body, still redolent with the perfume of the Holy Spirit, when that same Spirit gives life once more to this body for ever! Now is the time of darkness and death, then will be the time of radiant light and unending joy, and you will share in this yourself. So rejoice even now with us, earth, as we look forward to the day he leaves you and in gratitude grants you a share in the radiance of his transformed humanity." My friends, think of the promise in the words of Saint Paul. They are words inspired by the Spirit and they contain a promise that can calm our hearts: "the one who raised Christ from the dead will give life to your death-directed bodies."

Let us make these words our prayer: "See what love the Father has bestowed on us that we may be called the children of God. Yet so we are... Beloved, we are God's children now; what we shall be has not yet been revealed. We do know that when it is revealed we shall be like him, for we shall see him as he is. Everyone who has this hope based on him makes himself pure, as he is pure" (1 Jn 3: 1-3).

The Two Ways

Father Francis Martin

*"For if you live according to the flesh, you will die, but if by
the spirit you put to death the deeds of the body, you will live."*
(Rom 8: 13)

The collection of psalms in our Bible begins with the same vision we find in this statement by Saint Paul. Psalm 1 presents us with the only two possibilities of our existence: the way to life and the way to death. Psalm 2 presents us with the Messiah: the one set up for the rise and fall of many. Now that the Messiah has come and saved us by his death and resurrection and by giving us the Holy Spirit, the true contours and consequences of the choices presented to us at the beginning of the Psalter are now apparent. When we think that it took the suffering and death of the Son of God to save us from eternal death, we begin to get an idea of the seriousness of our situation. We Christians are brought up in our post-Christian world to think that "I'm OK, you're OK." If we need the grace of Christ, it is more or less for a cosmetic improvement, a touching up here or there: a little less anger, cut back a bit on our gluttony, be more careful with regard to chastity, be more generous with our possessions, etc. Paul, however, tells us that the two ways open to us are clear and serious: either put the drives of the flesh to death or (literally) "you are going to die." What is the secret, then, of "staying alive" and enjoying God's life? It lies in knowing the love of Jesus Christ for us and in the power of the Holy Spirit, reducing these drives toward darkness to an impotence, to a death. The arena of this conflict is our body, not our physicality, but the physical energy with which these sinful drives are endowed and which presses upon our consciousness. The means of victory are three: a consistent life of prayer, an honest and trusting life of repentance, and a sincere forgiveness of others. Obey the Spirit and yield to his energy "and you will live."

Father, you have set forth for all the world to see how great your love is. When we were still sinners, still at enmity with you, Christ died for us. We sing to you, O Lord: thank you for the cross. Never allow this overwhelming love of yours to become commonplace. At every Eucharist awaken us once again to your invitation to life.

Living in God's Family
Father Francis Martin

"For those who are led by the Spirit of God are children of God."
(Rom 8: 14)

An earlier verse in Romans tells us that if we yield to the Spirit and bring to impotence the sinful drives which express themselves in the acts of our body, we will live. We will not be brought to death, the place where there is no praise of God. Saint Paul now begins a new line of thought by explaining that those who are led by the Spirit of God are his children.

Notice, Paul does not characterize such children as merely "possessing" the Spirit of God, which is a precious first step, but of being "led" by the Spirit. From the moment of our baptism, the Holy Spirit is incessantly moving us to the Father. With an infinite enthusiasm he sweeps us along, if we yield, in his eternal and infinite movement of love toward the Father, identifying us with the movement of the Son. Saint Paul speaks here of a secret joy in yielding to the action of the Spirit: namely, we recognize that same action in others, we feel at ease with them and feel a bond with them. Association with such people brings about a joy and a sense of "family." Every time we meet such people there is a sense of mutual recognition; we see that resemblance to the Father, who has brought us to birth through the death of his Son. We come to a mutual recognition of the truth that "he willed to give us birth by the word of truth that we may be a kind of firstfruits of his creatures." (Jas 1: 18). This is a brief and tiny glimpse of what awaits us in heaven. Not only will there be no tears or suffering, no fear or sadness, there will be the joy of loving and being loved with a purity and sincerity that transpires with a freedom that we never tire of enjoying and never fear losing. We experience everlastingly that the Father is the One from whom all family in heaven and on earth takes its name. We are, all together, led by the Spirit and rejoice together in being the children of God.

Most Holy Father, the fountain of all that is good, we praise you for the plans you have for us. You share your Spirit with us and make us a family. Blessed are you, O God and Father of our Lord Jesus Christ.

Abba!

Father Francis Martin

"You did not receive a spirit of slavery to fall back into fear, but you received a spirit of adoption, through which we cry, Abba, 'Father!'" (Rom 8: 15)

When considering verse 14, we placed the accent on the communal aspect of being God's children by sharing his Spirit. There is no doubt that the accent in this verse, 15, is upon the intimate relation of each believer with God the Father. Abba is an Aramaic word expressive of love, reverence, affection, and admiration. It was used, for instance, by children in addressing their father, or by students addressing a revered master. We have no evidence that anyone used this word in addressing or speaking of God. On the basis of his own knowledge, Jesus revealed the true nature of God, and ultimately of the Trinity, by the way he spoke as well as by his whole attitude of love and obedience to the Father. He instructed his disciples to pray and trust in the same way: "When you pray, say: Father" [Abba] (Lk 11: 2). The early Christians had the habit of saying both the Aramaic and Greek words together: "Abba, Father." Saint Mark (14: 36) describes Jesus as praying in just this way in Gethsemane, and Saint Paul, both here and in Galatians (4: 6), teaches us that the quintessential work of the Holy Spirit is to so form in our hearts a knowledge and divine affection for the Father that we too pray as Jesus did: Abba! This prayer comes from the depth of our spirit under the movement of the Holy Spirit who had so moved the very heart of Jesus. Who can describe this still imperfect but captivating revelation of the Father's face? Who can speak of the joy, the comfort, the love, and spontaneous gift of self to the Father that springs from the depths of the human spirit when we meet him even in this veiled manner? The very Source within the Trinity – there is nothing greater, and he is love. There is with him not the slightest shadow of deceit or disappointment: he is the God and Father of our Lord Jesus Christ.

Father, who can describe your trustworthiness, your love, your delight in being loved by your tiny unworthy creatures? Your blessed Spirit moves in us, and we catch a vision, a presence, a joy that pulls us forward to a complete abandonment to you such that even in darkness and pain and doubt we can never turn from you or withdraw from you or forget your name.

So That We May Be Glorified

Father Francis Martin

"The Spirit itself bears witness with our spirit that we are children of God, and if children, then heirs, heirs of God and joint heirs with Christ, if only we suffer with him so that we may also be glorified with him." (Rom 8: 16-17)

The experience of the action of the Holy Spirit extends more widely than prayer. There are times when we rejoice in dying to self, in suffering for the Gospel, in loving and forgiving when we have no capacity for such love. All of this is an unmistakable experience of the movement of the Holy Spirit within us. Imagine: God himself, the Holy Spirit, is actually at work in us to bring us to eternal life! As these things happen to us and we yield to them, we are granted a tiny glimpse of the work of the Spirit in the great saints and martyrs. We are not alone, my friends; the Spirit of God is with us and in us and he raises our small capacities beyond themselves so that we live and act, think and feel, like children of God. This, then, is his witness along with our own spirit that we are in fact the very adopted children of the Father, loved by him and heirs to all his treasures. What does it mean to be an heir of God? It means that God plans to give us everything except his own divinity, and even then he has made us sharers "in the divine nature" (2 Pt 1: 4) so that we live eternally, body and soul, by the direct gift the Trinity makes of himself to us. If only we suffer with Jesus, join him in the pain of dying to sin, and in bearing the burden of those who have yet to hear the Gospel. There is no one on earth who does not suffer, yet how many have the privilege of offering their daily pains, their efforts to die to sin, and even the great sufferings that come in life, in such a way that others can draw life from these? This is the privilege of the baptized. We suffer with him so that we may be glorified with him.

The presence of suffering causes us fear and revulsion, as it did you as well, Jesus, in your agony in the garden. You embraced your vocation with the power of the Holy Spirit and the presence and co-suffering of your Mother. Teach us what it means to suffer with you, to love with you, and to know the support of Mary, looking forward in hope to the joy set before us. Mary, Mother of God, identify my spirit with every movement of your own.

The Glory to Be Revealed

Father Francis Martin

"I consider that the sufferings of this present time are as nothing compared with the glory to be revealed for us." (Rom 8: 18)

With this statement Saint Paul enters upon a new aspect of his teaching. It is a message of hope. In this verse, he enunciates the basic principle for the hope that is in us: it is the complete lack of any proportion between our present suffering in and with Christ, and the glory that will fill us for ever. In the lines that follow he will list four foundations of this hope. The first foundation, touched upon in the next verse, is the fact that we understand that the incompleteness of material creation, its groaning, is a promise of its completion one day. The second is our own experience of this incompleteness: if hope were not in us, death might frighten us but it would not witness to a future beyond itself for those who are in Christ. Even as we groan, we have a sure conviction that there will be a redemption of our bodies. The third is the witness of the Holy Spirit who enters into our groaning with a groaning prayer of his own. Finally, our understanding of God's complete plan grounds our hope for what is yet to come, namely, our conformity with the glorified Jesus Christ. How many times have we heard the saints say, even in this life, that the suffering they know (Saint Teresa said life was a night spent in a bad hotel) is really nothing in comparison with the joy they experience also in this life (Saint Thomas speaks of "unspeakable delights"). If such is the case even now, what must the joy of heaven be like? The Father, whose Spirit has enabled us to call out to him as Abba, will never disappoint us. This hope gives us courage in time of temptation and suffering not to turn away but to remain faithful and to pray with and exhort each other to remain faithful to the vision of the eternal joy we have been given.

Father, your Word is a promise, a firm invitation to eternal life. Through Paul, you have promised us that what awaits us, if we are faithful, is beyond the greatest joy we can know, even with you, in this life. Keep our hearts expectant; let us witness to others and be able to give to them a reason for the hope that is in us.

The Universe Called to Glory

Father Francis Martin

"Creation awaits with eager expectation the revelation of the children of God; for creation was made subject to futility, not of its own accord but because of the one who subjected it, in hope that creation itself would be set free from slavery to corruption and share in the glorious freedom of the children of God."
(Rom 8: 19-21)

With what a profound understanding of the created universe does Saint Paul begin this section. The material universe is awaiting a completion it lacks, but it cannot achieve this completion without the revelation of the children of God, and this awaits our glorification, the redemption of our bodies. Human beings are the high priests of the material universe, meant to give a human expression to the manner in which matter can give glory to God. Creation itself, however, has been subjected to frustration; it cannot achieve its goal because mankind, who shares its material nature, has by its spiritual sin misdirected it and continues to do so. Think of the waste, the ecological irresponsibility, the destructive use of energy, atomic and otherwise, by which the energies of the universe are turned from the goals they could achieve in order to serve sinful aims. This is the frustration already spoken about immediately after the first sin: "Cursed be the ground because of you! In toil shall you eat its yield all the days of your life" (Gn 3: 17). Much of the disorder that we experience is but the mirror image of the disorder within us to which we give expression through our bodies. The enigmatic expression "in hope," speaking of this subjection, probably means that God did not leave the frustrated material universe under the bondage caused by Adam's sin, but rather destined it to share in the freedom to be given to the children of God in the resurrection of their bodies: "Then I saw a new heaven and a new earth" (Rv 21: 1). At a moment in the future the full potential of the impact of Christ's resurrection will radiate through the universe and one great song of praise and gratitude will rise from the earth. We can, in faith, anticipate that song now when every day some small part of this universe becomes Eucharist, the risen body of the Lord.

Father, you have not only repaired our spirits, wounded by sin, but you will also restore our bodies, so much do you love us and respect all that you have made. We praise you, Lord, and in our song we want our bodies even now to manifest, with lifted hands and voices, the eternal destiny of our physical being.

Who Is My Family?

Father Richard Veras

"We ourselves, who have the firstfruits of the Spirit,
we also groan within ourselves as we wait for adoption,
the redemption of our bodies." (Rom 8: 23)

The Holy Spirit is the love between the Father and the Son. The love between two human persons is a precious thing – a relationship that we need to work on and be loyal to. For the Father and the Son, divine Persons, their relationship is not merely a thing, but a Person, the Holy Spirit who proceeds from the unity of the Father and the Son. It seems that the firstfruits of the Spirit is the desire to belong to the unity of the Trinity, i.e., to await adoption.

Are there families you know whose unity and familiarity with one another overflows to their friends? I had a college friend who came from a large family. Whenever I visited them I was made to feel a part of the family; in fact, I sometimes *wished* I were a part of the family, so attractive was the life they shared. Likewise I had a friend in high school who, during a difficult time, made my family his own, and he was welcomed as one of us. At that point in his life, that welcoming embrace was his salvation.

Redemption does not mean some independent perfection; redemption means belonging: like the belonging I longed for when I saw my friend's large family, the belonging my friend longed for when he saw the unity in my own family. The family of families is the Trinity. The Spirit made us a part of this family in our baptism. The fruit of the Spirit is that I long, i.e., I groan with desire to experience this Unity of all unities, this Belonging of which every other belonging is an echo.

I want to go to the source of that sweet echo, and to await every day the adoption for which my whole being is made.

Come, Holy Spirit, make me belong to the love of the Father and the Son.

The Seeing That Gives Rise to Hope

Father Richard Veras

"Who hopes for what one sees? But if we hope for what we do not see, we wait with endurance." (Rom 8: 24-25)

I hate wedding videos. They never seem to do justice to the magnitude of the event. The grandeur and the beauty are never captured; the reality of what happened on that day seems woefully trivialized and reduced.

I love wedding albums. My siblings and I would love to look through my parents' album over and over. The origin of our family lay mysteriously behind all those 8x10 black and white photos. A photo or a portrait seems to point discreetly yet surely toward the greater reality it portrays. It opens up a nostalgic longing and arouses memory in a way a video seems never to do in its attempt to capture everything so indiscriminately.

Why do we not see what we hope for? Perhaps the way we look at the future is somehow similar to the way we see the past. Perhaps our origin is a kind of image of our destiny. For in this life I have glimpses of the ultimate salvation I hope for. Natural beauty and the beauty of the arts give me portraits of a reality so much greater. All the saints who have walked before me point me to the One toward whom they have walked. Those persons in my life whose love sustains and saves me are living portraits of the One for whom I hope. The sacraments are the most discreet and most sure signs of the love for which I long.

My parents' wedding is rooted in the depths of my being, although my eyes did not see it. The wedding feast of heaven constitutes the depths of my being, though my eyes have yet to fully see. My hope springs forth from the certainty with which I await that great feast, as I see its glimpses breaking into the here and now.

Lord Jesus, may the continual portraits of your heavenly dwelling place continually give birth to my hope.

The Christian at Prayer:
Incapable Yet in Communion

Father Richard Veras

"The Spirit too comes to the aid of our weakness; for we do not know how to pray as we ought, but the Spirit itself intercedes with inexpressible groanings." (Rom 8: 26)

There is a story about two monks praying evening prayer together during a great storm. At a certain point when the trees are knocking against the stained glass and the wind seems about to blow the monastery over, one monk interrupts his recitation and turns to the other insisting, "We'd better put our breviaries down and start praying!" The other monk looks at him perplexed, for he thought that they already were praying.

So often I pray in a formal way without being present. So often I see my breviary or rosary or the Mass as something I have to do, and not as a tender invitation to me from God the Father. Sometimes when I try to be attentive I feel like I am not quite sincere in my begging or in my attempt to be sincere before God. Perhaps I have never prayed as I ought. Perhaps I will never know how. And so, perhaps, prayer is an even more radical dependence upon the Mystery of God than I have ever imagined.

When I find myself distracted or insincere, the problem is not that I need to rely on my unaided efforts. Rather, I have discovered yet again that without Christ I can do nothing, not even pray. Thus I recognize a reason truly to beg for the Spirit – because I have immediate evidence that I cannot pray as I ought.

When I look at my own weakness I feel alone, I am tempted to give up, and I question the value of my prayer. When I beg for the Spirit, my recognition of my distraction and lack of fervor in that moment becomes a reminder of my dependence, and I am aware that I am not alone. At that graced moment I can stop praying formally and really begin to pray, imperfectly yet in communion.

Come, Holy Spirit, renew my heart, enkindle in me the fire of your love. Send forth your Spirit that I may, once again, be created.

Love for One Is Love for All

Father Richard Veras

"We know that all things work for good for those who love God, who are called according to his purpose." (Rom 8: 28)

When he finished college, my brother bought an expensive car. He was deciding between a job offer in the suburbs and one in Manhattan. He didn't like the city.

His expensive car was stolen, and the Manhattan job offered him an apartment near the building where he would work. The unfortunate circumstances made his decision for him. He begrudgingly took the job in Manhattan.

Within two years, one of his colleagues at the non-preferred job became his wife. They now live happily in the suburbs with their two children.

My brother and sister-in-law owe their happiness to a car thief! My nephew and niece owe their existence to a criminal act! God can make *all things* work for the good of those who love him! Redeeming evil to bring about good is the work of God's mercy; and God's mercy on me becomes his mercy on the world. There is no such thing as a good that would be just for me, because I exist in relationship. I have a place in the great design of God. My brother's happiness was not just for him but for the good of his family, whose existence is also for the good of the Church and the world.

Think of Mary's joy in being the Mother of Jesus; there is nothing more blessed which could have happened to her. Yet it didn't happen just for her, it happened for all humanity, for all those destined to be God's sons and daughters. Her suffering at the cross was not without purpose; and her joy at the resurrection of her Son is shared with all of us who are touched by the risen Christ.

God's mercy on me is his mercy on the Church; and his mercy on any one of his sons or daughters is his mercy on me. In building up one of its members, God builds up the whole Church.

Lord, have mercy on me, a sinner; may your mercy upon me gloriously echo through the Church and unto the eternal harmony of your kingdom.

God Proposes to the Predestined

Father Richard Veras

*"Those [God] foreknew he also predestined to be conformed to
the image of his Son, so that he might be the firstborn of many
brothers. And those he predestined he also called; and those he
called he also justified; and those he justified he also glorified."*
(Rom 8: 29-30)

Have you ever noticed how vividly many couples remember
their first date, and the day and the way they got engaged?
I know one couple whose first date was dinner and the
movie *Crocodile Dundee*. They remember this well because she
remembered thinking it was a strange movie for a first date, while
he, on the other hand, had spent much time with his friends deciding exactly what movie he should bring her to. His friends also
helped him pick the restaurant... and what to wear... and what to
say...

Another friend tells of the elaborate evening he organized when
he proposed to his future wife. It involved a limousine arriving at
just the right time in just the right place; and a band at a jazz club
playing just the right song; and a guard at the Empire State Building allowing the newly engaged couple to go to the top just before
it closed.

As both of these stories were being told, the wives, i.e., the recip-
ients of all this planning and affection, were clearly quite happy to
watch and listen as their husbands told, for the umpteenth time,
all that they went through to win their bride.

In each case, the husband had predestined the wife; she was the
one he wanted, but he had to call her, because she was free. In each
case, the husband longed to glorify the woman he so loved.

God loves us, and he loves our freedom. He has predestined all
of us, but he puts himself in the position of having to call us. He
loves us so much he wants to justify us so that we may be worthy
to become the glorified bride of Jesus the bridegroom.

Imagine the joy and gratitude with which I would live if I was
aware of all the planning and wooing that God has done and is
doing out of his infinite affection for me.

*Lord, thank you for predestining me. Give me the grace to recog-
nize the ways in which you are calling me and the poverty of spirit
to allow you to justify me so that I may be made worthy to share
in the glory you have prepared for me.*

Pray for the Peace of the Penitent

Father Richard Veras

"If God is for us, who can be against us? He who did not spare his own Son but handed him over for us all, how will he not also give us everything else along with him?" (Rom 8: 31-32)

Hearing confessions is sometimes heartbreaking. It is not the sins that disturb me. For God can forgive sins. After all, Jesus offered himself on the cross so that we would not be slaves of our sin but rather sons and daughters of God who is Love.

Confessions are heartbreaking when you are before a penitent who has long stayed away from confession out of shame, and you see the long suffering he has caused himself by trusting his own measure more than God's mercy. Confessions are heartbreaking when you are before a penitent who doesn't seem convinced that he has really been forgiven by the grace of the sacrament, and so he remains a slave of his non-existent sin. Confessions are heartbreaking when you are almost certain that the penitent has something more he wants to confess but shame is holding him back. You fear that the shame will persist without the penitent having the experience of confessing his worst sin and still being looked upon like a beloved son or daughter.

Often I sit there and think, "This person is so lovable at this moment. There is nothing this person could confess which would make me draw back from him or desire anything less for him than all the love that God can give. If my petty heart could experience so much compassion for this person, how much more the heart of the Father?!"

Yet when I go to confession, often I am the dejected one who doesn't trust in God's mercy, and what I would like to say to my penitents I cannot say to myself. I need to hear it from another.

Is there anyone more against me than myself? How easily I forget what the Father and the Son did out of love for me. How sad when I am so lost in my empty notions of justice that I become unaware of the fullness of his mercy.

Lord God, may the memory of the cross of your Son Jesus Christ have victory over all that would keep me from running again and again into the ever outstretched arms of your mercy.

Love That Sustains Life

Father Richard Veras

"What will separate us from the love of Christ? Will anguish, or distress, or persecution, or famine, or nakedness, or peril, or the sword? [...] No, in all these things we conquer overwhelmingly through him who loved us." (Rom 8: 35, 37)

One day a dejected student tried to assert to me that his mother didn't love him. This was a son of a single mother who was scraping together thousands of dollars a year for him to attend a Catholic school instead of the dangerous public high school in his neighborhood. To make this outlandish assertion he had to ignore the love that paid his tuition, and that gave him clean clothes, and that fed him every day. His mother's love was so pervasive in his life, so bound up with his day to day well being that it was easy for him to miss it. His lament was inspired by his mother's strictness with him. So the very thing that he interpreted as a lack of love was really another sign of the love that sustained his life.

If his mother had heard this complaint, her son's ignorance and selfishness would still not stop her love for him. But if her son were actually aware of her love, how differently would he face life and conceive of himself and appreciate the meaning of the school where he studied and the clothes he wore and the food he ate, and the sacrifice of the things his mother would not allow him to do?

How differently would we live if we were aware of God's love that pervades our very existence? How differently might we face anguish and distress if we saw that these very things we interpret as God's absence are rather events through which God invites us to enter more deeply into the Mystery of his love for us? For the answer, just consider the martyrs and the saints, and any man or woman you have had the grace to know who lived through a deeply painful moment in life and did not lose faith or accuse God. Rather they were certain that nothing could separate them from his love.

Father, forgive my accusations. And may I recognize your forgiveness as one of the many signs of your love for me, through which I can conquer overwhelmingly.

Life That Expresses Love

Father Richard Veras

"I am convinced that neither death, nor life, nor angels, nor principalities, nor present things, nor future things, nor powers, nor height, nor depth, nor any other creature will be able to separate us from the love of God in Christ Jesus our Lord."
(Rom 8: 38-39)

I once asked a class of students what human beings need to sustain our biological life. The first thing they came up with was food and drink. Then they spoke of clothing and shelter. I kept pressing them for more. They started to speak about medicines. Finally, I had to go to the board and write… AIR!

I asked them why they didn't think of air! One student said because you don't have to worry about it, it's always there. Another said you don't have to pay for it.

Those students skipped over the most urgent need of biological life. I can go a while without food or water, but if my ability to breathe is hampered, my body will gasp and panic immediately! A bodybuilder will quickly be reduced to nothing if he has no air.

Consider our human existence, which is much more profound than mere biology. We have limitless curiosity and desire. We have an insatiable need for love. We have a sense of justice. We have a sense that we have a right to happiness by virtue of our very existence as humans!

I cannot get rid of my desire for happiness. I cannot stop my need for love even if at times it causes me great pain. I can numb but never eradicate my sense of right and wrong. I can't get rid of the sense that human beings have a right to happiness – as if it were promised to them.

These evident realities are at the core of my being, they make up my conscious existence, and yet they seem given by Another. These eternal needs make evident God's presence within me. God cannot be separated from me because he is inextricably bound up with the center of my being.

Nothing can separate me from the love of God in Christ Jesus our Lord, because my very human existence is the continuous and evident expression of his love.

Lord God, the very groanings of my inmost being are a continuous spring whose source is your love. Let me not forget you, but live a continuous dialogue with you by becoming aware of your urgent and continuous presence in me.

The Journey to Faith Begins with Sincerity

Father Richard Veras

*"If you confess with your mouth that Jesus is Lord and believe
in your heart that God raised him from the dead,
you will be saved." (Rom 10: 9)*

I asked the class of twenty-five students who of them were absolutely certain that Jesus is God. Three hands went up. I was not distressed or discouraged; I was thankful for their honesty. We now had solid ground on which to proceed.

The three who quickly professed the certainty of their faith were not such a surprise to me. I noted that these were three students who seemed secure in themselves and solid among their peers. They were students whose demeanor in class showed that they were not easily swayed by the changing ebb and flow of the class mood. They seemed to have a greater humanity and strength in front of the buffeting forces of our inhuman culture. They were already being saved by the risen Jesus in whom they believed.

Many of the rest were quite adept in their assessment of the state of the faith in their lives and in today's culture. Some said that they didn't think a lot of people who attend Mass would be able to say they were certain that Jesus is God. Others said that Catholicism is just something that people do without thinking much about it. Others believed, through hearsay, that salvation history is a fairy tale. Others said they already knew everything about Jesus yet, after superficial interrogation, honestly admitted that they didn't know much.

It was the most important lesson of the year. Because beginning from their honesty, and encouraging and praying for their openness, the students now had a shot at one day believing *in their hearts* that Jesus rose from the dead and is present in his Church. Without that lesson, their doubts would have remained unconfessed behind a façade of faith. The Christian proposal might have been learned academically, but never truly considered or verified in experience. Now, instead, that classroom might become the beginning of a journey; but only a beginning, because Christianity is not a lesson, but a life.

Lord Jesus, you say that where two or three are gathered in your name you are in their midst. May Christians throughout the world take seriously your promise and come together to verify it, so that the hearts of Christians may be truly awakened to faith.

Christ Is Present in Time and Space
Father Richard Veras

*"But how can they call on [the Lord] in whom they have not
believed? And how can they believe in him of whom they have
not heard? And how can they hear without someone to preach?
And how can people preach unless they are sent?"*
(Rom 10: 14-15)

Christianity is not an idea or a philosophy. Christianity is the
event of the Presence of Jesus Christ. Jesus lived in a certain
place in a certain moment in history. God is everywhere, but
God who is everywhere became flesh in Jesus. Jesus of Nazareth, in
his humanity, was not everywhere. He traveled around Palestine.
Through him, Jews and some Gentiles had the awesome possibility of encountering God in the flesh. They could look upon him
and touch him and hear his voice. In front of him they could freely
decide to follow or not, to believe or not. But never in history had
God awakened the freedom and the possibilities of the human heart
as he did through the humanity of Jesus.

Jesus desired that his humanity be spread throughout the world,
so men and women in all times and all places could have the possibility of encountering him in the flesh, in his humanity. For this
he promised to give the Holy Spirit to his apostles. For the Spirit
that made him flesh in the Virgin's womb would make him present in the flesh of his apostles and all of the baptized. Jesus sent his
apostles to baptize so that his Mystical Body could spread throughout the world.

Christianity is not merely agreeing with Jesus, but rather belonging to his body. Saint Paul understood this. For he was a Pharisee
who was likely more educated than the other apostles; yet he would
check with the apostles that what he was preaching was true. For
the risen Christ did not call Paul to an idea or a new religion; he
called him to his Body. Paul knew that to call on Christ in whom
he believed meant to call upon and follow his Body, the Church.

The Church is not everywhere, but wherever it is there exists the
possibility of encountering the humanity of Jesus who longs to
encounter us.

*Lord God, thank you for finding me. May I follow the commission
you gave to me in my baptism so that your saving humanity may
be known in that part of the world in which you have placed and
sent me.*

"My Jesus" versus the Real Jesus

Father Richard Veras

"Faith comes from what is heard, and what is heard comes through the word of Christ." (Rom 10: 17)

There is a Woody Allen movie in which the main character is on a date with a woman whom he has had his eye on for quite some time. The main character is a novelist; and as the woman is telling about herself he interrupts her. He tells her he already knows her because she has already appeared as a character in a number of his novels. The woman looks puzzled and offended, and tells her suitor, "You didn't write me."

Jesus could say the same thing to us. Many times we follow the Jesus of our imagination instead of the real Jesus. Many times we "write" Jesus, making him into the nicest person we could ever imagine. The problem is that this imaginary Jesus is nice according to our measure and our definition.

How do you know if you are following a Jesus of your own creation? If he never bothers you.

Those who were close to Jesus were frequently corrected by him. They were continually surprised by him. They could never predict him. He was simply not someone they could ever have imagined.

I was once teaching a group of students who were unchurched and had never heard the story of Jesus and the adulteress. It was beautiful, because I asked how Jesus would have answered the trap that the adulteress' accusers set for him – should they stone her and reject Roman law or let her go and reject Jewish law. The students had no idea; and they were surprised when I told them his response: "Whoever has no sin cast the first stone."

Jesus himself is the Good News, because he is ever new, ever different than our measures and imaginings. Anything new that comes out of the mouth of a Christian will always be traceable to the Word of Christ, the New Man who is the source of the new humanity present in the poor ones who love him.

Lord Jesus, let not my vanity and presumption value my own ideas more than your Presence in the Church and in the circumstances of my life.

The Glory of God and the Vainglory of Man
Father Richard Veras

"Oh, the depth of the riches and wisdom and knowledge of God! How inscrutable are his judgments and how unsearchable his ways!/ 'For who has known the mind of the Lord/ or who has been his counselor?'/ 'Or who has given him anything/ that he may be repaid?'/ For from him and through him and for him are all things. To him be glory forever. Amen." (Rom 11: 33-36)

I was once studying the Book of Job in a college class on ancient literature. At the end of the book, Job questions God as to why he allowed all the suffering that had happened. God responds to Job that he, as a creature, is not in a position to interrogate God. Job was not there when God created the world and Job is not capable of understanding God and certainly not worthy of taking God to task.

The young professor smugly told us that God's answer to Job seemed unsatisfactory at best and a cop-out at worst. We all smugly agreed. "Oh, that passé God!" "Oh, those backward Scripture writers!" How smart we all felt.

In order to sustain this arrogance, what did we have to ignore? We had to ignore the fact that the world around me, including the material world, does contain many things we cannot explain. We had to ignore the fact that reality does not seem to report to human beings before or after bringing on a hurricane or earthquake or cancer. We had to be oblivious to the fact that we did not give ourselves existence. We had to suppress these and other obvious data that would indicate that human beings are not the creators or arbiters of reality.

We had to refuse to entertain the reasonable thought that there might thus be something behind reality that I cannot understand. There might be an intelligence that is greater than mine. Their might be a love whose response to suffering is beyond what I could imagine. The inspired writer of Job certainly seemed to take many more factors into account than we budding academicians. Who was the adult here and who were the children?

God's love is way beyond me. For what kind of God stands by and continues to love us into existence even as our arrogant ignorance puts him on trial?

Lord God, the mysteries of the world are only mere introductions to the Mystery of Love that is you. To you be glory for ever.

Day to Day Martyrs

Father Richard Veras

"I urge you [...] to offer your bodies as a living sacrifice,
holy and pleasing to God, your spiritual worship."
(Rom 12: 1)

At the end of her life, Saint Thérèse of Lisieux exchanged letters with a seminarian named Maurice. He had dreamed of becoming a martyr. Thérèse shared with Maurice that she had the same dream.

Thérèse explained to Maurice that, as she matured, she realized that it was unlikely that God would give her the martyrdom that she dreamed about. In her maturity, she began to see that her day to day life was the martyrdom, i.e., the witness that God desired of her. The way she would offer herself to God would not be according to her own plan, but according to God's; only in this way is the offering true.

Maurice would discover the same thing as he became a missionary of Africa and found himself beset with the ordinary difficulties of a missionary, such as a rough terrain and a difficult relationship with his superiors. Ultimately, he would not die the glorious martyrdom of his dreams, but rather of an illness suffered by other missionaries of his order.

The big moments of life tend not to be the ones that wear us down. Even great tragedies sometimes bring about the best in us. What wears us down is the day to day and the hour to hour.

A missionary once came to our school and told the students of many dramatic life and death situations that required his heroic response. Many students were impressed, but one boy, Kevin, was disturbed. He said that the talk was quite amazing, but that he was a high school student in an ordinary high school. He wanted to know how he could have a dramatic relationship with Christ through the ordinariness of his life.

In union with Thérèse and Maurice and Kevin, let us offer our day to day lives as a living sacrifice, that the ordinary may be a place where his extraordinary Presence is revealed.

Jesus, help me to treasure the life you have given to me as the gift that it is. I offer to you my life so that it may not be the fruit of my plans, but the flowering of your love.

78

Obeying the Law of Conformity

Douglas Bushman

*"Do not conform yourselves to this age but be transformed
by the renewal of your mind, that you may discern what is
the will of God, what is good and pleasing and perfect."*
(Rom 12: 2)

S aint Paul knew how powerful the attraction of conforming to
one's culture is. To conform is a law of human nature ingrained
in our being by God. One need only observe children to be
convinced that they instinctively imitate the patterns of their family
culture. At later stages when they strive to break out of the conformity
of their early years, this is simply substituting one
conformity for another.

Like all dynamisms God has placed in us, the "law of conformity"
is meant to lead us to him. Jesus Christ is the essential reference
point for the fulfillment of the "law of conformity." Elsewhere Saint
Paul wrote, "Be imitators of me, as I am of Christ" (1 Cor 11: 1),
and, "Be imitators of God" (Eph 5: 1).

The "law of conformity" serves a higher dynamism, namely, the
need for love. Made in God's image, who is love, we are made to
receive love and to give love. So great is this need that people will
conform to expectations in order to belong, to be accepted. We are
masters at discerning such conditions, children at heart, and all too
quick to conform in order to be acceptable to others.

Jesus Christ established a new culture, a culture of life, truth, and
love. This culture is found in the Church. It is the communion of
saints, the bond of unity in faith, hope, and charity. In this communion,
the most fundamental of all human needs, the need for
love, finds fulfillment. Here alone conformity is not a means to the
end of gaining the love that all seek, but love itself.

To conform or not to conform, that is not the question. It is,
rather: to whom shall I conform? Saint Paul's exhortation not to
conform ourselves to the world challenges us to obey the "law of
conformity" by eschewing every kind of pseudo-love the world
offers and by imitating the love of Christ and his saints.

*Lord, renew my mind by the Gospel Saint Paul preached. Root out
of my heart any conformity to the world that keeps me from doing
your will, and give me an ardent desire for your culture of life, your
truth, and your love.*

To Know Thyself Know God's Love
Douglas Bushman

"I tell everyone among you not to think of himself more highly than one ought to think, but to think soberly, each according to the measure of faith that God has apportioned."
(Rom 12: 3)

It is fascinating that the subject Paul considers first regarding the "renewal of our minds" (Rom 12: 2) is our very self. He knew that pride, rooted in what we have inherited from the sin of Adam and Eve, makes us prone to overestimate our own importance. The Lord addressed this attitude when he confronted the apostles for debating who was the greatest (Mk 9: 34). The story of the Pharisee and the tax collector in the temple (Lk 18: 10-14) shows that even acts of religion can create a sense of superiority, dividing one against another.

Those who are renewed in the love of God revealed in Jesus Christ should have no need to exaggerate their self-importance. What greater sense of self-worth can there be than knowing that Christ "loved me and gave himself for me" (Gal 2: 20)? Self-aggrandizement can only mean that the love of Christ has not yet been allowed to complete the work of renewing my mind.

The Good News of God's love in Christ reaches to the innermost depths of our being. The "renewal of our minds" by faith allows us to see ourselves as we truly are. This confirms a teaching of Vatican II that was central in the thinking of Pope John Paul II, namely, that Christ fully reveals man to himself. The first and most fundamental thing he reveals is that God is love and we are precious in his eyes. We are the objects of God's love.

No service we perform can add to God's love for us. He loves us because he is love. Everything we do in faith is a response to the one who "first loved us" (see 1 Jn 4: 19). The Lord entrusts every one of us with a mission of service in the Church, but he instructs us all: "When you have done all you have been commanded, say, 'We are unprofitable servants; we have done what we were obliged to do'" (Lk 17: 10).

Blessed Saint Paul, through your intercession may God make me meek and humble of heart. May my motive for accomplishing the tasks of my vocation be to make a return of love for Christ's love for me, and to give glory to God.

Love Is the Soul of the Church

Douglas Bushman

"As in one body we have many parts, and all the parts do not have the same function, so we, though many, are one body in Christ and individually parts of one another."
(Rom 12: 4-5)

Saint Thérèse of Lisieux received the grace to perceive in a most profound and personal way the dignity and beauty of every vocation and function in the Church. Each was so appealing to her that she found herself unable to align her will with just one if this meant excluding the others.

This was an insight of mystical penetration into the doctrine of the Church as the Body of Christ. In her path toward the holiness to which God called her, this grace prepared her for another grace, the discovery that her vocation was *love*. Love is the soul of Christ's Mystical Body. Every vocation is rooted in and animated by charity. So, by embracing the call to the perfection of charity, Thérèse could embrace every vocation in its source.

The Church has confirmed her mission and her holiness, not only by proclaiming her Doctor of the Church, but also by assigning her the title of patron saint of missions. Though she was never a missionary, she possessed the fervor of charity that gives rise to and animates missionary activity. She not only recognized the legitimacy and dignity of every vocation, she embraced them all in love.

With the same inspiration, the Second Vatican Council reminded us that though not all are called to be martyrs, all are called to the perfection of charity that makes a person a martyr when forced to make the ultimate decision. Similarly, while relatively few in the Church embrace the consecrated life by professing vows of poverty, chastity, and obedience, all are called to strain toward the perfection of charity that makes the spirit of poverty, chastity, and obedience the rule of life.

Each of us is but one member of the Body of Christ in gift and function, yet every gift and function is present in the love that vivifies and unifies the Body's many members, making us all "individually parts of one another."

Lord, grant every member of the Church a deepened awareness of Saint Paul's vocation, a living sense of being united with all the members of the Body of Christ, and an increase in the love that gives life to every apostolic work in the unity of the Church.

To Know Good and Evil, Know Christ in the Eucharist

Douglas Bushman

"Let love be sincere; hate what is evil, hold on to what is good; love one another with mutual affection; anticipate one another in showing honor." (Rom 12: 9-10)

Could the Christian way of life be described more generally than in Saint Paul's injunction to "hate what is evil, hold on to what is good"? Everything depends on determining what is good and what is evil. This is the condition for being able to "love one another with mutual affection." The prerequisite to fulfillment of the commandment to love is accurately to define what is good and what is evil according to the wisdom of God. This requires a constant vigil of watching over our hearts in order to discern and reject any definition of good and evil that comes from the world and not from God.

Since the Church understands conscience to be an inner voice calling man to love good and avoid evil, Saint Paul is saying, in effect: "Be people of conscience." For those who heed his directive and strive to love others as God has loved us, it is consoling to know that Christ died in order to purify our consciences (Heb 9: 9-14). He revealed the full truth about good and evil, about God's love and goodness and the nature of sin. This makes it possible for us to call good and evil by their proper names, as John Paul II put it.

Baptism is initiation into active love for one another, since it is "an appeal to God for a clear conscience" (1 Pt 3: 21). The Church's baptismal faith informs our conscience about good and evil, and this faith, celebrated in the Liturgy of the Word at Mass, leads us to the Liturgy of the Eucharist and the celebration of Christ's sacrifice. Here is where the true definition of good and evil can be learned. Here the blood of Christ continues to purify your consciences. Here, in the Eucharist, the full truth about love, God's own love, can be known and received so that we may love one another as we have been loved.

Lord, purify my conscience for the sake of the purest love. May the Church present to the world the witness of sincere love, so that all people may be drawn to the Eucharist to learn the true meaning of good and evil, and discover here the fullness of love.

Reason for Hope in Time of Trial

Douglas Bushman

"Do not grow slack in zeal, be fervent in spirit, serve the Lord.
Rejoice in hope, endure in affliction, persevere in prayer."
(Rom 12: 11-12)

Saint Paul's exhortations reflect his awareness that Christians encounter difficulties and these can be the occasion for diminishing the commitment of faith. Trial, persecution, suffering, routine, the sheer length of the race – these can cause the original purity of purpose, intensity of dedication, and exuberance of new life in Christ to wane. Hope is the answer, supernatural hope that in times of affliction clings to God's promises and keeps the heart open to him in prayer. It is only through him, with him, and in him that we can endure.

It is the lesson of the parable of the sower (Lk 8: 5-15). In the life of faith a good start is only that, a good start. The commitment to follow Jesus must be confirmed every day, with every decision. Man's freedom can only be exercised in the flow of time. Every day is a gift from God intended to be an opportunity to ratify all that faith holds as true. If it seems that God is slow in keeping his promises, if what we experience seems far removed from what we had thought God had pledged, then we must realize that this is a trial meant to purify our faith.

Faith and hope are purified when there is no evidence in today's affliction that God is present and acting. We experience Christ's abandonment on the cross. Daily routines appear devoid of meaning, lacking any saving value. Suffering seems to confirm the fear that God is uninterested, or powerless. Persecution makes us feel forsaken.

Saint Paul's exhortations are credible because they were accompanied by his witness. There is no naïveté in an apostle who experienced shipwreck (three times), imprisonment, attempts on his life, opposition to his preaching, and backsliding among his converts. Through it all he had discovered a law of God's ways: "My grace is sufficient for you, for power is made perfect in weakness" (2 Cor 12: 9).

I bless you, Lord, and thank you for Saint Paul's example of unwavering hope. When I am fainthearted may his example strengthen me and his words inspire in me fervor of spirit, joyful hope, and constancy in prayer.

Living the Unity of the Church

Douglas Bushman

"Rejoice with those who rejoice, weep with those who weep. Have the same regard for one another; do not be haughty but associate with the lowly; do not be wise in your own estimation. Do not repay anyone evil for evil; be concerned for what is noble in the sight of all." (Rom 12: 15-17)

For Saint Paul, Church unity must be a lived experience. It cannot be limited to the liturgical professing of the one faith in the Creed and offering the one sacrifice in the Eucharist. First, it is a life of solidarity. Because we are "individually parts of one another" (Rom 12: 5), my joy and sorrow cannot be isolated from the other members of Christ's Body. They are my brothers and sisters, not just when gathering for worship, but always. "If [one] part suffers, all the parts suffer with it; if one part is honored, all the parts share its joy" (1 Cor 12: 26).

Second, faith is the foundation of the Church's unity, not social class, education, or economic status. If I avoid those who are not similar to me in these ways, might this indicate that these define who I am more than faith does? And third, if the eternal God not only stooped so low as to become man but stooped even lower still and communed with the lowly, by what pretext do I remain aloof from them?

Fourth, the wisdom of faith is not the privilege of an elite class. It is God's gift, and only the humble, who realize the insufficiency of any wisdom of their own, can receive it. Jesus rejoiced that God's wisdom is hidden from the clever and revealed to mere babes. Any wisdom other than that of faith introduces criteria for making judgments that are foreign to concern for the common good of Christ's Body, resulting in division.

Fifth, the Christian response to offenses is forgiveness, up to seven times seventy, for the sake of preserving the unity for which Christ prayed and died. This brings the eucharistic source of unity, God's own mercy, into the daily life of the faithful.

Last, with all eyes fixed on what is good and noble, the Church's members assist one another in imitating the virtues of Christ, making the Church the communion of saints.

Blessed Saint Paul, do intercede for me, that my thoughts, words, and actions may be inspired by a renewed awareness of the Church's unity and the call to love my neighbor as Christ has loved me.

Creating a Culture of Love

Douglas Bushman

"Do not look for revenge but leave room for the wrath; for it is written, 'Vengeance is mine, I will repay, says the Lord.' Rather, 'if your enemy is hungry, feed him; if he is thirsty, give him something to drink; for by so doing you will heap burning coals upon his head.' Do not be conquered by evil but conquer evil with good." (Rom 12: 19-21)

A culture that does not think in terms of the priority of relationships must become a culture of violence, death, and vengeance. Such a culture knows only two ways of looking at others: either they are threats to my pursuit of happiness, and therefore adversaries, or they are useful for it, mere tools. This is a culture of love of self to the exclusion of any other love.

Christ offers a counter-culture of love, life, and reconciliation. The "renewal of our minds" (cf. Rom 12: 2) in faith makes it possible to see what God sees in any "other" who may be an enemy. Faith sees loss, a cheapening of life *for me*. An enemy is a potential friend, an image of God who intended that my life be enriched by this "other" who now is my enemy. God made this person to be my brother or sister. I am deprived this relationship and the Church is deprived of his gifts. Faith makes me realize that I am suffering, not chiefly because of my enemy's hurtful actions, but because the mutual enrichment of communion in the true and good is lacking.

We are called to love our enemies because God "first loved us" (1 Jn 4: 19) in Christ "while we were enemies" (Rom 5: 10). Christ's suffering reveals that the rejection of love cannot be the last word. His loving "to the end" (Jn 13: 1) conquers the evil of love's rejection with the good of a more powerful love.

To love our enemies we must learn that mercy and forgiveness shown to an enemy is also mercy received. The father of the prodigal son showed mercy to his son and received him anew. The son regained a father, and the father also regained a son. When our love for enemies is a participation in Christ's suffering over the loss of relationships with those God loves, then it becomes powerful enough to conquer evil with good.

Lord, may the experience of evil and suffering be the occasion for men and women to seek an answer, and may their searching lead them to discover that your love, fully revealed in the paschal mystery of Jesus, is the power that conquers every evil.

God's Ultimate Authority

Father Donald Haggerty

"Let every person be subordinate to the higher authorities,
for there is no authority except from God, and those that exist
have been established by God." (Rom 13: 1)

Our Christian life is always subject to certain tensions. We live in this world but not of this world, bound to a time and place, yet possessed of eternal truths by faith. Our eyes turn toward invisible realities, especially in our contact with the Eucharist. But we also immerse ourselves in the tangible satisfactions of family and children, work and friendship, church and charitable activities. This tension of remaining in the world, yet ultimately pursuing a goal that transcends this life, provoked Saint Paul to reflect on the relationship of Christian life to the civil order. The Christians of his own time were subject to the governing authority of the Roman Empire. Although Roman hostility toward the Christian religion had already intensified by the time Paul wrote his Letter to the Romans, he nonetheless urged what might be called a qualified docility to the imperial authority of the state. Paul's understanding was that the rule of Rome persisted only by the favor of God. In using the expression, he trusted that divine providence permitted this authority for reasons that could be discerned partially but which ultimately were known only to God. Paul's urging of a subordination to the authorities can be viewed not just as an expedient compromise, a way to avoid danger. Much more, it would appear that Paul had a deeper spiritual sense of God making use of all realities, including the political reality of Roman governance. What would Saint Paul say to us in the current day about Christian responsibility toward government and civil authority? In the West, we do not live under tyrannical governments. Yet a subtle tyranny does exist in Western societies, namely, a deeply rooted spirit of moral compromise fostered by the legal system and democratic structures. In no way can we accept this as somehow within God's plan, but rather must struggle to overcome every grave injustice, with particular concern for the right to life of the innocent.

Father, in your wisdom, you have created all things to reflect your goodness. Grant me the gift of discernment to know right from wrong, and the courage to bear witness to a justice for all rooted in your divine will.

The Happiest Obligation

Father Donald Haggerty

"Owe nothing to anyone, except to love one another;
for the one who loves another has fulfilled the law."
(Rom 13: 8)

No one enjoys feeling obligated or under constraint in their actions, even if this is at times unavoidable. On the contrary, free actions are our delight, choices which we can pursue out of attraction. This is especially true of every virtuous life. Genuine virtue means choosing good actions because the appeal of their goodness draws us. We choose then, not primarily what we owe to morality, but what we have learned over time is a choice for happiness. For instance, who does not prefer making a donation to the poor rather than handing over a payment to reduce a debt? The generous action energizes and uplifts; the obliging action is often a reluctant one. Saint Paul was aware we cannot live a good life without being bound by morality. But he also knew that the Christian ideal of love transformed the notion of obligation, removing any oppressive sense of burden or imposition. The law of love, which is the law of the Gospel, sums up all obligation. Perhaps an illustration is helpful. It is a Christian maxim dating from the patristic period that the rich man's superfluity is the poor man's necessity. What the rich man may be enjoying frivolously and in excess, the poor man requires for sustenance. We might conclude that the rich man has an obligation to give alms to the poor man. True, but in a sense this is only justice speaking. The law of generosity is only fulfilled when the gift of alms is transformed by a more profound vision. When love motivates the rich man's gift, it is to Christ that he gives when he offers a gift to the poor. Acting from this spiritual truth as his motive, the rich man no longer gives to the poor man because he owes him a gift of alms; no, he gives ultimately to our Lord himself, who gives himself to us when we are generous in love.

Heavenly Father, teach me more deeply the law of your love, and grant me the generosity it requires so that I may find in a desire to please you the happiness I seek in life.

Armed with Divine Light

Father Donald Haggerty

"Let us then throw off the works of darkness [and] put on the armor of light; let us conduct ourselves properly as in the day." (Rom 13: 12-13)

The imagery of light and darkness was part of Jesus' own preaching. Most strikingly he spoke of himself in Saint John's Gospel as the light of the world, and he referred as well to the hour of darkness he faced at the end of his life. He urged us in turn to be children of light, lamps shining for all to see, implying that the darkness of unbelief would be present in every era of history and would require public witness on our own part to counter it. The image of light is indeed an apt metaphor for truth and the experience of it in our faith. In taking our flesh, the Son of God revealed the truth of God to us, not in a manner that removes all mystery, but making the divine mystery accessible to us through his humanity. Years ago I was given a mounted portrait of the face of Jesus from the Shroud of Turin lacquered onto a small piece of thin wood. Many times I have gazed on the features of this face of Jesus in death after the dark suffering of Calvary, finding myself on occasion in silent awe at the God who became a man. It is an experience of light that we receive in such moments of prayer. Somehow life itself then acquires a transparency it may not ordinarily have. The rough edges of life and its passing satisfactions mean far less. In the light that accompanies prayer, we are given certainty that our faith is a great gift and privilege – that it can never be a private affair but demands visible testimony, a correspondence between our religious conviction and committed actions reflecting our faith. We realize as well that faith is not a strenuous exercise, nor a burden; rather, in the gift of faith we have a constant strength and protection, an armor of light, we would not otherwise possess. We have God at our side.

Loving Father, fill my soul with your divine light that my life may always give witness to your truth, and so draw others to the recognition of your love for them and your call to them.

Clothed with Christ

Father Donald Haggerty

*"Put on the Lord Jesus Christ, and make no provision
for the desires of the flesh."* (Rom 13: 14)

For Saint Paul, this expression to put on Jesus Christ went far beyond simply dressing ourselves in the spiritual apparel of good deeds. Much more than simply following a teaching regulating our conduct, we are by our Christian faith to encounter the presence of a living person. Saint Paul was intensely convinced that our faith meant nothing less than Jesus Christ giving himself to us now, dwelling in our soul in an intimacy of divine presence. This conviction in faith of the real presence of God in the depth of the soul is a profound Catholic doctrine if we consider its spiritual implications. As long as we remain in a state of grace, we are never alone, never distant from God, never farther away than a whisper from the companionship of our Lord. It should be no surprise that Saint Paul, knowing this constant presence of God within his own soul, urges a lack of concern for the desires of the flesh. Of course this presupposes a renunciation of sins of sensuality. But Saint Paul also taught that an anxious attachment to the passing enjoyments that this world can offer will make us less receptive to lasting spiritual gifts. We cleave to the surface of life when our desire for pleasure is strong, when we indulge in expensive good food or unnecessary purchases, all to the detriment of deeper spiritual awareness. On the other hand, to put on Jesus Christ requires an interior effort of docility and receptivity, an openness to God in our daily life, impossible no doubt without a daily routine of quiet time with our Lord in prayer. To allow our aspirations and goals in life to be influenced more strongly by God means not to be anxious about assuring the continuance of our material comforts. God will take care of our lives, as only a provident Father can, but he asks us also to trust confidently in this care.

Father in heaven, help me to remain united to your Son in all my desires and aspirations. Keep me from being ever held bound by the passing seductions of this life, so that one day I may enjoy the blessing of your presence for ever in heaven.

Hidden Fruitfulness

Father Donald Haggerty

"None of us lives for oneself, and no one dies for oneself. For if we live, we live for the Lord, and if we die, we die for the Lord; so then, whether we live or die, we are the Lord's."
(Rom 14: 7-8)

There is no such thing as a Christian life in isolation. From the day of our baptism we are united to a reality far greater and more expansive than our own existence, incorporated into the mystical Body of Christ, which is another name for the Church itself. This word "incorporate" perhaps sounds like talk about companies established for business. But we should not miss its link to the Latin word *corpus*, meaning body. The baptized Christian remains permanently part of a body, a bloodline, a vast family, even if grace is lost or the faith itself is forsaken. The soul's mark of baptism is indelible, which is a reason to remain confident in hope that a person even in grievous spiritual danger will continue to receive graces for conversion that have a source in the prayers of the Church. How many mothers and fathers may need to know this if their children have abandoned the practice of the faith. There is a related truth as well, which is that the fruitfulness of our lives is never limited to our immediate personal contacts. A cloistered Carmelite nun, speaking from behind the iron bars that separated her from a visitor, once told me that the Carmelites learn early in their religious training that any power of intercession they may have for others comes not simply from graces due to their prayer but from their prayer joined to steady, unremitting sacrifice. The profound spiritual influence of such hidden lives, despite their restricted contact with people, can be enormous spiritually, graces stretching far beyond the few persons a Carmelite ever sees personally. Their lives are fruitful above all because of a dying to self in a union with Jesus' own offering on the cross. The giving up of self in love unites a soul with countless unseen lives, often no doubt for the sake of a mercy God pours out on souls in their last need before death.

Father, help me to die to myself that I may grow in love for you. Lead me to a spiritual fruitfulness, that in responding to your graces my life may contribute to your desire that all people come to know you.

Radiant Presence

Father Donald Haggerty

"The kingdom of God is not a matter of food and drink, but of righteousness, peace, and joy in the holy Spirit; whoever serves Christ in this way is pleasing to God and approved by others. Let us then pursue what leads to peace and to building up one another." (Rom 14: 17-19)

The kingdom of God is Jesus' own image for the gift God bestows upon us when we submit our lives to him in genuine fidelity. This gift is nothing less than God himself. If we cleave to him in faithfulness, the Father, Son, and Holy Spirit will take up their home within our soul, as Jesus promised at the Last Supper. The personal presence of God dwelling within our souls is indeed the kingdom of God within us. A divine kingdom of this nature implies a sovereignty and a demand for observance. But the rule in this case involves always a command of love that will unite us to others. Our Lord will lead us to recognize more over time his beloved voice returning with requests for the sake of others, while inviting us always to deeper companionship and a union with his own divine life. When Saint Paul urges us to direct our attention to a kingdom not of food and drink, but to righteousness, peace, and joy, he is surely concerned for spreading the truth of Christ's invitation to all souls. Joy and peace and goodness are captivating qualities, and every Christian life should radiate them. But where do they come from if not from God himself living within souls, radiating his own presence when souls are filled with God? A great privilege is at work in this, namely, that sometimes the presence of Christ can be mysteriously conveyed to others through our humanity. I can testify that my own vocation to the priesthood finally became a decision of certainty when I was working at a shelter for the homeless in the Bronx run by Mother Teresa's Missionaries of Charity. I had never seen such happy people as I did among the sisters and volunteers whose daily life was far from easy. The experience confirmed for me the one thing needful to pursue in life. And it joined me to certain souls for a lifetime.

Father, you give yourself to us in mysterious ways. Help me to know your presence in others and, by the joyfulness of my life, to radiate your love to all who are in search of you.

Putting Charity First

Father Joseph Koterski, s.j.

"We who are strong ought to put up with the failings of the weak and not to please ourselves; let each of us please our neighbor for the good, for building up." (Rom 15: 1-2)

Charity always proceeds by way of respect for our neighbors and their consciences. This might mean, for instance, ordering a soft drink rather than a beer when we are out with a friend who has trouble with alcohol. Or there might be a film on some mature theme that we could watch without being aroused to lust or cruelty but that would sorely try another person with more delicate sensibilities. The stronger should not knowingly put the weaker into temptations beyond their strength, but ought to forego or defer certain pleasures out of deference for others. The point here is not prudish fear, but simple respect for the fact that one person may be able to tolerate things that another cannot. One should not presume that everyone is blessed with the same strength.

But this sort of kindness toward those whom we know or suspect to have certain weaknesses should not be confused with a wimpish desire to be liked at all costs. Our charge is to build up the Christian community, and for Saint Paul this will often mean a readiness to undertake fraternal correction. There may, for instance, be a need to challenge a person who is overly confident about his abilities to watch sophisticated movies without endangering his own soul. The task, of course, is not to be a moral policeman, but to be responsive to the promptings of the Holy Spirit about the demands of practical charity. Finding the way to deliver an appropriate correction or to raise a helpful question will take a good sense of humor as well as a prudent sense of timing. But daring to make the criticism that another genuinely needs to hear is crucial to honoring Saint Paul's instruction here – we are to live not so as to please ourselves but to please the Lord, by our patience with the weak and our readiness to undertake really practical charity.

Blessed Lord, you know our strengths and our weaknesses. Give us the good sense to respect the weaknesses of others and to aid them from the strengths you have given us. And make us ever ready to use that strength in genuinely practical charity in your service.

Docility to Christ

Father Joseph Koterski, s.j.

"May the God of endurance and encouragement grant you to think in harmony with one another, in keeping with Christ Jesus, that with one accord you may with one voice glorify the God and Father of our Lord Jesus Christ." (Rom 15: 5-6)

Those who dissent from the teachings of the Church weaken the Body of Christ, and they do so not merely by the errors into which their wayward views may lead them personally. Their dissent can lead others astray and hurt the community, especially by the discouragement that comes from disunity. It can easily sap our strength. While the Church is resilient in defending personal conscience and in teaching that God requires us always to follow our conscience, she is equally forceful in insisting that our consciences must be properly formed.

In this passage, which comes quickly after a lengthy review of the moral requirements implied by Christian faith, Saint Paul prays God to send the grace necessary for real harmony of thought. He is praying for peace, but not for peace at any price. Rather, he prays for a harmony among Christians that will be genuinely rooted in Christ and that will glorify God the Father precisely by giving evidence that it is Christ to whom we must conform our lives and our thoughts, and not some idea of our own invention, let alone the latest fad.

Saint Paul's wonderful sense of the diversity of gifts that the Holy Spirit has bestowed on different members of the Christian community assures us that he is not intending some bland uniformity in his words here. Rather, he is testifying to the need for unity on the important questions – on those issues where our own penchants and inclinations could easily sidetrack us to prefer our own opinions to the truths of Christ, even if those truths strike us as hard to accept. The unity for which he prays will not be the unity of the lowest common denominator, but the unity that comes from conforming our minds and hearts to Christ – and thus a unity that may well require of us real conversion of heart where we do not spontaneously happen to see what Christ is teaching us.

Blessed Lord, stir up your grace in us to think with Christ and the Church, to submit our thoughts to your light and not to cherish private convictions that are opposed to your truth. By our unity in your truth may we praise you.

93

Divine Hope and Human Expectation

Father Joseph Koterski, S.J.

"May the God of hope fill you with all joy and peace in believing,
so that you may abound in hope by the power of the holy Spirit."
(Rom 15: 13)

Students always *hope* for good grades and may even have reason to *expect* them when they have studied hard. Workers *hope* for a raise, but their experience may teach them whether they can *expect* one. In general, human *hope* is measured by the degree of our confidence that something good is coming, and the more prudent among us know how to temper our *expectations* realistically.

Saint Paul here writes about something beyond human hope and expectation. He prays that God will give us the joy and peace of deep faith and fill us with hope through the Holy Spirit. The supernatural gift of faith is the grace of God that enables us to believe in him whom we cannot see. By such faith we can trust that he knows everything about us and that he is ready to give us whatever we need, including the knowledge that he exists and cares for us.

The prayer that Saint Paul voices in this verse pleads with God not only for the gift of belief, but even for joy and peace in believing. One could, after all, believe something and not be at peace about it. There are some people who find God's omniscient gaze terrifying – not necessarily because of a guilty conscience but simply because they prefer to be in complete control of things themselves. Which of us does not sometimes wish that God were not watching us quite so closely? In this prayer, Saint Paul calls us to open ourselves to God in a more mature faith, one that is at peace and tranquility in our belief and love of God, so that we can be ever more alert to the stirrings and promptings of the Holy Spirit, and ready to trust in the divine power of God that is so far beyond our personal strength.

Blessed Lord, we beg you to make us strong in faith and joyful in belief. Settle our souls with your holy peace, so that we may be ever more alert to the stirrings and promptings of your Holy Spirit, and that we may put our hope entirely in your divine strength.

The Mystery Hidden for Ages in God

Father Joseph Koterski, S.J.

"To [Jesus Christ] who can strengthen you [...] according to the revelation of the mystery kept secret for long ages but now manifested through the prophetic writings and, according to the command of the eternal God, made known to all nations, to bring about the obedience of faith, to the only wise God, through Jesus Christ be glory forever and ever." (Rom 16: 25-27)

Beneath this complicated syntax there is a simple and lovely truth. Paul praises God for bringing his saving plan to completion in Christ. Already in the Torah one could find references to God's providential design for the redemption of fallen humanity. But the disclosure of God's intention to carry this plan out through the sufferings of the Messiah became clearer in Isaiah's prophecies about the Suffering Servant. The plan includes not only Israel, but all the nations, and is only fully manifest through the life of Jesus Christ.

For someone like Paul, who grew up within the strictness of the Pharisees and their reverence for the law, the significance of understanding Jesus Christ as the eternal Son of God means that Christ can never be sufficiently praised. Not only did the Pharisees have a profound love for the Torah as a special divine gift to Israel, but they cultivated a vigorous sense of the many difficulties involved in keeping the law. What Paul came to understand by his own conversion was that keeping the law – even if one could manage to do that – was not enough. Hence his emphasis here on praising God as one whose graces strengthen us in ways that would be unattainable by our own efforts. Even comprehending God's plan is beyond us and requires God's disclosure of that plan through revelation.

God has also given Paul to understand that what is required of us is the obedience of faith. That phrase should remind us of the obedience of faith showed by Abraham. Forsaking his homeland, Abraham journeyed to the land that God promised him. Strengthened by grace, Abraham showed obedience by his readiness to sacrifice his only son. By the mercy of God he received that son back unharmed as well as the promise that he would be the father of many nations. For Paul, as a careful reader of the Torah, the person of Christ is the fulfillment of the promise.

Blessed Lord, we praise you for the abundance of your love for us. How often your ways exceed our understanding. Grant us, we beg you, a faith like that of Abraham and Paul, a faith rooted in your own fidelity, beyond our powers to ask or even to imagine.

The Call to Holiness

Father Joseph Koterski, s.j.

"Paul, [...] to you who have been sanctified in Christ Jesus,
called to be holy, with all those everywhere who call upon
the name of our Lord Jesus Christ, their Lord and ours."
(1 Cor 1: 1-2)

Paul's salutation is not merely some innocuous greeting. He testifies to what Christ has done to sanctify us, to our vocation to holiness, and to the efficacy of Christ's name for this purpose. Every Christian, regardless of one's state of life, has the vocation to holiness. Paul here connects our duty to seek holiness with what Christ has already done for us. By baptism we receive the grace that sanctifies us. Not only are we freed from original sin, but we are given sanctifying grace, a share in the divine life. But with these gifts comes a task – the call to holiness.

What does holiness require? The question is not about some minimal standard that would be just enough to get by. Whatever our walk of life, we are called to the fullness of Christian life and to the perfection of charity, to be perfect as our heavenly Father is perfect. Such a tall order would be beyond our strength if it were up to us alone. And so Paul mentions the community of all those who call upon Christ for his grace. In this way the salutation of this letter already announces some of its great themes, that we could never manage without divine grace, but that God will not save us without us, without our free response to his initiative.

The holiness for which we need to strive is twofold. We need to devote ourselves to the glory of God and to the service of neighbor. This lesson shines out with clarity in the lives of countless saints. We might think, for instance, of the superb hymns in praise of God that Francis of Assisi wrote to accompany his love of the poor. Or we can ponder the hours of adoration that Mother Teresa insisted upon for her sisters as a way to sustain them as Missionaries of Charity. Christian holiness, wherever it is found, glorifies God by imitating his own fidelity and generosity.

Blessed Jesus, we praise your Holy Name. Give us your grace to follow you day by day. We revel in being your followers and in being called Christians. Help us to live up to that name by a charity like your own.

Fidelity and Fellowship

Father Joseph Koterski, S.J.

"[Our Lord Jesus Christ] will keep you firm to the end, irreproachable on the day of our Lord Jesus [Christ]. God is faithful, and by him you were called to fellowship with his Son, Jesus Christ our Lord." (1 Cor 1: 8-9)

When asked what virtue they most need, people frequently answer "patience." It may have to do with the stress of modern life. Curiously, the traditional lists of Christian virtues rarely mention this virtue. When they use the word, it clearly means perseverance under trial and difficulty. Augustine has a wonderful treatise on the grace of perseverance, and prayers like the Hail Mary end with "pray for us now and at the hour of our death."

Paul reassures us that Christ's grace will always be available to us. Whether "the end" mentioned here be our bodily death and immediate judgment or the general judgment at the Second Coming, there is good reason for hope. But the ultimate reason for that hope is not our own strength. Paul can promise that God will make those who accept and embrace his will firm and even "irreproachable." The ultimate reason for that hope is God's fidelity.

Faith normally refers to our own belief in God and our readiness for resolute action and commitment. But far more resolute than any stance that we could ever take is God's fidelity. Even when Israel repeatedly broke its covenant with God, he stood firm. Through the prophets, he again and again recalled Israel to fidelity. The situation is comparable for each of us. Whatever our infidelities, God is faithful – faithful in his provision of the graces that we need and faithful in his recurrent insistence that we need to return to him.

This divine summons is highly personal. It is not just "being right with God" in some abstract way but a summons to fellowship with Christ. We are not just nameless members of some large corporation. Rather, by our baptism we have been made the brothers and sisters of Jesus. Our adoption as the sons and daughters of God has brought us into a fellowship with God that calls us to be perfect as our heavenly Father is perfect.

Holy and mighty Lord, we glorify you. We praise your fidelity through all the ages of history and through all the days of our lives. We beg you for the grace of perseverance and faithfulness until death. Make us, we beg you, firm and steady in our love, and grant us the graces that we need to honor you in all that we do and say and think.

Love of the Cross

Father Joseph Koterski, S.J.

"The message of the cross is foolishness to those who are perishing, but to us who are being saved it is the power of God."
(1 Cor 1: 18)

One picture is worth a thousand words. But much depends upon what is in that picture. Without the eyes of faith, all that one sees in a crucifix is the limp body of a man hanged, presumably for some terrible crime. There is no mistaking that the death was agonizing. There is no avoiding the pain – quite a lot of it. For someone without faith, this is failure and shame.

Yet Christians hold the cross in honor. The crucifix has a different message. As Paul urges, for those with faith it is a sign of God's love – a God who loved us so much that he sent his only Son to die for us. But it also conveys God's power. He raised up that only Son from death and opens for us a way beyond mortality to eternal life with God. By uniting ourselves to the Innocent One, our own innocence can be restored.

Unless one sees God's power there, the cross will appear as foolishness. If Christ did not truly rise, our faith is empty, our hope of immortality vain. Where there is no expectation of life beyond the grave, then only earthly life seems worth anything. Bodily death will seem the gravest threat, unmatched by any spiritual death of soul that might come from unrepented crime or sin. Seen in this way, there is no surprise when a culture like ours has trouble imagining that any war could ever be worth fighting or that public authority may need to use lethal force to protect the innocent, and yet tolerates some private right to take the lives of the unborn or the senile when they seem inconvenient. Everything in such a world is topsy-turvy, and the message of the cross seems foolish to those who are perishing. But in fact, the Innocent One has died for the sake of us who are guilty, and the power of God prevails.

Blessed Jesus, when we look upon your tortured body on the cross, we see your love for us. We praise you, O Christ, and we bless you, for by your cross you have redeemed the world. Help us, we beg you, to carry our own crosses and to trust you in everything.

Human Wisdom and Strength

Father Joseph Koterski, S.J.

"The foolishness of God is wiser than human wisdom,
and the weakness of God is stronger than human strength."
(1 Cor 1: 25)

There is no escaping the paradoxes of genuine faith – how can there be three persons in one God, or two natures in the one person of Christ? Expressing these paradoxes crisply helps us to ponder the mysteries of faith.

Paul begins here in paradox. How could an omniscient and omnipotent God ever be foolish or weak? It seems like a flat-out contradiction. But in light of Christ's assumption of our human condition, these words tell a profound truth. The divine generosity by which the Son did not cling to his equality with the Father but poured himself out for us will seem foolish by any human standards, much as the exuberance of any lover for his beloved will seem exaggerated by any rational calculation. The divine decision to take on every aspect of the human condition – from the vulnerabilities of nine months in the womb and the helplessness of infancy through the harshness of the passion and the pains of death – might seem like unnecessary pandering to human frailty. One need only imagine the spiteful insults that someone like Nietzsche would utter in contempt for a God who forgot his own magnificence and stooped so low.

Paul's phrases here answer the Nietzsches of this world. The foolishness of Divine Love in person is wiser than any human wisdom, for love's gift does not stand on ceremony but has measured our true needs. The true Divine Physician knows the right remedy, however counter-intuitive it might seem to amateur divinities. The assumption of our weaknesses by the Word become incarnate is the very condition of our healing, and the true Divine Physician has genuinely diagnosed our case.

With a power of expression like to that of Saint Paul, Saint Irenaeus of Lyons once said: "What Christ did not assume about our nature, he did not heal. But to heal us in every respect, he took on the whole of our nature. By his wounds, we are healed."

Blessed Lord, Divine Physician, we beg you to heal us. May no pride of ours prevent us from accepting your mercies. May we realize the depths of our need and cherish the graces you give. Come, Lord Jesus.

Divine Paradoxes

Father Joseph Koterski, S.J.

"God chose the foolish of the world to shame the wise, and God chose the weak of the world to shame the strong, and God chose the lowly and despised of the world, those who count for nothing, to reduce to nothing those who are something." (*1 Cor 1: 27-28*)

For Bernard of Clairvaux, humility consists in a reverent love for the truth. This means rejoicing in the truth of a well-earned compliment and praising God for having made us able to do well. But it also means accepting deserved criticisms without resentment and taking to heart the corrections we are given. In all such cases, humility requires that we reverently know and love the truth.

Understanding the paradoxes that Paul mentions here about the way God chooses his apostles and disciples requires humility. Where the wise of this world arrogantly think better of themselves than they deserve, God sometimes chooses those the wise regard as foolish to burst the balloon of their presumption. Where the strong of this world are inclined to think their own strength sufficient, God chooses the weak and shows what real strength is. And those whom the world counts as something, God humbles by his choice of those who seem to count for nothing.

Perhaps Paul was thinking of God's choice of Mary to become Jesus' mother. Perhaps he was reflecting on the simplicity of the other apostles. And certainly he was thinking of his own case and of all the strength of will and determination that had marked his own upbringing as a Pharisee. When he stood watch over the cloaks of those who stoned Stephen, Paul would have seen a martyr die. He might well have thought that martyr foolish for going to his death for a hopeless cause, a weakling in the face of greater strength. But when he himself was accosted by God on the way to Damascus, his pride was shattered and the apparent contradictions of these paradoxes suddenly turned out true. Only by being blinded for a while did he learn to see. And in his shame at having to go to those whom he had persecuted was he who had counted himself quite important reduced to nothing and then refashioned by God.

Blessed Lord, we praise you for your power and for your love. Where we are proud or headstrong, we beg you to make us humble. Where we are scornful or arrogant, we beg you to make us meek. In all things, we trust you to make us more and more like yourself.

The Mystical Body of Christ

Father Joseph Koterski, S.J.

"It is due to [God] that you are in Christ Jesus, who became for us wisdom from God, as well as righteousness, sanctification, and redemption." (1 Cor 1: 30)

To live in Christ Jesus is a blessing from God. Whether baptized as babies in the faith of our parents or as adult converts, it is God's grace that makes us Christians and members of Christ's mystical Body.

Paul here praises the gift of Christ for the human race. Whatever the possibilities of human learning, Christ is the gift to us of divine Wisdom incarnate. This is not at all to denigrate what human intelligence can creatively produce. It is simply to assert that no human minds have ever been able to imagine God's entire marvelous plan for our salvation through Christ.

Paul also explains here that it is Christ who justifies us and sanctifies us and redeems us. The loss of original justice with the Fall put us into the hopeless situation of being unrighteous. Now, when Paul was still a Pharisee, he seems to have thought that any one of us could in principle become righteous by keeping the law perfectly. But his conversion included the realization that none of us can ever make ourselves righteous. Rather, it is Christ as the incarnate Son of God who alone can restore us to right relation to God. While our debt to God was impossible for us by ourselves to repay, he has redeemed us.

All this talk of justification and redemption could perhaps be misunderstood as if it were merely a matter of doing the arithmetic and settling up our accounts. In fact, justification and redemption also refer to a profound transformation that God is working within us. God is at work in sanctifying us. Through the sacraments of the Church, God is at work restoring the image of himself in us that was shattered by the Fall. Through the reconciliation achieved in penance and the Eucharist, God is at work refreshing the likeness of himself that has been distorted whenever we sin. Through all of his graces to us, God is sanctifying us.

We praise you, Lord, for allowing us to be members of your holy Body, the Church. We glorify you, Lord, for restoring your own divine image and likeness within us. Let us show forth your charity in all that we say and do.

Knowing Christ Crucified

Father Joseph Koterski, S.J.

"I resolved to know nothing while I was with you except Jesus Christ, and him crucified." (1 Cor 2: 2)

Atop Pope John Paul II's crozier is an image of Jesus cruci-fied. The very angle of his arms tells much about the agony of the cross and the Christian meaning of human suffering. There is nothing stylized or dull about this figure, and the striking shift from the typical crucifixion scene can break us from presuming that we already comprehend this mystery.

The single-mindedness of Paul's resolve in this passage is com-parable. It is not a victory bulletin, as if he already understood every-thing that there was to understand about Christ's sacrifice. It is the simple statement of Paul's project during the visit he had made to the Corinthians. He had dedicated himself to looking upon Christ, to gazing at the mystery of Christ, to pondering what was told of Christ, and to contemplating nothing but Christ and especially his passion.

Perhaps we should think of what Paul was not going to do. He did not come to Corinth to see the sights, or to promote himself, or take advantage of the situation, or for any other purpose than to bring deeper knowledge of his Lord to this community. But to share the mercies that he had received and to explain what sur-passed any possible explanation meant the need to remain himself deeply focused on the mystery of Christ.

God is greater than anything that we can think or imagine. Yet, that none of us can encompass the mystery of God within our cat-egories does not mean that we can say nothing. For Paul, it means that the preacher needs to pray, the missionary to meditate, and the ambassador for Christ to dwell constantly in the presence of his Lord, regardless of where he goes. It is no surprise that John Paul II's walking staff bore so striking a scene of his Lord's cruci-fixion. Like his apostolic namesake, he needed to gaze upon the fig-ure of his Master wherever he went.

My Lord Jesus, Man of Sorrows, you did not shrink from the pains of the cross, so much did you love us. Grant us, we beg you, the grace to know you more intimately, to love you the more dearly, and to follow you the more closely, all the days of our lives.

The Indwelling of the Holy Spirit

Father Joseph Koterski, S.J.

"For the Spirit scrutinizes everything, even the depths of God. Among human beings, who knows what pertains to a person except the spirit of the person that is within? Similarly, no one knows what pertains to God except the Spirit of God. We have not received the spirit of the world but the Spirit that is from God, so that we may understand the things freely given us by God." (1 Cor 2: 10-12)

The pattern of our loves should have resembled those of the Trinity. But because of the Fall, our natural patterns of love are defective. Instead of having a generosity like the Father, who gave his Son everything that he is from all eternity, we tend to love only what we find attractive. Instead of loving with the Son's receptivity, a grateful love that flows from receiving everything from his Father, our loves tend to be halting. There is a kind of psychic inversion – fearing that we won't be loved unless we appear attractive, we are ready to be manipulative so as to appear love-worthy. Instead of loving with the joy of the Holy Spirit, taking delight in the perfect giving and receiving of the Father and the Son, we tend toward envy and jealousy. The weaknesses of mind, will, and desire flow from these defects in our loves.

But with baptism, recovery begins. There always remains more to learn about loving rightly, but the presence of the Holy Spirit from the time of baptism starts the restoration of God's image. What we have received is not the spirit of the world – a penchant for loving only what appears love-worthy, and for manipulating things to make us seem more love-worthy, and for being jealous over loves that we are not ourselves receiving. Rather, we have received the Spirit of God, who will help us truly to understand what God freely and generously gives, so as to know how to receive and how to take delight when we see others giving and receiving.

The Holy Spirit, Paul teaches us, knows everything, including what takes place in the depths of God. But when the Spirit begins to dwell within us, we are given what we need – the very presence in us of a Love who can set our loves aright and, if only we will let him, who can restore the shattered likeness of God in us.

Come, Holy Spirit. You who came to sanctify us at our baptism and who sealed your gifts in us at confirmation, we beg you – abide within us, and restore the image and likeness of God within us. Teach us how to love aright, to be generous without counting the cost, to be deeply grateful for all your gifts, and to take true joy in the things that most please you.

A Proportional Response

Father Raymond J. de Souza

"The one who plants and the one who waters are equal,
and each will receive wages in proportion to his labor."
(1 Cor 3: 8)

Saint Paul is a man who knows what it is to earn a living – even during his apostolic work he was careful to remind his readers that he worked in order not to be a burden on them. Writing to the Thessalonians, he was bold enough to say that those unwilling to work should not eat (2 Thes 3: 10). So it is not surprising to hear him insist that the laborer be given his due, and that no partiality be shown. The one who plants should not be favored over the one who waters. Both are necessary and they should be paid according to the just proportion of their labor.

We are generally quite good about insisting that we get what is coming to us. We know our labor; we expect our wages. We expect a just reward for lives lived in accord, as best as we can, with God's will. We might even think that God owes us something for our good behavior. We want our reward in proportion to our labor.

Yet the wages-for-labor analogy does not fit our relationship with God. It really is the other way around. God does not offer us the "wage" of salvation after evaluating our labors. He pays us, as it were, in advance. The gift of salvation, the promise of heaven, is already given to us before we have done anything. So the matter really ought to be turned around. It is not whether we are paid in just proportion to our labor, but rather whether our labor is a proportional response to the gift already given.

God's "payroll" does not fit our categories. He does not wait for us, and then respond in kind. He takes the initiative. He does not deal with us proportionately. His generosity is superabundant. It is for us to determine whether our response will be proportionate.

Almighty Father, we are not worthy of your generosity, but your Son Jesus has made us worthy. We ask for the grace to respond generously to the gift of salvation.

What We Can't Not Know

Father Raymond J. de Souza

"Do you not know that you are the temple of God, and that the Spirit of God dwells in you? [...] for the temple of God, which you are, is holy." (1 Cor 3: 16-17)

D o you not know? Saint Paul is putting the question somewhat provocatively, even aggressively. Perhaps, as a pastor, he is occasionally as exasperated as the father who says to his child: "How could you not know that?" Paul is reminding his readers of what he has already taught them. But there is a sense too that they should not need to be reminded, and perhaps not even taught, that the Spirit of God dwells within them. Do you not know?

Paul's Letter to the Romans is the scriptural locus for what we call the natural law – the natural knowledge of good and evil that does not require divine revelation. We may read Paul's words here in an analogous fashion. We should know that the Spirit of God dwells within us and that, housing the divine presence, we are like temples.

Looking out at the natural world, we see the wonders of creation and naturally just know that the creator must be even more wondrous. Saint Augustine said that we just look out at the beautiful and changing things of this world, and naturally seek after the One who is beautiful and changes not. So too it should be as we look at our lives and see the providence of God at every moment. We just can't not know that the Spirit of God is protecting us, sustaining us, guiding us.

In a skeptical age, we are wary of arguments that cannot be proven according to scientific criteria. Those arguments have their place, to be sure. Yet we should not discount those things we just know, not contrary to rational arguments, but prior to them. Those intuitions are themselves God's gift to us. Do you not know? Of course we do.

Almighty God, we know your providence calls us into being and watches over us at every moment. Grant that I may always know your presence in my soul and in my life.

What Is Hidden?

Father Raymond J. de Souza

"[The Lord] will bring to light what is hidden in darkness and will manifest the motives of our hearts, and then everyone will receive praise from God." (1 Cor 4: 5)

It's a terrifying prospect. One day all that is hidden now will be made known. Think of all the efforts we make to ensure that we present ourselves in the best light to those around us – the fashion and cosmetic industries depend on that! More important, think of the lengths to which we go to keep private or hidden all those embarrassing things we have done – our weaknesses, our failures, and even our sins. Surely the lines at the confessional would disappear if what was whispered in secret was later proclaimed from the pulpit!

Yet Saint Paul does not seem terrified by the prospect of everything being revealed. Why is that? Surely he must be embarrassed or ashamed of some aspects of his past.

In the preceding verses, Paul says that while he is not aware of anything of which he is guilty, he does not proclaim himself innocent. And he asks his readers not to judge him either. No, leave that task for God and, in time, he will reveal everything.

Paul goes further – he expects that such revelations will lead to God's praise. How can that be? It is because Paul has come to see things as the Lord sees them. Too often we look at our lives – our hidden lives – and see only the failures, the sins, the wandering away from the Lord. The Lord sees all that to be sure, but he also sees our struggle against temptation, our regret, our shame, our repentance, our desire to change, our good intentions, our faltering resolutions, our modest progress, our frustration, our perseverance – he sees it all.

Above all, he sees the work of grace in our lives, even if it remains hidden from us. When all is revealed, we shall not be pointing the finger at the embarrassing bits about others. We shall instead be wondering at how God's grace has ordered everything, including the embarrassing bits, for the good.

Lord Jesus, help me to see things as you see them, and to trust that your grace is sufficient to order all things to the good.

No Self-Made Saints

Father Raymond J. de Souza

"What do you possess that you have not received? But if you have received it, why are you boasting as if you did not receive it?"
(1 Cor 4: 7)

In Old World Europe, a prominent man is likely to emphasize the family from which he comes. In the New World, the reverse is true; the prominent and successful like to emphasize how humble their beginnings may have been. The latter wish to show they have achieved success on their own. They are self-made men.

Whatever truth there may be to that in the world of business, or politics, or sports, it is certainly not true in the spiritual life. There are no self-made saints. That's an obvious theological truth. It is God who takes the initiative, so even the saintly hermit in the desert is responding to God's gift. It's also an obvious spiritual truth – everyone receives the faith from someone else. We do not save ourselves.

Those truths should have consequences. We should be both grateful and humble. Grateful because we are nothing without the gifts of others; without the generosity of our parents we would not even have the gift of life. And humble, for we have no cause for boasting, as Saint Paul writes. Humility is to see things as God sees them. If we were able to do so, we would see not only a chain of causes behind each of our successes, but a veritable web of connections, in which everything we have accomplished is dependent on a vast array of factors, many of them unknown to us.

We are not able to discharge the debts of gratitude we have accumulated. But we can cultivate a spirituality of gratitude. Do we pray for the great-grandparents we never knew but who kept the faith alive in our family? Do we pray for the priest who baptized us? Do we pray for the teacher who instructed us in the basic truths of the faith? And are the words of Psalm 115 found often on our lips: "Not to us, LORD, not to us/ but to your name give glory."

Almighty God, apart from you I am nothing, and I can do nothing. I offer you my humble thanks for all that you have done for me, and for those people you have put in my life according to your providence.

Spiritual Fatherhood

Father Raymond J. de Souza

"Even if you should have countless guides to Christ, yet you do not have many fathers, for I became your father in Christ Jesus through the gospel. Therefore, I urge you, be imitators of me."
(1 Cor 4: 15-16)

How is a father different than a guide or a teacher? The guide or teacher attempts to instruct his pupil in some matter or the other. The father is concerned not so much with what the child knows, but with the child himself and with his total welfare. He sacrifices himself for his child. The good father tries to live as a model for his child. Indeed, the noble guide and the good teacher become spiritual fathers after a fashion.

Saint Paul is claiming a spiritual fatherhood. This text is often used to explain the kind of paternity proper to priests – a spiritual fatherhood from which they take their title, "Father." True enough, but spiritual fatherhood is a challenge for all Christian men.

It is not a secret that our culture is suffering from an epidemic of fatherlessness. Too many children grow up without their fathers, or even worse, not knowing their fathers. There is a similar crisis in spiritual fatherhood, one perhaps even older. Absentee spiritual fathers leave the things of religion to the women – the wives, mothers, grandmothers. Too many children grow up without seeing their fathers in the Lord's house. And it follows that too many young men think that the life of faith is women's work. Our parishes sometimes seem like someone has hung a sign outside: "No men allowed."

Spiritual fathers are as necessary as fathers in the family. Both boys and girls need to see strong men who are not too proud to kneel before the Lord. They need men who are willing to lead them in the ways of Christian virtue. They need to know that to lead is to serve, not to dominate. They need men in the mode of Paul – fearless evangelists, courageous witnesses, loyal friends, persevering companions. They need holy men.

Dear Saint Paul, intercede for me, that I might receive the grace to lead those in my care in the paths of holiness, for which you ventured all things with zeal and courage.

Clear out the Cupboards

Father Raymond J. de Souza

"Do you not know that a little yeast leavens all the dough? Clear out the old yeast, so that you may become a fresh batch of dough, inasmuch as you are unleavened. For our paschal lamb, Christ, has been sacrificed." (1 Cor 5: 6-7)

Most of us have something, perhaps at the back of a kitchen cupboard, that is well past its expiration date. Something we once bought and used at one time, but somehow got put away and forgotten. Now it is stale and good for nothing, yet it is still hanging around the kitchen. Saint Paul uses a kitchen analogy here, saying that while a little yeast is necessary to leaven the dough, the old, stale yeast is good for nothing. A little fresh yeast is sufficient to get the job done. But even a large quantity of stale yeast is useless. It is time to clear it out.

If we let our spiritual yeast go stale, we are going to end up spiritually flat. Perhaps there are prayers that once attracted us, or devotions to which we were, once upon a time, devoted. At one point they leavened the dough. Now they have lost their freshness and have become routine. They are still hanging around the cupboard, but no longer leaven the dough. It's time to clear them out and look for fresh yeast.

Of course we need discipline and routine in our spiritual lives, but we also need freshness and diversity. A good way to get that fresh yeast is through spiritual reading – masters of the spiritual life, lives of the saints, Fathers of the Church. An insight gained here, a new perspective there – it can bring fresh light to our existing prayer and sacramental life. Sometimes a phrase or verse picked up in spiritual reading can illuminate a passage of Scripture or part of the Mass, and we never look at it the same way again. Spiritual reading keeps us open to the riches of the Church's tradition, like the wise steward who brings out treasures new and old from his storehouse. A good spiritual book keeps us from going stale.

O Holy Spirit, guide me in the ways of your wisdom and of the holy men and women of every time and place, that the treasures, new and old, of the spiritual life may be open to me.

Let Not That Baby Sleep!

Father Raymond J. de Souza

"But now you have had yourselves washed, you were sanctified, you were justified in the name of the Lord Jesus Christ and in the Spirit of our God." (1 Cor 6: 11)

Sometimes a baby sleeps right through his own baptism, even while the priest is pouring the water over his head. What a pity! The baptism appears to have had no outward effect, when we know that in fact the soul has been changed for ever. (In some cultures, it is considered a bad omen for the baby to be so placid, so the mother or godmother might pinch the baby at the opportune moment to get a suitable response!)

It would be a wonderful miracle if we could somehow see a soul before and after baptism. We would see that it was different. We would not take it for granted.

Baptism makes a difference. Saint Paul speaks in the past tense – we were washed, we were sanctified, we were justified. It is also the passive voice – it is something that the Lord Jesus has done for us, not something we have done on our own. And what has been done to us makes us different. It makes us holy.

The astonishing good news about baptism is that, in receiving the Lord's grace, we in fact become holy, and are truly justified in the sight of God. It is not simply that the Father looks kindly upon us or treats us according to his mercy. It is more than that. He looks upon us differently, he treats us differently, because we are different. The grace of baptism makes us holy; it makes us worthy; it justifies us.

How could it not? We become part of the Body of Christ through baptism, and if we are part of Jesus, how can we not be holy? How can we not be pleasing in the sight of the Father? In baptism we have been changed, born again in the order of grace. So let that baby cry out with joy!

Almighty Father, send forth your Holy Spirit to stir into flame the graces of my baptism, that you may keep me faithful to your Son Jesus Christ, to whose Body I now belong.

Theology of the Body 101

Father Raymond J. de Souza

"The body [...] is not for immorality, but for the Lord, and the Lord is for the body; God raised the Lord and will also raise us by his power." (1 Cor 6: 13-14)

Check out any vibrant group of young Catholic adults today, and you will find talks, seminars, conferences on what is called the "theology of the body." It refers to the teaching of Pope John Paul II on how Christians should understand what it means to live in the body. The late Holy Father taught that, far from being a mere tool used by the soul, the body is an essential part of what it means to be a human person. The body, in fact, is the icon of the person – it is through the body that the person is made present and expresses himself in the world. That has important consequences for everything to do with the body, from the right to life, to marriage and sexuality, to the proper care of the dead. It has been characterized as John Paul II's most revolutionary legacy.

Yet there was an earlier version, as Saint Paul writes here, that the body is not for immorality, but for the Lord. Not only is the body not for immoral purposes, but it is for holy purposes – it is for the Lord. No denigration of the body here; no sense that it does not matter. To the contrary, the body is for God, and will find its end in him.

Saint Paul goes further: The Lord is for the body. The salvation the Lord brings is for the body too. The incarnation, passion, death, resurrection, and ascension are all, in a very concrete way, for the body. They have all exalted the body in its nature and in its destiny.

In ancient times, there were cultural currents that were infecting early Christianity, suggesting that what was done in the body was secondary, or perhaps even trivial. Those ideas have their contemporary equivalents today. The solution then was, Paul thought, a little theology of the body. So too did John Paul II.

Almighty and incarnate Lord, I thank you for the great gift of my body, which comes from you and is destined for you. Preserve my body from any defilement as I await the final resurrection.

The Dwelling Place of Glory

Father Raymond J. de Souza

"Do you not know that your body is a temple of the holy Spirit within you, whom you have from God, and that you are not your own? For you have been purchased at a price. Therefore glorify God in your body." (1 Cor 6: 19-20)

How can we glorify God in our bodies? Most of us do not think our bodies very glorious at all. Indeed, the fashion, weight loss, and cosmetics industries are rather dependent upon that view.

Yet our bodies are an essential part of who we are as human persons, and therefore our bodies are an essential part of our spiritual life. No body? No human life, physical or supernatural. No body? No kneeling in adoration, no singing in praise, no fasting in repentance. No body? No sacraments. No baptism. No Eucharist.

Saint Paul uses the image of the temple for our bodies. The temple is the dwelling place of the divine. Our bodies are just that, united to our souls which are animated by the Lord's grace. The temple imagery points to another way – the supreme way – that our bodies can glorify God. Jesus speaks about tearing down the temple, and his listeners think he is speaking about the great temple of Jerusalem. He is speaking instead about the temple of his body. The tearing down of that, and its subsequent resurrection, is the moment of his glory.

Martyrdom – the tearing down of the temple – is a moment of glory. It is the body's supreme testimony. It is the body's most complete way of giving glory to God.

Any bodily suffering too can be a way of giving glory. The suffering of the body can be united to the suffering of Christ. The holy person's bodily suffering amplifies the witness of his virtues.

Celibacy for the sake of the kingdom gives glory in the body. In renouncing the body's enduring stake in this world – children – the celibate points in his body to the life to come.

Marriage too gives glory in the body to God, for the union of the flesh is an icon of the communion of persons in God.

The body is a temple; the temple is the dwelling place of glory.

O Holy Spirit who fills the hearts of the faithful, come to dwell in my body so that it may give glory to God in the way in which he chooses and according to my state in life.

Chicken and Egg: Knowledge and Love

Father Raymond J. de Souza

"If one loves God, one is known by him." (1 Cor 8: 3)

In medieval theology, a central question was whether it was necessary to know someone before it was possible truly to love him, or whether it was necessary to love someone before it was possible truly to know him.

The great intellectual tradition of the Dominicans, led by Saint Thomas Aquinas, took the position that it was not possible to love someone who remained unknown. Love presupposes knowledge.

Another great intellectual tradition, that of the Franciscans, took the other view. Led by Saint Bonaventure, they argued that unless you loved someone, it was not possible truly to understand him. Knowledge requires love.

Both are defensible positions. Both find support in our common human experience. Who are the ones we know best? The ones we love. Who are the ones we love most? The ones we know best.

Think of a mother and her child. She loves him even before she knows him. Indeed, from the first moment she knows that she is carrying a child, she loves him, without knowing anything at all about him or her. As time passes, and the child grows up, she is interested in all things about him, because she loves him.

On the other hand, consider a young man courting a woman. At first he knows little about her, but over time what he discovers leads him to love her more. And if things should lead to marriage, it is because, in getting to know each other better, they discover that there is a basis for enduring love.

Which comes first, love or knowledge? In God, the two go together, in the same moment. For us, it depends. Sometimes our love outpaces our knowledge, and sometimes our knowledge leads to love. We need both, of course. When it comes to God, we need to learn more about the One we love and, at the same time, come to love more the One we know.

Almighty God, grant me the grace to love you more dearly and know you more clearly, that you may always be the object of both my heart and my mind.

One God. One Lord. One Life.

Father Raymond J. de Souza

"For us there/ is one God, the Father,/ from whom all things are and for whom we exist,/ and one Lord, Jesus Christ,/ through whom all things are and through whom we exist." (1 Cor 8: 6)

There is one God. One Lord Jesus. For this all exists. Everything else is secondary. It is rather easy to say that – another thing to live it. The moment of death is one at which much about life becomes clear; secondary things give way to primary things. Consider the example of a recently-beatified Spanish martyr.

On October 2, 1936, Blessed Bartolomé Blanco Márquez was executed for his fidelity to the Catholic faith during the anti-Catholic persecutions in Spain. The day before he was martyred he wrote the following to his girlfriend, Maruja: "My body will be buried in a grave in this cemetery of Jaen; while I am left with only a few hours before that definitive repose, allow me to ask but one thing of you: that in memory of the love we shared, which at this moment is enhanced, that you would take on as your primary objective the salvation of your soul. In that way, we will procure our reuniting in heaven for all eternity, where nothing will separate us. Goodbye, until that moment, then, dearest Maruja! Do not forget that I am looking at you from heaven, and try to be a model Christian woman, since, in the end, worldly goods and delights are of no avail if we do not manage to save our souls."

The salvation of souls is the primary thing. It is what the one God, the Father, desires above all for us. It is what the one Lord, Jesus Christ, has accomplished for us. Saint Paul reminds us of what Blessed Bartolomé learned well: apart from God, nothing has value. Everything else is secondary.

Blessed Bartolomé lived this in an extraordinary way. He reminded his girlfriend that she was to live this in a more ordinary way. That's our task. It is the Christian task.

Lord Jesus, you are the only Son of the one Father, and you have come to lead us home to the one God for ever. Grant me the grace never to let anyone, or anything, come between me and your gift of salvation.

Christ Is Not a Costume

Father Raymond J. de Souza

"To the weak I became weak, to win over the weak. I have become all things to all, to save at least some. All this I do for the sake of the gospel, so that I too may have a share in it."
(1 Cor 9: 22-23)

The man who is different things to different people is not one about whom we say good things. On the contrary, we judge him to be superficial, or even disingenuous, a man who changes depending on his circumstances. The chameleon is not the exemplar of good character.

Saint Paul goes further – he has become all things to all people. He does not concede this as a matter of weakness; it is a boast of evangelical zeal. How can this be? The secret lies in Paul's Letter to the Galatians: "I live, no longer I, but Christ lives in me" (Gal 2: 20).

The man who adopts different characters for different situations is an actor, one who wears a different costume for different roles. If he does too much of this, his own identity fades away and only the costumes are left.

Christ is not a costume. Christ is the one who reveals to us what it means to be truly human. To the extent that Christ lives in us, we become more fully who we are meant to be. A costume changes our outward appearance, and leaves the inside unchanged. Christ lives in us, and therefore our outward appearance becomes more of him, and less of us.

Jesus Christ can be all things to all people because he is both divine and human. The eternal Son of the Father, he became one of us that he might save us. He did not pretend. His human nature is no costume.

Our evangelical task is to become more like Christ that, being more Christ-like, we draw others not to ourselves, but to Christ. Pretending to be someone we are not is a trick that will eventually be exposed. Becoming more like Christ is not a trick, but rather a witness, that Christ might show forth. To present ourselves is not evangelism. To present Christ is. And he draws all men to himself.

Lord Jesus, you already live in me by the grace of the sacraments. Grant that others may not see me instead of you, but rather you in all that I say and do.

Bearing Our Humanity

Father William M. Joensen

"Whoever thinks he is standing secure should take care not to fall. No trial has come to you but what is human. God is faithful and will not let you be tried beyond your strength; but with the trial he will also provide a way out, so that you may be able to bear it." (1 Cor 10: 12-13)

Despite our recourse to measures designed to protect us from our own vulnerability, Saint Paul recognizes that we cannot escape the trials that accompany being human. Our attempts to be invincible can obscure the truth that the author of our humanity remains faithfully turned toward us. God stands ready to supply the strength we need and lead us out from our pride-induced predicament.

A young couple's five-year-old daughter succumbed to an infection following heart surgery. The father of the girl took up cycling as an outlet for his anger and grief, eventually spending hours a day training and regularly winning elite competitions. This all changed when, during a dawn ride, he was struck by a car and almost died. He lives, but the long road to recovery will require several surgeries and much spiritual stamina.

Is he bitter? No. He even regards the near-death experience as a blessing in disguise: "I am so lucky – all that time I took away from my wife and other kids. I get a second chance to make up for it."

This man knows what it is to be brought low from a high level of performance and prestige. From this new vantage point, he recognizes persons whom he had ignored in straining to avoid the emptiness and pain of his daughter's death. He has rediscovered his true identity in relation to his family – and, we might infer, God. He has embraced the place that we too easily pass by as we attempt to escape. But, sadly, we often amplify our restlessness, the sense of competing – above all, against ourselves – and draw others into the vacuum where a spirit of solidarity should reside.

Still, try as we might to run away, God keeps pace with us, bearing the burden we add to the weight of our humanity. God waits until finally we let Christ's cross pry open our pride and our pain, lifting us up, providing a way out.

Jesus, you know my humanity from within; you never fail to draw close to me in the midst of pain and weakness. Protect me from seeking false refuge in things that would only amplify my self-reliance and bring me the strength your cross so readily supplies.

Corporate Presence

Father William M. Joensen

"The cup of blessing that we bless, is it not a participation in the blood of Christ? The bread that we break, is it not a participation in the body of Christ? Because the loaf of bread is one, we, though many, are one body, for we all partake of the one loaf." (1 Cor 10: 16-17)

In the mutual presence of would-be disciples to one another, Jesus has all he needs to initiate a new mode of life. His own presence becomes a source of unity and inexhaustible love. The Lord activates a life where believing and being in communion is possible, perpetual. But we must allow our sense of independence to yield to even a fraction of humility and longing that will supply all Jesus needs to bind us together and compose us into a Church worthy of his name.

A middle-aged man who wanted to get back into shape contemplated the prospect of running with some women from his office. He shared his plan with a male co-worker, who was skeptical of the idea. The man then asked his wife if she had a problem with his prospective running partners; she responded, "I don't like that idea at all. If you want to run, run with me!" The man laughed and thought to himself, "That's why I love her so much."

The husband did not view his wife as possessive or unduly suspicious. Rather, he appreciated that in willingly binding themselves to one another, they had laid claim to each other's lives in a way that they could call one another to even deeper connection, sharing, sacrifice, presence. Belief in the body God forms means giving one another access to one's heart, to the options one is entertaining, the possibilities one might pursue. It means calling each other back to the unity where freedom is founded on trust that the other can guide us and help heal and seal us in the love that lasts for ever. Belief in the mysterious, sacramental presence of Christ in the loaf and cup is met by the same belief that this merciful presence is sustained as we elect to dine with one another – and even run with one another.

The loaf and cup are the means by which we together meet your lavish love, Lord. As I participate in your eucharistic presence, may I become fully transparent in all my comings and goings, so that I, too, may confirm and deepen the bond of unity that you have fashioned among us.

Indoor Plumbing

Father William M. Joensen

"Be imitators of me, as I am of Christ." (1 Cor 11: 1)

The mythic Narcissus errs not only by being smitten with the watery reflection that he regards as "other." He also mistakes this surface appearance for the substance of his own self. The self-absorbed person actually discounts rather than overestimates his own lovability. He settles for layers that hardly begin to fathom the depths that evoke God's contemplative devotion to his chosen creation. God loves us in loving his own being, and yet truly cherishes us as other than himself. We, typically, have to rediscover our true selves in relation to Christ before we can begin loving what God loves in us.

Saint Paul is no narcissist. The invitation to imitate him is not a form of self-flattery, but succeeds the plumbing of his own soul. Though converted, Paul still cries again and again out of his own personal depths. The waters of his own felt unworthiness part as he beholds Jesus bending toward him, impressing upon him the image of a beloved that penetrates to the marrow and mesentery of his "I."

Through generations, a household rite of passage is repeated: a proud father both chuckles and cherishes the moment when his young son, standing with him before the bathroom mirror while shaving, asks if he, too, might apply the cream and stroke his unstubbled face. The father hands the son a razorless shaver, so as not to hurt himself while mimicking dad.

In the household of faith, the Son, the perfect image of the invisible Father, entrusts himself to Paul and equips him with the Word, a two-edged sword that cuts both ways. This Word exposes both the bearer and the one for whom it is wielded – surely, swiftly laying bare the hidden recesses of our being. And yet, this is God's great mercy to us for, in the process, we discover who we truly are. We come to know Paul's great delight, to declare, "I am… of Christ."

Jesus, you are the perfect reflection of your Father. You invite me to face you without flinching or shrinking away in fear, so that I might come to know the depth of your love, and thereby come to know myself. My delight is to be found in you for ever!

Sharing God's "To-Do" List

Father William M. Joensen

"I received from the Lord what I also handed on to you, that the Lord Jesus, on the night he was handed over, took bread, and, after he had given thanks, broke it and said, 'This is my body that is for you. Do this in remembrance of me.'" (1 Cor 11: 23-24)

More bread and wine does not necessarily lead to true feasting. Jesus inaugurates a new age in which we know that God has come to us in human form, healing past wounds. Jesus also anticipates the hungers and trials to come. Persons whose pilgrim migration is toward and with the Lord at Mass rejoice as they realize that God meets us in our conscious needs, only to raise awareness of other needs for which he has made provision. The Eucharist calls forth expressions of charity that would otherwise remain concealed. Persons who are willing to be instructed by Saint Paul and by the needs of others discover this mysterious dimension of God's own self-donation. In contrast, those who are set only upon trying to find and fill themselves, who are unwilling to believe, remember, and receive from another, end up tired, disoriented, frustrated.

The Eucharist is the worthy means that God in his wisdom has chosen for us to be filled with his life. Eucharist is Jesus Christ made flesh and blood for our sake. He is the way through whom God consults with us, informs us by shaping our minds, wills, and hearts into his own. The anamnesis at the altar triggers our recollection of everything else that we are to do in Christ's name.

The Eucharist is to enable rather than impede access for all as we hand ourselves over to fulfill Christ's mandate. Persons are freed from circling around the house or the city, trying to get a glimpse of what is going on inside. Instead, we are drawn into the very center of a community who itself becomes our body and lifeblood, essential to our existence as the place that supports and sustains our mutual desire. The Church is this eucharistic home where Jesus hands himself over to us in perpetual presence, where he likewise receives our own desires as we gratefully recall that he is for ever "for us."

Lord Jesus, you are the center of a genuine feast. In forming a Church of the Eucharist, you call me not to hold back, but to hand myself over gladly for the sake of your Body. Mold me by the mystery which I share, so that I never forget to make the needs of my neighbor my own.

Sudden Death, Enduring Life

Father William M. Joensen

"In the same way also the cup, after supper, saying, 'This cup is the new covenant in my blood. Do this, as often as you drink it, in remembrance of me.' For as often as you eat this bread and drink the cup, you proclaim the death of the Lord until he comes." (1 Cor 11: 25-26)

In the realm of athletic competition, few things capture our attention as much as those tournaments where each game is an all-or-nothing affair, where the fear of being "one and done" heightens the significance of every performance. There are few things in life where everything counts on one condition, one decisive act, one form of fulfillment. And yet this is Saint Paul's claim in proclaiming the character of the eucharistic act, which should not be taken for granted despite the frequent opportunity for feasting in this Christ-conferred manner. No matter how many times we have participated in Mass, we do not lose our focus, for we must be able to count only to one: one cup, one covenant, one blood poured out in the one death. Oh, we do it often, but we know that in the divine dispensation it is an all-or-nothing affair: either Christ performs his one saving service of love for our sake on the cross, a sacrifice that endures to the end, or we do not pass go; rather, we perish.

Thankfully, gloriously, this is not the case. The One who bends down to our humanity hands himself over in a singular, profound gesture of love. We can for ever count on Christ. Jesus can command us to do what we do in the Eucharist because he is both the first-born Son and the first to offer himself in a comprehensive act of love. We hardly know the height and depth and length of love that passes into our hands, mouths, and hearts. There is no rival worthy of Jesus' own offering. But we gain a clearer understanding, a firmer grasp, as often as we do it. We cannot feign ignorance; we know what we are to be about. What is handed to us in proclamation and performance draws us along, stirring our will to hand ourselves over, progressing step by step until death comes, and our covenant share in the unceasing life who is Christ is complete.

Christ Jesus, how easily I compound and construct conditions by which I will serve you. Dissolve my reluctance and rebellion by the pure simplicity of your saving sacrifice. Allow me to drink in your life and love as I take up the cup again and again, so that I may perform today the work you have set before me, until you come to me once and for all time.

Circulating the Spirit

Father William M. Joensen

"And no one can say, 'Jesus is Lord,' except by the holy Spirit."
(1 Cor 12: 3)

Humans continue to try to build things on alternatively larger and smaller scales, all in an attempt to decipher and master the universe. This is the motivation behind the building of the world's largest particle collider to date. It is composed of a circular tunnel extending for many miles that has been described as a kind of Babel built underground. Dozens of countries manufactured its components and provided scientific expertise, all speaking different native tongues, but united in the common purpose to reduce the world to its most minute particles, including a long-postulated particle that imparts mass to all others.

Even if and when they are successful in overcoming their Babel-like origins and achieving their aim, investigators who would thereby claim to have explained the universe would ignore dimensions of reality that cannot be accelerated into existence by mere mortals. This mysterious dimension is met only by the will expressed in words such as: "Jesus is Lord." "Let it be done to me." "Only say the word and I shall be healed." "I baptize you." "Speak, Lord, your servant is listening." "I absolve you." "Teach us to pray."

These words are entrusted to the people of God. Some are pronounced exclusively by ministerial priests, and some are said by all who exercise their baptismal priesthood. These words are taken to heart and kept there. God's people are "kept" people. But they are not prisoners; they are truly free, with the freedom of the children of God.

The realm of Spirit is not inherently opposed to matter. Rather, it is the dimension of God's being encircling all that is, imparting meaning and transforming all that the Spirit touches: water, oil, bread, wine, and human beings. The Lordship of Jesus is grasped by the only beings whose own flesh may become the dwelling place of the living God. We are remade by the Spirit, and are capable of making the Lord known.

Master of the universe, you overcome the chaos that we humans encounter, and that we ourselves create. Allow me humbly to yield to the movements of your Spirit in my life, so that I may be a channel of Spirit and life for others, as all my being declares that you alone are Lord.

Baby Talk

Father William M. Joensen

"There are different kinds of spiritual gifts but the same Spirit; there are different forms of service but the same Lord; there are different workings but the same God who produces all of them in everyone." (1 Cor 12: 4-6)

Good babysitters and daycare personnel come at a premium these days. There is something gifted about the person who can overcome the sadness and fear experienced when mom or dad drops a child off and steps away. Part of the task is to redirect the child's attention to something colorful, curious, entertaining in that moment – some partial good that can distract the child from his or her own sadness, the awareness of the absent good. There is something charismatic about the manner of a worthy babysitter, the creativity of a devoted daycare provider. Who they are is not a diversion, a surrogate, but a participation in – a reference to – the love and presence of the parent. Trust and peace are engendered not simply in the learned awareness that mom or dad will return at the end of the day; rather, because the caretaker is there, the parent has not truly left. Sadness yields to security, and allows the longing for reunion to be a source of expectation, hope, and joy.

The Spirit is no surrogate, but the alter ego for Christ's activity of mutual service, secure belonging, and enduring presence. The Spirit does not level difference into an uninflected monotone, but parses and punctuates gifts for the good of everyone who is to produce and partake in the varied activity of Spirit.

The one who seeks to fill himself first ends up only being full of oneself. In contrast, our primary work is to be an ongoing refraction of the Spirit's sufficiency. We communicate the tenderness of a God who is always present as parent, lover, friend. We realize that no one is meant to be more than a heartbeat away from the cadence of God's compassion, the embrace of mercy. Child of God care is the consecrated service produced in everyone generated by God – the God whose sameness is not something profane, but the point of departure for diverse gifts to be expressed.

Spirit of the living God, your presence wells up in me as I will to witness on your behalf. Endow me with strength; counsel me with creativity and insight; grace my gestures and speech with your gentleness and love. Do not abandon me, but draw me ceaselessly into the company of the Father and the Son, the same God now and always.

Benefit Package

Father William M. Joensen

"To each individual the manifestation of the Spirit is given for some benefit." (1 Cor 12: 7)

God's love is expressed in manifold, amazing ways. Yet it is a tribute to God's own humility that this love is not forced upon us, but remains dependent upon men and women who are willing to drink in the Spirit of Christ and allow this Spirit to sift and stir their lives for the benefit of others – and for their own salvation. Every moment when God's passionate love for humanity is met in the life of a person such as Saint Paul, who is ready to let God order his desires, to lay down his life for the sake of this love, is a privileged, powerful event. Every time God's passion meets our own is simultaneously both Pentecost and "Epiphany" – manifesting the Spirit in new and variegated ways.

God's ultimate *pro bono* work is to send us an Advocate constantly to remind us that we are meant for life on a scale the world cannot even imagine. In the process of being revived, we look around and see others who have been similarly graced, along with those whose passionate longing has yet to be satiated. Either way, we realize that we belong to one another in a new respect – as parts of a Body larger than our own. To our great delight, we know that we are never alone.

And from this recognition, a new docility emerges in relationships among the people of God, in whom the Spirit dwells: in works of ministry and mercy, in steadfast fidelity and long-suffering, when the squeeze of a hand says far more than words can. Though this Spirit work may fall far short of what the world deems "success," prayerfulness and presence will participate in the salvation of the world, launching human longing before the Father of Mercies, and benefiting those who search for some reason to believe in God's love.

Passionate God, release your Spirit upon me in the measure you will. Stir and sift my soul, removing anything that would keep me from pouring myself out for the benefit of persons you place in my path today. May I reveal you and assist your Spirit in bringing them peace.

Body Casting

Father William M. Joensen

"A body is one though it has many parts, and all the parts of the body, though many, are one body, so also Christ. For in one Spirit we were all baptized into one body." (1 Cor 12: 12-13)

God's goodness seems so unevenly distributed at times, in ways that can leave us frustrated, jealous, spiteful. We sometimes lose track of the good sense that reminds us of God's intimate, individual intentions on our behalf. As a result, we forget that we are enlisted as one key part within God's spiritual script.

Those who are baptized are charged to overcome dispersive tendencies that would tear us apart from one another. We resist looking upon the neighbor with a spirit of covetousness or, alternatively, with a sterile pity that affords us easy self-absolution. We refrain from curious regard for the prosperity or plight of another as a mere source of entertainment with which we quickly weary.

God's Spirit helps us rediscover our company in Christ. We dare not capitalize on distinctions that matter little in God's sight: distinctions such as who comes from within and who from without; who can purchase the E-Z pass of remote recognition and those whose needs for assistance are glaringly apparent; or those who nonchalantly return our favor versus those who press us to go further than our customary comfort zone would allow.

At baptism we are inducted into an organic reality that, far from being exclusive, is eminently elevated. The Church is the site where the universal call to holiness is realized, though only as each individual accepts that there is a personally elected role to undertake. The dignity of persons is intensified in the theater of faith. God's preferential option for the human is activated when we respond to a casting call from above. Our felt poverty of spirit should liberate us rather than paralyze us with spiritual stage fright. Justice and charity will then surge into the aisles, so that all might shine in the ambiance of the Son. We tend toward Christ, insofar as we are responsive to our baptismal calling, not by autonomous choice, but diversified and designated as God would have it.

God of my baptism, you help me slip beyond an isolating comparison of myself with others, and draw my attention to Christ. Grace me with a spirit of self-forgetfulness that accompanies my willingness to take up my part in the dramatic gap between what presently is and what you will to be performed.

Spiritual Anatomy

Father William M. Joensen

"If [one] part suffers, all the parts suffer with it; if one part is honored, all the parts share its joy./ Now you are Christ's body, and individually parts of it." (1 Cor 12: 26-27)

Saint Paul is no mere optimist, who glances away from the half-empty, painful aspects of life. The Body of Christ must be anatomically correct, composed of both suffering and joyful parts, if the Gospel is to be alive in us.

A senior married couple (not estranged!) sent out separate Christmas letters, offering different perspectives on the previous year. The first letter was written by the husband, who related that at eighty years he still played golf regularly, that together they had a new adopted grandson, and other grandchildren who had begun college. Their own son, paralyzed twenty years earlier in a bike-auto accident, remained unable to speak or care for himself, but able to communicate with his eyes and facial expressions. Nonetheless, there was much for which to be grateful.

The wife's letter also expressed gratitude for family and named the adopted grandson. But she proceeded to mention a fellow parishioner whose unrecognized depression led him to take his own life, leaving a wife and four children. A daughter-in-law had undergone major surgery for cancer, and a son-in-law had lost his job. Oh – and Merry Christmas and a Happy New Year!

Were these simply good news-bad news letters? Or, did they limn the realities of life, recognizing where there was reason for gratitude, as well as where they must simply lift up and press on in petition, trust, hope? Had they simply given different accents to a mystery that envelops us and sends us seeking our part in the Gospel proclamation? In the process, we remain attuned to the whole of life: those parts that are vividly attractive, and those aspects that perplex and pierce our hearts. We reclaim joy in the presence of our beloved family, friends, and those for whom we pray. Though we still suffer anxiety, fear, and sadness, as the parts press upon one another, we are incorporated by a God who is with us in ecstasy and in exile.

The bruises and blessings of life are not foreign to you, my God, for you are familiar with everything that causes us both pain and joy. The mystery of suffering pales before my greater wonder at how you love us in your Son Jesus, who honors us with his presence, and builds us up into his Body.

Filling Fissures

Father William M. Joensen

"If I have all faith so as to move mountains but do not have love, I am nothing. If I give away everything I own, and if I hand my body over so that I may boast but do not have love, I gain nothing." (1 Cor 13: 2-3)

The Saul who would become Saint Paul was every bit the "mover-and-shaker." His fierce faith, his comprehension of the law, and manner of exacting justice left folks shaking in their sandals. But it was not until he was stopped in his tracks and arrested by love that Paul became capable of doing what was pleasing in God's sight. Until he gave himself over to Christ, he had nothing truly to boast about.

A prominent developer in a scenic region laid claim to some prime real estate perched below a bluff. Despite opposition stirred by a sense that his planned condominium project would mar the pristine beauty of the site, he pressed ahead. Crews hammered pilings relentlessly into the rock foundation – until it became apparent that the disturbance was producing fissures in the face of the bluff, shearing off large portions of rock that tumbled into the valley below. The project was not only about to alter the natural contour of terrain created thousands of years before, but would undermine its own basis for being. The work came to a halt; the "mountain" was respected not simply for the external advantage it afforded, but for what mattered within.

Pope Benedict XVI speaks of how God's love for those whom he created descended into the bowels of the earth, into the void opened up by human self-righteousness and hollow efforts to leave one's mark upon the world. Jesus passionately seeks out a people who were busying themselves into oblivion, buried in self-seeking. In Christ, love "turns back on itself," simultaneously giving itself away and claiming the beloved in one grand gesture on a hill that is transformed from hideous to holy. Jesus alone fills the fissure in our hearts, for in him our faith meets love face to face. We pause and reverse course, retracing steps sketched by Christ, the path Paul takes. The crucified one nullifies even our loveless faith, and restores our reason for boasting.

Faithful God, I do not want merely to move mountains, for though I believe in you, my pride would too quickly undermine what you accomplish through faith. Allow me to descend with you into places where love is lacking, to reclaim the beauty that my own projects and efforts cannot achieve unless your love fills them.

Rendering True Love

Father William M. Joensen

"Love is patient, love is kind. It is not jealous, [love] is not pompous, it is not inflated, it is not rude, it does not seek its own interests, it is not quick-tempered, it does not brood over injury, it does not rejoice over wrongdoing but rejoices with the truth."
(1 Cor 13: 4-6)

To sit with Shirley, an accomplished painter, in her dying days, was to be willingly held captive as she proceeded, one by one, to describe her eight grown children (whose portraits were lined up by birth order on her dresser) in great detail: their achievements, struggles, relationships, progeny, and peccadilloes. She did not soften or spin their life stories according to her own hopes or expectations, inflating or deflating their stature depending on whether they had met the measure of her own sacrifices and steadfast fidelity. Shirley knew well who her children were, and who they were not – a group of thoroughly unrelated persons could scarcely have been more diverse! Though the rigors of disease racked her body, her soul remained a receptive canvas, molded by the unfolding, unique relationship she possessed with each one of her offspring. The only gloss was the grace of seeing them as God does, with a gaze of unqualified love.

It is much easier, even for Saint Paul, to describe what love does and does not do, than to grasp what love is in itself, for unlike the common conception of love as a "feeling," love is something located below the surface of the sensible, dwelling in the souls of those who love. This form of love must be contrasted with the smoldering, sullen residue of resentment at the wrongdoing of another that lurks below the surface of loveless persons who merely seem to get along. Unlike this latter lack of love that draws its toxic energy from the occult confines of a misbegotten joy over misfortune suffered by another, true love, in contrast, cannot contain itself. Love longs to manifest itself, to lay itself down for the sake of the beloved. Oftentimes love is most luminously displayed in the patient, wholehearted acceptance of the beloved. Real charity conforms itself to the truth of the person presented to us and reckoned by the awareness of how God's love conceives that person.

There is nothing I desire more, Lord Jesus, than to love with all my being, yet there is nothing that so readily escapes me. Receive my heart as the studio of your ongoing work within me. Release me from the false joys that occupy hidden niches within me, so that I may receive my brothers and sisters as you do, and love them freely, faithfully, truly.

Much More Than a Cliché

Rebecca Vitz Cherico

"[Love] bears all things, believes all things, hopes all things, endures all things./ Love never fails." (1 Cor 13: 7-8)

If you have ever been to a Catholic wedding you are probably familiar with this line from Saint Paul, since it is a very popular reading at nuptial Masses. As a result, it can seem almost like a cliché, when it is actually far from it. Anyone who has ever fallen in love feels this passage to be true – you can believe and hope all things when the excitement of a new romantic interest is in front of you. Bearing and enduring all things – waiting for that new love to call you back, dealing with periods of separation – who does not recognize that experience? In the giddiness of new love, you can even believe that your love for the other person will never fail.

But the other, deeper, layer of this passage reveals itself over time. Time reminds you that you cannot bear all things or hope all things alone. Time often generates a cynicism about love; after a while, you see the limitations of your beloved (if not your own). You may not know how you can endure all things. And how can love never fail? Our feelings of love can, certainly. This is where the passage begins to speak to us in its fullness. Love – in order to be true to itself, in order to be truly love – must be in Him. We cannot truly love on our own, because our own love is weak; it cannot bear or believe all things. Love never fails, only because love is God's. Our own love is a sign – a sign that even we who are weak can know what is good, and a constant reminder that our love needs to be perfected in our relationship with Christ. True love is only possible because of God.

Let us pray today that our love be perfected in Christ. Lord, help us love you, and in our love for you, to believe, and bear, and hope, and endure all things. Remind us that you alone never fail us.

Objects May Be Further Than They Appear
Rebecca Vitz Cherico

"At present we see indistinctly, as in a mirror, but then face to face. At present I know partially; then I shall know fully, as I am fully known. So faith, hope, love remain, these three; but the greatest of these is love." (1 Cor 13: 12-13)

Saint Paul's reference to knowing only indistinctly – as in a mirror – is at first a bit strange for us, since contemporary mirrors are almost too sharp in their reflections. We see all too well with our mirrors. But whether our mirrors are clear or vague, we know that their images are always second-hand; what we see is not the object itself but its reflection. Although we can see things perfectly well in a mirror, it is disconcerting to know that what we observe is not the object itself (one of the reasons most of us prefer to turn around when driving in reverse). We like to see things directly – not just their reflections. When we are separated from loved ones for long periods, we may bring pictures of them with us. Even when the photos are clear and accurate, they are never as good as really seeing those we love before our very eyes!

The nature of our fallen world is such that we do not see fully; we do not see truly. Rather, we are given signs – partial images that suggest the fullness of the truth without revealing it to us completely. Our knowledge of life and of ourselves, even, is fundamentally second-hand. Not having made ourselves or our world, we do not totally understand who we are or what the nature of reality itself is. Now I can see him only partially through his world, but one day I hope to see him as he sees me. But that full knowledge is only meaningful in love, which is why Paul tells us that love is the greatest of the theological virtues. Love involves our whole will – we can accept faith with our minds, we can agree to hope, but we cannot truly love unless our entire self is at stake.

Lord, let me love you more completely today. May all the things that I see open me to loving you and the world in which you placed me, with a fuller heart and sharper vision.

Spiritual Envy

Rebecca Vitz Cherico

"So with yourselves: since you strive eagerly for spirits, seek to have an abundance of them for building up the church."
(1 Cor 14: 12)

Here Paul reminds us that envy is possible in the spiritual realm as well as in the material one, and he distinguishes between a desire for spiritual gifts that is a help, and one that is a hindrance. We sense that the Corinthians Paul was dealing with were pretty interested in "spirits" and acquiring spiritual gifts. Sometimes, they may have been too preoccupied with those gifts. But instead of condemning them for focusing on the wrong thing, we see how Paul puts into practice Christ's command to test everything and retain what is good. It is a good thing to strive for spiritual gifts, because it demonstrates a desire to be closer to Christ, and to witness to the faith. So Paul encourages the Corinthians in this desire. But he also reminds them what those gifts are for – just as the Spirit comes from God, his gifts must be used to serve him. Otherwise, wanting spiritual "talent" can be a temptation – a temptation to envy and pride.

Paul helps us make sense of piety: it is good when it serves his Body, the Church, and when it builds up everyone. It is bad when it serves only to build up myself. Such a simple and true principle! Thus Paul helps us recognize piety that is moved by him, and piety moved by "yours truly." It is all too easy to want to be holy or gifted as an extension of our pride, instead of out of love for him. We can transpose all of our normal failings into a sort of exalted spiritual realm – but they remain failings all the same. Instead of wanting to be rich, or beautiful, or smarter than everyone else, I may want to have spiritual insights. But those insights are no different from being rich or beautiful if I do not use them in his service. But if I do, they become the source of joy and wonder for everyone.

Lord, help me to desire gifts that build the Body of Christ, instead of seeking my own self-interests. Help me to see that what I truly desire will be fulfilled only in you.

No Eyewitness, but a Witness Nonetheless

Rebecca Vitz Cherico

"I handed on to you as of first importance what I also received: that Christ died for our sins in accordance with the scriptures; that he was buried; that he was raised on the third day in accordance with the scriptures; that he appeared to Cephas, then to the Twelve. After that, he appeared to more than five hundred brothers at once." (1 Cor 15: 3-6)

One of the most striking things about Saint Paul's conversion and belief is that he did not himself know Jesus. Paul was not one of the Twelve, and never met Jesus of Nazareth in the flesh. But it almost seems silly to mention it, when we consider his importance in the early Church and the strength of his commitment and conversion: Paul certainly knew Christ. Paul is a great person for twenty-first century Christians to look to – who, more than Paul, understand the situation of those who come after – those whose faith is based on trusted testimony and on the experience of a newness in life whose origin is in him. Saint Paul, as a former persecutor of Christians, is uniquely qualified to witness to Christ. If a Jewish man who never knew Jesus personally and even hated and distrusted Christians can be converted, then the evidence for believing in Christ must truly be convincing.

Paul handed on to the early Christians what had been handed on to him – he is not an eyewitness, but he is truly a witness nevertheless; a witness who was told by Jesus himself that persecuting Christians was the same as persecuting him. While he did not see Christ risen in his human form, he heard his voice and witnessed his saving power in dramatic ways and places: in his own conversion; in the Areopagus; and in many other miraculous events. But he knows that all that has happened to him depends on the truth that he received – the truth that Jesus came, died for our sins, was raised, and was seen, both by his first followers, and then by many more. This is of first importance, because everything else we believe depends on it. We have inherited a truth that we can now verify in our own lives; let us not shrink from the task that is set before us.

Lord, let me remember the truth of your sacrifice. Do not let my remoteness from your Son in time and place confuse me; he is with me today if I will only seek him out. Help me to recognize you in my present reality and witness to you today.

True Humility and True Worth

Rebecca Vitz Cherico

"For I am the least of the apostles, not fit to be called an apostle, because I persecuted the church of God. But by the grace of God I am what I am, and his grace to me has not been ineffective."
(1 Cor 15: 9-10)

Those of us schooled in the conventions of modesty can find Saint Paul's way of speaking of his virtues rather uncomfortable. When Paul talks about his abilities, it is unsettling. Why does he think he is so great? But why must we resist talking about ourselves as great? Some of it is because, deep down, we really think we make ourselves. We think we owe all our great qualities to our own hard work, and so it would be tacky to point out our superiority. But even in the most extreme scenario, we have only improved on what was already given us to start with. A priest I once knew – whose simplicity and holiness were outstanding – remarked that we all need to understand the difference between self-image and self-worth. Our self-image should be low, because we must recognize the pitiful state that we are in and our serious limitations. Our self-worth, on the other hand, must be monumental, because I know that even if I were the only person on the planet, Christ would have died for me. This is the value that I have as a person. Recognizing this value, and the true origin of my being, is hugely freeing. I can acknowledge my virtues because I know where they come from. In this context, I can see my faults in a new light as well, because I know that even my weakness has been given to me to help me grow closer to Christ.

Here, Paul seems to start out modestly enough – he is not fit to be an apostle. But then he reminds us that God's grace in him has not been ineffective. In this vein I can see Paul's apparent lack of humility differently – as a testimony to the Lord who made him and continues to re-make him. That grace is something at which Paul himself marvels – knowing himself, he knows what God's grace in him has wrought. And it is good.

Lord, help me to recognize my true origins in you today. Help me to look at myself honestly and recall my need for you and the grace that you freely give when I call on you.

It's a Sin

Rebecca Vitz Cherico

*"If the dead are not raised, neither has Christ been raised,
and if Christ has not been raised, your faith is vain;
you are still in your sins." (1 Cor 15: 16-17)*

In some languages, and in some parts of the United States, it is a commonplace to say, "It's a sin" rather than, "It's a shame." When something should have turned out well and it does not, or when some promising young man becomes a ne'er-do-well, "It's a sin." There was the hope of something good; the sense that something great would happen, but it did not. There is a truth in this: the idea that sin keeps things from fulfilling their promise, it keeps things from being all that they can. In the broken natural order of the world, things often do not fulfill their promise – but Christ does. Only what we give to him can be saved from death.

Divine power alone can save things from the grave, and Paul reminds us that our faith is pointless if we do not believe that Christ really redeemed us. Paul also reminds us of the logical consequences of faith, or the lack thereof. Either Christ has been bodily resurrected or he has not. And if he has not, then there is no hope for us either; our faith is wasted, and we are deluded. Belief in Christ is a radical proposal, and we must make a decisive choice: yes or no.

By explaining this to us in clear terms, Paul also reminds us here that Christ did not come to do away with our human ability to reason, but to fulfill it and push it to its limit; believing in Christ means believing that his resurrection was not simply an amazing historical event, but one that changed the world. Our reason can grasp this, and we recognize that many dramatic changes follow as logical consequences. We have been given our hearts and our minds so that we can fully comprehend the grandeur of Christ's promise. We don't need to be afraid of the extreme nature of Christ's proposal: it is radical, but it is not nonsensical.

Lord, let me follow you down the path on which you are leading me, however surprising it may be. Show me how you will fulfill the desires of both my heart and my mind, and help me to put all my trust in you, knowing that my trust is well-founded.

Firstfruits and Transformations

Rebecca Vitz Cherico

"Christ has been raised from the dead, the firstfruits of those who have fallen asleep. For since death came through a human being, the resurrection of the dead came also through a human being."
(1 Cor 15: 20-21)

I once read a very wise book of advice for those writing dissertations in which the author insisted on writing every day, first thing. She herself had received this advice from another writer and had not realized the other woman meant it literally until she had the chance to spend a weekend with her. When she saw this respected author wake up and get to work every morning, she realized she was really serious. It was not just a work ethic – getting the hard stuff over with right away – it was also a way of orienting the day. It is easier to write again later in the day if you have already written something that morning. What comes first is often a sign of what is to come – one of the reasons we try to start our day with prayer – what we place first in our time tends to pull the rest of the day with it.

First things are foremost in our minds and in our hearts. The firstfruits are the part of the harvest given to the Lord. Christ is the firstfruits; he has been given to God already and is risen and alive in him. Christ's resurrection is what leads us to hope and believe that our own resurrection will, one day, follow. Just as we all know death because of one man, we will also know everlasting life through another. In this sense, Paul's reference to those "who have fallen asleep" is no mere poetic phrase – even death is not as real as we think. Death is only temporary, while the life that God gave us, and Christ redeemed, will last for ever. What was formerly impossible has already happened in Christ, which gives us a new certainty. What seemed impossible has happened. Just as it seems impossible that the way I start my day should have the power to transform it – but it does.

Lord, let me put you first today, in both my day and in my heart. Help me continually to begin again in you and may my whole life be sanctified though your presence.

Much Greater Blessings

Rebecca Vitz Cherico

*"For just as in Adam all die, so too in Christ
shall all be brought to life." (1 Cor 15: 22)*

One of the punishments that routinely frustrates students in high school is when the class gets in trouble for the misbehavior of a few individuals. And yet, it is sometimes difficult for teachers to do otherwise when the miscreants' identity is unknown to them. When I taught in a high school and students complained to me about this (rarely, of course), I would ask them to consider all the times they had done something bad and gone unpunished. It was not much of a consolation. Even though my students knew it was true, they wanted to be punished when they really deserved it. It is much rarer for a class to be rewarded collectively: stellar pupils are usually recognized as exceptional and rewarded specifically. Very seldom does an entire class receive special treatment because of what a few easily identifiable people have done. We tend to give rewards to those (few) whom we think deserve them. In sports events, we have a small glimpse into the rewards that a few can bring to the many – a team may become great because of the contributions of a few individuals; even so, one great player does not make a team.

But God is much more generous with his blessings than we are with ours. So much more generous, in fact, that many have considered Adam's sin and our fall a fortunate one for having given us the chance at so marvelous a redemption. Christ's victory is a victory because it is not just for him, it is for everyone; we did nothing to deserve Christ's offering and yet it is given for us. Like a sudden windfall, our lives are transformed by this one man. Fortunately for us, God's ways are not our ways, and his math is not our math – the redemption is much bigger than the sin.

Lord, let me live today with a generosity of spirit inspired by your gracious redemption. Even when I hit obstacles on my path, let me remember that your resurrection is fully real, and freely given to all who will accept it.

135

Incorruptible and Changed

Rebecca Vitz Cherico

*"We will all be changed, in an instant, in the blink of an eye,
at the last trumpet. For the trumpet will sound, the dead will be
raised incorruptible, and we shall be changed."*
(1 Cor 15: 51-52)

Incorruptibility is often seen as a sign of sanctity. A person whose body is found to be intact some years after death is clearly a special case. Incorruptibility thus points to both something completely true – the person is true to himself by remaining unchanged in death – and something wonderful, since in the natural order, all bodies decay. Saints known as "incorruptibles" are often the subjects of special veneration; their bodies are generally encased and put on display for all to behold. They are clearly a reminder of God's marvels. Some years ago an acquaintance of mine, who was going through major life changes similar to my own, exclaimed to me, "We are changing!" It was a somewhat unusual comment and struck me as somewhat funny; her excitement at our changing made me think there was something wrong with the way we were before. There was! God made us; but he also made us to be changed; our very being is in motion. Our need to change is not an expression of distaste; it is a recognition that the fullness of our being can only be realized in time. We love our children, but we want and expect them to become adults. Just as we cannot anticipate the way that a child will be changed into an adult, we cannot know exactly how we will be transformed. But the knowledge that this transformation will occur is a source of wonder and excitement; we know that, with God's grace, something beautiful and true will emerge. We cannot imagine how this will be, but our experience of life shows us that radical transformations happen, both within the natural order of things and as manifestations of the divine. Just like the incorruptibles, one day we will be witnesses in the flesh to the truth and wonder of God's power.

Lord, let us pray that we be changed today in the way you want us to. Do not let us cling to old forms and old ways when Christ is seeking to transform us.

The Clothes Make More of the Man

Rebecca Vitz Cherico

"That which is corruptible must clothe itself with incorruptibility, and that which is mortal must clothe itself with immortality." (1 Cor 15: 53)

We live in an image-conscious culture that is saturated with clothing advertisements. Perhaps that is part of the reason that clothing seems so superficial to us; something shallow and extraneous. While much of our obsession with clothing may be trivial and materialistic, clothing is also a sign and can be an agent of transformation. Changing our clothes may also change us in some bigger way – many act differently when in uniform. Children do not separate clothes from the wearer as readily as we do, which is most conspicuous around the Halloween season. Many small children are frightened by costumes and are terrified by people with masks. Sometimes, even if you show the child the costume, and show her that you are only wearing a special outfit, she is still deathly afraid. The costume-wearer has been transformed into a monster in her eyes – no wonder she is scared! Other children are thrilled by the possibility of dressing up at Halloween, since it gives them the opportunity to be something they yearn for: the chance at being a fireman, a princess, or a superhero. Children's costume choices reflect the transformation we all desire for ourselves. Children usually want to be something dramatic – they want to be transformed into something permanently and astonishingly impressive. Many of the figures children imitate are larger-than-life; they do great things and last for ever: Spiderman always beats the bad guy, and he never dies. It is no wonder that superheroes and figures from fairy tales are some of the most common costume choices – who else can claim to be as heroic or as eternal?

Christ has given us that opportunity to be transformed. In him, we are given the chance to be immortal. What we have all longed for since childhood – heroism and eternity – has been given expression in our carnal reality. But unlike a mere costume, when we put him on, we are given the opportunity to be fully and permanently changed.

Lord, help me to see where my corrupt nature is being called to change in you. Let me be transformed in you and through you.

Killing Us Slowly…

Rebecca Vitz Cherico

"The sting of death is sin, and the power of sin is the law. But thanks be to God who gives us the victory through our Lord Jesus Christ./ Therefore, my beloved brothers, be firm, steadfast, always fully devoted to the work of the Lord, knowing that in the Lord your labor is not in vain." (1 Cor 15: 56-58)

The idea that something that does not kill makes you stronger has become a common notion in our culture. We have the sense that something difficult but not excessive will inevitably lead to personal improvement and enrichment. This is the principle behind many trying experiences that are done deliberately: part of the logic behind boot camp, running marathons, and climbing Mount Everest. But when this idea comes up, I like to recall that there are also things in life that kill you very slowly. Some trying things are also damaging, as health professionals speaking about the cumulative damage of lifetime stress will remind us. So it is with death and sin – sin kills, but slowly. When we consider our own death or that of a loved one, we can feel overwhelmed by the apparent futility of life: what is the point, we wonder, if it will all come to an end when I die? This sense of uselessness and waste is a huge part of death's poison. Life loses its sweetness because of the shadow of death looming over it. But Christ has taken away that shadow. I still fear death, but it no longer has the upper hand.

The poison of death is sin, and death takes hold of us as sin does. But what initially appears as an inevitable biological necessity is transformed through Christ. Human work appears in a new light: no longer is life merely the cycle of birth to maturity to decrepitude and then death. The work that we do in our lifetime is not condemned to die with us; we have been freed from the limitations of sin. Paul can honestly tell us that our work is not in vain, because our work is in Christ. How freeing! Now that death does not have us in its clutches, we have the possibility of building something that will last, just as we ourselves will last in him.

Lord, help me cling to what is lasting, and remind me of your victory over death. May I always remember what you have won for me, and be faithful to your work and your love.

Surprised by Love

Rebecca Vitz Cherico

"Be on your guard, stand firm in the faith, be courageous,
be strong. Your every act should be done with love."
(1 Cor 16: 13-14)

One thing that always surprises me in Saint Paul is the connections he continually makes between his exhortations and love. I find myself confused by his references to love after encouraging the Corinthians to be strong. When I hear Paul talk about being firm in the faith, I first think of silent, self-sufficient types. It is encouraging to hear what Paul says about the source of this strength; a great reminder of this saint's wisdom. Paul was a man who bore a tremendous amount out of his love for Christ. He traveled, went to prison, settled arguments, ended up beheaded… this is no soft sentimental man who talks about love. He doesn't tell us to love out of a vague piety. When he tells the Corinthians to be on their guard and stand firm in the faith, he knows what he is talking about, and what that requires. The unexpected answer is love. Our own capabilities may be great or small but, in the end, they will not be enough to sustain us. Only Christ will. It takes love to be courageous and strong in the face of persecution. It takes love to withstand the trials that many early Christians faced. The strength that we require will emerge out of our love for Christ. While our own lives may not be challenged by the same type of persecution and trials that the Corinthians dealt with, we have our own. And the answer to our sufferings is the same one it has been for every generation of Christians: deeper love for the one who made us. Our own courage as individuals will not be enough – but our love, sustained by him, will be.

Lord, we pray to be strengthened today. Let us grow in our love for you, and be strong in you and through you.

The Father of Compassion
Father J. Augustine Di Noia, O.P.

*"Blessed be the God and Father of our Lord Jesus Christ,
the Father of compassion and God of all encouragement,
who encourages us in our every affliction, so that we may
be able to encourage those who are in any affliction
with the encouragement with which we ourselves
are encouraged by God." (2 Cor 1: 3-4)*

There isn't one of us who has not at some time had to comfort a friend, a brother or a sister, a child, a colleague in a moment of distress, or illness, or loss. Often our approach is to get them to look at the bright side of things. To a colleague who has lost her job we point to the abilities and experience that may suit her for other employment. To a brother who is seriously ill we give the name of just the right physician or new treatment. We try to cheer up our friend who has broken up with her fiancé by introducing her to another circle of friends. But sometimes, there isn't a bright side: some sorrows are intractable. What can we say to comfort a colleague who is permanently disabled by an injury, or a child whose father has been killed in the line of duty, or a brother whose illness is untreatable? And as occasions for comforting others multiply, what about the comfort-givers? Where do we get the insight and the energy to provide the right sort of encouragement or consolation? Saint Paul assures us that the source of our capacity to comfort others is the Father of compassion and, what is more, the comfort that we give to others is identical to the comfort we have received ourselves. Saint Paul is speaking from experience. In the background are his own many troubles. Experiencing almost uninterrupted affliction himself, Saint Paul has also felt the continuous compassion and encouragement that comes from the God and Father of our Lord Jesus Christ. This is precisely the same comfort that he wants to share with his readers and, moreover, that he wants us to share with one another. What we have to give others is not just a look at the bright side, but the inexhaustible divine comfort that we have received from God and that no affliction can overwhelm.

Blessed are you, dear Father of compassion and God of all encouragement. Give me the strength to comfort others with the comfort I have so often received from you through Jesus Christ our Lord.

Embrace Christ's Sufferings

Father J. Augustine Di Noia, O.P.

"As Christ's sufferings overflow to us, so through Christ does our encouragement also overflow. If we are afflicted, it is for your encouragement and salvation; if we are encouraged, it is for your encouragement, which enables you to endure the same sufferings that we suffer." (2 Cor 1: 5-6)

The Dominican Saint Catherine de Ricci used to tell her nuns that they should embrace their trials joyfully. Many saints have been known to give similar advice. If you don't have trials – they seem to be saying – you are being neglected by God. Let's be honest: to most of us, this seems to be a very strange notion. We want to avoid troubles, not seek them, and certainly not pray for them. What is this strange wisdom of the saints? It goes beyond the common wisdom that suffering can make us stronger: "no pain, no gain," as the popular saying goes. There is something deeper at stake in the Christian wisdom that commends the embrace of life's difficulties. For the Christian, as Saint Paul affirms, the trials and difficulties of life are nothing less than a participation in Christ's sufferings. In this manner, we are assured a share in the benefits of his own passion and death: our salvation. Not only will the apostles like Saint Paul be afflicted, but, according to Christ's own words, whoever wants to follow him must take up the cross. It is only in this way that we can experience the purification from sin – from our attachment to sin and from the consequences of our sins – which is made possible for us by the passion and death of Christ. The salvation Christ won for us takes hold and transforms us over the course of our lives as we share daily in Christ's sufferings and are made strong, not just at a natural level, but in the grace and strength of the Holy Spirit. Christ himself showed us that there is no way to glory except through the cross. The joyful embrace of our trials, which the saints commend, makes perfect sense for those who are advancing on the road to glory.

Blessed are you, Lord Jesus Christ, who did not hesitate to give your life for my sake. Grant me the grace to bear the difficulties of my life united to your sufferings and the strength they impart.

Trust in God Who Raises the Dead

Father J. Augustine Di Noia, O.P.

"Indeed, we had accepted within ourselves the sentence of death, that we might trust not in ourselves but in God who raises the dead." (2 Cor 1: 9)

It's all well and good to talk about embracing our trials for the sake of Christ, but what if the trials we are facing are so extreme that they threaten to overwhelm us? Some trials are just too difficult, some obstacles are seemingly insurmountable, some sorrows simply unbearable. We have all known people who have had to face situations like these. Maybe some of us have faced them ourselves. And, even if we have no direct experience of such difficulties, we can imagine what it would be like to be helpless in the face of such situations. Saint Paul seems to be referring to just this sort of experience – probably when he faced, and escaped, a dangerous and menacing mob in Ephesus. It was a situation whose remedy was far beyond human ability – where human ingenuity and resources count for nothing. An extreme situation, in other words, where self-reliance is just not enough. In such a situation, what can one do? The immediate Christian response would be to trust in God. This is correct as far as it goes, but Saint Paul goes further when he speaks of trusting "in God who raises the dead." Certain situations of affliction are so extreme that only the God who raises the dead can rescue us. Moreover, these situations teach us something very important: that to rely on our own strength and ingenuity can only lead to failure and collapse. When we face situations like these – feeling, as it were, under "the sentence of death" – we learn not to trust in ourselves but in God who is more powerful than death. Confidence of this kind is unshakeable and renders the Christian invincible. What trial, or obstacle, or sorrow, or affliction can overwhelm the man or woman who trusts in the God who raises the dead?

Blessed are you, Father, who raised Jesus from the dead. Grant me the grace to trust in your constant help even in the moments of greatest difficulty.

The Divine Yes

Father J. Augustine Di Noia, O.P.

*"The Son of God, Jesus Christ [...] was not 'yes'
and 'no,' but 'yes.'"* (2 Cor 1: 19)

S ome of us sometimes say "yes" when we mean "no." We want
to be nice, so we give the desired response, knowing nonetheless that it can't or won't be fulfilled. Some of us sometimes
say "no" when we mean "yes." In this case, we really do want something, but we're embarrassed or afraid to say so. Most of us, most
of the time, say "yes" or "no" and try to mean it. In important
matters, this is not always easy. Christ is not like this, Saint Paul
declares in one of his most famous lines: "The Son of God, Jesus
Christ, was not 'yes' and 'no,' but 'yes.'" At the most basic level, Saint
Paul here affirms that in Christ there is none of the dissimulation
that often obscures and tangles our communications with one
another. We can count on Jesus Christ to speak simply and directly,
with the luminosity and transparency that characterizes the divine
truth that subsists in the Word of God and Son of the Father. What
is more, Saint Paul describes not only the mode of Christ's *speech*
but the mode of his *being and action*: Christ *is* "yes" and *enacts* "yes."
The backdrop for this remarkable assertion is the whole economy
of salvation, looking back to the creation of the world and forward
to the consummation of the divine plan. God's desire and intention to share the communion of Trinitarian life with human
persons could not be thwarted by the sin of our first parents, for
he immediately undertook to remedy the harm caused by this original sin through a plan of salvation that unfolded as promise after
promise – one "yes" after another – was fulfilled. These promises
culminate in God's definitive "yes" – Jesus Christ who *is* the content of these promises and who *enacts* the salvation they prefig-
ured. There's no wavering or vacillation here, but fulfillment and
reality – only a resounding divine "yes!"

*Blessed are you, Father of our Lord Jesus Christ, constant and
unwavering in your promises. Bring to fulfillment in me the
redemption begun at the moment of my first baptismal grace.*

The Fragrance of Christ

Father J. Augustine Di Noia, O.P.

"Thanks be to God, who always leads us in triumph in Christ and manifests through us the odor of the knowledge of him in every place. For we are the aroma of Christ for God among those who are being saved and among those who are perishing."
(2 Cor 2: 14-15)

In Saint Paul's day, it was customary in Rome to welcome a victorious general with an elaborate civic and religious ceremony called a *triumphus*. Only a genuinely significant military victory would merit a triumph starting outside the walls of Rome, entering the gate reserved for such occasions, and following a designated route through the city streets. Led by the Senate, this grand procession would include the conquered enemy leaders and other captives followed finally by the victorious general – called the *triumphator* – and his whole army. Roman citizens would line the streets and shower the *triumphator* with flowers until the procession reached its conclusion at the temple of Jupiter on Capitoline Hill. When Saint Paul speaks of "God, who always leads us in triumph in Christ," he undoubtedly has this traditional Roman ceremony in mind as he imagines the sweet fragrance of flowers arising from the streets through which the triumphal procession has passed. In this way, Saint Paul depicts our role in the transmission of the knowledge of Christ using the image of the aroma or fragrance of the garlands strewn upon the triumphant victor. It is an aroma that is sweet-smelling to the victors (believers) – "those who are being saved" – but repulsive to the defeated (unbelievers) – "those who are perishing." The sweet odor of Christ prevails because his victory is definitive and irreversible, even for those who turn away from him or reject him. But how can we be the aroma of Christ? The task seems quite beyond our limited powers. Yet Saint Paul's words bear this unmistakable sense. It can only be through the grace of God "who always leads us in triumph in Christ" that we will receive the energy, insight, and courage to be instruments of the knowledge of Christ in a world that longs to breathe in its fragrance.

Blessed are you, Lord Jesus Christ, triumphant victor over sin and death. Grant me the grace to lead others to you through the example of a life fragrant with holiness.

From Glory to Glory

Father J. Augustine Di Noia, O.P.

"The Lord is the Spirit, and where the Spirit of the Lord is, there is freedom. All of us, gazing with unveiled face on the glory of the Lord, are being transformed into the same image from glory to glory, as from the Lord who is the Spirit." (2 Cor 3: 17-18)

The idea that we are being transformed from one degree of glory to another is hard to grasp. When we look at ourselves in the mirror, especially those of us who are getting older, it looks more like we are sinking into decrepitude than advancing to glory! But, appearances to the contrary notwithstanding, through the eyes of faith we can glimpse the transformation that is underway. Remember the moment of the Transfiguration, when the apostles were permitted to see the glory of the Lord with unveiled faces? Why did Christ reveal himself in this way? One reason surely was that, having seen the glory that lay beneath, their faith would remain strong even as they witnessed the terrible defacement he was to undergo on the cross. Another reason was that the Transfiguration would reveal their own destiny. Just as they would be conformed to Christ in his sufferings, so they would share in his glory. Saint Paul's fundamental point here is that we are being refashioned in the image of Christ by the Holy Spirit at work in us. The Father sees in his only-begotten Son his perfect image, giving rise through all eternity to the love that is the Holy Spirit. Our transformation follows the reverse path: the Holy Spirit reshapes us in the image of the Son so that the Father welcomes us into their communion of love as his adopted sons and daughters. The Father sees and loves in us what he sees and loves in Christ. This is what Saint Paul means when he says that we are being transformed *into the same image* from glory to glory, as from the Lord who is the Spirit. Our whole life as Christians is a process of transformation that is really a conformation as our adoption into the life of the Trinity reaches its fulfillment from glory to glory.

Blessed Father, I pray that, in the grace of the Holy Spirit, you will see and love in me what you see and love in your beloved Son, our Lord Jesus Christ.

Be My Light

Father James Martin, S.J.

"God who said, 'Let light shine out of darkness,' has shone in our hearts to bring to light the knowledge of the glory of God on the face of [Jesus] Christ." (2 Cor 4: 6)

The title of Mother Teresa's posthumous collection of letters is *Come Be My Light*. Yet ironically, her letters speak more about darkness than light. For the last fifty years of her life, the woman now called Blessed Teresa of Calcutta suffered from an intense sense of spiritual darkness. Her prayer seemed empty, futile, fruitless. God seemed absent. This "dark night" was all the more striking given the mystical experiences that she had enjoyed earlier in life. In 1946, she literally heard the voice of Jesus asking her to leave the Sisters of Loreto to found a new religious order, the Missionaries of Charity.

What was Mother Teresa's response to this long interior darkness? Fidelity. She maintained the commitments she made to God, who had asked her to "be my light" among the poor. In time, Mother Teresa realized that the darkness was one way of experiencing the abandonment that Christ faced on the cross, and that the poor face daily. And the Albanian-born nun recognized that the very longing for God is a sign of God's presence.

Many of us, when confronted with darkness in life – spiritual, emotional, professional, or otherwise – mistakenly believe that it is a punishment from God. Sometimes we even use it as an excuse not to do the hard work of the Christian life – being compassionate, loving, and merciful. Mother Teresa's arduous but ultimately joyful life shows us that following Christ depends not simply on our emotional experiences, important as they are, but on our fidelity, our trust in God's will, and our ability to surrender to the future that God has in store for us. And then, in the midst of the darkness, we are able to be God's light.

Loving God, sometimes the way is so dark and it is so hard to find you. Please help me to trust in you even when you don't seem present. And help me to see your presence in my life soon.

My Friend Alice

Father James Martin, S.J.

"But we hold this treasure in earthen vessels, that the surpassing power may be of God and not from us. We are afflicted in every way, but not constrained; perplexed, but not driven to despair; persecuted, but not abandoned; struck down, but not destroyed; always carrying about in the body the dying of Jesus, so that the life of Jesus may also be manifested in our body." (2 Cor 4: 7-10)

During my Jesuit training, I worked for two years in Nairobi, Kenya, with the Jesuit Refugee Service. There, in the midst of a bustling city, thousands of refugees from across East Africa had settled, after fleeing poverty, famine, and violence. My job was to help the refugees start small businesses to support themselves. We sponsored tailoring shops, small restaurants, a bakery, and even a little chicken farm.

Whenever I read these lines from Saint Paul, I think of Alice Nabwire, a Ugandan refugee. Alice had migrated to Kenya in the 1980s, while still a young woman, fleeing the violence in her home country. When I first met her, she was running a thriving tailoring shop, along with two friends, out of a wooden shack in one of the city's worst slums. Like every refugee, Alice had seen great misery in life. And it seemed unlikely that she would ever earn enough money to return home.

Yet she was one of the most joyful people I've ever met – energetic, resourceful, even playful. When we opened up a shop to sell refugee handicrafts, she would bring her colorfully patterned dresses, and if I bought two, asked why I didn't buy three. And if I bought three, why not four? Once, when I told her that another refugee was planning on naming her baby after me, and that I was going to pay for the baptism clothes for the newborn child, Alice laughed, "If you keep doing that, there will be many babies named after you!"

Alice was "struck down, but not destroyed." Whenever I feel tempted to despair, I think of Alice, who reminds me of the "surpassing power" of God, who can fill us with hope, even in the most desperate circumstances – if we are open to accepting it.

Compassionate God, I am often fearful and weak. Yet my weakness is a doorway to understanding my reliance on you. Help me to trust in you. And help my earthen vessel be a carrier of your grace.

Dying to Self

Father James Martin, S.J.

"For we who live are constantly being given up to death for the sake of Jesus, so that the life of Jesus may be manifested in our mortal flesh." (2 Cor 4: 11)

Almost twenty years ago, I first heard the expression "dying to self." At first it sounded morbid. Why would anyone want to die at all?

Ultimately, it began to make sense. "Dying to self" means letting go of the parts of ourselves that prevent us from moving closer to God. By embracing these small "deaths" we find ourselves experiencing new life. In this way, we can experience the mystery of the resurrection.

One example in my life came as I was preparing to work with Mother Teresa's sisters in Kingston, Jamaica, among the poor. Despite the fact that Jamaica has a thriving medical community, I was terrified of getting sick there. What would happen to me? Food poisoning? Malaria? Something worse?

The night before my departure I confessed my fears to an elderly Jesuit. He said, "Why not just allow yourself to get sick?" In other words, sickness is part of being human. So why not allow yourself to be human? The part of myself that was obsessed with not getting sick needed to "die," so that I could follow God more freely. That's not to say that I was foolish in caring for myself, but I needed to let go of the need for perfect physical health at all times. My friend's advice helped me not only to relax, but also to find God more easily after I arrived in Kingston. (And I never got sick!)

This is part of the continual death that Saint Paul is talking about. Finding God depends on being free enough to do this. Can we allow ourselves to die these small deaths in order to experience new freedom? These "deaths" are one of God's important invitations to us – because they lead to new life.

Loving God, you sometimes invite me to let go of something that prevents me from following you. Help me to embrace these small deaths so that I can experience new life in you.

Looking forward to Heaven

Father James Martin, S.J.

"The one who raised the Lord Jesus will raise us also with Jesus and place us with you in his presence." (2 Cor 4: 14)

It has become common to say that Christianity is not simply about "pie in the sky when you die." In other words, Christianity is not simply concerned with meeting God in the afterlife. It is *also* about experiencing God in our lives on earth. The kingdom of God, as Jesus reminds us, is among us.

But one result of emphasizing the presence of God in our daily lives can be overlooking the fundamental importance of the afterlife. After all, part of the Creed that we recite on Sundays says, "I believe in the resurrection of the dead." Catholics believe that, after their deaths, those who have led loving and faithful lives will enjoy eternal life. This part of our tradition is a comfort for anyone who has ever lost a loved one, or anyone who fears death – which is to say, everyone.

A few years ago, one of my favorite spiritual directors died suddenly, at age sixty-five. He was someone who I would call my "spiritual father," the person who taught me how to pray. During his funeral I was almost as sad as I had been years before, at the funeral of my father. But in a few months my sadness was replaced with a surprising new feeling: I was looking forward to seeing David again. Like my father, David had led a good life, and I trusted that he was in heaven. This wonderful feeling of anticipation has remained. Though I hope it's not for some time, I almost can't wait to see David again.

This belief is not only theologically sound, but sensible. When people question the afterlife, I ask them this: Why would God sever the relationships he has with us? God the Father, who loved Jesus, and gave him new life, loves us as well, and will, as Saint Paul said, "raise us also with Jesus."

God of eternal life, sometimes I fear the death of my friends and family. Sometimes I fear my own death. Help me to believe in the resurrection and help me to look forward to heaven, when I will be reunited with all of my friends and family.

God Likes You

Father James Martin, s.j.

"Everything indeed is for you, so that the grace bestowed in abundance on more and more people may cause the thanksgiving to overflow for the glory of God." (2 Cor 4: 15)

Did you ever think about God liking you? Christians are so used to hearing that God *loves* us that we need to be reminded that God *likes* us, the way that friends like one another, and wish only the good for one another. God likes you.

When I was a boy, I used to ride my bike to school. In the mornings, as I neared school, I had to pedal over a bumpy dirt path through a small meadow. During the spring and early summer the meadow was bursting with life. Bordered by tall oak trees, filled with wildflowers and tall grasses, and buzzing with grasshoppers and honeybees, the little meadow was my favorite spot in the whole world. One morning, I paused in the middle of the meadow to smell that warm summery smell that the earth gives off. As I stood beside my bike, a monarch butterfly flew past me silently. I remember feeling that I wanted to stay there for ever.

When I recounted that memory to a spiritual director, he said, "God takes delight in you!" God was showing me, through my experience in the meadow, not simply how much he loves me, but how much he likes me, and wants me to be happy, in the same way that we want our friends to be happy.

"Everything indeed is for you" is not an expression of arrogance, as if the whole world revolves around you. Rather, it's an expression of the abundant love God has for us. God likes us so much that he wants us to enjoy the whole world: the meadows, the flowers, the trees, the oceans, the towns, the cities. Everything. Once we realize this, it's easy to be grateful for God's generosity, and to "overflow" with thanksgiving. And to like God in return.

God of surprises, help me to see the ways that you take delight in me. And help me to take delight in you.

Everyone's Call

Father James Martin, S.J.

"We have a building from God, a dwelling not made with hands, eternal in heaven. For in this tent we groan, longing to be further clothed with our heavenly habitation if indeed, when we have taken it off, we shall not be found naked. For while we are in this tent we groan and are weighed down, because we do not wish to be unclothed but to be further clothed, so that what is mortal may be swallowed up by life." (2 Cor 5: 1-4)

Nobody feels completely satisfied with his or her life. Even the most successful, accomplished, popular among us still feel a certain degree of incompletion and of longing. A sense that there is something more to life.

Not long ago, I was invited to work with a group of actors who were putting together a play based on the story of Jesus and Judas. The play would be produced at a prestigious New York theater, and among the cast were some successful actors, directors, and playwrights. When I first met them, I imagined that they were probably leading a charmed life. After all, a few had reached the pinnacle of their professional lives, and had many admirers. Yet after a short time with these wonderful people, I realized that their lives had a full measure of joys and sorrows, like anyone else's. While others might imagine them having perfect lives, they certainly didn't see it that way. Like all of us, they had to face our "poverty of spirit," the realization that in this lifetime we will always long for something more.

That "something more" is God. The deep longing that we all experience is the desire for God, a desire that will only be completely fulfilled when we meet God face to face, after our deaths. So while we "groan" in this "tent," that is, while we may face frustration in our daily lives, we can be consoled by knowing that the longing for God comes from God. These desires are a way that God has of drawing us nearer. For those who say that they've never felt themselves called by God, this is the call.

Creator God, sometimes I feel so incomplete. Sometimes I don't even know what I want. Help me to see that this longing is from you, that it is for you, and that it is leading me, gently, toward you.

The Courage of Faith

Sharon Mollerus

"We are always courageous [...] for we walk by faith, not by sight." (2 Cor 5: 6-7)

Saint Paul's statement is straight and bold, and he backs it with his life. Walking by faith put him in the daily dangers he catalogued. No one could yet envision that the ragtag Church would not only survive but triumph over the might and rage of the Roman Empire. The challenges may be different today, or not so different depending on what part of the world we live in, but we can draw on the same courage from Christ that prompted Saint Paul's observation. Teresa Cejudo, one of the newly beatified Spanish martyrs, was the mother of a ten-year-old when she was killed for her faith. She worked with a Salesian school in a small town, distributing food to the poor and teaching illiterate children. Before being executed in a cemetery, she spent a month in jail where her daughter visited her without understanding that her mother would be taken from her. Teresa asked not to be blindfolded because she wanted to look death in the face, and she asked to be the last to be shot so as to encourage the others to stay strong in their faith. She stated that she was not afraid of dying for God. Her daughter later married and had eleven children, and was said never to have harbored resentment over her mother's death – a remarkable fruit of a mother's courage that strengthened even her child despite this cruel deprivation. We are invited to an impossible certainty that what we see now is not the last word; instead the resurrection is the final event of the world. We are helped to live this certainty through the sacraments and our companionship in the Church with the saints and our fellow Christians. Just as Teresa Cejudo encouraged her fellow martyrs, we can stir each other to this courage on the path that peers into heaven.

Lord, grant me the courage today to follow you, despite my apprehension and pride. Help me to trust you through all the circumstances you give to bring me closer to you.

The Fullness of Life

Sharon Mollerus

"We must all appear before the judgment seat of Christ, so that each one may receive recompense, according to what he did in the body, whether good or evil." (2 Cor 5: 10)

This statement is hardly the hot topic these days. Presumption, the Pollyannaish wish that heaven is due us regardless of faith or actions, is the prevailing attitude toward the last things: death, judgment, heaven, and hell. It may not be that we lack the images for a miserable eternal existence so much as that death and the afterlife mean so little to us now. The devaluing of life affects even committed Christians in subtle forms. Our common culture has lost the joy in children, the tenderness for the ill and handicapped, and the priority given to bonds of family and friendship over personal comforts. Life seems disposable and haphazard, and we must continually counter this defeatist mentality in ourselves which contracts our hope for living fully and for always. We have been barraged with appeals to reduce our desires to the mundane and easy reaches in the world and to bow out gracefully when our time or luck is up. In our times, we don't factor in absolute fulfillment or total loss as the real stakes for each of us personally. Regardless of our perceptions, the life given to every human person, born or unborn, rich or poor, loved or abandoned, is a glorious gift of eternal worth, a fact that should raise dread and wonder in us and a reality which we cannot diminish by the most callous carelessness or indifference. God's mercy awaits the recognition of our dependence on him to give us this well of living water, this life which we could neither grant ourselves originally nor guarantee to ourselves after death. This understanding should engage the whole of our reason and freedom, rather than cause us to succumb to irrational fear and denial. It can push us unreservedly to embrace the whole promise of eternal life extended to us through Christ's sacrifice.

Lord, thank you for the great gift of life that you give. Help me to see the full value of my life united to yours, that I may consecrate all to you.

An Impossible Exchange

Sharon Mollerus

"[Christ] indeed died for all, so that those who live might no longer live for themselves but for him who for their sake died and was raised." (2 Cor 5: 15)

What parent, in front of a sick child, is not ready to exchange their life for the child they love more than themselves? Grandparents, when they see their once rebellious children suddenly transformed into solicitous parents, then recall their own progression from youth to maturity. Something that we at first think so foreign to our nature is, on the contrary, exactly the natural attitude of parent to child. God the Father gives his Son for our sake and raises him up, so that we would be redeemed and also raised. He who does not spare himself his only Son, his Everything, shows that life with him is rooted in this self-giving. Our tortuous efforts to make life meaningful, to follow our dreams and plans, can be quickly crushed. We may find the world unfairly adverse to our plan to live for ourselves. Instead, we learn we can only find our personal fulfillment through this total gift of ourselves to the One we belong to and his people. We see this consistency of love especially in those who love us, those who, like true fathers and mothers, are able to care more for us than we do for ourselves. These friends and loved ones value our destiny more than our comforts. We have been reclaimed for God, we who as sinners had no rights to forgiveness or happiness. If we honestly assess our machinations to make happiness, we can be sure that these fall short of the grace of salvation offered to us by Christ's sacrifice and available not only in heaven but now in a bounty of grace. As God loved us for our final destiny in him, so we see that it is in self-giving that we will be truly united to the One who calls us to fulfillment.

Lord, help me to let go of my selfish plans to cling to your love. My life is yours; make it fruitful for your kingdom.

Seeing with New Eyes

Sharon Mollerus

"Whoever is in Christ is a new creation: the old things have passed away; behold, new things have come." (2 Cor 5: 17)

The world is transformed in front of the eyes of the new lover who has just discovered the one he hopes to be with always. A new spring is revealed. The sky is suddenly bright blue, the clouds white and billowy, the foliage green and fertile. To the one who loves, obstacles only incite the desire to see her again, and the world is suddenly full of signs of the beloved's dear presence. The sacrifice of sleep or time or money will not be calculated against the chance to stay with the one he loves. After a restful, focused Sunday, it is easy to forget in the Monday rush that the old things have actually passed away and that the triumph is now, even in the midst of difficulties and the weariness we endure from labors both physical and emotional. After returning from a retreat or holy hour, we can feel that we have left the best behind and must wait until the next sacred occasion to be fully united with Christ again. But the new things are for every day and are meant to transform all the given circumstances into one path of happiness. The presence of the One who loves us can be welcomed again at any moment as he is always with us. We have to recognize a new criterion for life which makes us curious and unafraid. Instead of being defeated by obstacles to this new attraction, we can accept every opportunity to stay with the beloved. The way continually to revive this new life is to access Christ's presence in the sacraments and to stay close to those who reveal Christ's living presence to us. Then we will let the old things go and will see more and more the newness that is the fresh nature bestowed on us by Christ.

Lord, today let me see again the new spring you are bringing into my life. Let my memory of your goodness hold throughout this day.

What Stops Us

Sharon Mollerus

"God was reconciling the world to himself in Christ, not counting their trespasses against them and entrusting to us the message of reconciliation. [...] We implore you on behalf of Christ, be reconciled to God." (2 Cor 5: 19-20)

We seem to tolerate a host of obstacles to this full reconciliation with Christ that Saint Paul urges. They vary from gnat-like worries that swirl around our heads to larger life-changing challenges to living the Christian life fully. While we try to ignore them, at the same time we avoid the Presence that awaits us just beyond these concerns. Such encumbrances keep us from the one thing necessary, Christ himself. What holds us earthbound? It may be a grudge, habit, preoccupation, relationship, or even a crushing pain that prevents our opening to Christ and our happiness. We may feel we need to call pest control first to set our house in order, but instead it is acknowledgment of our bottomless need that brings us back to this direct encounter with Christ and makes change possible, in God's time. He does not catalog trespasses against us, but waits for our pleas and contrition. He offers us every means to union with him, through the sacrifice of his Son, daily renewed and awaiting us in the Eucharist and the sacrament of reconciliation. In the moment that Christ saw Zacchaeus and told him, "Today I am coming to your house," the tax collector, in his fascination with this man, found all his usual preoccupations had fallen from first place. He was immediately ready to shed pride, property, and position, to make restitution for his thefts, and to replace self-aggrandizement with discipleship. To see the face of Christ again is to become unfettered from all that has held us back. The message entrusted to us is the Good News of freedom available to ourselves and to everyone. We can only testify to this relationship with mercy by our own joy and serenity, and in the forgiveness and friendship we then extend to others.

Lord, please remove all encumbrances to this total embrace with you. Grant me the courage to seek and hold to you always.

The Scandalous Sacrifice

Sharon Mollerus

*"For our sake [God] made [Christ] to be sin who did not know
sin, so that we might become the righteousness of God in him."*
(2 Cor 5: 21)

The things that most disgust us about ourselves and others are those things Christ crucified in the wounds of his body and the expiration of his breath. Beaten, bloodied, naked, Christ was nailed on the cross bearing every outrage and shame known to mankind. There is no human anguish that Christ did not participate in with his final sacrifice. He surrounded himself with the likes of Zacchaeus and Mary Magdalene, a thug and a prostitute, and praised them for the great love that comes from gratitude for being forgiven much. Perhaps the larger scandal is when we don't recognize the triumph in our own case, when our own sins weigh us down and seem unforgivable in our isolating pride. The leper Naaman, a Syrian military officer, was told of Elisha the prophet by a servant girl, a captive from Israel, who waited on his wife. When Naaman went to Elisha, the holy man asked him to bathe in the River Jordan seven times. The great man at first resisted the simple request because of his pride, until his servants convinced him that if he was prepared to do something more difficult in exchange for healing, why not simply obey what the prophet had asked. The leper was healed by the waters of the Jordan, as we are in the sacraments of baptism, reconciliation, and the anointing of the sick. We can imagine in a sad self-sufficiency that God himself is not great enough to remove this shame and restore us to wholeness, yet we are simply invited to accept this offered healing. We need a sober assessment that recognizes our dependence and lets go of the tendency to control our own lives. A peaceful gratefulness, a childlike trust, is all that is asked in exchange for the unimaginable sacrifice of God for man that rescues and changes us.

Lord, give me this confidence and joy in your forgiveness. Help me to return to you again and again without hesitation.

The Paradox of Life

Sharon Mollerus

*"We are treated as deceivers and yet are truthful;
as unrecognized and yet acknowledged; as dying and behold
we live; as chastised and yet not put to death; as sorrowful
yet always rejoicing; as poor yet enriching many; as having
nothing and yet possessing all things." (2 Cor 6: 8-10)*

What human nature would divide, divine grace restores in whole harmony. Sorrow and joy are compatible, although this contradiction surpasses the limits of our human understanding. Everything that happens in time is restored to its rightful place and lifted out of a span of meaninglessness. Although it is evident on honest examination that riches and fame can never meet the measure of our hunger for goods, it is absurd and wonderful that the poor and unknown will trump the world's rulers in the final distribution of fortune and honor. And if Christ, goodness incarnate, was hated, how much more will we be with our irritating failings, even while our weakness remains a sign of his continuing redeeming intervention in our lives. If our greatest saints can be vilified by cynics, as we have seen with Mother Teresa, nevertheless the truth of holiness finally will be revealed and acknowledged. For those who are honest, even now the wisdom of the Church's teachings, considered difficult and even hated by many, has been demonstrated to yield a fruit of happiness and stability. The sacrifices demanded for wholeness can be welcomed instead of shunned, because they are evidently fulfilling. Similar to replacing the easy highs of sugar and caffeine with substantial food and drink, what at first seems a privation becomes satisfying because it is in accord with our nature as made by God. The mortal self-sufficiency that rules most of the world's opinions and policies, the human accounting of little things and small values, will be definitively overturned as creation is recovered. God himself, revealed in the design he displays across the days of our lives, is sufficient for us; and we can only know this by a path of daily discipleship. Our certainty grows in Christ, even as we yield confidently to the vagaries of the path we are sent on.

Lord, help me endure the contradictions in my life with new confidence in you. I offer you the difficulties you have seen necessary for love of me and mine.

Inevitable Sorrow

Sharon Mollerus

"Godly sorrow produces a salutary repentance without regret, but worldly sorrow produces death." (2 Cor 7: 10)

Sadness is inevitable, for we are made for an infinite which we do not yet fully possess, and all the good luck in the world won't calm this restless longing. The death of worldly things is the law of the finite; it is as predictable as the boredom that follows the excitement for each new thing we wanted, received, and cast aside for the next fancy. All depends on the object of one's sorrow, desire for God, or worldly worries. Fortunately, we have many examples of conversions that show a repentance that does not stop at regrets, but moves forward to joyful attachment to Christ and bold new sacrifice for the kingdom of God. Saint Paul himself can say this after being an accomplice to the murder of his future brothers in the faith. Saint Peter could take the reins of the newborn Church and preach the Gospel fearlessly and publicly, after three times denying the only person who could save him from death. A new blessed, Franz Jägerstätter, was reputed to have led a wild life before his dramatic conversion on a trip to Rome with his new bride. The Austrian family man later chose martyrdom rather than cooperate in the evil of the Nazi regime when he was drafted into the military. Although nearly everyone, from spiritual advisers to family members, tried to dissuade him from his uncompromising stance, he saw clearly that the Gospel calls for a whole commitment to Christ, and he embraced death without regret. Conversion changes our heart's object, our desire. When we mourn over the things that pass in this world, instead of our sinful escapes from God's presence, we don't find our heart's true companion. Distress rooted in the disappointment of our images of success and comfortable circumstances keeps us from the dependence on God that frees us and gives us gladness in him alone.

Lord, I offer you all the attachments that point me to my need for you. Let my sadness bring me closer to you today.

The Wealth of the Poor

Sharon Mollerus

"You know the gracious act of our Lord Jesus Christ, that for your sake he became poor although he was rich, so that by his poverty you might become rich." (2 Cor 8: 9)

The disruption of the original order in the world, that natural dependence of creature on the Creator upset by sin, requires that a new mindset be practiced and learned. It is not intuitive to fallen nature to exchange our self-security for fullness in God. All our lives we have been urged to be cautious and hard-working to secure a footing in an uncertain world. This leaves us ever troubled as we try to volley the circumstances thrown to us to our personal advantage and build bulwarks of resources to protect ourselves and our families against want and misfortune. Christ came into the world as a naked baby to a poor couple who were defenseless in front of the vagaries and violence of their times. Forced to migrate for the census at the time of imminent birth, turned away from decent shelter, hunted by Herod, they were as vulnerable as the least ones on the earth. Still nothing happened to the Holy Family that wasn't guided by the Father's will. They did not rely on their power or worldly leverage even to protect the divine child. Help was given them in messages of warning and direction. A stable was provided for the child's birth, and the kings and shepherds were invited to come and adore him in a field beneath the heavens. We learn that the things and happenings of the world have a larger purpose, and we need not control or put these in opposition to their Provider and the others given to us. Our peaceful entrusting of all to God, as Christ gave his life into the hands of his Father, allows us to inherit all that has been promised, the riches of life as God's true children. We see that the materials of living, precious as they are for their purposes, are subject to the Father's sufficient provision for his children.

Lord, I kneel at your crib in wonder of your way of coming to us. Help me to become a child before the greatness of all you offer of your love.

Leveraging Littleness

Sharon Mollerus

"Consider this: whoever sows sparingly will also reap sparingly, and whoever sows bountifully will also reap bountifully."
(2 Cor 9: 6)

We are always invited by Christ and the apostles not to hold back in our response of love to God's love. We can read such a passage and be discouraged by the idea that some superhuman effort is required which we don't feel up to. Instead, we are invited to give all that we have, the widow's mite, and not to be afraid of our smallness. The bountiful sowing is the great confidence, the size of a mustard seed, which allows God to make us fruitful instead of our relying on our own generosity and good will. This faith pushes us to risk without calculating the result, trusting in the Lord to bring all to fruition, especially the most hidden goods. Anxiety about our achievements, even spiritual ones; dubious calculations of our impact on others; the wrangling and worrying we do to fix the efforts we believe we have bungled: these are all counterproductive to the work Christ wants to do through us. Absolutely everything is useful, all that passes through the quirks of personality up to and including the contrition for our sins. There is nothing that God cannot use to the good if we trust him to reap us. Saint Thérèse of Lisieux led an uneventful and short life in an ordinary family and later as an unassuming Carmelite nun. Her offering of the whole of her small portion, her unremarkable sacrifices in her provincial milieu, catapulted her into a super-saint, a Doctor of the Church and Patroness of Missions. She leveraged her patience with the sisters' foibles and the acceptance of minor slights to heroic sanctity; she dared even to offer her naps in chapel for love of God. For her, love had no ceilings but could soar ever further. Nothing was wasted in her exuberance to live as a child of God in dependence and boundless gratitude.

Lord, give me the faith to return all to you with all boldness. Use my weakness to reap your work in me.

Learning to Give

Sharon Mollerus

"Each must do as already determined, without sadness or compulsion, for God loves a cheerful giver." (2 Cor 9: 7)

God, who needs nothing, awaits our gift. He asks that we trust in him as provider, rather than depend on our own clever schemes to manage our future security. Paul knows our human weakness, that resolve will be undermined by worries. A joyful surrender teaches us God's care for us which is always surprising and definitive. Some stories amaze us, of impoverished African women with AIDS who took a collection for the victims of Hurricane Katrina, or the Iraqi police fund taken up to help those who lost homes in the San Diego fires. These small, shining gestures demonstrate a freedom that doesn't come easily to those of us who presume we can take care of ourselves and our own without help. It seems a strange thing to grudge a gift to a lover or parent. Yet, we can suffer from the sadness of the miser, who hoards because of his fear of want. Our energies are consumed with the anxiety of managing possessions instead of being free gratefully to receive and open-handedly give of the blessings we receive. Why do we place God, from whom we continue to receive everything, at the bottom of the Christmas list? If our gratitude and generosity rightly go out to spouses, parents, children, and even their teachers, how do we continue to minimize our debt to God, using for excuse his abundance instead of mourning our distance from his love? For Christians, giving is all done in his name so that it has a value far beyond that of charitable projects meant to assuage a guilty prosperity. The Lord is the One who gives the increase to what we joyfully return to him, however small. The discipline of releasing what has already been offered allows us to take these small steps in learning dependence on the Father for our daily bread.

Lord, help us to grow in dependence on you for all things material and spiritual. Grant us the courage to place all things in your hands to be worked by your merciful bounty.

God's Yield in Us

Sharon Mollerus

"God is able to make every grace abundant for you, so that in all things, always having all you need, you may have an abundance for every good work. The one who supplies seed to the sower and bread for food will supply and multiply your seed and increase the harvest of your righteousness." (2 Cor 9: 8, 10)

In his Letter to the Corinthians, Paul was trying to encourage a community that had experienced painful division instead of a fruitful unity. Adversity can appear to overwhelm our best efforts, especially during those conflicts which often arise among the well-intentioned who should be closest collaborators. As the cynical saying goes, "No good deed goes unpunished," and it can seem that our attempts to do the right thing are often unwelcomed and unfruitful. Sometimes we are even despised and ridiculed for what we must say and do to be faithful to the Gospel. We feel ourselves absurd in front of the utilitarian logic of a society that measures people by statistics instead of by love. Persecution is thus added to the hundredfold promised us, as Christ indicated. The true harvest in the world is goodness brought by God's grace building on our efforts offered to him. It takes an engaged faith to trust Christ to bring the yield of truth forward. His is the courage given to us and the result he brings to the labor in a place that is openly hostile to God's plan of love. Paul asks his congregation to believe that God will make the impossible possible and that he will deny us no means to live faithfully and to produce this good itself. We can trust God to see us through the work of restoring creation for which he has employed us at a late hour. Of course, no one wishes to waste his life and see the product of his toil withered and trampled upon. But we need not be disconcerted by appearances: the crucifixion itself, the evidently colossal defeat, becomes the glorious victory itself. It is no different for the Church shining through the witness of the lives and deaths of her saints and martyrs.

Lord, I know that all is yours which I take up and use today for your world. Please bless my efforts and give my work increase for the sake of your kingdom.

A Vision of God's Love

Father Vincent Nagle, F.S.C.B.

"Who is weak, and I am not weak? Who is led to sin, and I am not indignant?/ If I must boast, I will boast of the things that show my weakness." (2 Cor 11: 29-30)

It was just a moment, but everything changed. Late at night, correcting the mountain of papers from my students at the Moroccan school where I was teaching, feeling the hostile relationship that existed between us, I complained to myself how they did not *deserve* this sacrifice on my part. Then everything changed. Up to that moment the world had seemed to me a place where, if you just identify the problems and get the power to stop the people causing them, you can make everything perfect. The question was power. Then God gave me a vision. I clearly saw myself as a baby in the arms of my mother, sick, late at night. She, as weak as she was, with five children older than me, and another only a year younger, walked and walked with me in her arms. Why? Because I deserved it? No. It was because I needed it. That's all. I had been shown what lay at the heart of life. It was need, not eliminating problems. What was interesting, then, was not power, but to see how God was answering our need for love, life, beauty, and truth. Where do these things come from?

Saint Paul too had been set on eliminating problems, starting with the Church. He too had had a vision (infinitely greater than my own). And these mysterious words – "Who is weak, and I am not weak? Who is led to sin, and I am not indignant?" – come from his discovery of life as need and its magnificent answer. Life for Paul, for us, is the presence of the answer to that need. Life is Christ. How could he not then identify as his own the weakness and shame of others? Since his joy is the love of that one who has come to answer this need, logically enough, he cries out, and we with him, "I will boast of the things that show my weakness."

My Father, grant me the grace to discover my need in encountering the one you have sent to answer this need. Let no one's shame be repugnant to me, rather may it incite me to turn ever more to your Son, who on the cross embraced our shame to redeem us.

Who Is a Saint?

Father Vincent Nagle, F.S.C.B.

"That I might not become too elated, a thorn in the flesh was given to me, an angel of Satan, to beat me, to keep me from being too elated. Three times I begged the Lord about this, that it might leave me, but he said to me, 'My grace is sufficient for you, for power is made perfect in weakness.' I will rather boast most gladly of my weaknesses, in order that the power of Christ may dwell with me." (2 Cor 12: 7-9)

When I read this passage of Saint Paul, I go back to a moment that has guided my personal dramas of sin and grace ever since. I was listening to a priest speaking to several hundred university students who had come to spend a few days with him in the Alps. At one point a girl stood up to ask a question. She said, "When I am with my friends (of this Catholic movement), I am good. When I am not, I am bad." We all felt struck by the courageous clarity of this statement. The answer surprised me very much. The priest said, "First, stay with your friends. Second, imagine a man who has a weakness, we won't speculate what it is. Each morning he arises with confidence in Jesus and his Mother, light-hearted in his hope not to fail that day. He does fail, repeating that mistake arising from his weakness. He goes home full of tears and repentance, praying to Jesus and his Mother for compassion, forgiveness, and healing. Again, he awakens the next morning full of gratitude, and the pattern repeats itself. And this goes on for years, perhaps for the rest of his life. What do we call a man like that?" There was silence. The priest, speaking forcefully now, insisted, "What do we call him?" Again silence. Finally he said, "A saint. He is a man alive entirely through his recognition of and confidence in the presence of Jesus and the prayers of his Mother. These define his entire reason for living. They define who he is. This is the definition of a saint."

Saint Paul is humiliated by this weakness of his. But it only opens him more deeply to the truth of himself, which is the grace of Christ, his communion with the Father through the Son. And so too, our humiliations are not our defeat, but our own doorway to a new humanity in Christ.

All perfect God, how I suffer because of my defeats. How I squirm under my humiliations. Give me liberation through fixing my hope, not on myself, but upon your Son, who has changed disgrace into redemption.

The Usefulness of Uselessness

Father Vincent Nagle, F.S.C.B.

"I am content with weaknesses, insults, hardships, persecutions, and constraints, for the sake of Christ; for when I am weak, then I am strong." (2 Cor 12: 10)

For my patients in the hospital where I was chaplain, often the hardest thing to bear was not their pain, traumatic as that could be. Instead it was their weakness, and the sense of uselessness and being a burden to others. The anger and frustration about being in such a position, and the prospect of remaining in this position, could be overwhelming. I would point out that a major reason why the disciples followed Christ was that he was all-powerful and all-good and thus all-useful. Watching him expose lies and hypocrisy, heal the sick, raise from the dead, they had big plans for the kingdom to come. The reason they ran away at the crucifixion, then, was not simply that they were afraid, but also that this inexplicable weakness on Christ's part seemed so scandalously useless. "What could be the use of his letting himself be taken and tortured like that?" they were thinking.

I would then take out a crucifix, and we would look at it together. Then I would say, "Is this useless? Was his weakness useless? Is ours?" We would talk about the victory and hope it brought. We would rediscover our gratitude for his being with us in our weakness, so that it not be an end for us, but a path to victory with him. It seemed like the most useless thing, but it turned out to be the most useful thing ever. I would ask, "Is he here now, winning his victory with you? Are you not the most useful person in the world right now?" I would often see their faces change from an expression of someone trapped, to someone making a mature assent. We can feel like escaping, deciding that there is no quality of life in our weakness. But when someone recognizes Christ's victory in us, we see that we are chosen, useful. Then we can say with Saint Paul, "When I am weak, then I am strong."

God, my Father, let me not be scandalized by my uselessness. Rather, make me one with your Son in his "useless" act on the cross, so that, offering myself to him, I may be brought into his act of salvation.

By What Power Do We Live?

Father Vincent Nagle, F.S.C.B.

*"[Christ] is not weak toward you but powerful in you.
For indeed he was crucified out of weakness, but he lives
by the power of God." (2 Cor 13: 3-4)*

I was moving from strength to strength, in his name, in what seemed like a series of conquests for his kingdom: completing a license in Islamic studies, preparing for ordination, and starting a mission in Africa. I was in a movement in the Church bursting with life and reaching out to the whole world, and one of the first priests of a new missionary society. Then I got sick. It was sheer exhaustion. And then for the next couple of years I did almost nothing.

I lay in the dark with a rosary in hand.

But even at the beginning, I was sure that it was not just an evil chance. Why had my strength been taken away? I suspected what it was that he wanted to give me. I had been so keen on what I was accomplishing in his name. But at center stage it was always me. What he wanted to give me was a new center, himself. He did not want my life to depend on what I was doing. He wanted it to depend on what he was doing.

What was he doing? Offering his love. He was offering me the chance to simply be the one who was saying, with his help, "yes" to being loved by him. And that is all. Everything. Anything else did not depend on me. It was his. I just had to say "yes" to him. Only by embracing my weakness as a gift could I begin to live as I desired, as one who is, unworthily, loved.

Christ had been willing to be emptied, to be weak, so as to be lifted up by the Father. Saint Paul says Christ is not weak toward you but powerful in you. For indeed he was crucified out of weakness, but he lives by the power of God. By what power, then, do we, each one of us, live?

My God and Creator, you are all mighty, and any power of mine is nothing in front of you. Let the power of your mercy be my only boast. I ask this through your Son who gave himself up for me, and through the Spirit who unites me to him.

167

It Changes Everything

Father Vincent Nagle, F.S.C.B.

"Examine yourselves to see whether you are living in faith.
Test yourselves. Do you not realize that Jesus Christ is in you?"
(2 Cor 13: 5)

One of the tricks my brothers and I used to play on each other was hiding in a room we knew the other would come into, letting them settle in thinking they were alone, and then jump out. You often got quite a reaction, especially when, as one of my brothers did a couple of times to me, you hide behind the shower curtain in the bathroom. The point is, discovering the presence of another person, especially when we thought we were by ourselves, changes everything. Everything changes when we discover that we are not alone.

And this is how Saint Paul is referring to faith. He says, "Examine yourselves to see whether you are living in faith... Do you not realize that Jesus Christ is in you?" Faith is the recognition of the presence of another, of that other who is the Son of God made flesh, Jesus Christ. It changes everything. Thus we find Saint Paul insisting with his wayward children in faith on two points. The first is that they cling fast to that relationship, that human community, in this case Paul, that allowed them to recognize the presence of Christ. "Living in faith" means living in that human story, the Church, that shows you Christ. Secondly, he challenges them to see that, in belonging to that community, they are not acting alone but are intimately in his presence. This is Paul's own experience with them. Paul's presence among them gave birth to the Church, something he could not by himself produce. He was not acting alone. So, even though they are surrounded by temptations and different voices, they do not have to be afraid. Let them be aware that Christ is in them. For us too, we do not depend upon the changing winds of fashion. We have another starting point, all the time. He is here. We are not alone. This changes everything.

Lord God, this life can seem such a solitary journey. Liberate me and change everything through increasing my awareness of my communion with you through the presence of your Son, alive within me by the power of the Holy Spirit.

He Is Our Peace

Father Vincent Nagle, F.S.C.B.

"Mend your ways, encourage one another, agree with one another, live in peace, and the God of love and peace will be with you." (2 Cor 13: 11)

After a long letter of warnings and pleadings to his beloved community in Corinth, Saint Paul comes to the end saying, "Mend your ways, encourage one another, agree with one another, live in peace, and the God of love and peace will be with you." After all of his encouragements about faith in Christ, and of being weak for the sake of letting Christ be strong in us, is he letting go of all of his talk about Christ and simply saying something like what a man famously called out during a riot: "Can't we all just get along?"

Actually, he has not stopped talking about Christ at all. To explain this I like to think about a mother at a shopping mall at Christmas time, when everything is crowds and chaos. At a certain point she loses track of her three-year-old child, and runs off to the authorities for help. As she is waiting for word, a person tells her that they have just announced that there are no more murders being committed. Yet she does not have peace. Other announcements are made about an end to injustice and hunger, and yet she has no peace. When does she have peace? When they bring her baby and she enfolds him in her trembling arms. Real peace is like that. It is a presence, not an absence of unpleasant things. When Saint Maxmillian Kolbe was put in an underground bunker at Auschwitz to die with his fellows, in that place of supreme injustice and violence, there was peace in that room, for Kolbe made clear the presence of Christ.

When Saint Paul tells us to agree, he is telling us to find Christ in our midst. Telling us to mend our ways means to follow Christ in our midst. Encouraging means to help each other recognize him. Thus, to live in peace means to live with God, for he, in his Son, is our peace.

How many things disturb my peace and trouble this my heart made for you, my God. Let me not be tempted to do violence to attain my peace, but rather let me recognize it already here in your Son, the Prince of Peace.

Outside the Box

Father Vincent Nagle, F.S.C.B.

"The Lord Jesus Christ [...] gave himself for our sins that he might rescue us from the present evil age in accord with the will of our God and Father, to whom be glory forever and ever."
(Gal 1: 3-5)

A person once showed me a box pattern of dots, three down and two across, and asked me to link them up with just three straight lines. I tried a few times and, not very good at these things in any case, gave up. He took up the pen and quickly drew three lines connecting all the dots. In contrast to mine, his lines extended beyond the pattern of dots. The only thing that made all the dots fit was to go beyond, outside the box. It had not entered my head, nor would it have, had he not shown me.

So it is with our lives. Unless this world is all about another world, something beyond, then it is impossible to make all the elements fit into an acceptable whole, especially in times of deep trial. Indeed we even rebel at the mere thought of any thinkable plan that would include the pain and evil of this world. So we are left in chaos, with wrecked and meaningless lives. We live in a time that does not think "outside the box" of human science. We do not hear discussions of "the truth," of "the meaning of everything," rather it is just accepted that there are many irreconcilable truths. What, then, indeed can deliver us from this present evil age? Like the lines that united the dots in the box, it has to be something beyond, a world beyond the limits of this world, this age, that comes and intersects it, reconciling all things. Since we cannot imagine this new thing, it must be something that we can meet, that shows itself to us in a human, flesh and blood experience. On our own it all doesn't make sense. But in sharing the life of him whose love, life, and presence is so outside the box, we find ourselves being, impossibly, reconciled to everything in our lives. We are delivered from this present evil age.

Creator of all things, the evil of this world bewilders me. Let me live in this world, already sharing the kingdom where you are all in all. I ask this through your Son, whose kingdom is our hope.

Even the Very Last Atom

Father Vincent Nagle, F.S.C.B.

"[God], who from my mother's womb had set me apart and called me through his grace, was pleased to reveal his Son to me, so that I might proclaim him to the Gentiles." (Gal 1: 15-16)

Saint Paul describes himself entirely in terms of his vocation. As he prepares to plead his case to his misled Galatian children in the faith, he presents himself to them anew, reviewing his qualifications, the nature of his vocation. "[God], who from my mother's womb had set me apart and called me through his grace…," he says. Paul is pointing to something for which all of us, explicitly or implicitly, are making entreaty to God. He is putting into words that experience when, through grace, we become certain that there is a plan for us. We become convinced that our lives have been and are desired, known, and cherished by that Mystery from whom creation is born and returns.

I can still remember the sensation that came over me when I received my vocation, after years of energetically hedging my bets. Meditating on all the mad, improbable elements that had conspired to bring me, interiorly and exteriorly, to this impossible point where I could hope to say yes with my whole heart, for my whole life, I had an intuition that has remained. It rushed into my consciousness how for me to be standing there, receiving the definitive form of life God desired to give me, then the whole universe must have been arranged to bring it about. So many were the absolutely chance meetings, gratuitous acts, and miraculous events that were necessary from the beginning of the world to bring me to where I was. Somehow even the movement of the last electron in orbit in the last atom on the edge of the swirling mass of galaxies moved only to fulfill the plan that had my destiny as its source and center. Truly Christ is the Word through whom all things were made.

Do we not all, then, need to entreat the grace to say, with Saint Paul, "You, who have called me from my mother's womb"?

God, I cannot see the details of your plan, but only the face of your Son in whom your plan is fulfilled. Bring me into the meaning and destiny of all things by letting me share the life and mission of him who lives and reigns with you and the Holy Spirit, for ever and ever.

Not Escape, but Salvation

Father Vincent Nagle, F.S.C.B.

*"I have been crucified with Christ; yet I live, no longer I,
but Christ lives in me; insofar as I now live in the flesh, I live by
faith in the Son of God who has loved me and given himself up
for me." (Gal 2: 19-20)*

I once overheard a discussion among some highly educated and widely read and traveled men. They were excitedly discussing the progress of humanity toward its goal, which, they agreed, was autonomy. They pointed out, happily, that with advances in technology, the human person was ever less required to rely on others. Technology, they hoped, would allow a person to fulfill even his affective and reproductive needs without involving himself in messy relationships. Are they wrong? Due to sin, weakness, and madness, a relationship can apparently require giving up what we want, suppressing with violence, open or subtle, our identity. And so we seek autonomy. But is that what we want? To be alone? Could that ever be happiness, even with wonderful technology?

Saint Paul shows how it is only through faith in Christ that personal connectedness and individual identity can be saved. It is the opposite of autonomy. "I have been crucified with Christ. I live, no longer I, but Christ lives in me." The presence of the other, this particular other, Jesus Christ, does not suppress Paul's identity but *saves* it. How? Because Christ is what he wants, and how else do we know who we are, except by discovering what we truly want. Why is Jesus what he wants? "I live by faith in the Son of God who has loved me and given himself up for me." Isn't this what we all want? To be perfectly loved so that the other even gives himself up for us? Recognizing in faith the presence of the one loving him is Paul's very identity. Because this presence shows him what he wants, it also shows him who he is. But, as Saint Paul points out, it comes through crucifixion. It comes, that is, through our wounded relationships. Our crucified relationships are the place where our identity will be saved, by recognizing through faith the one loving us. Let us not seek escape, but beg for salvation.

Father, you know how I want to flee, to be not touched or hurt. But you want to come close. Show me your love in your Son, so that I may be conquered and say yes to communion with you.

He Is the Answer

Father Vincent Nagle, F.S.C.B.

"I do not nullify the grace of God; for if justification comes through the law, then Christ died for nothing." (Gal 2: 21)

I was once listening to a great teacher in the faith speaking about Jesus. At a certain point he affirmed that Christ is the one who has the answer for our lives. I was uncomfortable with this and said, "No, Christ is not the one who has the answer for our humanity. Christ himself is that answer." He asked, "What's the difference?" I said, "For example: If a student is studying for an exam and finds someone who has the answers, then what he needs to do is to get them from that other person. But then the student does not need that other person any more. He can pass the exam without him. But if that other person is himself the answer, then the student must stay with that person. Separation is not an option."

Christ does not come first of all as lawgiver. He himself, his life, is the fulfillment of the law. What we need in the first place are not the examples and words Jesus gives us. Rather what we need is him, his life, himself.

Saint Paul is trying to make the same point to his misled followers, who have begun to center upon the law as their answer, a way of conceiving Christianity still very present today. Many of us are at least sometimes guilty of "nullifying" the grace of God, as Saint Paul puts it. Do we not get so excited about finding the truth that we concentrate all of our energies on applying God's true law? Don't we get so excited about having received true answers that we set our whole heart on our putting them into practice? Don't we forget to ask for him, himself? What occupies the center is how we, and others, are doing and not what he is doing, namely, offering salvation, offering himself. Saint Paul wants to save us from being preoccupied with ourselves, and turn us to being occupied by Christ.

Father, what a temptation it is for me to try to "live to the plan." Let desire for your Son fill me so that his presence will be my only plan.

Knowing the Truth Is Not Enough

Father Vincent Nagle, F.S.C.B.

"Christ ransomed us from the curse of the law by becoming a curse for us. [...]/ Before faith came, we were held in custody under law, confined for the faith that was to be revealed. But now that faith has come, we are no longer under a disciplinarian. For through faith you are all children of God in Christ Jesus. For all of you who were baptized into Christ have clothed yourselves with Christ." (Gal 3: 13, 23, 25-27)

As we sat in the darkening room at evening, a person very close to me declared, a little out of the blue, "It has to be said that it is only the Catholic Church that teaches the truth about the human person." Astonished, I asked, "But then, why don't you come into the Church?" "Oh," she answered, "the truth and I parted company a long time ago. I'm just not up to it. I have to live according to my limits, and so we go our separate ways." I was silent. Her experience had been that encountering the truth judged her in her failings, judged her in her weaknesses. Knowledge of the truth had not set her free. It had made her feel condemned. She fled.

A couple of years later the founder of my missionary society came for a visit. They met for a couple of short conversations, not very extensive for they had no language in common. A few weeks after that, on a bright morning, she said to me, "Take me to meet the local priest." We went and a couple of hours later, after having her confession heard and receiving the sacrament, she came out a Catholic. "Why now," I asked, "after all these years?" "Well," she said slowly, "when your founder was here, I saw how much the Church loves you." She wanted to be a part of that, to belong like that.

The shocking discovery that the truth exists can leave us examining our lives in a new way, and can leave us sadly on the outside looking in, wretched. But, as Saint Paul powerfully reminds us, the truth, known in the law, is not content in his glory, but has become a curse to share that glory with us. The real discovery is not that the truth exists, but that he loves us and invites us in, even as we are, to be clothed in himself.

Mighty Father, my sinfulness makes me flee from your holiness. Let me give up measuring myself, and accept instead with gratitude the invitation of your Son, to share friendship with him for ever.

An Impossible Discovery

Father Vincent Nagle, F.S.C.B.

"There is neither Jew nor Greek, there is neither slave nor free person, there is not male and female; for you are all one in Christ Jesus. And if you belong to Christ, then you are Abraham's descendant, heirs according to the promise." *(Gal 3: 28-29)*

It was December and the beginning of summer vacation for the students in Kenya. Myself and a missionary priest I had just met were standing in a field far from Nairobi waiting for the students to start arriving for a vacation together. I had arrived in the country just a couple of days before for the first time, to begin a new mission. As I stood there I could not have felt more estranged. I did not know anyone coming, I did not know the language, I had never been to sub-Saharan Africa, and there was almost nothing planned for the days ahead. And as the young men and women started to wander in, bedraggled from hard travel, and we had a first bad meal together, my anxiety increased.

Then, after dinner, some of the students, the teachers, the priest, and I, all sat down together. We asked, "What do we want from these days ahead?" What strongly emerged among us was that we wanted to meet Christ that week. We wanted the One in whom we see our destiny to become visible among us. We wanted him, the meaning of everything. What had seemed alien to me now was familiar. They wanted what I wanted. What they had encountered and had brought them to that place was precisely what had brought me.

After that I have always been able to hear the stupefaction in the words of Saint Paul as he describes what is impossibly unfolding in the people before him. Their hearts, touched by Christ, are one. Gulfs once believed unbridgeable, between mentalities, histories, and cultures, are joined in the unity of an identical commotion in their hearts. Their desire has become one, him. Differences no longer have the last word. The encounter with Jesus Christ has revealed for each the heart of the other. In all our estrangements, let us beg for Jesus to reveal himself, giving us our communion with all.

Dear Father, how many good reasons I have to keep my distance from others, for their differences threaten me. Let me see your Son, and so discover again the heart common to us all, redeemed by the blood of that same Christ, our Lord.

Through the Tenderness of a Mother

Holly Peterson

"When the fullness of time had come, God sent his Son, born of a woman, born under the law, to ransom those under the law, so that we might receive adoption. As proof that you are children, God sent the spirit of his Son into our hearts, crying out, 'Abba, Father!' So you are no longer a slave but a child, and if a child then also an heir, through God." (Gal 4: 4-7)

This passage from Saint Paul's letter cannot help but fill the heart of the simple reader, the reader who is open, with overwhelming gratitude. What tenderness we see in God, our God – like no other god in history – that he would choose to become flesh, become one of us, become a real companion with us in our journey. And what a mother we find in Mary, in the "yes" of that young girl; a "yes" that was merely a breath in front of the impossible question. That whisper of a "yes" that was full of unimaginable consequences; that "yes" that changed history in a way that no other "yes" in history has ever impacted the world. Saint Paul writes that her obedience led to our ransom. From what are we ransomed, from what are we liberated? We are liberated from what binds us, what holds us back; from that which keeps us from loving and living intensely the moments and circumstances of our day; from saying yes to the real. Her "yes" made it possible for our own freedom to move into relationship with the Father who intimately adores us, a Father to whom we can say, as Saint Paul says later in this same Letter to the Galatians, "It is no longer I who live, but you who live in me." It is no longer my measure, my calculation of how things should be, or the measure of the law that matters, but it is a relationship with you who have "ransomed" me by becoming man; you who had the tenderness to save me from the slavery of my own tyranny, and have allowed me to call you Abba, Daddy, Father. Whose heart does not long for such a Father! Through the tenderness of our Mother we know the overwhelming love of the Father who has made us his heirs.

Loving Father, help us to see that you are not far and unknown, but a Father to whom we can say "you" with the same tenderness with which we speak to our own fathers.

An Impossible Freedom

Holly Peterson

"For freedom Christ set us free; so stand firm and do not submit again to the yoke of slavery." (Gal 5: 1)

F reedom: probably one of the most misunderstood words in any language. How often we use this word without understanding the depth of what it signifies, and yet Saint Paul writes that it is precisely for the possibility of freedom that Christ came. The common reduction of the word freedom became clear one day when I asked my high school students to share their ideas of freedom. What ensued was a string of "no's": no responsibilities, no school, no obligations, no parents around, etc. But, when I asked them to describe a moment when they felt free, they responded with a myriad of experiences: getting a license, going away with best friends, completing a big project, or skiing in the Sierra Nevadas. They were free in moments when they *engaged* with life and responded to their obligations! How true it is that when we look at our experience of freedom, being free usually implies an engagement with reality and not an idea about reality or what it is for. Paul writes that freedom is what Christ came for, what he acted on our behalf for, so that we might know him and really live! Knowing Christ doesn't bring us a freedom for a moment or a day or a weekend, but a freedom that is possible always, in every day, in every moment. The taste of freedom we begin to experience in the mundane and not so mundane details of our life lived *with* him leaves us not slaves, but free men and women. He has set us free from the slavery that tells us we can achieve happiness alone with our ideas of success, achievement, or acquisition. He came to help us see that ultimately freedom is the fulfillment of the infinite needs that constitute us, which can only be filled with something infinite!

Thank you, Lord, for using your freedom to help me understand that my only hope for profound happiness is in you. Free me from the slavery of the solitude that comes from not following you but my own ideas of happiness.

A Great Gaze

Holly Peterson

"Through the Spirit, by faith, we await the hope of righteousness. [...] In Christ Jesus, neither circumcision nor uncircumcision counts for anything, but only faith working through love." (Gal 5: 5-6)

In the first century, the Church challenged Saint Paul about baptizing those who were uncircumcised. At the Council of Jerusalem we know that Paul argued fervently his belief that faith alone, and not adherence to the law, saves (Acts, chapter 15). Thus, in his Letter to the Galatians he continues the theme, but this time he points to the fact that faith must work through love. What does it mean to say, "faith working through love"? A Christian sees the same things others do, wants to do well in work as others do, plans his or her finances and lives in relationships as all do, but we are different. We strive for the supreme ideal and maximum beauty like others do, but our ideal is Christ, and giving witness to him. The ideal is that every gesture undertaken is underpinned by the desire to love the person or the thing in front of us, for it is given by Christ. This is righteousness, is justice. Without the Spirit, instead of hoping for righteousness, hoping for a greater love of others, we would be left to our own abilities and efforts, and ultimately alone. We know that we are incapable of loving as we would like, or of pursuing righteousness fully, as we are burdened by weakness and incapacity that will never be fully overcome. But, as Saint Paul reminds us, it is because of the Spirit that we await in great hope! This hope we wait for is not a wish for something unknown, like a far-off aspiration, but rather a certainty for the future because we have experienced his present goodness now; a certainty that he will show his face again and again! This is what the Spirit gives us – this great gaze on the future that is not optimistic, but realistic!

May you send us your Spirit, Lord, so that our awareness of your presence might generate in us a great hope and a positivity that is impossible without you!

An Affectively Attractive Presence

Holly Peterson

"The flesh has desires against the Spirit, and the Spirit against the flesh; these are opposed to each other, so that you may not do what you want." (Gal 5: 17)

The Christian community was no longer bound by the Mosaic law, but that did not mean that lawless abandon to material goods, or the conduct of the world, was the new morality. The Spirit, Paul writes, is what guides us, and not the desires of the flesh. The desires of the flesh remain because we live in a fleshly world – things attract us! Paul begs the question though as to whether the objects that we see that fulfill our desires are ends in themselves. Are they interesting only as long as our sentiments tell us? Or are the objects of our desires *signs* of the need for the Infinite; signs through which we are being called to the Infinite? One place where the desires of the flesh and those of the Spirit are clearly identifiable is in the relationship between man and woman. Certainly the desire for the other is a gift – far from profane – but how easy is it to think of boyfriend or girlfriend or spouse in a reductive way, possessing them not in accordance with the Spirit. As soon as the other disappoints or does not behave in accordance with what we want, we become angry or defensive, or even go looking for another! But this is not the purpose of the desire God put in the heart of man for woman, and vice versa. The desires of the flesh, in positive terms, draw us to Christ who becomes an affectively attractive presence *through* the other. (If he did not, Christianity would be rules to follow or laws to obey!) He or she is Christ's way of saying, "I adore you." When the object of our attraction is seen as a gift, as his presence, then the desires of the flesh are not opposed to those of the Spirit, but are guided to their proper design – to draw us to the Ultimate attraction.

Lord, thank you for giving me so many ways to see your attractive presence today. Open my heart so that I might see you in the things that I desire; see you calling me to yourself.

The Initiative of Another

Holly Peterson

"The fruit of the Spirit is love, joy, peace, patience, kindness, generosity, faithfulness, gentleness, self-control." (Gal 5: 22-23)

In the liturgy, the communication of God's Spirit is called *Donum Dei Altissimi* (Gift of the highest God). The gifts that Saint Paul refers to are not the result of human construct, merit, or effort. They are pure gift. The dynamic of this gift is similar to what happens when we receive a gift; when the doorbell rings and we find standing in front of us a delivery person with a bouquet of flowers. In front of an event such as this we are surprised – moved by the event of something unexpected, something that is completely the initiative of another person toward us! And so it is with these gifts of the Spirit: they are an event which occurs within us, a total surprise which happens within us which is not the result of our doing but of the initiative of Another. If we catch ourselves in action, that is, if we look at our experience, how moving is the initiative of Another in us! When we behave according to the Spirit, when we see ourselves responding with patience or kindness, where does that capacity come from? If we are reasonable, if we are simple, if we are honest with ourselves, we cannot help but acknowledge that these gifts are the initiative of an Other, as we are incapable of such virtues on our own with our weaknesses and limits. The surprise of God's presence mysteriously enters into our human frailty and makes us, as Saint Paul writes later in this letter, "a new creation" (Gal 6: 15). The gifts we find within us, and coming through us, are living signs of his intimate presence and companionship. Thus, solitude vanishes. When we find ourselves behaving in accordance with the Spirit we know that he is accompanying our humanity in a most intimate and personal way – two thousand years vanish as he happens again in our flesh.

Jesus Christ, let me see the gifts of your Spirit that will be given to me today, and let me see you and acknowledge you as the Giver.

A New Life Wrought in the Spirit

Holly Peterson

"Those who belong to Christ [Jesus] have crucified their flesh with its passions and desires." (Gal 5: 24)

The Church teaches that as Christians we share in Christ's suffering, death, and resurrection through baptism. Those who are faithful to him, the Catechism says, are led by the Spirit and follow the Spirit (CCC 2543). When we look at the first century of the Church, as recorded by Saint Luke in the Book of Acts, we see numerous examples of those whose passions and desires had been transformed to a singular purpose – that of giving witness to the One to whom they belonged: Paul himself, Barnabas, Ananias, and so many more. The first martyr, Saint Stephen, boldly admonished the people of Jerusalem: "You stubborn people, with uncircumcised hearts and ears... You are always resisting the Holy Spirit!" His life is a witness to us of one's passions and desires transformed to a singular purpose – that Christ be known. It is not by chance that the Church put the date of this great saint's feast on December 26, reminding us that if we truly abandon ourselves to the Christ child a "crucifixion" will be required. Though most of us will not become martyrs to the point of shedding blood, the baptized Christian is called to the same singular goal as Stephen. The Christian man or woman experiences this crucifixion by willingly putting their fleshly identity to death through the choice of baptism. Concretely belonging to him not only gives us a share in his cross, but gives us a new way of life, a possibility of a richer life because it is now ontologically, in its very nature, connected to him. We see the marvelous witness of this transformation each year at the Easter Vigil in the lives of the newly baptized – men and women transformed by their baptism! The new life wrought in the Spirit is what really changes our passions and desires – alone we are incapable!

Heavenly Father, fill my heart and mind as one baptized into your Holy Spirit with the single-minded desire that through my life you might be known and made known.

Moved by His Presence

Holly Peterson

"If we live in the Spirit, let us also follow the Spirit."
(Gal 5: 25)

Paul writes to the Church that they can live without being subject to the law of Moses if they follow the Spirit. The Church in the first century, as described in the Acts of the Apostles, did just that. Saint Luke describes the Church community, after living in fear and hiding following the resurrection, as men and women changed by the occurrence of the Pentecost. "They devoted themselves to meeting together in the temple area and to breaking bread in their homes. They ate their meals with exultation and sincerity of heart, praising God and enjoying favor with all the people" (Acts 2: 46-47). They, as Saint Paul describes, followed the Spirit; they lived by the Spirit. It is not that their circumstances were changed by Pentecost (remember that nearly all of the apostles suffered a martyr's death!), but something changed in their way of living their circumstances. There was a boldness and a certainty present in them that was not present before Pentecost. What happened? Generated by the Spirit, they began to live according to the Spirit. The Spirit comes today in the very same way, not in tongues of fire, but through the face of a friend or the voice of a student or colleague. Christ moves us today within reality, just as he did the apostles, and moved by his presence one begins to live in his presence; to live in the Spirit. The question is, am I open and simple enough to recognize his Spirit in the way he comes? Or, to put it simply, am I willing to take seriously the encounters that come to me every day, *certain* that they are him? The promise is that those who continually follow and sincerely commit to Jesus will feel the strength of his proposal in all of its intensity.

Jesus, give us a simplicity that allows us to see you move throughout our day, full of certainty that you are there waiting to meet us.

He Alone Can Make Things New

Holly Peterson

*"Bear one another's burdens, and so you will fulfill
the law of Christ."* (Gal 6: 2)

The law of life is charity. When asked about the greatest commandment, Jesus responded that it was to love God and, second, to love one's neighbor as one's self (Mt 22: 36-40). When Saint Paul told the Galatian community to "bear one another's burdens," he called them to fulfill that commandment; to care for their neighbor. What is a charitable friend in front of our burdens of marital difficulties, financial problems, death, illness, or struggles at work? It is not the one who tries to eliminate our burdens, or fix our problems. A friend is one who reminds us of our relationship with Christ. Looking at our experience, how rarely do we see the burdens and difficulties that we face as a problem of religiosity – that is, a relationship with Christ? Our struggles often have little or nothing to do with Jesus and a rapport with him, and we therefore bear them without awareness of his presence. It is natural, especially with those we love, to want to alleviate drama and sorrow from his or her life. But isn't it precisely during difficult times that we can truly develop a dramatic relationship with the Mystery? Christ himself didn't come to erase problems; he came only to put us in the correct position in front of what weighs us down. It takes humility to bear the burdens of another by reminding them that God alone can make all things new, and then to accompany them in the discovery of that newness. It is God who placed within us the heart that only he can generate, this is the best possible way to bear one another's burdens. Thus, to introduce one to Christ is the greatest love one can have for one's neighbor.

*Lord God, the maker of my being, give me the heart of a child, ready
to carry the burdens that cross my path each day and ready to
accompany my friends in their journey toward you.*

Everything Can Be Made Anew

Holly Peterson

"Make no mistake: God is not mocked, for a person will reap only what he sows, because the one who sows for his flesh will reap corruption from the flesh, but the one who sows for the spirit will reap eternal life from the spirit." (Gal 6: 7)

Paul, the champion of spreading the concept of salvation by faith alone, exhorts the Galatians by telling them that, although they are not bound by the Mosaic law, they are not without a law, and their actions do matter. How they choose, and what they choose, will determine what they reap. We too are confronted with the option of sowing in the flesh or sowing in the Spirit. To sow in the flesh means to live instinctively with regard for self only, and living in such a way leaves one in solitude. There is a balance in the universe; every inch of its fabric was put in motion by God; his laws and rules are always operative and there is nothing that we can do to stop them. Ultimately, he will win! However, in front of his dominance we are free – we can sow in the Spirit, following his attractive presence, or we can sow on our own. Our freedom characterizes every human act and we can never be coerced (CCC 1732). So where is the good news if he ultimately will win? In the fact that he has the power continually to make all things new. Unlike what happens in nature, when leaves fall from the limb and rot and remain rotten, he can take corrupted flesh and make it anew. If through the Spirit one desires to begin again, then anything – bad choices, greed, unfaithfulness – can be made anew. Paradoxically, through sin we can become aware of his great love and mercy. "Oh, happy fault" that where there is sin grace abounds (CCC 412). Therefore nothing, not even our own corruption, can be against us. Everything and everyone is a possibility to encounter him! God who "will not be mocked" can even use our faults to reveal his glory, giving us eternal life in the Spirit.

Loving God, help us to beg each day that your Spirit might infuse us with the audacity to find you amidst our own corruption.

The Piece of Reality That Belongs to Him
Holly Peterson

"Let us not grow tired of doing good, for in due time we shall reap our harvest, if we do not give up. [...] Let us do good to all, but especially to those who belong to the family of the faith."
(Gal 6: 9-10)

J esus Christ said that he would be with us "always, until the end of the age" (Mt 28: 20). This can be taken to have merely a spiritualistic meaning, and thus remain abstract, not belonging to the world in which we live, or it can be seen as a fact in time and space. Christ, who is a fact in time and space, remains with us in the flesh, and he can be found in the flesh today, in time and space. The Church, the Body of Christ, is this place where he remains with us; his presence is within a concrete people who identify themselves as belonging to him. This people of Christ, Saint Paul writes, are the first to whom one must be charitable, must treat with goodness and help in the concrete needs of every day. In this exhortation, written to a mature Christian community, Paul encourages a practical manifestation of love, first by taking care of those in the Body of Christ who bear the burden of teaching the word of God to others, and then by taking care of the needs of the other needy. Why does Saint Paul show a preference to the family of faith? Certainly not as a comparison to say that others outside of the Church are less important. The hallmark of the first-century Church was their generosity to others: "They would sell their property and possessions and divide them among all according to each one's need," the Acts of the Apostles records (2: 45). Instead, in taking care of the family of God, of those who bore the faith to others, who passed on the message of Jesus Christ, one was taking care of his most objective presence on earth; and in doing so, would take care of all those whom the Church cared for. Christians are thus exhorted to take care first of that piece of reality which belongs totally to him, and not to neglect anyone else in the process of generosity.

Jesus Christ, may my time, treasure, and talent today be used to edify your Church, and so the world.

185

Offering As Prayer

Holly Peterson

"May I never boast except in the cross of our Lord Jesus Christ, through which the world has been crucified to me, and I to the world." (Gal 6: 14)

Paul, in contrast to the proselytizers of his time, writes that his boast is nothing other than Christ. He arrived to the point of saying nothing of his personal efforts or accomplishments, of his scourgings or converts for the kingdom, but only of Christ's triumph. Clearly, Christ was the consistency of his person, of his "I." In our contemporary rationalistic mentality, the Mystery, Christ, has been reduced to a deity to call upon when problems arise, or someone who "plugs up the hole" when things go awry. As a friend pointed out, we don't need Christ when we are on vacation in the Bahamas! (That is, until our tire blows out!) In short, Christ is separate from life and its circumstances, from the nitty-gritty of our every day. Looking at our experience, however, do we need the person we love only when we have problems? Or when we see an unexpected sunset, or hear a beautiful piece of music, or see a provoking film? Within a great love everything reminds us of the beloved, and we want him or her to be with us all of the time. This is how it was for Paul, who boasted and spoke only of him. What is the resistance in us? Ultimately and paradoxically it is a resistance to beauty. Desiring him we are afraid to say yes to his attractive presence – to, as Pope Benedict wrote, "the Incarnate God who attracts us" (*Deus Caritas Est*, 14). The antidote to this resistance, the Church tells us, is offering; asking him to come in and win us over, to help us breathe. Offering, or begging, is the most reasonable form of prayer one can pray, as we are capable of nothing without him. Offering means to beg him to overwhelm us with his beauty, so much so that we too can echo with Paul, "We boast of nothing but the cross of Christ."

Christ, all of my person needs you to breathe today: let your beauty draw me near to you and save me from any resistance that I may have in front of your beauty.

Responding to His Choice

Holly Peterson

"Blessed be the God and Father of our Lord Jesus Christ, who has blessed us in Christ with every spiritual blessing in the heavens, as he chose us in him, before the foundation of the world, to be holy and without blemish before him. In love he destined us for adoption to himself through Jesus Christ, in accord with the favor of his will, for the praise of the glory of his grace that he granted us in the beloved." (Eph 1: 3-6)

This hymn tells us of God's choice and our election. Our adoption was the result of his initiative, but he didn't choose us when we were reconciled through his Son but *before* the beginning of the world; before we merited anything! His choice is an abundant sign of his overwhelming love for us. For Christians, the outward sign of this choice is baptism. Baptism is the encounter with a Presence that changes life, that makes us part of his body, makes us participants in his same mission in the world. Because of our baptism every circumstance is the place *par excellence* where we respond to this choice. His choice and our "yes" to the baptismal call alleviates the tendency toward dualism – where there is one's relationship with Christ and *then* there are the important things of every day where our hopes, dreams and desires rest, where the details of my life are. Living dualistically, the two paths don't cross! Instead, because of our election, responding to the objective details of every day is a possibility to encounter him, to respond to his choice. A relationship with him comes through sweeping the floor or making decisions in a boardroom; every instant, bar none, is an encounter with him! What tenderness, to choose us "in accord with the favor of his will" even though we were yet nothing, capable of nothing! The sign of our gratitude for this choice is our free and simple "yes" to him each day. The Church encourages us to begin the day with the great prayer to Mary, the *Angelus*, and to echo her words: "Be it done unto me according to your will." The chosen person who says "yes" is a *homo viator*, a man on a journey; one graced by the companionship of the Beloved.

Open the eyes of our mind, Lord, to help us understand the hope to which you have called us: to the riches of his inheritance you have given us through our adoption. Give us the heart of a child that we might dwell in this belonging today and always.

Pardon and Peace

Monsignor James Turro

*"In [Jesus Christ] we have redemption by his blood, the
forgiveness of transgressions, in accord with the riches of his
grace that he lavished upon us. In all wisdom and insight, he has
made known to us the mystery of his will in accord with his favor
that he set forth in him as a plan for the fullness of times, to sum
up all things in Christ, in heaven and on earth." (Eph 1: 7-10)*

"In Christ we have redemption by his blood, the forgiveness of
transgressions…" How desperate must be the mood of the
man who has no hope of throwing off the guilt he has
incurred through some misdeed or other. He must resort to all
manner of involvement, games, amusements, a fervent pursuit of
knowledge, or some other earthly distraction. But all in vain. He
must see that his guilt endures, there is no way of dousing it.

The best news of all for such a man must be the bold fact with
which the Letter to the Ephesians confronts us, namely: in Christ
we have "forgiveness of transgressions." And to be sure, God is not
sparing in the remission he delivers to anyone who has sinned, he
is forgiven "in accord with the riches of his [Christ's] grace." It is a
comfort to realize that Scripture has abundant evidence of God's
readiness to pardon: "Let the scoundrel forsake his way,/ and the
wicked man his thoughts./ Let him turn to the LORD for mercy;/ to
our God, who is generous in forgiving" (Is 55: 7). It makes sense to
conclude that the pardon I receive so liberally from God should be
made to travel beyond me to those who have offended *me*. It would
not be amiss to emulate God's readiness to forgive. To err is human,
to forgive divine. I consider with surprise that the only petition in
the Lord's Prayer that has a condition attached to it is: "Forgive us
our trespasses as we forgive those who trespass against us." Like
God, I must be richly forgiving and be ready to forgive "not seven
times but seventy-seven times." God's forgiveness may be wildly
undeserved, yet it is always forthcoming. Consider the parable of
the Prodigal Son. Though the long-suffering father's kindness was
cruelly tried, the father welcomes the returned wastrel most warmly.
All is forgiven. A person is never so beautiful as when he forgives.

*Dear God, thank you for your ready forgiveness and your unmer-
ited goodness to me. Grant me pardon and peace and give me as
well the strength of character to forgive those who have wounded
me in one fashion or another.*

The Purpose Driven Life

Monsignor James Turro

"In [Christ] we were also chosen, destined in accord with the
purpose of the One who accomplishes all things according to
the intention of his will, so that we might exist for the praise
of his glory, we who first hoped in Christ."
(*Eph 1: 11-12*)

"In Christ we were also chosen... so that we might exist for the praise of his glory." How many times are people left wondering at the meaning of it all. What is the point of our existence? How bleak and gross even is the answer the world gives back to that question. It maintains that we have no particular role to play at all in the world. We are simply pointless – we just are, period. If that be so, is there any wonder that some people under severe pressure from a grave illness or from the sheer routine of day-to-day living decide to end it all? The purposeless life is not worth living.

But as God first chose the Jews to spread the good news about him and to praise him, so God expects no less of us – that we do just that – "that we might exist for the praise of his glory." What an exalted goal to have in life: the glorification of God in all we say and do and are. A backward look at our lives – an examination of conscience – may sadly reveal that we have been quite negligent in this regard, that is, in making Christ better known within our family, our circle of friends, our co-workers. One's life cannot have a more exalted thrust than that – to first understand and then to proclaim to all and sundry that God made us "to know, to love, and to serve him in this life and to be happy with him for ever in the next."

God, give me the sharpness of mind and the force and clarity of speech to witness to you in every venue in which I may find myself.

He Leadeth Me

Monsignor James Turro

"May the eyes of [your] hearts be enlightened, that you may know what is the hope that belongs to [God's] call, what are the riches of glory in his inheritance among the holy ones, and what is the surpassing greatness of his power for us who believe, in accord with the exercise of his great might, which he worked in Christ, raising him from the dead and seating him at his right hand in the heavens, far above every principality, authority, power, and dominion, and every name that is named not only in this age but also in the one to come." (Eph 1: 18-21)

For the wicked, the fact of God's omnipotence is devastating. But for the virtuous, God's power is reassuring and fortifying. The supreme instance of God's power at work is found in the resurrection of Jesus. Such power could never be attributed to the capability and genius of man. How right and wise then it is to submit to God, the All-Powerful. Conversely, how foolhardy to run counter to his will.

One of the great consolations that can come to a person is the thought of God presiding over one's present life and over eternity. One must not allow oneself to be threatened by all manner of fears and worries. These are vain and unnecessary apprehensions – "God's in his heaven, all's well with the world."

The corollary to the goodness and greatness of God is trust in God. Consider "the surpassing greatness of his power for us who believe." Here the Scriptures are eloquent in urging total reliance on God. "I wait for you, O Lord… in you I trust; I do not fear what mere mortals do to me" (see Ps 25: 1-2). "Trust in the LORD forever! For the LORD is an eternal Rock" (Is 26: 4). "Do not let your hearts be troubled. You have faith in God; have faith also in me" (Jn 14: 1).

The person who has embraced Christ in faith can think of himself as the most secure individual – far beyond the reach of harm or intrigue.

With profound gratitude I acknowledge your uniting solicitude on my behalf.

I in You and You in Me

Monsignor James Turro

"[God] put all things beneath [Christ's] feet and gave him as head over all things to the church, which is his body, the fullness of the one who fills all things in every way." (Eph 1: 22-23)

"The Church which is his body." Jesus Christ fills the Church with his reality. I must adjust my thinking and my behavior to that fact. I must not drive a wedge between Christ and the Church as one tends to do when one focuses exclusively on the human side of the Church. To be sure, the Church is made up of human beings with their attendant shortcomings, but that fact does not tell the whole story. These human beings live as the Body of Christ.

The fact that the Church is the Body of Christ creates a comforting proximity of Christ to me. He is not far off, he is truly, strongly present in the Church of which I am part. My link with Christ is much richer and more intense than I would have dared to imagine; I am enlivened by him as blood enlivens a body.

Further, all this means that the intentions of Christ must be carried out by me who am his hands and feet.

What more ennobling factor could there be in my life and actions than to be a member of Christ's Body the Church?

There is in all this a most powerful reason for loving my fellow Christian who is part of the sacred Body of Christ and merits the respect that I would give to a limb of Christ.

Grant me the grace deeply to feel the closeness to Christ that is mine as a member of the Mystical Body.

Into Your Loving Hands,
I Commend My Life

Monsignor James Turro

"But God, who is rich in mercy, because of the great love he had for us, even when we were dead in our transgressions, brought us to life with Christ (by grace you have been saved)."
(Eph 2: 4-5)

"The great love he had for us." If one thinks of it, there is much in life that is worrisome. The sheer spitefulness of some people toward us, the raw cruelty of others, accidents, unforeseen illnesses – we could compose a whole litany of the menacing contingencies one has to contend with in life. To dwell on this fact is to lapse into dark depression.

But such gloom is unwarranted because, however threatened life appears to be, one must take into account the abiding love God has for every individual one of us. Contrary to all appearances, he stands by us in every circumstance, to guide and protect us.

What a huge debt of gratitude we incur for God's love and concern for us. How can it ever be repaid?

In return for God's love and care of us, it would not be misconceived for us to emulate God in his concern for us – for us in turn to be a channel of his love into the lives of others.

Since we are so staunchly supported in life by God's love for us, we can afford to face the challenges of life with courage. God stands at our side to ward off all real harm.

Once again we must realize that we are a long way from deserving the abundant grace and care that God expends on us.

Lord, make me an instrument of your loving care for all those who cross my life and are in pain.

Love Divine All Loves Excelling

Monsignor James Turro

"[God] raised us up with [Christ], and seated us with him in the heavens in Christ Jesus, that in the ages to come he might show the immeasurable riches of his grace in his kindness to us in Christ Jesus." (Eph 2: 6-7)

"His kindness to us in Christ Jesus." Once again Paul is found enthusing over Christ's love for us. Yet in a sense Paul's obsession with this fact is not surprising. If one has even the slightest acquaintance with the daily news or even if one examines one's conscience, it is indeed cause for surprise that God is as good and kind as he is to such undeserving persons as we tend to be.

Paul would not have us think of God's love for us as a tepid, measured little affection. It is vast and strong. How inappropriate then for me to return his love and care in a weak and perfunctory way. Christ died for me.

God is love. Before creation there was Father, Son, and Holy Spirit. The Father loved the Son; the Holy Sprit is the love which the Father bore the Son. Following creation, God fixed his love on us, his creatures. It was this unquenchable love that brought him from heaven to die out of love for us who sinned. It is that same love that keeps God here still in the Eucharist.

I, the recipient of all this richness, must stand witness to the world of God's kindness to me in Christ. I am the member of the Church that has this as its thrust and goal – to witness to and to celebrate God's unbounded goodness and love poured out in present times and in ages to come.

Lord, help me in my daily struggle to become ever more deserving of your massive love for me.

A Generous God

Monsignor James Turro

*"For by grace you have been saved through faith,
and this is not from you; it is the gift of God." (Eph 2: 8)*

"This is not from you, it is the gift of God." Perhaps there is not a more deep-seated, urgent desire in man than the desire to be self-sufficient – not really to need anybody or anything – God included. This of course is a fond hope. Consider that though we as a race have mastered space and in large part defeated physical illness, however we have not been able to vanquish death nor have we succeeded in achieving untrammeled and unending happiness. Clearly we need God and the happiness and security he alone can confer. Humbly we must acknowledge that we are not equal to the task of acquiring much of what we require to lead a fulfilled and successful life. We have a desperate need of God and his gifts for us to lead a fulfilled life.

We must look beyond the happiness that God confers upon us to countless other gifts and favors with which he brightens our lives. One thinks of the faith – in every way, a gift of God. It is the faith among other things that puts balance in our lives. It makes us aware of God and the things of God. It gives us to understand that just about everything short of God is limited and flimsy; only God can truly, deeply satisfy.

As one reflects on God's generosity toward oneself, a not inappropriate resolve is to emulate God's lavish generosity in our dealings with other people – an imitation of Christ.

Faith, this great gift of God, must be prized and jealously guarded. We must never jeopardize this faith in any way – not by the thoughts we think or the life we lead. It should be a hardy faith – not a faith that one possesses but a faith that possesses one. A mere profession of faith honors God because, when all is said and done, it is taking God at his word.

O God, you have heaped high the graces which you have been pleased to offer me; give me one thing more – a grateful heart.

And the Almond Tree Blossomed

Monsignor James Turro

"We are [God's] handiwork, created in Christ Jesus for the good works that God has prepared in advance, that we should live in them." (Eph 2: 10)

"We are his handiwork..." If ever there is a time and occasion when we can indulge in legitimate pride, it is when we realize that God is our Maker. It is a pride of origin. We can take deep satisfaction in this for, as it is sometimes vulgarly put, God does not make trash. We ought straightforwardly to acknowledge our origins at God's creative hands. We are God's property. This is no small boast. We ought to recognize our deep indebtedness to him.

We could rightly think of ourselves as a living advertisement for God. By observing us, people can learn something about our Maker. In our caring, considerate attitude toward people, they should be able to discern something of God's love and goodness. Our very existence affirms the greatness and kindness of God. There is a story told about Saint Francis of Assisi who one day as he passed by an almond tree called out to it and said, "Speak to me of God." And the almond tree blossomed. We must blossom and so declare the greatness and splendor of God.

There is a deep down assurance that we can feel because if we are God's creation then we live under his loving care of us. We must be important to him or else he would not have called us into existence.

From the fact of our creation by God it also follows that God has provided the wherewithal for our continuing existence. Our needs are more than adequately provided for.

Part of the high purpose for which we were created is to perform good works. These are to be done not only as a response to God's initiative but also as an expression of God's power within us.

Dear Lord, grant me the grace to be aware of your presence within me urging me on to glorify your name by all I say and do.

And Who Is My Brother?

Monsignor James Turro

"But now in Christ Jesus you who once were far off have become near by the blood of Christ." (Eph 2: 13)

"You who once were far off have become near." Christ by his cross and resurrection has taken the edge of strangeness off people that otherwise would be totally alien to me. Thanks to the blood of Christ, they have become brothers to me. This is a result that is passionately desired by people of good will – the collapse of the barriers that keep us apart. A common denominator now links me to other persons however removed from my world and culture they may be. The blood of Christ redeems them every bit as much as it redeems me. I must weave this face into my normal behavior toward people; I am no longer dealing with rank strangers but with persons now identified as brethren. What a transformation that makes in my world. I can let my guard down, the edge of strangeness is gone from people whose culture and upbringing may be ever so exotic.

I must resign myself to the fact that my benevolence toward others will not always be reciprocated to me. That is understandable: after all, they may be unaware of Christ and his unifying life and death. Or if they do know Christ, their understanding of him may be minimal or even distorted. There is in most people an unacknowledged urge to fraternize, to be on easy terms with everybody, even with "strangers."

In the A.D. epoch, that is, after the coming of Christ, there is now a basis for giving vent to this urge to fraternize with all and sundry. We have been made brothers and sisters to one another.

Dear Lord, thank you for the warmth of togetherness that the shedding of your blood has made possible for us.

In Unity There Is Strength

Monsignor James Turro

"For [Christ Jesus] is our peace, he who made both one and broke down the dividing wall of enmity, through his flesh, abolishing the law with its commandments and legal claims, that he might create in himself one new person in place of the two, thus establishing peace, and might reconcile both with God, in one body, through the cross, putting that enmity to death by it."
(Eph 2: 14-16)

"He who broke down the dividing wall of enmity." Togetherness is highly prized by people. We like to belong. This is just what Christ achieves for those who embrace him in faith – belonging. Differences are minimized. Elsewhere Paul put it as bluntly as one could want: "There is not male and female; for you are all one in Christ Jesus." (Gal 3: 28). Difference is most often off-putting to people. They do not seem to know how to relate to someone who does not share a common racial background, education, or upbringing. But these differences evanesce or are made to seem superficial when one considers the radical unity that exists among those who have embraced Christ.

It is axiomatic that there is safety and strength in unity – one for all and all for one. Someone who has embraced Christ in faith has good grounds for feeling safe in a community with others who have similarly committed themselves to Christ.

It is not just poetic metaphor to conceive this life as warfare. The conscientious believer must struggle to safeguard his values in a world that for the most part derides the Christian ethos. It is not very encouraging to have to wage a lonely battle. There is much more hope and vitality in a warrior who feels the presence of fellow soldiers behind him, before him – on all sides. They are caught up in a common battle.

Thank you, O Christ, for the companionship of dedicated men and women – believers in you – who share life's journey with me.

I Am the Way

Monsignor James Turro

"[Christ] came and preached peace to you who were far off and peace to those who were near, for through him we both have access in one Spirit to the Father." (Eph 2: 17-18)

"Through him we both have access to the Father." What indeed if there were a rich treasure buried in a field but no avenue of access to it at all. Obviously that wealth would have no impact whatsoever on our lives. We could hanker for it, but in vain. But in fact there is a way, one that we too seldom take into account. It is Christ. He is the Way that leads to the richness that is God –indeed, he *is* God.

Can we stand idly by and be satisfied just to acknowledge the possibility of actually meeting with God in Christ? This face (God in Christ) ought not only to be acknowledged but celebrated as well. It should be acted upon by us. Indeed, God has himself facilitated a loving embrace of him by us in the Eucharist. Through the Eucharist he makes himself reachable. We nod, not worship, from afar.

What is the meaning of God's proximity to us in the Eucharist? It is a mind-boggling expression of love for us. If God were indifferent to us – not caring whether we ever resorted to him or not – he would hardly have approached so near to us as he does in the Eucharist. Can such a regard, such love of us, be ignored or taken for granted? It would surely be crass for us not to respond to the unimaginable overture that God has made to us.

O God, forgive my indifference to your closeness to me in the Eucharist. Let me experience ever more acutely the warmth of your eucharistic presence.

Belonging

Monsignor James Turro

"So then you are no longer strangers and sojourners, but you are fellow citizens with the holy ones and members of the household of God, built upon the foundation of the apostles and prophets, with Christ Jesus himself as the capstone." (Eph 2: 19-20)

"You are no longer strangers and sojourners." One of the most comforting life experiences is the sense of belonging. Without it we are left to develop doubts. We feel insecure and adrift. We suppose that we are somehow wanting and incomplete. We envy those who are within the inner circle. They are accepted; we for whatever reason are not. It's all so depressing. And so we become hellbent to belong. To belong is safe. There is a warmth and a sense of well-being in belonging – "we are no longer strangers."

How different is one's approach to a stranger compared to the way one approaches a friend. One comes to the stranger full of doubts and hesitations. This need never be the case in my approach to God. He has defined himself as a friend, warm and well-disposed toward me. He is open to my needs and desires.

This guarantee from God – that he does not see me as a stranger – is most welcome and most fortifying. Sometimes it seems that each news report reveals new cause for alarm. Life seems threatened on every side, if not by global warming then by the increased crime rate or the irresponsible use of nuclear power. In these times, belonging to God and the confidence that belonging engenders is most strengthening.

Thank you, O God, for your exquisite care of me. I would want every breath I take to be a "thank you."

Daddy Taught Me

Father Peter M. Girard, O.P.

*"In [Christ Jesus] you also are being built together into a
dwelling place of God in the Spirit." (Eph 2: 22)*

I can clearly recall the winter afternoon when my then six-year-old niece told me how she loved to pray the rosary. When I asked her why she loved this prayer, she answered: "Daddy taught me how to pray it." Here out of the mouth of babes came the truth of how Christian families are meant to be the "domestic church," a spiritual edifice "being built into a dwelling place of God in the Spirit." For my niece did not love the rosary simply because of the beautiful wooden beads that I had given to her, but rather it was the experience of having *her father teach her* how to be close to Jesus and Mary.

The Church teaches us that the family remains the "sanctuary of the sacred" where the gift of human life is nurtured and protected. As the first heralds of the Gospel, parents nourish the physical, intellectual, emotional, and spiritual lives of their children. So while our Catholic schools serve an invaluable function in the education of our children, *the love of the truth* communicated from parent to child remains unsurpassed and irreplaceable.

Saint Paul reminds us that the Christian family remains the primary place where children learn to love the truths of the faith. While civil governments may attempt to redefine the nature of marriage and family, it is the domestic church, under the care of father and mother, which best serves the wholesome development of children. The spiritual edifice of the family instills the love of the faith in a unique and irreplaceable way. I am quite sure that when I have long left this earth and my niece is in her eighties, she will be quietly whispering the Hail Mary while holding her beads because "Daddy taught her."

Jesus, font of all wisdom, help our fathers, mothers, and children respond to your wondrous graces so that we may be built into a spiritual edifice in the power of your Holy Spirit.

Kneeling before the Father's Throne

Father Peter M. Girard, O.P.

"I kneel before the Father, from whom every family in heaven and on earth is named, that he may grant you in accord with the riches of his glory to be strengthened with power through his Spirit in the inner self." (Eph 3: 14-16)

It is said of Saint Dominic that while he elevated the host and chalice during the consecration of the Mass, tears could be seen streaming down his cheeks. I am convinced that Saint Dominic wept because he was able to perceive what truly takes place each time Jesus becomes truly present upon our altars. Although the Second Vatican Council and the Catechism of the Catholic Church teaches us that the Holy Eucharist remains the "source and summit of the Christian life" (LG 11, cf. CCC 1324), perhaps some of us have lost the sense of awe and wonder that imbued Saint Dominic when he stood at the altar.

Perhaps the best way for us Catholics to rediscover our appreciation for the Mass is to recall that it remains much more than merely a gathering of human beings. As the risen body of Christ and the power of his eternal sacrifice upon the cross are made truly present upon our altars, the Mass transcends space and time itself! His Precious Blood, flowing from his sacred wounds, reaches down through time and history to sanctify all of creation. At every Mass, therefore, *all of creation* kneels at the throne of the Father, worshiping the Lamb made truly present in the power of the Holy Spirit. Amazingly, at each altar where the Mass is celebrated, within each tabernacle and at the center of each monstrance, we have all the souls in purgatory and all of the angels and saints in heaven gathered with us!

Saint Paul reminds us that at the very center of our Christian life, "we kneel before the Father's throne of glory," worshiping the Son truly present to us in the Holy Eucharist, responding to the graces given through the Holy Spirit. May we always have the sense of wonder that captivated Saint Dominic as he wept each day at the Father's throne.

Jesus, Priest and Victim, truly present within the hands of the priest and within every tabernacle in the world, give me the grace to appreciate the beauty and holiness of each Mass that I attend.

A Basket of Roses

Father Peter M. Girard, O.P.

"[May Christ] dwell in your hearts through faith; that you, rooted and grounded in love, may have strength to comprehend with all the holy ones what is the breadth and length and height and depth, and to know the love of Christ that surpasses knowledge, so that you may be filled with all the fullness of God."
(Eph 3: 17-19)

Each year my nieces' school hosts a colorful All Saints parade during which the younger children dress as saints of their choosing. One year I arrived at my brother's house to see my younger niece diligently assembling her costume as Saint Elizabeth of Hungary. As is traditional in iconography, my niece was carrying a beautiful, overflowing *basket of roses*. I soon came to realize that these flowers were a symbol of "the love of Christ that surpasses knowledge."

Born to King Andrew II of Hungary in 1207, Saint Elizabeth was a princess, wife to a German prince, and mother of three children. While many others of her station may have been content with a life of exclusive privilege, Elizabeth sought to be filled with "the breadth and length and height and depth" of the love of Christ. It was the embrace of the love of Christ that surpasses all human knowledge which gave the princess the spiritual eyes to respond to the needs of the destitute of her homeland. At her mountaintop Wartburg Castle in central Germany, Saint Elizabeth sold her royal jewels to build a hospice at which she personally cared for the sick. In response to a widespread famine, she supervised the giving of meals to nine hundred people each day from the castle refectory. When her husband attempted to limit her generosity, Saint Elizabeth responded that the loaves of bread she gave were truly a *basket of roses* for the poor, at which point an overflowing of these fragrant flowers poured forth.

The sight of my little niece carrying a basket of roses reminded me that the graces of Christ are an overflowing, inexhaustible gift offered to all human beings. Saint Paul reminds us that by saying "yes" to these "roses," we become instruments of the love of Christ that surpasses all human understanding.

Jesus, ever-flowing font of love, give us the grace to respond to the needs of our suffering brothers and sisters, especially the hungry and those with terminal illnesses.

One Little Yes
Father Peter M. Girard, O.P.

"To [God] who is able to accomplish far more than all we ask or imagine, by the power at work within us, to him be glory in the church and in Christ Jesus to all generations, forever and ever. Amen." (Eph 3: 20-21)

Jesus can do so much with so little. All he needs is our little "yes" and he can accomplish the most wonderful works through us. As a newly ordained priest, Saint John Bosco discovered this truth vividly as he prepared for Mass one morning in Turin's cathedral in 1841. It seemed to be just an ordinary day. However, after a homeless boy had come into the sacristy just before Mass, Father Bosco invited him to learn the Catechism daily. What began as a simple, seemingly ordinary invitation to one boy, emerged within months as the Oratory of Saint Francis de Sales, with eight hundred boys attending Mass, classes, and learning productive trades (and *mama* Bosco served as the cook!). This most fruitful work for the destitute youth of Italy was not "planned" in the formal sense. Rather, Saint John gave his little "yes" in response to grace, and a most wondrous ministry emerged.

None of us can say "yes" to Jesus of our own effort. He gives us the grace to say "yes" each day to his plan of holiness for us. And yet, there are certain key moments when he will visit us, asking us to embrace his plan of love. These moments might appear insignificant, but the Lord beautifully arranges our day with opportunities to respond to his grace. Jesus unfailingly visits us at these moments, giving us the opportunity to respond with a generous "yes."

Saint Paul helps to realize that there are no "ordinary" days according to Jesus' plan of happiness and holiness for us. Each moment is a singular and unrepeatable opportunity to give our little "yes," ready to blossom with the most miraculous fruit. Imagine what can happen in your life when you say "yes" to him, even on the most "ordinary" of days.

Jesus, source of all holiness, help me to see each hidden invitation to respond to your grace, so that the most wondrous works may be accomplished in me and through me for others.

A Dad's Job

Father Peter M. Girard, O.P.

"I, then, a prisoner for the Lord, urge you to live in a manner worthy of the call you have received, with all humility and gentleness, with patience, bearing with one another through love, striving to preserve the unity of the spirit through the bond of peace." (Eph 4: 1-3)

My brother is a dedicated husband, attentive father, and a hard-working man. In response to the graces of Christ, my brother strives to "live in a manner worthy of the call" he has received. One of the victims of the loss of jobs after September 11, 2001, he had taken on three part-time positions in order to put food on the table and pay for Catholic school tuition. For ten months, my brother got no more than four hours of sleep each night as he worked to provide for his wife and children. No matter how tired or sick he was, he embraced his vocation as father of the family with "humility, gentleness, and patience."

I can recall clearly one day asking my brother about all of the hours he was working. His response was pressed indelibly upon my mind: "I have to do several jobs now, but *my primary job* is to make sure that my wife and children make it to heaven." Those of you who have younger brothers can perhaps understand my wonderful amazement at seeing someone I once viewed as a boy now fully embracing the graces of Christian manhood! Here my brother was, giving his "yes" in the midst of great hardship, a "prisoner for the Lord" if you will, as he provided for the needs of his family.

Saint Paul reminds us that Christ gives us the grace to grow in virtue according to our specific vocations. With humility as a foundation and patient endurance as the anchor, we bear one another's burdens so that we might all journey toward heaven. Responding to the Lord's most wondrous graces, we live in a manner worthy of the call we have received. Acting as the instruments of Christ's selfless love for one another, our families grow closer and stronger, preserving the unity of the Spirit in the bond of peace.

Lord Jesus, strength of all who labor, give us the grace to live in a manner worthy of the vocation you have given to us, bearing with one another so that our families may grow ever stronger.

God Is Our Father

Father Peter M. Girard, O.P.

"One body and one Spirit, as you were also called to the one hope of your call; one Lord, one faith, one baptism; one God and Father of all, who is over all and through all and in all."
(Eph 4: 4-6)

Recently, while visiting a retreat house, I came across a group of people praying what appeared to be the rosary. While the participants were indeed holding beads, the prayers had been changed to reflect a spirituality of solidarity with "mother earth." "Blessed be thy beauty and abundance, Mother Earth," the retreatants prayed. It became clear to me at that moment that these well-intentioned but misguided Catholics considered the Father-hood of God to be an *accidental quality* rather than essential to his nature.

Today, some claim that since the Scriptures were written in a "less enlightened" age, we need to transcend the texts' restriction of assigning "fatherhood" to God. To continue to refer to God as "Father," they claim, we are excluding those who cannot relate to God in this way. However, the Lord himself refers to God as "his Father," and Saint Paul states that we all have "one Father who is over all and through all and in all." Saint Paul emphasizes that the One who is Lord over all is properly referred to as "Father" and not as "mother" or "parent."

The Judeo-Christian revelation teaches us that God is a Father not merely in an accidental sense. Just as a mother is *part* of her creation in the natural order (the child grows within her), a father is notably *other than* or *apart from* his creation. God is a Father because in his creation of the universe he remains essentially other than us. We do not emanate from God's essence like ripples in a pond. Rather, we are created as *imago Dei*, reflective of his glory but decidedly *apart* from him. So whereas God has *motherly char-acteristics*, he is properly called "Father" by all Jews and Christians.

Lord Jesus, Son of the eternal Father, give us the grace to call out "Abba" as we claim our inheritance as adopted children.

The Fountain of All Holiness

Father Peter M. Girard, O.P.

"Grace was given to each of us according to the measure of Christ's gift." (Eph 4: 7)

If you have ever visited the city of Rome, you know that one of its ancient and most spectacular characteristics is the preponderance of beautifully flowing fountains. There are many hundreds of fountains in Rome, each perpetually gushing with water around the clock and throughout the year, a seemingly endless supply of crystal-clear water. What most people do not realize, however, is that these beautiful Roman fountains are not mechanically powered. Using aqueducts to allow the assistance of gravity, the abundance of fresh water is carried without human effort from the mountains to gush into each of the fountains.

One day while sitting in a certain piazza of Rome, I realized that the rushing stream of water into the fountains was a powerful symbol of every grace that we receive. Just as the source of fresh water for the Eternal City is the mountain, so the source of grace remains in the inner life of the Trinity, the "mountain" where God alone dwells. Just as the pure water rushes down through aqueducts, so living water flowed from the temple of heaven in the incarnation of the Son. Just as water gushes forth from the fountain, so every grace that you and I receive "gushes forth" from the sacred wounds of the crucified Christ. *Jesus is the fountain of all holiness* and his hands, feet, and side are the portals through which we receive the gushing and purifying waters of salvation.

Saint Paul reminds us that the graces of Christ, poured forth from his sacred wounds, remain limitless and eternally flowing. The "fountain of all holiness" never runs dry but flows with crystal-clear, life-giving water for each thirsty soul. Let us be ever mindful that his Precious Blood is ever flowing to purify and heal us.

Jesus, fountain of all holiness, may I never doubt that your wonderful graces, poured forth from your sacred wounds, will always be there for me, especially in times of trial.

A Mother's "Word-Box"

Father Peter M. Girard, O.P.

"And [Christ] gave [...] teachers, to equip the holy ones for the work of ministry, for building up the body of Christ, until we all attain to the unity of faith and knowledge of the Son of God, to mature manhood, to the extent of the full stature of Christ, so that we may no longer be infants, tossed by waves and swept along by every wind of teaching arising from human trickery, from their cunning in the interests of deceitful scheming."

(Eph 4: 11-14)

I had always considered my sister-in-law to be an outstanding Christian mother, lovingly attentive to the needs of her children. One day I noticed something that helped me to understand a deeper dimension of the vocation of motherhood. As her elder girl was soon approaching school age, my sister-in-law decided to begin teaching her reading and vocabulary skills. Not willing to allow the television to do such important work, this loving and attentive mother developed *her own word game* (she called it the "word-box") that was designed specifically to address the needs and temperament of her first child. It was so wonderful to see this child so excited to learn new words as Mommy taught her using the "word-box."

In his 1988 encyclical letter *Mulieris Dignitatem*, Pope John Paul II described the uniqueness of the vocation of the mother as one who "is filled with wonder at this mystery of life and understands with unique intuition what is happening inside her." Indeed, my sister-in-law was responding to the graces of Christ in nourishing and educating her children, ever attentive to their particular needs.

Saint Paul reminds us that Christ gives his holy ones the graces to build up his Body, the Church. When we participate in the building up of the spiritual edifice which is the Church, we are preserved from the emptiness that the world offers. When parents respond to the graces of their vocation, their children grow in knowledge and love so that they can resist worldly deceptions. My sister-in-law, in responding to the graces given to her with her "word-box," was building up both her own family and the whole Body of Christ in knowledge and love.

Lord Jesus, giver of the gift of motherhood, grant that all mothers may respond to your wondrous graces as they care for their children.

Living the Truth in Love

Father Peter M. Girard, O.P.

"Living the truth in love, we should grow in every way into him who is the head, Christ, from whom the whole body, joined and held together by every supporting ligament, with the proper functioning of each part, brings about the body's growth and builds itself up in love." (Eph 4: 15-16)

The One who is all Truth, the perfect reflection of the Father's glory, gives us many opportunities each day to respond with love toward our neighbor. In responding to this invitation of grace, we are perfected as members of his Body, building up the Church in love until he comes again in glory. I can remember once being called to a hospital on a very busy evening. I had barely enough time to visit a sick person before attending various meetings. The One who is "Head of the Body," however, had different plans for me! As I pushed the elevator button in the hospital lobby, I beheld an elderly, bespectacled lady who appeared rather confused about the floor on which she found herself.

While a seemingly insignificant moment, this was rather a tremendous opportunity Jesus was giving me to respond with love. I could have easily ignored her, preventing myself from being detained by a confused old lady, especially on an evening busy with church "business" at home. However, in responding to the Lord's invitation to speak to her, I learned that her husband was spending his last hours on earth in intensive care. I was then able to bring him who is Head of the Church to this dying soul through the celebration of the sacraments. The little old lady's husband left this earth a few hours later after being spiritually cleansed, nourished, and prepared for that final journey.

Saint Paul reminds us that as Head, Jesus does not neglect any member of his Body, the Church. He had not abandoned the elderly husband nor me as his priest! Rather, when I responded to his gift of grace with selfless love, Jesus accomplished a most wondrous work through me.

Jesus, Head of the Church, help me to recognize each opportunity to respond to your wonderful gifts of grace, becoming your instrument in building up the Body which is the Church.

Embracing the Virtuous Man

Father Peter M. Girard, O.P.

"You [...] were taught in [Christ], as truth is in Jesus, that you should put away the old self of your former way of life, corrupted through deceitful desires, and be renewed in the spirit of your minds, and put on the new self, created in God's way in righteousness and holiness of truth." (Eph 4: 21-24)

In its opening paragraphs, the Catechism of the Catholic Church reminds us that since all human beings are created "by God and for God," we discover the truth for which we long only in his embrace (CCC 26). Whenever we embrace the truth about our creation in his image, therefore, we find happiness and fulfillment even in the midst of life's trials and tragedies. Conversely, when we embrace falsehood as the measure and inspiration of our moral conduct, we discover only misery and a denigration of the human person, even if surrounded by earthly comforts.

Growing in holiness, therefore, necessarily involves a "putting away" of our habits of sin and striving for holiness through the embrace of virtue. Saint Augustine understood this well once he began to say "yes" to the Lord's wondrous graces. After convincing himself that a secular life alone could bring him fulfillment, the thirty-two-year-old Augustine began to listen to the sermons of Saint Ambrose in Milan's great cathedral. After reading Saint Paul's exhortation to reject vice and embrace virtue, in Romans (13: 13), Augustine gave his "yes" to embracing the "new self." In his famous *Confessions*, we see Saint Augustine as the model of the one who put away the old self so that he might emerge as a new creation through grace.

Saint Paul reminds us that only through the graces of Christ, poured forth in his Precious Blood, can we put away the "old self" and embrace a life of virtue. Like Saint Augustine, we may well have spent years living in the darkness of vice. However, since we are created fundamentally "by God and for God," *it is never too late* for us to begin embracing virtue!

Lord Jesus, Beauty that is ever ancient and ever new, my heart remains restless until it rests in your own Sacred Heart. May I seek your truth each day as I respond to your hidden opportunities of grace.

Embracing the Truth

Father Peter M. Girard, O.P.

"Putting away falsehood, speak the truth, each one to his neighbor, for we are members one of another. Be angry but do not sin; do not let the sun set on your anger, and do not leave room for the devil." (Eph 4: 25-27)

Let me tell you about a seminarian of mine who helped me to realize that only the embrace of Truth brings us happiness and fulfillment. A few days after grading final exams, this seminarian came to my office convinced that I had made an error on his paper. "You gave me a *B+*," he said, "but I think that you meant to give me an *A*." I told him that I had not made an error and that I thought his paper was good but not deserving of the highest grade. The young man angrily responded that he had shown his paper to other students and even other professors, all of whom agreed that he should receive an *A*!

Now here came the moment at which Jesus was asking me to respond to his grace. I knew that if this young man was to be ordained, he needed to be first of all *a man of truth*. So I addressed the seminarian in this way: "Young man, if you want this *A*, then I will give it to you and there will be no further questions." "Really?" he enthusiastically yet cautiously responded. "Yes," I said, "if you really want that *A* then I will place that mark on your report and I will not hold this against you."

However, just as the young man turned around with a smile and was about to leave my office, I added: "Of course, you will have to live the rest of your life knowing that you gave yourself this grade, *that it is really a lie*. If you can spend the rest of your life living this lie, then leave now and you will receive the highest grade." The seminarian paused for a moment as he considered whether or not, as Saint Paul encourages us, to embrace the Truth. He turned around and said quietly: "I will take the *B+*." I knew at that moment he would be a wonderful priest.

Jesus, source of all holiness, give me the strength to reject the false-hoods of the devil and embrace your Truth. May I be granted the courage to speak the Truth even if this means a sacrifice.

A Fragrant Offering

Father Peter M. Girard, O.P.

"Be imitators of God, as beloved children, and live in love, as Christ loved us and handed himself over for us as a sacrificial offering to God for a fragrant aroma." (Eph 5: 1-2)

When we live in a country where we can freely practice our religion, we can sometimes forget that many Christians around the world are persecuted and even martyred for embracing Christ. As Christ willingly became that perfect, sacrificial offering for the forgiveness of sins, so many persecuted Christians today become part of that "fragrant aroma" through their incorporation into his suffering, death, and resurrection.

On September 17, 2006, gunmen killed Sister Leonella Sgorbati, aged sixty-six, a nurse and teacher at the SOS Kindergarten Hospital in Mogadishu, Somalia. Having been a religious sister generously caring for the sick in the missions for forty-two years, this beloved Bride of Christ was assassinated simply for being a Christian.

After a bodyguard was killed instantly in the attack, Sister Leonella was rushed back into the children's hospital having been hit four times in the chest. As physicians raced to save her life, they could see that she was mouthing some words. A nurse bent his ear to her mouth and he heard a whisper that proved to be her last words on earth: "I forgive you…" Here, Sister was a perfect imitation of Christ, a *catechism of selfless love* as she forgave her attacker.

Saint Paul reminds us that we all are united to Christ who was the fragrant, perfect, sacrificial offering for sins. Whereas most of us will likely not be called to physical martyrdom, each of us is asked to become a "fragrant aroma" by allowing our sufferings to be incorporated into the Paschal Mystery. In addition, we should never fail to pray for those Christians, like Sister Leonella, who give their lives for the glory of his Holy Name.

Lord Jesus, perfect offering, may my sufferings be incorporated into your Paschal Mystery, that I may bear the most wonderful "fragrant aroma" for the good of my soul and the salvation of others.

211

Darkness and Light

John Janaro

"You were once darkness, but now you are light in the Lord. Live as children of light, for light produces every kind of goodness and righteousness and truth." (Eph 5: 8-9)

O nce we "were darkness" but now we "are light in the Lord." When baptism makes us Christian, it indicates first of all a change at the level of our personal being itself. The "darkness" that once defined us is replaced by Christ's life and light in which we are enabled to see the truth of God's plan for us and follow it in love. What is "darkness"? It is the darkness of fallen humanity, a world dominated by the sin of our first parents. Without the transforming grace of Christ, fallen man is alienated from God and cannot accomplish God's will in the world. Man seeks God, but is distracted by contrary desires and the selfishness of his fallen human nature. Still, man's fallen nature has not been entirely ruined, and fallen man, aided by the grace that is meant to lead him toward faith and baptism, stumbles in the darkness toward a light he does not yet know. No wonder the world we live in displays both the good and the evil of human effort. There are, on the one hand, the advances of science and technology so beneficial to mankind. On the other hand, there are the pervasive attacks on the dignity of the human person: violence and hatred, abortion and pornography. Human nature seems trapped in distortion and contrary impulses. The world will always reflect the "old man," laboring in darkness in Adam's fallen nature. In baptism, however, we put away the old nature: we are freed from original sin and endowed with a participation in the life of Jesus in the Spirit. We are no longer imprisoned by the darkness of the fallen world, for we are members of Christ, the light of the world. Baptism introduces us into a "new world" by empowering us to live as "children of light" in Christ and to come to resemble him through works of "goodness and righteousness and truth."

Almighty God, grant us the grace to live by the light of your Son, our Lord Jesus Christ, received at baptism. Christ the light of the world has given us a share in his life. Grant that Christ's light might shine in our hearts, so that we might bear witness to his love in the world.

Works of Darkness

John Janaro

"Try to learn what is pleasing to the Lord.
Take no part in the fruitless works of darkness;
rather expose them." (Eph 5: 10-11)

The "world" dominated by the sin of Adam is a world of darkness. It is darkness because it produces illusion, generates blindness, and ends in nothingness, which is to say the utter impoverishment of our being. Without the grace of Christ, even man's naturally good desires cannot lead him to the fullness of truth and life willed for him by God. Instead, he is sure to become lost in conflict, frustration, and pride. Darkness is the consequence of human pride, and it permeates the realm where man seeks the eternal through his own domination of the things of this world: the things that come to be and exist in time, and the things that man himself makes. By the strength of his own intelligence, his own energies, and his own work, man seeks to determine and to dominate his destiny. He longs to stretch to infinity realities that are destined to pass away: to make gods of wood and stone, or of the products of his labor, or the energies of his nature, or the clever constructions of his own mind. The light of faith exposes the works of darkness. Faith, hope, and love adhere to the redeeming and sanctifying action of Christ, and engender a new way of approaching all of reality. On the one hand, man begins to see that the purpose of his life is neither the exaltation of his own humanity nor the abandonment of his dignity to a slavery to false promises that would betray his ineradicable desire for infinite happiness. On the other hand, man begins to recognize the realities of the world for what they really are. Created things reflect the mystery of God the creator, and from this fact comes all of the goodness and attractiveness they possess. Thus created things are not ends in themselves, but are meant to be "signs" that point to man's true life in God, or to use another metaphor, "steps" that direct his path to eternity.

Almighty God, teach us what is pleasing to you. Never let us be deceived by the darkness that would lead us to forget that you and you alone are our true happiness.

The "Light" of Faith and the Light of Christ

John Janaro

"Everything exposed by the light becomes visible,
for everything that becomes visible is light."
(Eph 5: 13-14)

Faith is often contrasted to vision, and with good reason, because the mystery of God, even in faith, is known only indirectly by analogy via words and concepts that are fitted to the mode of human understanding. Man's mind is *finite*, even when supernaturally elevated by grace and revelation. Yet at the same time, we speak of a "light" of faith that raises up our minds to the contemplation of divine things, and that constitutes, in its vital relationship to hope and charity, a foreshadowing of beatitude. The truth of revelation is more than "abstract" or academic in our lives. It generates *experience*, which is the reflection of faith's light. We hold revealed truth firmly because we know that it is the truth about the God we love. And we begin to recognize the *supernatural* value, in God's light, of our work, our affections for people, and especially our suffering. The light of faith, working through love, conforms our lives to the holiness of God. And God accomplishes our salvation by connecting us to a real man who lived in history, a man who was, in himself, the holiness of God. Living faith brings us close to God by uniting us with Jesus Christ. Christ is the light of the world; he is the One who fully reveals both the mystery of God to man and the mystery of man to man himself. Communion with Jesus sheds light on everything, because relationship with God in Christ is the ultimate concrete purpose of man's personal existence. The reason why each and every human being is created *is Jesus*. Everything and every person we encounter in our lives finds ultimate concrete meaning in Jesus. He is our light, and in him we come to recognize what our lives are all about. No other person, no thing, no ideology, no mere effort of man's own natural mind can take his place.

Jesus, draw us into a deeper share in your risen and glorified life.
May our faith in you enable us to see that everything that happens
to us in the world is meant to lead us to your glory.

Give Thanks for Everything

John Janaro

"Be filled with the Spirit, addressing one another [in] psalms and hymns and spiritual songs, singing and playing to the Lord in your hearts, giving thanks always and for everything in the name of our Lord Jesus Christ to God the Father." (Eph 5: 18-20)

True life in the Spirit leads us to embrace all the circumstances that make up our days, because we know that every moment of life comes from Jesus and is intended by his wisdom to deepen our relationship with him. Nothing is meaningless, extraneous, or undignified in the Christian life, even if our present experience of a given event or circumstance might suggest otherwise. So often our lives seem confused, or even incomprehensible. God does not seem to hear our prayers. We feel wounded by failure in our work, by our own suffering, or by the suffering or death of a loved one. We cannot see with our human eyes nor grasp with the merely human power of our understanding how such circumstances could be part of God's plan for us. Yet it is these moments that enable our trust in God to grow. By surrendering ourselves to his grace, we become able to bear and even to accept lovingly the trials of life. We learn too that the joyful and contented moments of life cannot be grasped and held by our human selfishness, but can only be embraced with true joy by being surrendered to God. It is faith working through love in the depths of our soul that allows us to thus be shaped and transformed by Jesus in the Spirit. As we consecrate to God our relationships with one another, our love for each other in the most ordinary circumstances becomes a true offering of worship. It is not that we are being exhorted to speak continually about religious subjects; rather, it is a matter of recognizing that the life of the Spirit makes it possible for every human gesture to become a tone in a hymn of thanksgiving in which God's love is acknowledged and made manifest. This is the meaning of our existence in this world: to worship and give glory to God through Jesus Christ in the Spirit, in all that we are and all that we do.

Lord, give us the grace to recognize that every moment of our lives is in your hand, and designed by you to lead us to eternal glory. Enable us to consecrate our lives to you, so that our daily activities might be lifted up to you in worship and thanksgiving.

Love and Service

John Janaro

"Be subordinate to one another out of reverence for Christ."
(Eph 5: 21)

This text establishes the ultimate context not only for the most intimate human relationships (those within the family, and especially those between husband and wife) but also for all human relationships. Human beings are called to live in communion with one another with a unity that comes from God and reflects his glory. Thus human relationships witness to the mystery of God insofar as they are constituted by love. Love is simple, and yet in this life it seems so complicated even for Christians. We are commanded to "love one another" and yet this love seems like an ideal to strive for rather than an established reality among us (thus we are exhorted to "forgive one another" continually). The "new law" of life in the Spirit is, indeed, a *law of love*. What is the real mystery of love? The law of love is self-giving. It is affirmation of the other person in a way that makes the lover transcend himself and place himself "at the disposal" of the beloved. The radical nature of love in any relationship consists in each person giving himself to the other in love, and divesting himself of self-centeredness in order to "make space" for the one who is loved. Thus each person becomes capable of giving himself fully and receiving the gift of the other person by "emptying" himself. Christian "subordination" is defined ultimately by the self-giving love of Jesus Christ. The One who created all things freely took the lowest place in order to give himself to everyone and make space within himself for everyone. Human beings find themselves in a variety of relationships that imply different kinds and different levels of "authority" and "obedience." Christian love transforms both into self-surrendering love of Jesus, in whom we discover that "to serve is to reign."

Almighty God, transform all our relationships according to the pattern of Jesus' obedience to you and to the gift of himself to us.

Jesus Protects Us from the Evil One

John Janaro

"Draw your strength from the Lord and from his mighty power. Put on the armor of God so that you may be able to stand firm against the tactics of the devil." (Eph 6: 10-11)

What do we think about "the devil" in our world today? For some time there has been a tendency either to reduce him to some vague, malevolent "force," or to limit his activity to the most malicious and destructive persons and the terrible events they set in motion: Hitler, Stalin, terrorism, genocide, concentration camps, etc. Many consider "the demonic" to be a subconscious "dark side" within our own nature, or a kind of "insanity" to which can be ascribed all the evils that human beings commit. The truth is that the devil is a created being that we cannot see with our eyes, but who nevertheless is involved in the lives of each one of us. There are in the universe fallen and irredeemable spiritual intelligences that hate us and interfere with our lives. Their natures and their power are superior to our human nature, and because their being transcends sensible reality entirely, we only know of their existence by faith. The devils are liars and murderers, as Jesus said. They hate our happiness and seek to rob us of our destiny by tricking us to follow false paths that end in destruction. The devil's "tactics" would outwit our natural intelligence if we were left to ourselves. But the good news of the Gospel is precisely that we are not left to ourselves in the fight against the devil, or the distractions of the world, or the weight of our own selfishness. By his death and resurrection, Jesus has made us a new creation and incorporated us into his Mystical Body. Therefore, there is no place in the Christian life for a morbid fear of the devil, provided that we "stand firm" with Jesus. Jesus has defeated the devil in the desert and, above all, on the cross. His flesh is the armor that will protect us so that we are not driven away from our own happiness.

Lord Jesus, in your mercy, shield us and defend us against the malice and deception of the devil.

This Present Darkness

John Janaro

*"Our struggle is not with flesh and blood but with
the principalities, with the powers, with the world rulers of
this present darkness, with the evil spirits in the heavens."*
(Eph 6: 12)

Saint Paul stresses that the "world rulers" of fallen humanity, of that fallen world we call "darkness," are "principalities and powers" that are superior (in their nature) to man ("flesh and blood"). They are the "evil spirits," those mysterious but real spiritual intelligences that Scripture calls "angels." They are *fallen* angels who refused to serve God "in the beginning" when God created "the heavens." (Gn 1: 1). They are the enemies of the human race, and by leading man into sin, they gained a certain "power" over the fallen world. This power should be recognized, but not exaggerated. God rules even the fallen world and, especially since the victory of Christ, he limits the influence of the devil. However, each of us must recognize that these malevolent beings can and do seek to take advantage of our wounded nature and lead us to ruin. Why, then, does God permit the devil to act in the world at all? Why does he permit Christians to endure the temptations of the devil? It is clear that beings superior to human nature who are evil, intelligent, and ruthless have a hand in the affairs of the world. This can be seen even by looking at historical events, in which it is clear that individuals and groups have surrendered their wills to some superior, sinister power, with the result being the perpetration of evil on a monstrous scale. How else could such inhuman violence and such hatred for human life prevail in our world? God also allows Christians to be tempted; yet God always gives us the grace, in Christ, to overcome temptation. Jesus himself was tempted in the desert, and his victory is the basis for our hope. The threat of the Evil One moves us to let Jesus penetrate every aspect of our lives, because wherever the risen and glorified Jesus is recognized and loved, the devil is defeated.

Loving God, may your grace penetrate our whole lives so that we might adhere more deeply to the Mystical Body of Christ. Grant that the triumph of Jesus over sin and death might drive away the wickedness of the devil.

Hold Your Ground

John Janaro

*"Put on the armor of God, that you may be able
to resist on the evil day and, having done everything,
to hold your ground." (Eph 6: 13)*

Saint Paul uses the imagery of war to describe our struggle against the devil. It is important to note, however, that the Christian takes a decidedly *defensive* posture in the struggle with Satan. Courage and steadfastness here preclude any presumptuous ideas of going forth into the devil's territory and conquering him by our own weak human capacities. The Christian believes that Jesus *has already* conquered the devil, and that the key to the Christian person's sharing in that conquest is to abandon his life to Jesus. Jesus is the new Adam, the "new man," the head of the "new" redeemed human race. The first Adam listened to the deceptions of the devil, disobeyed, and brought sin and death to the world. Fallen nature was, in principle, "defenseless" against the devil's power. However, God, in view of the promised Redeemer and in his merciful love for man, protected man, nurtured his aspirations for the infinite, and prepared the world for the coming of his Son. In Jesus' death and resurrection, the defeat of the devil – promised from the beginning – was accomplished. It has now become possible for us to participate in this victory. The "armor of God" is an image for the new life in Christ given in baptism and nourished by the life of faith in the Church. We are exhorted to "put on" the armor of God: this very physical image conveys to us the concreteness of allowing every aspect of our lives to be renewed in Christ. If we "wear" Christ, if we let him live in us and through us, we will persevere in the face of any assault. The armor of God is Jesus living in us and making manifest his defeat of the devil, and his Lordship in our lives and in the particular circumstances in which we live. Through the mystery of the Church, the triumph of Jesus and the defeat of the devil extend to every place and time.

Merciful Jesus, we abandon our lives to you. Give us the grace to hold fast to your love in the temptations and tribulations of life.

Faith Is Our Shield

John Janaro

"Stand fast with your loins girded in truth, clothed with righteousness as a breastplate, and your feet shod in readiness for the gospel of peace. In all circumstances, hold faith as a shield, to quench all [the] flaming arrows of the evil one. And take the helmet of salvation and the sword of the Spirit, which is the word of God./ With all prayer and supplication, pray at every opportunity in the Spirit." (Eph 6: 14-18)

Here, particular aspects of the image of the "armor of God" are set forth. We note that the Christian is outfitted to "stand fast." He must adhere to the Gospel; thus in his own person he participates by the grace of Christ in defending the kingdom that Christ has won at the price of his blood, a kingdom that has begun to manifest itself even in this present age. It is the Evil One who is on the attack with his "flaming arrows." God permits this so that the Christian might grow closer to Christ, and so that he might recognize that his salvation depends on God's grace. Truth and righteousness – it is baptism and the living out of baptismal grace that initiate and sustain these gifts in us. It is faith – that trusting, loving faith by which we abandon ourselves to the Lord whom we cannot see – which shields us from the flaming arrows of temptation. Our sword is the Sword of the Spirit, the Word of God that reveals both the truth about God's love for us and the lies of the Evil One. Clad in this armor, what are we to do? Pray! At every opportunity we must pray "in the Spirit"; we must beg God to sustain us in the salvation that has been won for us in Christ Jesus. Christian life reveals to us that it is we who are weak and God who is strong. We must pray continually, in words and in thought and in life. We must acknowledge him and thank him for his saving power which continually protects us on our journey to him. Without God's grace, the arrows of the devil would penetrate us and destroy us. *Worship* is the proper response to the one who is all-powerful, and *gratitude* is the prayerful recognition that he has given himself to us. This present life is a struggle, but God provides us with what we need, and we must continually turn to him and adhere to him through Jesus, in the Spirit.

Almighty and Eternal God, clothe us with your armor, so that in Jesus' name and by his strength we might prevail against the attacks of the devil. May the Sword of the Spirit, your Word revealed to us, make manifest the lies of the Evil One and your love for us.

Freedom and Grace

John Janaro

"I am confident of this, that the one who began a good work in you will continue to complete it until the day of Christ Jesus."
(Phil 1: 6)

Many of us misunderstand the true nature of Christian life, which is a life of healing, elevating, and empowering *grace*. How often we underestimate the role of grace, God's transforming gift of love to us that shapes our whole lives. It is easy to turn Christianity into a list of things that *we* must accomplish and avoid, and then to rely on our own efforts and the strength of our own human will to "win" God's approval. In such a scenario, "grace" is reduced to an occasional factor, a vague divine "help" that gives us an added "push" when we face some difficulty. We think of grace as *God cooperating* with *our* human and self-driven efforts to implement the Christian "program" in our lives. Of course, God's mercy is greater than our misconceptions. God knows our hearts better than we do, and he teaches us, sooner or later, that everything comes from him. Let us reflect, however, on how different the essence of the Christian life really is! We are healed of original sin and raised up to the status of sons and daughters of God by baptism. This is a gift from God that we cannot possibly merit by our own finite actions. We belong to God through Jesus Christ in the Holy Spirit. On the arduous path of life, it is God who anticipates us with his empowering grace that enables us to desire and will to embrace human circumstances with acts of supernatural love. We live by the power of God; thus grace fashions and accompanies every work we are called to accomplish. *We must cooperate* by surrendering ourselves to God, by abandoning our self-will, and by trusting in him always. We adhere to him by a faith vivified by hope and charity, and by prayer. Prayer is man standing before God in need of everything, but also with trust that God will give everything, and bring us to the fulfillment he has destined for us.

Heavenly Father, by your grace, bring to fulfillment the goodness and love you have instilled in us in Jesus Christ. Sustain us in the hope that you will complete the good work you have begun in us. Open our hearts to the Holy Spirit who works within us, and enable us to cooperate with his transforming love.

Ardent Love

John Janaro

"For God is my witness, how I long for all of you with the affection of Christ Jesus." (Phil 1: 8)

Saint Paul speaks about the affection of Christ, an affection in which Saint Paul shares by grace and which attaches him to the Christians of Philippi with "longing." In the Christian life, grace enables us both to will and to perform the good deeds that are called for by the circumstances of life or by God's specific command. Here, we must remember, however, that grace lifts up the whole person to the status of adopted sonship. As we grow in the Christian life, we become more "God-like." The transformation of our whole personality in Christ extends to every aspect of our humanity, conforming the senses to the rule of reason and instilling a rightly ordered and zealous ardor into the affections of the heart, so that the whole man might respond to the supernatural good. The mature Christian life is not one in which the will and the intellect adhere to God, while the affections of the heart irredeemably go their own way. It is true that a dissonance within the person exists at the beginning of Christian life in a way that requires struggle and asceticism. Yet the human person is a unified whole – soul and body, with a mind and a will, but also with a "heart," with affections and with the physical senses. Redemption is destined for the whole man. The exercise of supernatural virtue, however, brings about more and more the healing of the person, so that his affections, rather than diverting and distracting his will, begin to support and strengthen Christian love. God's transforming grace changes not only the will, but penetrates the whole man, bringing into the sphere of divine life the affections and the movements of the senses. The mature Christian person is able to bear witness to God's love ardently, patiently, courageously, and joyfully.

Merciful Lord Jesus, true God and perfect man, by your grace, bring together the broken pieces of our lives, so that every aspect of our humanity might rejoice in your glory.

Discerning What Is of Value

John Janaro

"This is my prayer: that your love may increase ever more and more in knowledge and every kind of perception, to discern what is of value, so that you may be pure and blameless for the day of Christ, filled with the fruit of righteousness that comes through Jesus Christ for the glory and praise of God." (Phil 1: 9-11)

Faith lives by love and is strengthened by hope. The "theological" virtues interpenetrate one another in a sense, so that the whole Christian person might become "pure and blameless" and "filled with the fruit of righteousness" in Jesus Christ. God has revealed his love for us. He is the beginning, sustenance, and fruition of everything we are, everything we do, and every circumstance we encounter. Faith opens up our reason to this tremendous truth, and so with mind and heart, we hold fast to Jesus Christ, the One who has accomplished God's design through his unfathomable self-giving love that extends to every human person and to the whole world. Through the death and resurrection of Jesus Christ, God has revealed and established that the whole world, and every reality in the world, finds its ultimate meaning and value in his plan of salvation. In the beginning of Christian life, faith reveals how God's love truly penetrates everything, but the experience of this fact takes time, and follows the road that leads to God himself. Saint Paul prays that "love may increase." Even after revelation and supernatural faith, we are a long way from seeing God face-to-face. But in charity we can, here and now, reach God and "taste and see" his infinite goodness and wisdom. Love is the impetus that generates a greater adherence to God, "ever more and more in knowledge and every kind of perception." As we thus grow closer to God, our minds are opened more and more to God's wisdom and his plan to bring all things under the headship of Christ. Living the Christian life brings about a whole new way of looking at the world, of judging the value of worldly things, and of embracing the circumstances of our own life with purity, innocence, and compassion.

Almighty God and Father, grant us the gift of wisdom, so that in Jesus Christ we might show forth the glory of your steadfast love in all the world.

Dying to Live

Father Gary Caster

"For to me life is Christ, and death is gain." (Phil 1: 21)

I used to boast, somewhat proudly, that I was ready to die, that I was fully prepared to meet the Lord. I imagined this placed me squarely within the company of Saint Paul. Then, four years ago, my younger sister showed me I was wrong. She let me see how this just put me in the company of fools (and not the ones who are that way for Christ). She taught me all of this while she was dying. I learned how we gain Christ by the way she approached that final end which claims us all. She wasn't eager to die. She was concerned with living. She embraced each new day with gratitude, recognizing the opportunity it presented: the possibility of being freed from anything that limited her openness to God, her love of others, and her appreciation of reality. For my sister, each new day offered her the chance to die to herself, so she gladly welcomed the occasion of putting to death whatever prevented her from having a deeper, richer experience of Christ. My sister lived squarely within the company of Saint Paul because she knew that he was speaking not of our final end, but the way we must approach it. She understood that in order fully to be alive, "to gain Christ," she had to let go of herself. Each day I could see her letting go. Each day I was reminded how much of me must die. I didn't want my sense of self to be so narrowly determined that there was little room for Christ. I discovered that, in some respects, I had been afraid of dying in the only way that matters, the way Christ champions in the Gospel. My sister taught me how to live by the way she chose to die. She taught me just what Saint Paul was teaching the Philippians.

Lord, let me live each day with a willingness to die, and die each day with a willingness to live. Let my life so radiate your love that others may come to know and experience what I myself have found in you.

Choosing to Remain

Father Gary Caster

"I long to depart this life and be with Christ, [for] that is far better. Yet that I remain [in] the flesh is more necessary for your benefit." (Phil 1: 23-24)

Every child knows the longest day of the year is Christmas Eve. Once night falls the anticipation of the morning becomes so intense that time almost stops. The lingering darkness of night is tolerated because of the hope of what will be. Every child waits, however anxiously, knowing that eventually the new day will dawn. The experience is the same once we have discovered the truth about human destiny revealed by Christ. Like Saint Paul, our hearts become filled with the desire to be fully and for ever within the life of God. We long to experience perfectly and without any limitation the love made flesh in the incarnate Son of God. We long for the everlasting satisfaction of the deepest desires and needs of the human heart. And with Saint Paul, we learn that our hope for the dawning of eternal life is secured in a particular way through the network of relationships that constitute the Body of Christ. Remaining in the flesh is indeed of benefit, because the act of following Christ is not a solitary, isolated, private endeavor; neither is eternal life. Our life with Christ here and now, and hereafter, is meant to be lived out in communion with others. Our desire for eternal life should therefore determine how we take our place and live our lives within the world and as members of Christ's Body. Remaining in the flesh alive with the hope of eternal communion and filled with the Holy Spirit extends the gift of Christ's presence to the world. The whole Body of Christ derives great benefit from those who remain in the flesh with a commitment to serving others in love and strengthening them in the Holy Spirit. With Saint Paul, we can live in the flesh through the long night of waiting because the Love that secures our hope is truly at work in the hearts of those who believe.

Heavenly Father, let my desire for eternal life determine my life here and now. Let my love for you be of benefit to all members of Christ's Body, even to all the world.

225

Family Ties

Father Gary Caster

"Conduct yourselves in a way worthy of the gospel of Christ, so that, whether I come and see you or am absent, I may hear news of you, that you are standing firm in one spirit, with one mind struggling together for the faith of the gospel, not intimidated in any way by your opponents." (Phil 1: 27-28)

Saint Paul's words to the Philippians remind me of something my parents used to say to me and my brothers and sisters whenever we were going to be away from home or out on our own: "Behave yourselves." This was their simple way of reminding us to be the persons they raised us to be, and not to be "intimidated" by whatever conflicting influences we might encounter. Unfortunately, there were times I failed to do so. It was then they would point out how my behavior didn't faithfully reflect the way I had been raised. Saint Paul uses similar words to encourage his spiritual children. He wants them to remember that in all ways and at all times they are members of the Christian family. Their conduct should therefore reflect "the way of the Gospel" in which they have been raised. As sons and daughters of God, their actions should depend – not on whether Paul is with them – but solely on the truth of who they are in Christ. Standing firm in this is a positive safeguard against difficult situations and opposing voices. Saint Paul knows they don't have to be told how to behave; they simply need to be reminded who they are. As Christians, our conduct should flow naturally from the one spirit that binds us together as a family. The way of the Gospel requires a unity that goes beyond personal preferences, social bonds, or individual comfort levels. As members of God's family, we have an obligation to one another, one that draws us together in good times and in bad, in sickness and in health, in riches and in poverty. Only as a family united in mutual and loving concern, only as a family – one in mind and heart – can we live in peace undisturbed by those who fear, reject, or are opposed to the way of the Gospel.

Heavenly Father, through the power of your Spirit, let me always live according to the truth of who I have become in Christ, never forgetting who I am, standing firm before the world ever confident in your love.

Love and Suffering

Father Gary Caster

"To you has been granted, for the sake of Christ, not only to believe in him but also to suffer for him." (Phil 1: 29)

The first letter I received from Blessed Teresa of Calcutta frightened me. She wrote, "Since you love Jesus, be prepared to suffer." I wonder if the Philippians had the same reaction to Saint Paul. The straightforward language he uses to educate them about the true nature of Christian belief is alarming. And yet, however startling his words may be, they actually point toward a method for believing wholly determined by Christ. Saint Paul makes it clear that the life of Jesus establishes the boundaries of what is reasonable, adequate, and necessary when formulating truth claims and theological propositions. Whatever is claimed by faith must correspond with the life of the man Jesus. This is the reason for the incarnation. Christ's humanity sets out for us the rule for measuring our own. The yielding of our minds and hearts entails a willingness to judge the claims of faith according to the innate desires of our hearts and the experience of our humanity. It also entails a willingness to have our human experiences judged according to the life of the Son of God. Christian belief is more than an intellectual activity; it is an affair of the heart, a total giving of oneself to Christ. Following this method of inquiry demands nothing less, because at the core of Christ's life is his willingness to suffer. He reveals love in the experience of the cross. Every moment of his life was directed toward this comprehensive act of suffering, and is only fully understood from its perspective. Paul is right in saying belief entails suffering. How could it be otherwise when Jesus reveals his belief in us as love? For him, they are one and the same. Mother Teresa knew that suffering for Christ isn't something one seeks out, it is something one can expect the moment one says, "Yes, Lord, I believe." Or when one says with Saint Peter, "You know everything, Lord, you know I love you."

Lord God, in the gift of your Son you have revealed the depth of your love for us. Grant that I respond by giving myself totally to you, for Christ and for all the world.

Complete Joy
Father Gary Caster

"If there is any encouragement in Christ, any solace in love, any participation in the Spirit, any compassion and mercy, complete my joy by being of the same mind, with the same love, united in heart, thinking one thing." (Phil 2: 1)

There are events in our lives – hopefully many – in which everything is perfect, when nothing further need be added. The people and place, the setting and atmosphere, the conversation and camaraderie, everything's right just as it is. There are moments in our lives we wish would never end, moments that come to define and characterize for us what it means to be happy, content, and fulfilled. These moments often come unexpectedly, without detailed plans or careful orchestration. We know we aren't always able to anticipate or determine when they will be, so we celebrate them when they come and hold onto them in our memory. We also know that at times the events we would like to be perfect fail to fulfill our expectations. Saint Paul knew this. Like every one of us, he longed for that sense of contentment that comes with being filled with joy. He also knows that he cannot generate this on his own. Knowing Christ to be the real cause of his joy, he appeals to the community that constitutes Christ's Body to make his joy complete. Paul sees and loves in the Philippians what he sees and loves in Christ; he wants them to do the same. That's why he encourages them to be of the same mind, united in heart and filled with love. In their communion with Christ and one another, a communion fixed in the Holy Spirit, the Philippians can truly give Paul the joy for which he longs. Saint Paul isn't asking them for something that is not possible. He's simply asking the community to live the truth they have become in Christ. Their unity with each other will certainly console him, for genuine communion completes every human heart. Nothing need be added to such an experience except the hope that it will last for ever. In Christ we know it will.

Sustain within me, O Lord, that joy which comes from being one in mind and heart with the members of your Body, living united with them in love all the days of my life.

The Unimagined Gift

Father Gary Caster

"Do nothing out of selfishness or out of vainglory; rather, humbly regard others as more important than yourselves, each looking out not for his own interests, but [also] everyone for those of others." (Phil 2: 3-4)

Have you ever received a completely unexpected gift that showed how well the person giving it knew and cared about you? Have you ever been given a gift that touched your heart enough to change the way you thought about yourself, others, and what it means to give? Saint Paul has this kind of experience in mind when describing how the Philippians should live in communion with each another. The "humility" that is the source of Christian communion is generated by the unexpected and undeserved love of God. He offers this pure gift in the person of Christ. This humility is a virtue not acquired through human initiative, but instilled according to the response one makes to the offer of God's love. Recognizing that the gift of God's love corresponds perfectly with the instinctive desires of one's heart cultivates a radical change of perspective. There is no longer any need to look out for oneself and one's own interests; God is looking out for them. This fundamental shift in disposition enables us to live with our minds and hearts genuinely concerned with the interests of others; not as a duty or obligation but as a way of life. The "humble regard" that sustains Christian communion is born of the desire to share with others the gift we have received. With the needs of our hearts being satisfied by the love of God offered us in Christ, we become free for others in such a way that they do become "more important" than ourselves. There is, then, nothing greater or more fulfilling than extending to others the love we have received. In fact, the love of God offered us in Christ compels us toward others in a way so wholly compatible with our humanity that our lives become wonderfully and perfectly fulfilled.

Lord, help me accept the gift of your love, always trusting in your care. Let me look past myself, fixing my gaze solely on the needs of others.

Christian Motivation

Father Gary Caster

"Have among yourselves the same attitude that is also yours in Christ Jesus,/ Who, though he was in the form of God,/ did not regard equality with God something to be grasped."
(Phil 2: 5-6)

A skilled actor or actress knows that the key to a successful performance is an accurate understanding of the character's motivation. A competent director helps them discover and explore this. As a result, the dialogue and action flow more naturally, insuring the believability of the performance. Acting with the right motivation assures both the audience and the performers a rewarding experience. Saint Paul is a good director. He shows this in his concern for the Philippians. He wants them to experience a full, abundant, satisfying life and he knows that having the right motivation will guarantee this. So Paul describes for them how the key for living as a Christian in the world is something they already possess: the "attitude" of Christ. Their incorporation into his Body has bestowed on the Philippians the same disposition that shaped and determined the life of Christ. This "attitude" they share with Christ derives from the truth of who they are in him, a truth not to be held onto but to be handed over. The life of Christ is not merely an example of how to live, but the source and possibility of truly living. Just as Christ did not use "his equality with God" to manipulate, control, or dominate the lives of others, neither should the Philippians use their relationship with Christ to do so. The way of the Christian in the world is the way of Christ in the world. It is the way of letting go, of surrendering. Knowing who he was in God gave Jesus the freedom to be himself in the world, open to and concerned about others and secure in peace. Knowing who they are in Christ will give the Philippians this same freedom, opening their lives to others and to the whole of reality. Having the attitude of Christ means trusting completely in the One whose life we share. That alone should be our motivation.

Heavenly Father, help me relinquish my life to your loving care so that I might live in the freedom of being your child.

Humility and Obedience

Father Gary Caster

*"[Christ Jesus] emptied himself,/ taking the form of a slave,/
coming in human likeness;/ and found human in appearance,/
he humbled himself,/ becoming obedient to death,/
even death on a cross."(Phil 2: 7-8)*

One of the great joys in watching children play is the ease
with which they take familiar things and use them in
unimagined ways. Children see hidden potential in playing cards, plastic containers, paper bags, and other ordinary objects.
The objects are "emptied" of their common purposes and given
new and greater significance. These new possibilities are limited
only by the creativity and imagination of the child. What children
do at play provides an insight into who they are, what they are thinking, and how they feel. The self-emptying of Christ Jesus provides
similar insights with respect to God the Father. By "taking the form
of a slave," Jesus allows the unbounded creativity of the Father to
be revealed. The humanity of Christ, so familiar and recognizable
(even unto death), is used in an unimagined way: the "way of the
cross." This new way of Christ Jesus makes possible the self-emptying of our humanity, so that we can be filled solely with the
Father's imaginative purposes. Our humanity, enslaved by sin, is,
in Christ Jesus, reconfigured according to the Father's design. We
are given new significance and greater purpose because Christ Jesus
willingly abandoned himself to the Father. Jesus wholeheartedly
took upon himself the limits of the humanity he assumed. Jesus
became enslaved by time, place, and circumstance, so that in time
and place and circumstance the loving initiative of the Father's will
would be made known. The humility of Jesus is demonstrated in
his willingness to serve the Father with and in terms of his body.
His obedience to the Father unto death becomes the way for us to
live our humanity in freedom. The power of Saint Paul's words lies
in the truth to which they testify. The Father has taken what is most
familiar to us and in Christ Jesus used it in the most unimaginable
way.

*Lord, help me empty myself as you did, so that I might be filled
with the Father's love and order my life according to his purposes.*

What's in a Name?

Father Gary Caster

"God greatly exalted [Christ Jesus]/ and bestowed on him the name/ that is above every name,/ that at the name of Jesus/ every knee should bend,/ of those in heaven and on earth and under the earth,/ and every tongue confess that/ Jesus Christ is Lord,/ to the glory of God the Father." (Phil 2: 9-11)

The name "Jesus" identifies more than a religious figure from the past. The name summarizes the whole record of God's action in history on behalf of the human family. At the same time this name also points ahead to the destiny which determines the life of every man and woman. The action of God in time has always been about our future, a preparation for an eternity that is more than an endless succession of days. The name "that is above every other name" moves us toward a timeless "now" in which we will no longer be burdened by what was or anxious about what will be. The name "Jesus" champions a love revealed in ancient signs and wonders, a love condensed in a unique human life that was born from the history of God's chosen people. The man who bears this name lived his life entirely for others, sacrificing even his flesh and blood for a future that no man or woman could ever have imagined, constructed, or sustained. In the man who bears this name before which "every knee should bend," God has definitively answered the question posed by Moses when he stood before the burning bush: "Who are you?" To the most profound question found in the Bible, "those in heaven and on earth and under the earth" can now confess together the glorious way God has chosen to formulate his reply. The name "Jesus" is more than a word used to identify a man that at one time lived among us. This name identifies a man who just happens to be God. This name, therefore, conveys such a sense of mystery that all those who comprehend not only reverently bend their knee, but gladly fall down in adoration.

Heavenly Father, help me bend my will before your Son and celebrate with my life the love his name commands.

The Work of Fear

Father Gary Caster

"Work out your salvation with fear and trembling.
For God is the one who, for his good purpose, works in you
both to desire and to work." (Phil 2: 12-13)

In the "work" of salvation there are two kinds of fear. The first is a type of anxious concern that originates from a sense of danger. This type of apprehensive fear cripples and incapacitates, eventually causing a person to shut down and disengage. It is the kind of fear that fosters timidity and in time leads to the burying of one's talents in the ground. There is, however, another kind of fear, one that derives from a sense of awe. This reverent fear animates and excites. Since it's generated by the recognition of "God's good purposes," it moves a person to take a chance, to risk everything and to trust in what's been given. It fosters confidence and ultimately leads a person to rely solely on God. The first kind of fear makes a person recoil, quivering and quiet and not yet fully alive. The second kind of fear makes a person stand tall, trembling with eagerness and enthusiasm, alive and enriched with possibility. The first kind immobilizes because a person is consumed with the possibility of failure. The second kind invigorates because doing nothing is not an option. Saint Paul understands this second kind of fear, the kind that's needed if we are to "work out our salvation." This is the fear that's born of an appreciation and acceptance of what's been given by the God who works in us, a fear that keeps alive the thought of what can be. This fear brings one's humanity to new life because it moves a person toward God and never away from him. It arouses a confidence in the human heart that allows a person to run the race, to work until completion, to make up for what's lacking, to surrender completely to God. The fear that is born of reverence allows God's work to continue in us as he sees fit for it fosters a docility of heart that allows for the satisfaction of our deepest desires.

O Lord, let my life be captivated by a reverent fear that opens me to your redemptive work, and excites my heart with the rich and creative possibilities that are born of your love for me.

Zeal for Souls

Father Gary Caster

"Do everything without grumbling or questioning, that you may be blameless and innocent, children of God without blemish in the midst of a crooked and perverse generation, among whom you shine like lights in the world, as you hold onto the word of life, so that my boast for the day of Christ may be that I did not run in vain or labor in vain." (Phil 2: 14-16)

The affection Saint Paul has for the Philippians reveals the true nature of zeal for souls. He knows his life to be so inextricably bound to theirs that he cannot possibly imagine "the day of Christ Jesus" apart from them. Because Paul cannot think of or envision his own relationship with God apart from the Christian community, he runs his life for others, seeking to build up the children of God according to the same word of life that changed his own. Paul encourages the Philippians to do the same because he encountered this word of life in a man whose flesh and blood perfectly communicates the Presence of the Mystery that is God. Paul is pleading with them from his heart, trying to persuade them according to the truth which is also in theirs. His singular concern and the effort of all his labors is that the Philippians will faithfully adhere to Christ, "without grumbling or questioning," because trust is the hallmark of Christian discipleship. Paul knows that if they trust, if they hold fast to Christ in the act of following him, their lives will "shine like lights" and become beacons of hope for the rest of the world. Paul has seen for himself and can testify how the very light of the Son of God radiates from those who labor according to God's wishes, serving him with gladness and freedom of heart. Paul knows that Christ has not left the world, but remains present through his Body, the Church, in an active and vital way. The hope for any generation lost in the perversions that result from the disorders of sin is to be reborn as sons and daughters of God. To remain "without blemish" is truly possible to the extent that one remains open to the Word of life and continues to explore what Christ makes possible in the act of following him.

Heavenly Father, your zeal for us is revealed in the life, death, and resurrection of your Son. Let my heart be consumed by this same zeal so that others may come to know and experience what I have found in you.

Heavenly Libation

Father Gary Caster

"Even if I am poured out as a libation upon the sacrificial service of your faith, I rejoice and share my joy with all of you."
(Phil 2: 17)

With the use of one word, "libation," Saint Paul vividly draws our attention to the fundamental nature of Christianity. In Christ this ritual outpouring of wine has literally come to life. When Jesus poured out his blood on the altar of the cross, what was once only a symbol of man's desire to be at peace with God has become the sacrament of man's redemption. Jesus spent his public ministry preparing the apostles and those who followed him for the moment of his self-sacrifice. Their education in this new covenant began at a wedding in Cana when Jesus changed water into wine. This first miracle shapes the whole of Jesus' ministry and comes to fruition the night before he dies. During the celebration of Passover, Jesus takes a cup of the ritual wine and changes it into his blood. At this sacred meal he establishes the means by which all future generations will have real access to the death he undergoes the following day. After receiving the promised Holy Spirit, the apostles and company of Jesus' followers will never think of water, wine, or blood in the same way. The celebration of the Eucharist becomes the center of their life as a community. Their willingness to serve the Lord will be for ever nourished by the gift of his body and blood. Their faith in this gift allows Christ to "pour himself out" in a perpetual act of thanksgiving. In the new covenant between God and man, Jesus' blood truly is the perfect "libation." With one word, Saint Paul clearly shows us that the Eucharist must be more than something we receive with the rest of the community. It must determine how we live. Just like Christ we are "to be poured out as a libation," one for another, expending ourselves in love, even to the point of shedding our blood. The completion of human joy is found in "sacrificial service" of God and neighbor.

Lord Jesus, teach me how to pour out my life as you did, in loving service of my brothers and sisters. Let me always find my joy in serving them.

The Advantage of Losing

Father Harry Cronin, C.S.C.

*"I even consider everything as a loss because of the supreme good
of knowing Christ Jesus my Lord. For his sake I have accepted
the loss of all things and I consider them so much rubbish,
that I may gain Christ and be found in him, not having
any righteousness of my own." (Phil 3: 8-9)*

Rubbish is a record of human progress. It is a harsh record: unyielding and sometimes unpleasant. Rubbish is what we used in the past. Rubbish is what we once thought was important – but no longer. It is what we discard as our lives move on. Rubbish gives us a good record of where we have been, what we used to be like, what used to be important to us; but this very accurate record – our rubbish – tells us nothing about the future. It only tells us about the past – a past we may wish to forget.

That is why Paul is so willing to consider all his human learning – which must have been substantial – as rubbish. We know that Paul studied under the great teacher Gamaliel; but he realized, in some way, that everything he knew, all his knowledge, was about the past. He also sensed – and this must have been shattering – that what he had learned was useless.

It is easy to study the past. But what about the future? Is it possible to learn anything about the future? The answer, of course, is "yes." In Christ we have access to the future. In Christ, the future is more than a series of events which have not yet happened. In Christ, the future is a promise, one that is unbreakable.

Paul came to know Christ on the road to Damascus. It was a meeting that directed the remainder of Paul's life – and led him finally to a martyr's death. Paul realized that the event that began in Damascus had to continue and mature. Knowing Christ had to progress. His knowledge of Christ had to change every day, because Christ is not a formula. He is a person. Paul's knowledge of this person had to become deeper and more compelling. Knowing Christ had to become the force that drove his life.

*Jesus, Brother, Friend and Savior, help me to view disappointments
as progress. Help me see with your eyes and love with your heart
because, in your sight and in your love, nothing is lost.*

What It Means to Rise

Father Harry Cronin, C.S.C.

"Depending on faith to know [Christ] and the power of his resurrection and [the] sharing of his sufferings by being conformed to his death, if somehow I may attain the resurrection from the dead." (Phil 3: 9-11)

If you have ever watched someone die, you know that it is a struggle. Very often the ordeal of dying is slow and the person sometimes "hangs on" for days. It is a process that is especially painful for loved ones and survivors. It is a necessary struggle, however, because life is what we want to hold on to – both consciously and unconsciously. At our deepest core, we want to live. It is for this reason that we hold on to life, sometimes with hope, sometimes with desperation.

There is a significant lesson for us here. If it is so difficult to die, there must be a similar process – and perhaps a similar struggle – to rise from the dead. The power that left the body must return. The flesh, blood, soul, and spirit must be reclaimed and reanimated.

Paul knew with absolute certainty that he would conquer death, that he would, like his Savior, rise from the dead. But he knows this will be a process. It begins with the simple actions of knowing Christ, proceeds to touching him and hearing him, and, finally, joining him and being linked to his suffering. Christ came to the moment of resurrection through the painful path of torture, death, and the descent into hell. Paul realizes that he must take a similar path. What was true for Christ must be true for Paul.

Paul invites us to place our faith on one simple fact. Life is not a movement toward death. It is a movement toward rising from the dead. The life we are now living is a movement toward another, greater, more intense and more wonderful life; it is not a movement toward life's cessation.

Paul believed, with all the prophets and patriarchs, that the God he worshiped was truly a living God. The one and only gift of this God is life.

Jesus, giver of life, be close to us, especially when we are nurturing despair or doubt or fear. When we play with these dangerous toys, we are playing with death. Like a good parent, take us away from our dangerous toys.

Pursuer Becomes the Pursued

Father Harry Cronin, C.S.C.

"I continue my pursuit in hope that I may possess it, since
I have indeed been taken possession of by Christ [Jesus]."
(Phil 3: 12)

Christ took possession of Paul when he experienced the frightening and illuminating vision on the road to Damascus. He was thrown violently from his horse and struck blind. He stayed blind for days, haunted by the words of Christ. The words were terrifying. The voice of Christ in the vision had told Paul that his relentless attack on Christianity, his desire to destroy this divisive sect, was in fact a personal attack on Christ himself. Me, Christ says. You are persecuting me. A blind Paul lived for days with that dark accusation: Paul, you are persecuting me.

Paul's sight is restored in more ways than one. He is once again able to see the physical world: the sky, the trees, and the clouds. His real vision, however, extends far beyond that. For the first time in his life, he sees clearly who and what he is – and who and what Christ is. This is the vision that bought him salvation.

The only way Paul can respond to this vision is by preaching rather than persecuting. He preaches Christ Jesus with the same intensity, the same fervor, and the same passion. Paul's mission to preach the Gospel is a path for self-healing. It is a way for him to escape his past – a past which he can no longer endure.

The experience on the road to Damascus was not an end, but a beginning. He sees it in particularly brutal terms: a manhunt. He is pursing Christ, he is chasing after Christ. But in this pursuit, it is Paul himself who is overtaken.

What happens then? What happens when the pursuer becomes the pursued? What happens when Paul is caught and captured by Christ? For Paul, it was a painful, traumatizing process of being broken and renewed, of being literally taken apart and put back together. This gives Paul an important and amazing realization. In Christ we are all made new.

Jesus, you blinded Paul so he could truly see you. Take away from our sight everything that blurs our vision of you. Peter didn't sink in the water as long as he watched you because, in that watching, he found a faith that let him walk on water. Help us to believe – and to keep watching.

A Power beyond Dreaming

Father Harry Cronin, C.S.C.

"Our citizenship is in heaven, and from it we also await a savior, the Lord Jesus Christ. He will change our lowly body to conform with his glorified body by the power that enables him also to bring all things into subjection to himself." (Phil 3: 20-21)

A power will invade us. A power will take us over. It will be the power of Christ alive, the very same power that created and ordered the world. When the universe was created, Jesus Christ was the model, the format, and the template of all creation. In the prologue to his Gospel, Saint John says very bluntly that all things were made in Christ. All things. No exceptions. Saint Paul is telling us that this same unique, immense, and immeasurable power is ours. It belongs to us. The power that transformed chaos into the universe will transform you and me as well. The creative power of God literally floods over us. This flooding, however, is no destructive force. It is a loving embrace. It changes and transforms us. We are embraced and flooded by the creative power of God, even though that embrace sometimes seems to us a kind of darkness or pain. That power possesses us right now. When we die, the possession will be complete. God will be sole owner. Death will have a new and mysterious meaning. It will be for us the quiet opening of a new door into a new life. The body that we have now will be wonderfully changed. We will not exchange it for a later model, as we might buy a new car. The very body we live in now will undergo a change, which has already begun. It will not be destroyed. We will not throw our old bodies away and get new ones. The very body we have now will be renewed – by Christ's power. Our bodies are made by the love of God for the love of God. They are the precious containers of eternity.

Christ says, "I live." You and I say, "I live." These two statements become one. They have the same meaning. I live and Christ lives – by the same life.

Jesus, help us to ready ourselves for the new life that will be ours. Remind us, however you can, that this new life will be the real life. What we experience now is a fading dream. We will wake from this dream and find a reality beyond our dreams, even the wildest and most improbable.

The Duty of Being Glad

Father Harry Cronin, C.S.C.

"Rejoice in the Lord always. I shall say it again: rejoice!
Your kindness should be known to all. The Lord is near."
(Phil 4: 4-5)

It is a very strange command. Be happy. Rejoice. Be glad. It is important to realize that Paul's words are indeed a command. He is not making a suggestion. He is giving the people of Philippi an order, a very serious command. Paul is telling his followers – commanding them – to be happy. He is telling them to be happy in the same way he would tell them to be holy, to be righteous, or to be just. Be happy, he tells them. Be happy always, at all times, in every circumstance.

The underlying truth, of course, is that happiness is a choice. We choose to be happy in the same way that we choose to be sad. We might think that happiness is a disposition that comes about when everything around us is the way we want it to be. When all our circumstances are according to our preferences and desires, when everything is right and pleasing, when we have no displeasure and no pain – then we are happy.

We don't have to live very long, however, to realize that this supposition is a dangerous lie. Happiness is not a result of getting our own way. Happiness does not result when all our circumstances are right or pleasing or well arranged.

Happiness is singing with God. Happiness is harmonizing our voice, our wishes, and our will to God. Happiness is ours when we discover – with joy – that we are singing God's song, when we allow his music to move our hearts, when we give all our strength and all our breath to singing his song. God's song is always a love song. Sometimes it is a sad song, because love is sometimes sad. Sometimes it is a happy song, because love is what brings us peace and joy and serenity. But it is always God's song.

Jesus, you teach us what joy is through the example of your life.
You rejoiced when you cured the sick, you rejoiced when you raised
from the dead, you rejoiced in doing your Father's will. Bring us
into this joy.

The Disease Called Anxiety

Father Harry Cronin, C.S.C.

"Have no anxiety at all, but in everything, by prayer and petition, with thanksgiving, make your requests known to God. Then the peace of God that surpasses all understanding will guard your hearts and minds in Christ Jesus." (Phil 4: 6-7)

None at all. None. Have no worry, no anxiety at all. It's hard to imagine a life free of worry, but that is what Paul wants us to do. Banish worry. Throw worry out the window. Worry and anxiety have no place in our lives. Get rid of it. Paul tells us this bluntly, directly, and with no ambiguity.

Worry is like cancer. It eats away at our serenity, our sense of ourselves, our wholeness. Worry is a violent destroyer. The reason for this is both simple and frightening. Worry is fear – but fear on the offensive. Worry is not passive. Worry attacks and pursues. Worry is the guest we put up for a night who turns out to be a serial killer. Worry is fear that we invite into our lives and nourish.

Worry attacks us where we live. That is why it is so damaging. The root of worry is our awareness – a false awareness as it turns out – that we know how things ought to be. We all have created plans and drawings for the architecture of our lives. Worry is what happens when the plans – for whatever reason – are not working out. When the workers don't show up, when the supplies are delayed, when the foundation caves in, and when a hurricane breaks all the windows – when that happens in the architecture of our lives, that's when we worry.

We are left with one infallible fact. Worry will definitely and without doubt make everything worse. Worry is a bad response to disaster because worry saps our strength and assures us that we will deal with the disaster badly. Worry assures us that we will make the wrong decisions or take the wrong course.

Don't worry about money, don't worry about family, and don't worry about your job. Don't worry about anything. Don't worry at all.

Jesus, give us whatever we need to eliminate fear and worry and doubt. They work against your grace and they set up barriers to your gift of life. Help us be rid of them and help us replace them with wonderful hope.

The Obligation of Beauty

Father Harry Cronin, C.S.C.

"Whatever is true, whatever is honorable, whatever is just, whatever is pure, whatever is lovely, whatever is gracious, if there is any excellence and if there is anything worthy of praise, think about these things." (Phil 4: 8)

Fill your lives with what is true, what is good, and what is beautiful. But be wary. These are not qualities that float around in the air like clouds or disembodied spirits. We embrace what is true and good and beautiful through human contact. Beauty is not in the eye of the beholder, as some think. Beauty is the mirror of God which is planted in all God creates, especially human creation. We recognize and experience the beauty that is truly there. People are not beautiful because we recognize their beauty. They are beautiful in themselves, in the simple fact of their creation by God.

We can cut ourselves off from that beauty. That is the modern tragedy. Here's an example.

They were both in their thirties. He was dressed in impeccable Brooks Brothers. She was dressed in the latest from Nordstrom's. They were both sitting at a table across from each other and both of them were on their cell phones. The waiter comes up to take their order and they stare at him blankly. He stands there. They both fumble with the menus, not really looking at them. They both point to something on the menu, nod blankly to the waiter, never letting go of their cell phones. The waiter writes down what he thinks they ordered and leaves disgusted. The conversations continue. They are sitting across the table from each other. They are having lunch together. But not really. In the midst of what seemed to be human company, neither of them has had any human contact. They were not "together" in any sense. It all seemed so natural. It seemed like the way things should be done. Our cyber-obsessed world does everything to defeat human contact. As long as we lack that contact, there is no way we can see beauty and – tragically – no way we can recognize it.

Jesus, please open our eyes. Allow us to experience the beauty that unites our world with your creative power.

Always One with Us

Father Harry Cronin, C.S.C.

*"Keep on doing what you have learned and received and heard
and seen in me. Then the God of peace will be with you."*
(Phil 4: 9)

On one level, it certainly seems arrogant. Paul puts himself forward with a boldness that, on one level, is difficult for us to comprehend. He sets himself up as a model for everyone else to follow and an example for everyone else to imitate. Make me your model. Make what I have said your rule. Do what I do. Accept with absolute truth all that I have told you.

It would be arrogant, were it not for the fact that Paul was absolutely convinced of a broader, more comprehensive, and more amazing truth. When he tells the Philippians to make him their model, he is proclaiming his own faith in the truth that Christ has become one with him and he has become one with Christ. Christ lives in Paul. Paul lives in Christ. The same Jesus Christ, the Lord, the Messiah, the Son of God – that Christ lives in Paul of Tarsus. For this reason, it is perfectly reasonable and right for Paul to tell the Philippians that if they follow him – Paul – they will follow Christ.

It's not arrogance on the part of Paul. It is supreme generosity on the part of Christ. The grace that comes from Jesus is not merely supernatural first aid, or psychological advice, or spiritual comfort. What comes to us from Christ is Christ himself. He gives us his presence. He is with us. Sometimes this presence is silent, sometimes it is confusing. The presence of Christ never reduces the human condition or banishes human pain. The presence is there along with the pain. To believe in Jesus Christ is to believe, as Paul did, that Jesus Christ is always here. Right here. Always with us, always central, and the most vital reality in our lives.

It is a beautiful truth. There is a mysterious and mystical identity between Christ and his followers. Let us live there.

Jesus, you are close to us and one with us in a way we can't comprehend. We can't be one with any other human being in the same way we are one with you. Help us to walk in this union, to live in this oneness, and to realize every day that it is only because of your love.

How We Are Strong

Father Harry Cronin, C.S.C.

*"I have the strength for everything through him
who empowers me."* (Phil 4: 13)

As human beings, we feel strength from within. We feel strong and energetic and this gives us the assurance we need to exercise our strength outside ourselves. We jog or go to the gym because we feel we have the strength to do it. Without that feeling, we stay home and watch television.

Paul tells us about a strength that comes from the outside. This strength is hard for us to imagine. It is contrary to our ordinary experience of strength. This is a strength that comes from the outside, a strength that is given to us, that we realize suddenly that we have. It is important for us to have this new awareness because it is important that we realize that it is not our strength. It doesn't come from within. It is not ours. It is the strength of Christ that is given to us. The strength of Christ comes from the outside because it is not our strength and we must have a deep and thankful realization of this fact.

A famous Academy award-winning actress, Mercedes McCambridge, once said that at certain moments when she was performing and when she was truly inspired, she was able to do what she was not able to do. She was able to act above and beyond what she knew her abilities were.

It is the same with the strength that comes from Christ. We are able to do what we are not able to do.

The strength of Christ is like that. It is not limited by our abilities, by our imagination, or even by our desires. It is strength without limits, a power without boundaries.

Martyrs give up their lives for God. That is the strength of Christ. Christ wants us to give our lives as well. In order to be truly strong.

Jesus, you are our strength. It is in you that we are able to do our work. It is through you that our work will become works of wonder.

Rich in Christ

Father Harry Cronin, C.S.C.

"My God will fully supply whatever you need, in accord with his glorious riches in Christ Jesus. To our God and Father, glory forever and ever. Amen." (Phil 4: 19-20)

Wait a minute. The riches of Christ. What riches did Christ have? Wasn't he supposed to be a poor man, a day laborer? Didn't he once tell his perspective followers that he didn't even have a place to sleep? Didn't he tell his followers at another time that he was worse off than wild animals? He didn't even have what the little foxes had. They had lairs. And he didn't have what the birds had – they had nests. So what is this about the "riches" of Christ?

Jesus once said, with a fiercely radical boldness, that a camel could pass through the eye of a needle easier than a rich man could enter heaven. Jesus was not only a man without riches, he was a man who held riches in contempt. When he died, he had only the clothes on his back, and even they were taken away. He died naked and poor, with no hope.

Or so it seemed.

When we allow ourselves to be poor as Jesus was poor, there will be a change in our hearts. For the first time in our lives, we will be truly able to embrace. When we embrace someone, when we throw our arms around them, when we hug them closely and joyfully – we have to be free. Embracing is one thing we can't do half-heartedly. Never embrace someone unless you're sure you want to embrace them. Half-hearted embraces don't work.

It is the same when we embrace God.

To embrace God and to be embraced by God, we have to be free. This freedom is precisely the riches of Christ that Paul describes. The riches of the world deprive us of freedom. The riches of the world take away our freedom.

The riches of Christ free us from the riches of the world. Wealthy in Christ, we can be truly free.

Jesus, give us the courage to be rich in you and you alone. Your life is our wealth, your body and blood in the Eucharist is our fortune. Give us rest and peace in your richness.

The Great Grace of Hope

Father Harry Cronin, C.S.C.

"We have heard of your faith in Christ Jesus and the love that you have for all the holy ones because of the hope reserved for you in heaven. Of this you have already heard through the word of truth, the gospel, that has come to you." (Col 1: 4-5)

The first victim of any disaster is hope – whether that disaster is natural or man-made. Whenever things go monstrously wrong, the first casualty is always hope. It is fragile, like rare cut glass. We can lose it so easily. Saint Paul tells us that, for those who follow Christ, there is someone who protects and saves our hope: the Father of Jesus. Saint Paul tells us that our hope is safe with God. It is well beyond any damage that can be afflicted by human disaster or natural cataclysm. God truly holds our hope and guards it.

The Gospel records only three times when Jesus raised from the dead. Each time he did so, he used words. Simple words. He only spoke. He called – probably shouted – at Lazarus to come out of the grave. He told the daughter of Jairus just to "get up." And he told the son of the widow of Naim to "rise." Jesus always used words when he spoke to the dead. He called the dead back to life with the sound of his own human voice. When Paul says that we have heard this hope, he is making an important statement. Hope is always something we hear. It becomes a cycle. When we hear it, we experience it, and when we experience it, we speak it. We cannot hope because of what we think or what we read. We hope because of what is said to us – by someone.

Of course, it makes a great difference who it is who speaks hope to us. It has to be someone who has hope, someone who has found hope in his life. We must hear hope from one of those rare persons who have looked unflinchingly at the despair and destruction of the world and said: that is not all there is. There is something beyond, and that "something" is hope.

So let us speak hope, with strong words.

Jesus, our hope, give us what we need to face failure, disgrace, disappointment, and despair. Give us the grace of hope, which cleanses our hearts from fear and anger, and allows us to greet you with arms and hearts truly open.

Wisdom and Knowing

Father Harry Cronin, C.S.C.

"We do not cease praying for you and asking that you may be filled with the knowledge of [God's] will through all spiritual wisdom and understanding to live in a manner worthy of the Lord, so as to be fully pleasing, in every good work bearing fruit and growing in the knowledge of God." (Col 1: 9-10)

The human mind is a wonder. What it cannot comprehend is as important as what it can. Saint Paul reflects on two of the most important gifts of the mind: wisdom and knowledge. They are not the same. Wisdom is constantly moving, constantly engaged in a journey that takes our minds beyond mere knowing. Wisdom knows about knowing. Wisdom is knowledge about knowledge. To be wise is to understand what knowledge is, to understand the true nature of knowledge; and, most importantly, to understand the very real – and sometimes, very tragic – limitations of knowledge. Wisdom sees where knowledge comes from and where knowledge is going. Knowledge is "knowing about." Wisdom is simply "knowing." Wisdom carries with it everything that knowledge produces and everything knowledge implies. Wisdom, however, goes beyond knowledge. Knowledge is the promise of wisdom. Wisdom is knowledge made whole.

Wisdom tells us what we cannot know. Wisdom defines the limits of knowledge. Wisdom, however, always points us to a place and a purpose beyond knowledge. Wisdom takes us where knowledge can't go: to the thoughts of God and the mind of God. The summit of knowledge is to know God's will. That is the only knowledge we really need. The only knowing that is ultimately worthwhile is to know what God wants in our lives. What God always wants for us is love and the fruits of love. This summit of knowledge is the doorway to wisdom. Knowledge permits us to approach the will of God. Wisdom allows us to know God, as God truly is, the "self" of God, the heart of God, the mind of God. We live in a world where knowledge is valued and wisdom is scorned. In our world, knowledge has an ally, a terrifying ally. In our world, knowledge is power. We are obsessed with power. Followers of Jesus must be different. We must be obsessed with wisdom.

Jesus Christ, beginner and origin of wisdom, cleanse our knowing from what is dangerous. Make our knowing an instrument that searches for your will and our wisdom the awareness of your act of love in our lives.

Living in the Light

Father Lawrence Boadt, C.S.P.

"Strengthened with every power, in accord with his glorious might, for all endurance and patience, with joy giving thanks to the Father, who has made you fit to share in the inheritance of the holy ones in light." (Col 1: 11-12)

The Letter to the Colossians is Paul's manifesto about how to "live in Christ." It constantly stresses the difference between living in darkness and the wonder of living in the light. It is no accident that Paul would choose this contrast between darkness and light for describing the possibilities of a new life as a Christian when he writes to his converts in western Turkey. First of all, Paul's own personal experience, the most intense of his life, centered on being overcome by an overwhelming blast of light as he was approaching Damascus (Acts 9: 3; 22: 6). In Acts (26: 13), Paul says it was brighter than the sun! Although blinded, he had begun already to see differently. Before, he had been a zealous, dedicated, and fearless defender of Jewish orthodoxy as he understood it against these new Christian heretics, but now he was being summoned by Jesus himself to become one of them. Suddenly he realized that he had been living in darkness and ignorance of God's work around him, and a new understanding and a new light by which to live were opening up for him. He had heard the testimony of Stephen before the Sanhedrin explaining God's new salvation in Jesus, and then given approval, out of hatred, to his martyrdom. How blind he had been. From this moment forward, Paul never turned back, but always pressed forward in this new light he had received. Secondly, he knew the people of the region of Colossae gave great reverence to the temple of Apollo in the neighboring town of Hierapolis, where a sulfurous fissure in the earth was honored as the mouth of Hades, the land of darkness and evil spirits. Paul wanted the Colossians to know they need never fear those spirits of darkness because they had the light of life in Christ. It is a lesson vital for us also today.

O God, Creator of light on the first day of your creation, enlighten our minds to hear the message of love and faithfulness you have revealed through your prophets and apostles, and rid us of the fear that paralyzes our trust in you.

Living in the Kingdom of God

Father Lawrence Boadt, C.S.P.

"[God the Father] delivered us from the power of darkness and transferred us to the kingdom of his beloved Son, in whom we have redemption, the forgiveness of sins." (Col 1: 13-14)

Paul prepares for his great hymn of praise to Christ, the "first-born" of all beings (Col 1: 15-20), by offering an extended prayer (Col 1: 9-14) that the Colossians may be filled with the "knowledge" of God's will, and with "wisdom" and "understanding." This "knowledge" of God's true intentions for humankind and of the proper way to live a life worthy of their faith in Christ is the chief purpose of Paul's letter. He is aware of their fascination with the doctrines of the two powers for good and evil in the spirit world, and wishes to steer them away from such false teachings of the Gnostic tradition. Paul does not actually tell us much about these false teachers, but they clearly proposed a way of salvation different from Paul's Gospel of complete redemption in and through Christ alone. Before he reaffirms in his great hymn the primacy of Christ above all things, he pointedly repeats his doctrine of salvation: Through the gift of faith and their baptism into Christ, God has taken them out of any loyalty to the forces of darkness and the need to serve evil spirits, and brought them into the kingdom of God's Son. This is Paul's fundamental proclamation to all his churches. It is the language of conversion from darkness to light (see also 1 Thes 5: 4-5; Eph 5: 8). Once in Christ, we have redemption (Rom 3: 24-26; 5: 9; 1 Pt 1: 18-19) and forgiveness of sins (Mt 26: 28; Heb 9: 22). It is God the Father who has rescued us from our enemy and entrusted us to the care of his risen Son until the end comes, and Christ hands all back to his Father (explicitly explained by Paul in 1 Cor 15: 24-28). The lesson Paul draws is for all of us to trust completely in Christ, to know his Presence and his Spirit in our midst, and to live in imitation of him in all we do.

O God of all truth, give us the knowledge and wisdom to find your Presence everywhere in our world, and the courage to live as disciples of Jesus, your Son, who teaches us how to know you in knowing him.

Living in the Image of God

Father Lawrence Boadt, C.S.P.

"[God's beloved Son] is the image of the invisible God, the firstborn of all creation." (Col 1: 15)

Scholars tell us that the hymn to Christ in Colossians (1: 15-20) probably was already sung by the early Christians before Paul borrowed it to make his own point in this letter. It is amazing to realize that such profound proclamations of faith were well-established as regular hymns in the weekly liturgy within twenty years of the time Jesus died and rose. When Paul declares that Jesus is the image of the invisible God, the firstborn of all creation, he is not making a well-intentioned generality like we might when we say that all good people are God's children. This is a powerful claim that God has chosen to make himself available and knowable to us through another human being like ourselves. If we think for a moment that God in his very being is infinite and eternal, without material body or limitations of any kind, we should naturally ask, "How could we weak creatures of this world ever know him intimately or personally?" Are we not for ever doomed to look longingly to the greatness and perfection of a creator who is not of our nature, and whom we can never understand? This is the perpetual human dilemma posed by the Book of Job in the Bible itself. The only hope would be if God himself approached us and offered to be known. The Old Testament is the story of God's revealing his will and his love in action toward Israel and all peoples of the earth, but God still remained at an awesome distance. Paul and the Christian Gospel proclaimed that now God had indeed planned a way that we would be certain of his loving commitment and engagement with humanity – by sending his own divine Son and self to dwell with us in our human estate. Do we want to know God as deeply as possible as a friend and partner as well as master? Then we must come to know Jesus Christ as our Lord and friend and partner.

Father, you have sent your Son into our world that we might come to know our heavenly destiny of eternal life with you more fully in his life as one with us in our human struggles and in his sharing with us the power of his resurrection. Help us to know him more deeply each day.

Christ, the Master Plan of Creation

Father Lawrence Boadt, C.S.P.

"In [God's beloved Son] were created all things in heaven and on earth,/ the visible and the invisible,/ whether thrones or dominions or principalities or powers;/ all things were created through him and for him." (Col 1: 16)

P aul's vision of the world and its operations is rooted in the conviction that God directed all things and brought them into being out of his divine goodness and love. God had a master plan in which all things would work together for the good as he intended them. In Romans (8: 28), for example, he passionately asserts that, "We know that all things work for the good for those who love God, who are called according to his purpose." Chapter 1 of Colossians is the description of this "master plan." Jesus is the model for this plan. Already in verse 15, he has insisted that Jesus is the very image of the invisible God. We come to know and "see" God in the life of Jesus, in both his earthly life and his risen empowerment as Lord at the right hand of the Father. In Paul's thought, this unity and harmony of creation can be discovered in the total obedience and faithfulness of Jesus for us, but is threatened by the pagan religious views that the Colossians held from before their conversion to Christianity. In their thinking, the world was torn in conflict between the forces of evil spirits and good spirits. Many of the evil spirits were believed to come from the underworld in order to assault humans and lead them into sin. Paul makes it clear that all spiritual beings are under God's control. The principalities, thrones, dominions, and powers represent a sample of such angelic beings, but Paul declares that all are obedient to God's will. All beings, worldly and spiritual alike, were shaped into existence because God intended their purpose in light of Christ's saving work of healing the world and bringing it into one, as Paul will say in verses 19 to 20. Paul is so convinced of this centrality of Jesus to God's plan for the world that he says in verse 16 that everything was created "in" and "through" and "for" Christ.

Lord God, you have made the world good, so the power of evil may never have control over those who recognize your Presence and goodness in its creation; give us a greater love of your Son, Jesus, who reflects that goodness in the possibilities of our human life.

In the Beginning Is the End

Father Lawrence Boadt, C.S.P.

*"[God's beloved Son] is before all things,/ and in him
all things hold together." (Col 1: 17)*

Genesis, chapter 1, sets the theme of all of Scripture when it describes God's act of creation as (1) completely planned out and unfolding in perfect order day by day; (2) completely good and according to God's love as he beholds it come into being; (3) completely capped in its harmony by the creation of human beings in the very image of God; and (4) leading to the total praise of God as God and humans contemplate its wonder. Indeed, the ancient Israelite thought was that humans, who have been given a share in God's creative power and governance over the universe, form the critical center point where the unity and harmony of this world with God stand or fall. Genesis tells us as early as chapter 3 that when humans sin, not just they but all of creation is alienated from God. The rest of the Old Testament (forty-eight more chapters of Genesis and forty-five more books) is the story of how God brings healing to the world and leads it back toward union with himself. Paul understands that this healing has reached its fulfillment in the atoning death of Jesus for all sinners, so that both humans and their world will be brought back together as one to God through the risen Christ. Paul borrows a conviction of the Wisdom Books of the Old Testament that Wisdom, understood as an actual spiritual being, was God's first-born, and acted as God's architect and master planner for all that was made (Prv 8: 22). Paul sees this Wisdom passage as a prophetic revelation of the pre-existent Christ, who was with the Father from the beginning, and served as the model for what humanity should be and become and how it should view all of creation. Paul thus reinforces his point that we must live in Christ, act according to Christ, and see all things in Christ. We thus share in his reconciliation of the world to God.

O Lord of the Old Testament, you revealed your constant desire to heal this broken world and reconcile us to yourself in age after age until you gave us complete forgiveness in the person of your Son Jesus. Help us to learn his lessons of forgiveness toward others in all our relationships.

The Many Heads of Christ

Father Lawrence Boadt, C.S.P.

"[God's beloved Son] is the head of the body, the church./
He is the beginning, the firstborn from the dead,/ that in all
things he himself might be preeminent." (Col 1: 18)

P aul has clearly affirmed in the previous verses that Christ is not just first in honor or power, but in the very order of existence itself. Perhaps he was familiar with the thinking of the great Jewish teacher, Philo of Alexandria, who was still alive when Jesus was born, and who related the great truths of Jewish faith to the philosophy of the Greek world. Paul would have found the prophetic key from the Scriptures in Proverbs (8: 22), but would easily relate it, as Philo had done, to the Greek idea of the eternal *logos*, or principle of existence. Christ can never be on the same level as other humans, but for Paul, Jesus was not only the divine pre-existent one, he was also the "head of the body, the church." He is the first in authority, the sole leader of the Church, and Paul teaches that we must have absolute loyalty and obedience to our head. Thus he is continuing his argument to the Colossians that they must avoid any loyalty to such other powers as thrones or dominions, etc. Paul never forgets the central saving mystery of the cross and resurrection in his explanation, and adds that his preeminence is not only for the living members of the Church, but encompasses those who have died as well, so that he is now in power as chief over all creation. Because Paul also calls the Church the "Body of Christ," there is a second sense to being the "head," beyond the role of authority. He is the source of life and thinking for the Church just as the head rules the rest of the physical body. He is also the "beginning" because by his death and resurrection, a new creation has begun, a new order of universal salvation for us all. Saint Paul again confirms that we need look no further than Christ for guidance and leadership in our lives.

God our Father, you have given us Christ your Son to be the source of our life as a community of disciples; give us the help we need to remain faithful to him and to walk always in his ways so that we may truly be his Body, the Church.

Hail the Conqueror of Death!

Father Lawrence Boadt, C.S.P.

"In [God's beloved Son] all the fullness was pleased to dwell,/ and through him to reconcile all things for him,/ making peace by the blood of his cross." (Col 1: 19-20)

P aul will say later in this same letter, "for in him dwells the whole fullness of the deity bodily." This can help explain his use of the term "fullness" in this verse: God's exercise of power and divine purpose to heal humankind is to be found only in Christ. Paul may be reflecting on the great vision of Isaiah's call as a prophet, which opens with Isaiah standing in the temple and saying, "All the earth is filled with his glory!" (Is 6: 3). The risen Christ is understood by Paul to be the fullness of God's glory revealed to the world. More pointedly, it is only through the mystery of his cross, with all of its horrible aspects of evil, that God has brought the universe in its entirety into wholeness again. Paradoxically, Christ's apparent defeat in death was the occasion in God's plan to bring victory over the power of evil. Jesus took on the very sign of evil's victory over human life, death itself, and defeated it when God raised him alive from its grip. "Peace" (in Hebrew, *shalom*) has the sense of more than just freedom from enemy attack; it includes the harmony and right relationship among all things. True peace will come only when we accept the death of Jesus as an act of love that embraced the suffering of the whole world and gave it meaning by his identification with all sufferers. Paul adds that this healing includes even the heavenly beings. No doubt he is thinking once again of those spirits to whom the Colossians are so attracted. Paul calls on all of his hearers to live the words of Jesus reported in the Gospel that "whoever wishes to come after me must deny himself, take up his cross, and follow me. For whoever wishes to save his life will lose it, but whoever loses his life for my sake and that of the gospel, will save it" (Mk 8: 34-35).

Lord God of all creation, you have brought the gift of peace to our world by offering us the vision of a restored relationship of mutual love with yourself given to us by the complete self-gift of your Son's death for all; grant that we may learn to sacrifice ourselves out of love for the good of others.

Walking the Walk in Christ

Father Lawrence Boadt, C.S.P.

"You who once were alienated and hostile in mind because of evil deeds [God's beloved Son] has now reconciled in his fleshly body through his death, to present you holy, without blemish, and irreproachable before him, provided that you persevere in the faith." (Col 1: 21-23)

Paul has completed his great hymn to Christ as God's preeminent presence and agent in the divine plan of salvation for all ages: for the past time of the Old Testament revelation, during the lifetime of Jesus on earth, and in the present age of the Church. He now turns to outlining the main argument for his letter. In verses 21 to 23, he directly addresses the Colossians and reminds them first that they were once alienated from God, but, second, now they have been transformed by their faith, and, third, that they must persevere in this new way of life. He also sets forth the three main points he will develop in the rest of the letter: (1) explaining how the saving work of Christ has made them holy and able to live according to Christ; (2) the need for them to be faithful to the Gospel they have heard; and (3) the need to be loyal to Paul who proclaimed that Gospel to them, and not to be led astray by other teachers. In true Greek rhetorical style, he will develop each of these points in the reverse order: loyalty to him (1: 24–2: 3); fidelity to the true Gospel (2: 5-23); and life in Christ (3: 1–4: 6). So this short passage contains the whole purpose of Paul for writing to the Colossians. In verse 21, it is God who reconciles us by the "fleshly body" of Jesus, that is, by his human suffering. Since through his human existence Christ has saved us, so we receive that salvation in our bodily living, and so it must take effect in the way we live and what we do. Paul suggests that Christ continues to work in us to make this holiness happen if we will persevere in our faith. The meaning clearly is that faith is not just belief but a full reliance on Christ's strength to enable us to live according to his commands.

Father, you watch over us each day in your loving providence and send us the grace we need to remain faithful to your commandments. Give us today the knowledge and guidance of your Son, Jesus, that we might walk always according to his teaching and example.

Bonding in Suffering

Father Lawrence Boadt, C.S.P.

*"Now I rejoice in my sufferings for your sake, and in my flesh
I am filling up what is lacking in the afflictions of Christ
on behalf of his body, which is the church." (Col 1: 24)*

In verses 24 to 25, Paul begins the defense of his ministry as the apostle charged with proclaiming the Gospel to the Colossians. Because he fears that they have been turning away from what he had taught them to follow the Gnostic teachings of some other "false apostles," Paul wants them to understand he is not just another teacher, but has been commissioned by God to be their apostle and has suffered in obedience to God's command in order to bring them that Gospel. The claim that he is completing what is lacking in the sufferings of Christ on behalf of the Church has led to many questions as to what Paul really meant. He has just told us that, without any exception, Christ has completed the fullness of God's plan by his death (1: 19-20). So how can Paul add to this? The answer lies in Paul's union with Christ. He is the apostle, the "one sent" as the voice and word of the sender, and so he is one in mind and purpose with Christ and shares in this life in the proclamation of the mystery of the cross of Jesus, while he lives out that Gospel until Christ will come again to bring to completion the message of the cross at the end of time. This is reinforced by the great suffering Paul actually experienced in the persecution and violence against him by Jewish opponents and in the terrible hardships of constant traveling in the service of the Gospel. Paul realizes the truth of Jesus' warning that before the end, "They will hand you over to the courts. You will be beaten in synagogues. You will be arraigned before governors and kings because of me" (Mk 13: 9). Paul helps us see that the worst suffering he must endure is the knowledge that his proclamation of the Gospel that brings life to so many also stirs up violent hatred in others. Can we also embrace it?

Father of our Lord Jesus Christ, unite our hearts and spirits to him in accepting the sufferings of this life and remaining steadfast in times of trial or temptation so that we might never be separated from him by fear or cowardice before evil.

God's Hidden Strategy

Father Lawrence Boadt, C.S.P.

"The mystery hidden from ages [...] has been manifested to his holy ones, to whom God chose to make known the riches of the glory of this mystery among the Gentiles; it is Christ in you, the hope for glory." (Col 1: 26-27)

Paul calls the contents of the Gospel that he has brought to the Colossians the "mystery" of God. This choice of expression suggests that God's intentions were hidden from our understanding beforehand. In Ephesians (1: 9-10), he explains more fully that "[God] has made known to us the mystery of his will in accord with his favor that he set forth in [Christ] as a plan for the fullness of times, to sum up all things in Christ, in heaven and on earth." Paul believes that the mystery was God's "plan" built into creation from the beginning. Just as God created the beauty and unity of all things in the image of his Son, he also planned for their eventual reconciliation and healing through the Son. The role of Christ as the pre-existent model of humanity's relationship with God and of his future role as its restorer was not made known to the inspired writers and prophets of the Old Testament, but they were given preliminary insights in the great salvation events in Israel's history. But that knowledge of God as Savior was limited to the Jewish people who held to God's covenant. Because Paul sees the death and resurrection of Jesus as a revolutionary act of salvation that provides a new way of salvation for the Gentiles, a way never allowed by the Old Testament, it is a mystery made known only by faith in Jesus Christ. Paul often attributes this faith to the work of the Holy Spirit. In Ephesians (1: 11-14), for instance, he speaks in the same manner as here but adds that it is known by the gift and seal of the Holy Spirit. But here, he attributes the knowledge of the mystery to the action of Christ himself in their midst. Life in Christ is life in the Spirit – the two work together in us as one, creating union "with" Christ and power to live "in" Christ.

Almighty God, you guide all things that you have created according to your will and divine purpose, and place in us the grace to recognize your hand in all things. Help us through your Holy Spirit to deepen our awareness of the mystery of your plan of salvation in Jesus Christ, your Son.

A Vision for Everyone

Father Lawrence Boadt, C.S.P.

"It is [Christ] whom we proclaim, admonishing everyone and teaching everyone with all wisdom, that we may present everyone perfect in Christ." (Col 1: 28)

When Paul says that he "proclaims" Christ, it is the very term used throughout the Acts of the Apostles for the preaching of the whole Gospel (see Acts 17: 3, 23, for example). His proclamation then is not just that Jesus is Messiah and Savior, but includes his instructions about how they must live according to the Gospel. Teaching and admonishing cover both the saving truths they must believe as well as the correct behavior they must adopt. Strikingly in this short sentence, Paul uses the word *pas* in Greek, meaning "all," four times to emphasize the universality of God's mysterious plan. It was not reserved for the Jews only, or for Gnostic groups who had special knowledge of secret ways to obtain life after death. Paul presents the message of the Gospel in such a way that anyone can receive it and be welcomed to accept its truth and commit themselves to live its commands. The Christian message summons people wherever it finds them. This is in sharp contrast to the many pagan "mystery religions" which flourished in the Roman Empire, such as the cults of Demeter, Isis, Mithras, or Cybele. They promised a way to escape bodily limits, especially death, by following a secret body of knowledge that would free a person's spirit from the world of flesh. Paul never permits a division between body and spirit in God's salvation – both are transformed and freed by the life, death, and resurrection of Jesus. When Paul says that he hopes to present all of them "perfect in Christ," he means in both our body and soul, just as Christ the risen Lord is perfect in both. We are encouraged fully to unite our spirits with Christ, to discipline our bodily behavior according to his teachings, and to accept suffering willingly in communion with his suffering. This was how Paul himself lived, and he asks that we imitate him (1 Thes 1: 6; 1 Cor 4: 16).

Father, you have sent your Son to dwell as one with us that we might see and love in him what we have heard and known of you. Help us to imitate his filial love and thus come to know you more deeply.

A Labor of Love

Father Lawrence Boadt, C.S.P.

"I labor and struggle, in accord with the exercise of [Christ's] power working within me." (Col 1: 29)

Paul frequently notes his great labors for the sake of the communities to whom he preaches (see 1 Thes 5: 12; 1 Cor 16: 16; Rom 16: 6). His Second Letter to the Corinthians is almost entirely a lengthy defense of the difficulties under which he had to work to bring the Gospel to so many places. He opens with a beautiful thought on this subject: "For as Christ's sufferings overflow to us, so through Christ does our encouragement also overflow. If we are afflicted, it is for your encouragement and salvation; if we are encouraged, it is also for your encouragement, which enables you to endure the same sufferings that we suffer" (2 Cor 1: 5-6). Paul does not depend on his abilities or inner strength but on the power of Christ working through him. He pleads with the Corinthians that, "Whoever is confident of belonging to Christ should consider that as he belongs to Christ, so do we." (2 Cor 10: 7). And in Galatians (2: 20) he exclaims, "I, live no longer I, but Christ lives in me." Here in Colossians (1: 28-29), Paul does not mention the necessity for *faith* on the part of the hearers, but it is presupposed as the way by which one comes to accept the Gospel. Paul assumes that God provides such an offer of faith to all who hear his preaching because the power of Christ is at work in him. Because it is the divine grace of God, it has no limits and can reach the hearts of even the most difficult people anywhere. And yet Paul knows that many will not be converted by his preaching. As he says about his fellow Jews, "a hardening has come upon Israel in part, until the full number of the Gentiles comes in, and thus all Israel will be saved" (Rom 11: 25-26). Sharing Paul's vision, we need to pray for all peoples to hear the Gospel and for understanding between Christians and Jews.

God, who has given your covenant to your beloved people Israel as an enduring pledge of your love and extended it to all nations through the work of your Son Jesus, give us the faith and the courage to welcome all people in your love and be reconciled together through repentance of our sins against them.

Check Your Roots

Sister Genevieve Glen, O.S.B.

"As you received Christ Jesus the Lord, walk in him, rooted in him and built upon him and established in the faith as you were taught, abounding in thanksgiving." (Col 2: 6-7)

Born with a notable lack of green thumbs, I looked at my potted ivy in despair. It drooped like a tired old woman; its leaves were fading from green to yellow; dead leaves littered the windowsill around it. "But I *watered* it!" I protested to my mother. She produced new potting soil, plant food, and watering instructions. Like a miracle, the plant revived. "If you want it to grow," she told me, "you have to plant it in good soil. Then you have to feed and water the roots." In this passage, Saint Paul suggests we check our roots. At baptism, we not only "received Christ Jesus the Lord," we were securely rooted in him, but, unlike the ivy, we sometimes pull up spiritual stakes and put down roots in other ground. Jesus provided us with a sound test: "By their fruits you will know them" (Mt 7: 16). A conscientious gardener checks often. If our daily examination of conscience shows that our lives are bearing the fruits of the Gospel, especially increasingly selfless love of God and neighbor, then we know that we are well rooted in that deep place where the grace of God and our response in faith are firmly intertwined in Christ. If we see other fruits appearing, then we know the time has come for a little pruning and perhaps a better sort of food. What we take in from what we read, watch, listen to, or mull over in our minds determines the quality of the fruit we bear. Poor nutrition produces fruit that might look appealing but will feed no one. Saint Paul reminds us that the best nutrition comes from the faith we were taught and continue to deepen through prayer, reading, study, the company of other believers, and the sacraments, especially the Eucharist. A tree well rooted and well fed in Christ has every reason to produce lasting fruit, including an abundant crop of thanksgiving!

O God from whom all life comes, you have rooted me in Christ and built my life upon him. Grant that I may grow daily in the faith with which you nourish me, so that, strengthened, I may walk in Christ. For this and all your gifts, I give you thanks and praise!

Empty Space for God

Sister Genevieve Glen, O.S.B.

"For in [Christ] dwells the whole fullness of the deity bodily, and you share in this fullness in him, who is the head of every principality and power." (Col 2: 9-10)

To be filled, something must first be empty, as anyone knows who has started to fill a water glass at table, gotten distracted by conversation, and gone on "filling" the glass when there was no empty space left for the water. Saint Paul writes elsewhere about Christ's self-emptying. What he calls to our attention here is the need for our own. We cannot share in the fullness of the deity that fills us as Christ's Body unless we make room by emptying ourselves of anything that offers no space for God. Saint Paul's words call to mind the holy of holies, the room at the heart of the Jerusalem temple kept all but empty to receive God. We sometimes build other rooms in our inmost self and furnish them for other gods. The prophet Ezekiel described an "idol room" in the much-desecrated Jerusalem temple of his day. Do we have an idol room, where we keep all the false gods whom we honor with our obedience and our sacrifices? Their name is legion: public opinion, unnecessary financial gain, self-satisfaction, pleasure, comforts of all sorts. They are all demanding of our time, our attention, our energy. We recognize them best when they decree that we have no time to pray, no time for Mass, no time to do a kindness, no time to listen to our children's stories or our aging parents' laments, because we must be at the beck and call of a TV program, an exercise class, a golf game, overtime work to pay for things we don't need... you know them. There is room for only one God in the inner temple of the Christian self – the one "who is the head of every principality and power." With his help, let us drive out that other crowd, with all its demands, so that our inner emptiness may be filled not with their clutter but with the fullness of God in which we share through Christ.

O God, empty my heart of everything that crowds you out of my awareness and out of my desires. Fill my emptiness with the fullness of your presence in and through Jesus Christ, so that he may rule my mind and heart with your love.

Buried Alive!

Sister Genevieve Glen, O.S.B.

"You were buried with [Christ] in baptism, in which you were also raised with him through faith in the power of God, who raised him from the dead." (Col 2: 12)

Every news announcement of another mining accident evokes a certain terror. What must it feel like to be buried alive, not knowing if rescue will arrive in time? We seem to unite in breathless prayer for the courageous rescue workers digging through the rubble in search of survivors. And you can almost hear the universal cheer when a gritty, exhausted team of rescuers brings a living person to the surface. Baptism, by comparison, seems a ludicrously tame sort of ritual, celebrated with neither danger nor suspense to chill the onlookers. Yet, as Saint Paul tells us, we were indeed buried alive in baptism. Baptism by immersion highlights that truth vividly, but whether we were baptized by immersion or sprinkling, as adults or infants, all of us died and were buried in the baptismal waters. We were not buried alone: we were buried with Christ, who tasted to the full the death we so fear. And God came to our rescue. By the gift of faith – either our own, if we were adults, or the faith of the Church if we were infants – we were able to grasp the hand of God's power and be raised up with Christ (Catechism of the Catholic Church 1282). When someone is rescued after being buried alive, the person often says that the experience is like returning from the dead, with a chance to start life over with new purpose and new perspective. By virtue of our baptism, this same gift has been given to us. Every morning, we awaken to the opportunity to live our new life in Christ, with its new purpose and new perspective. To discover the possibilities it opens to you daily, read the Scriptures. You might choose one of the readings from today's Mass, for example, and ask the Holy Spirit to show you what God is offering you and asking of you now. You may be surprised at what you discover.

O God of the living, you carried me from the death of sin to new life in Christ through the waters of baptism. Renew in me today the life you have given me to lead. Open my eyes to see your will for me, and grant me the courage, wisdom, and love to live it faithfully in Christ.

A Fresh Page

Sister Genevieve Glen, O.S.B.

*"Even when you were dead [in] transgressions [... Christ]
brought you to life along with him, having forgiven us all our
transgressions; obliterating the bond against us [...] nailing it
to the cross." (Col 2: 13-14)*

The advent of the personal computer has saved many trees
from writers who constantly crumple up a draft gone awry
and start over with a fresh page. There is no equivalent when
we read the current chapter of our life's story with a dissatisfied
eye. Blotted with mistakes, covered with scratched out intentions
that have never borne fruit, disfigured by marginal notes on a plot
that seems to be going nowhere, the draft makes us yearn to tear it
up and start again with a clean piece of paper. We fail to see that
God has already thrown away the old pages and started a new one.
At baptism, God tore up the transcript of our sin – original sin and,
if needed, personal sin. God's forgiveness is more than juridical.
It does not simply write a writ of absolution for our sins, it actually destroys the record of the legal claims that have accumulated
against us by virtue of our transgressions, says Saint Paul, using
courtroom language. God nailed that record to the cross, where it
has been dissolved in the blood and water from the pierced side of
the Crucified. That dramatic metaphor makes clear how clean is
the page on which we now write our story. Moreover, it lays the
groundwork for hope when we feel we have again blotted our man-
uscript with sin. By means of the many forms of penance available
in Christian life, especially the sacrament of penance, God provides
us again and again with a fresh start. Let us also remember that the
story we are writing is not ours alone, nor are we its sole author.
We have been given our new life in Christ. Our personal stories are
chapters in Christ's story. That story is God's work. We are collaborators in the writing. Through God's mercy, there will always be
enough pages for us to complete the work.

*O God, the author of life, you have forgiven my sins again and
again, and given me a fresh start so that I can become the Gospel
story live in the unique flesh of my own time, place, and personality. Keep me faithful to this work of writing the Gospel with my life
so that all I am and do may praise you.*

The Treasure Hunt

Sister Genevieve Glen, O.S.B.

"If then you were raised with Christ, seek what is above, where Christ is seated at the right hand of God. Think of what is above, not of what is on earth." (Col 3: 1-2)

Your heart follows your treasure, said Jesus (see Mt 6: 21). Your feet follow your heart. Remember all those adventure stories of young seekers risking their lives in a quest for the treasure buried at the spot marked X on the pirates' map? For the youthful treasure-hunters, the quest itself was the real treasure. It rescued them from everyday humdrum, gave them a purpose worth the investment of their lives, furnished them with a zest for living, and matured them, whether or not they ever found the gold. Saint Paul sends us off on an adult quest for treasure far greater than gold when he urges us to "seek what is above," meaning Christ in his risen glory. He is not launching us into space. The tradition of vertical geography that locates heaven physically above our heads describes a theological, not a spatial, relationship. Heaven is where God is, and God is everywhere. God lives in the hearts of the just. However, to imagine heaven as "up high" is to acknowledge God's transcendent holiness. At baptism, we were "raised with Christ," but, paradoxically, we are still on the way toward where he is "seated at the right hand of God." The time between baptism and death is the time of our quest. We have a map: the Scriptures. We have a compass: our conscience. We have food for the journey: the Eucharist. Let us not let familiarity dull the edge of the adventure. Christianity has sometimes been accused of promising "pie-in-the-sky-when-you-die" but nothing much before that. The truth is that our treasure does not lie only in some distant future. Saint Paul tells us to think of what is above, but we discover it all around us as we go, always accompanied by the Christ we seek. The saints invite us to open our eyes as we travel: "All the way to heaven is heaven" (Saint Catherine of Siena).

Our Father in heaven, you allowed your only-begotten Son, Jesus Christ, our Lord, to be buried in the earth, but you raised him to glory at your right hand. You have called me to seek him, your hidden treasure, who has already found me and set me on the way. In your mercy, make me faithful in the quest and bring me to its goal in heaven.

Hide-And-Seek

Sister Genevieve Glen, O.S.B.

"You have died, and your life is hidden with Christ in God. When Christ your life appears, then you too will appear with him in glory." (Col 3: 3-4)

Gather up some kids, put them in an old house abounding in nooks and crannies, and, in no time at all, you have a lively game of hide-and-seek in progress. The game rewards those best skilled in hiding. Children play at what they need to learn for a successful adulthood. As adults, heirs of Adam and Eve, we seem to have a great need to hide all our vulnerabilities: we hide our fears, our wounds, our dreams, our loves. Internet sites invite users to choose a persona, sometimes complete with name, face, and history, behind which to hide their true identity. But choosing a persona is nothing new. We have all learned to hide behind whatever masks have worked for us: a tough exterior, a camouflage of compliance, an aura of success, a youthful look. In a world made hostile by sin, we do indeed sometimes need the protective armor we put on like a suit of clothes in the morning. The problem arises when we mistake the mask for the reality, the borrowed armor for the truth, the clothes for the person, and allow them to deform us. In truth, we have a far better hiding place than we could ever invent for ourselves: through baptism, our life is hidden with Christ in God. Our inmost reality is concealed from all comers by the protective love of God made flesh in Jesus Christ. The psalms speak rightly of God as our refuge, our shelter, our shield. But Christ is more than a mere protector. At baptism, we were planted in him as seed in good soil. And, in that soil, the seed changes. Concealed even from ourselves, we are slowly transformed into his image embodied in our own unique truth. When Christ, in whom we live, appears, we too will appear not as the frightened children who hid but as we truly are, the sons and daughters of God, clothed in Christ, our glory.

O God, my refuge and my strength, you have hidden me with Christ in the protection of your life-giving love. As I live and grow in him, transform me day by day into his image through a life of humble and faithful love, prayer, and service until my true dignity as your beloved child is revealed when he appears in glory.

Defeating the Snake

Sister Genevieve Glen, O.S.B.

"Put to death, then, the parts of you that are earthly: immorality, impurity, passion, evil desire, and the greed that is idolatry." (Col 3: 5)

As small children, my brother and I were playing in my grandmother's driveway when we saw a creature we had never seen before. White with black rings, it looked like some kind of giant worm. We called our grandmother to come and look. One look was enough. This large, peaceful, fiercely protective Irishwoman moved faster than we knew she could. Before we grasped what was happening, she had dashed into the garage, snatched up a shovel, and made short shrift of the snake. Paul's ferocity matches hers. He, too, sees a danger his flock perhaps does not recognize. The aspects of our humanity he lists as belonging to the unredeemed earth are more lethal than any snake. Acted out, they destroy us more effectively than the most deadly venom. Now as then, the world around us provides a number of attractive invitations to the items on his list. However, Saint Paul does not direct our violence against the lures. Rather, he demands that we put to death the responses they evoke in us: immorality, impurity, passion, evil desire, and the greed that worships whatever god is offering us the satisfaction we crave. These are the teeth of the snake lying quiet within us until stirred. Saint Benedict († c. 547) provides a practical way to protect ourselves from the fangs. Knowing that action begins with thought, Benedict borrowed an image from Psalm 137 to urge us to move like my grandmother at the first sign of the thoughts that lead to these deadly behaviors, before they are even old enough to seem harmful. Root them up, he says, and dash them against the Rock who is Christ. Make the sign of the cross, call on the name of Jesus, pray a simple prayer. My grandmother knew that there was no time to make the snake's acquaintance. She killed it without mercy or remorse before it could bite. Saint Paul would have us do likewise.

O God my help, you defend me from evil. Send your Holy Spirit to defend me from the evil that lurks within me, waiting to destroy. Grant me the wisdom and the courage to root it up and dash it against Christ before it can harm me, your child.

The Green Grass and the Brown

Sister Genevieve Glen, O.S.B.

"But now you must put them all away: anger, fury, malice, slander, and obscene language out of your mouths. Stop lying to one another, since you have taken off the old self with its practices and have put on the new self, which is being renewed, for knowledge, in the image of its creator." (Col 3: 8-10)

Who does not long to become a "new self"? Judging by the unflagging popularity of self-help books, we all do. The temptation is to look for the "quick fix" – immediate weight loss, instantaneous halt to aging skin, rapid makeover, instant conversion. Saint Paul himself bears witness to the possibility of the sudden, dramatic moment on the road to Damascus that changes life for ever. However, he speaks here of the slow, delicate season of conversion begun but not yet completed in which most of us live. In baptism, as the rite itself suggests, we have already stripped off the old sinful self and put on the new redeemed self clothed in Christ. However, the deep change wrought by baptism takes time to transform the surface. Old habits linger awhile before new ones are firmly formed. In spring, there comes a moment when the fields of wild grass seem to turn overnight from brown to green. If you look closely, though, you will see that the change is not so sudden. At first, the new shoots of tender green grass are there, but the old dead grass partially covers and protects them until they are strong enough to flourish on their own. Then the old brown grass falls away. This pattern of nature encourages all of us who live between baptism and the final resurrection to learn patience. If we give all our attention and energy to uprooting the old habits, we may find ourselves with nothing left. If we keep our attention and our energy focused on strengthening the new habits of Christ-like thinking and doing that bear outward testimony to the Christ-life growing within us, we will discover that the old habits of sin slowly fall away under the impact of grace. Of course we must check the old growth, but hope burgeons with the new and pushes us forward to our goal, selves renewed entirely in the image of our creator.

O God our creator, you have made me for yourself. Grant me the long patience of faithful perseverance as you transform me once again into your image, through Christ our Lord.

Christ All in All

Sister Genevieve Glen, O.S.B.

"Christ is all and in all." (Col 3: 11)

"Big Brother is watching you." The omnipresent figure of Big Brother haunts the frightening world of *1984* imagined into being by George Orwell in 1948. In the story, no one recalls ever having seen Big Brother, but everyone fears the consequences of displeasing him. For too many people, Christ is like Big Brother: present everywhere, knowing everything, even the innermost thoughts of the heart, disapproving of all but the impossibly holy. For such people, Saint Paul's words, "Christ is all and in all," conjure up a spiritual totalitarianism like the political state Big Brother represents. Yet, for Saint Paul, the belief that "Christ is all and in all" is good news, not bad. It is the ultimate comfort in a threatening universe. Those who fear otherwise have the story tragically backwards. Evil is Big Brother prowling everywhere to confound and destroy us. Guilt that knows no remission is Big Brother's minion, sucking all hope out of us as do Big Brother's servants in *1984*. Christ is the ever-present, ever-watchful, ever-active love of God made flesh, crucified and risen to deliver us from their oppressive regime. He is the hero of the human story, not its villain. Where sin and death abound around and in us, Christ is present as the fountain of life that never dries up. Where we shiver in our soul's boots at the awareness of our disobedience, Christ knows our every thought and forgives us again and again at the slightest hint of repentance. Where we can hardly bear our flawed selves, Christ sees beyond the wrinkles and cracks to the image of God budding in our depths and labors without wearying to restore us to our true selves. Christ is the heartbeat of the universe, its origin and goal. In his presence, we have nothing to fear and everything to cheer for, like the citizen-slaves of a totalitarian state when they find themselves suddenly, wonderfully, astonishingly set free.

O Father in heaven, you have made me your child in Jesus Christ, your Son, the elder brother for whom my fears and doubts cry out in time of trouble. Through the liberating power of his death and resurrection, deliver me from all the bonds of sin and death, that I may for ever live in him who is all and in all for your glory.

Clothed in Christ

Sister Genevieve Glen, O.S.B.

"Put on then, as God's chosen ones, holy and beloved, heartfelt compassion, kindness, humility, gentleness, and patience, bearing with one another and forgiving one another, if one has a grievance against another. [...] And over all these put on love, that is, the bond of perfection." *(Col 3: 12-14)*

In a town with few Catholics, a child of around six clearly did not know what to make of my religious habit. She hung back staring until she had worked it out to her satisfaction. Then she darted up and announced triumphantly, "You're a *church* lady." Clothing often announces to whom we belong. Members of religious orders and organizations, particular professions, branches of the armed services, ethnic groups, even age and social groups all wear identifying garb of one sort or another. At baptism, we too received identifying clothing. We put on Christ, as Saint Paul says elsewhere. Some clothing is worn only on certain occasions, but we "wear Christ," as it were, every day of the week, not as a set of clothes we put on and take off but as a way of being. But what does "wearing Christ" look like? What do onlookers see when they meet us in the store, or anywhere for that matter? Saint Paul lists the essential "Christ-wardrobe" in this passage. Uniforms of any kind generate expectations of their wearers. Saint Paul's list names what kind of behavior onlookers should see in those who are clothed in Christ. To get a more concrete picture of what each item should look like, we might look for Gospel passages that show Christ modeling it. Then we might find inspiration in seeing what it looks like on other people, either recognized saints or people living Christ-like lives around us. Finally, though, we must try each item on for ourselves. What does Christ's gentleness look like on me? What particular shape and feel does patience have when I'm the one displaying it? Because each of us is a unique expression of God's creativity, each of us wears the Christ-wardrobe with a flair uniquely ours. But all our delightful diversity is woven together into the seamless robe of love that covers the entire Body of Christ and radiates God everywhere we go.

O God, Creator of the universe, you have clothed me in Christ so that I may bear witness to your love. Grant that I may never disfigure my Christ-clothing with behavior unbecoming to a Christian, but may wear it always and everywhere in such a way that those I meet will themselves desire to be so clothed.

Peace Begins at Home

Sister Genevieve Glen, O.S.B.

"Let the peace of Christ control your hearts, the peace into which you were also called in one body [...] be thankful. Let the word of Christ dwell in you richly, as in all wisdom you teach and admonish one another, singing psalms, hymns, and spiritual songs with gratitude in your hearts to God." (Col 3: 15-16)

"Please, go away and leave me in peace!" pleads the weary mother beset by a horde of toddlers, all clamoring for her attention. She echoes the cry of all those who seek relief from demands they cannot meet, from attentions they do not want, from hostility they cannot withstand. In fact, all of us tend to imagine peace as the cessation of something – demand, disturbance, suffering. However, peace is not an absence but a presence. Real and lasting peace is the fruit of disorder put right. The peace of Christ is the fruit of the cross through which Christ righted the order of a world gone mad in sin. To enter into Christ's peace, we must seek out that right order. Saint Paul tells us here to seek it by allowing Christ's word to dwell in us richly. Taught by those entrusted with the ministry of the Word, admonished by one another as we share in one another's wisdom, formed by worship – "singing psalms, hymns, and spiritual songs" –, shaped by the Eucharist, whose name means "thanksgiving," our hearts will gradually abandon all the sources of disorder that tear us apart, and will grow into the right order of the Gospel. As the peace of Christ, born of a life of selfless love for God and neighbor, takes hold of our hearts, it will strengthen the bonds that unite us to one another as members of Christ's Body. Thus individuals and Body confirm one another mutually in a growing peace which can spread outward to embrace family, neighborhood, workplace, and world. The work is slow. The disorder is deep. Individually and together we will fall out of peace again and again as we struggle. But God is faithful, the promise is sure, and one day Christ's peace will prevail. Our task in the meantime is simple and humble: "Let the word of Christ dwell in you."

God of all peace, you have called me to live Christ's peace in a troubled world. Strengthen your peace within me through the wisdom of Christ's word dwelling in me and in those with whom I share my faith, worship, and life, so that I may be a living sign of hope amid violence and despair.

To Thine Own Self Be True

Sister Genevieve Glen, O.S.B.

"And whatever you do, in word or in deed, do everything in the name of the Lord Jesus, giving thanks to God the Father through him. Whatever you do, do from the heart, as for the Lord and not for others, knowing that you will receive from the Lord the due payment of the inheritance." (Col 3: 17, 23-24)

"Robert," asked the religion teacher, "can you give me a quotation from one of the saints?" Robert, who was studying the notes for his English test under his desk, blurted out, "To thine own self be true." "And which saint said that?" inquired the teacher. "Saint Paul?" guessed Robert hopefully. "No," replied the teacher, who had seen the notes, "they were written by Shakespeare." "I bet he copied them from Saint Paul!" Robert countered. Shakespeare didn't copy the words from Saint Paul, of course, but he might have, had he read today's passage from Colossians carefully. Saint Paul is indeed exhorting us to be true to ourselves in whatever we do. However, to glean that meaning from the passage, Shakespeare might first have had to consult an older source. The ancient Greek philosopher Socrates was fond of quoting the oracle of Delphi: "Know thyself." To be true to oneself, one must first know oneself. One of Saint Paul's favorite phrases is "in Christ." That captures our root identity: we are members of Christ's very Body. To act as our truest selves, then, we must act always "in the name of Jesus Christ" because we have been so intimately joined to him. We can safely act "from the heart" because our hearts belong to Christ who forms them in grace. We need not flounder through ancient philosophies or English literature, though, to discover what it means to speak and act from a heart rooted in Christ. The Gospel is the benchmark against which we test the authenticity of our words and deeds. We seek to be true to ourselves by being true to Christ, not for others' sake, but for his. To be true to him is our grateful return for his love. And only by being true to him can we genuinely serve others. The reward is great: we who are Christ's Body are heirs to his glory. Let us always give God thanks!

God our Father, I give you thanks that you have made me one with Christ as a member of his Body. Keep me always faithful to what you have called me to be, that I may give glory to you and Gospel service to my neighbors in Christ's name and for his sake.

Prayer and Fasting

Lisa Lickona

"Persevere in prayer, being watchful in it with thanksgiving."
(Col 4: 2)

Recently I was teaching my eight-year-old son Max about the angels. We read several passages from the Bible in order to learn more about how these heavenly beings can help us, guide us, and protect us. Then we read about Satan, the fallen angel, and the temptations he placed before Jesus in the desert. As I re-read this familiar scene with my son, I marveled at the way it depicts temptation with psychological acuity. Aren't the temptations that Satan places before Jesus precisely the ones that I face every day! First there is the simple attack on the passions: aren't you hungry… why not just turn these stones to bread? Then there is the attack on the intellect: doesn't Scripture say that the angels will protect you? Finally, there is the all-out assault on the will, on the love that binds one to God: just worship me, says Satan, and I will give you everything. Every day we find ourselves assaulted by the tempter in each of these ways. How many times have we snapped at our spouse because we were hungry? How many times have we justified our actions with a "word from God," even when we knew better? How often do we avoid doing what is right because we are tempted to worship a strange god – our public image, our reputation, our material possessions. This constant assault of the enemy is why Paul never tires of encouraging his dear children to be persevering and watchful in prayer. It is prayer alone that will enable us to counter the onslaught of the enemy. Christ himself would only meet the temptation of the evil one after his forty days of prayer and fasting. We can do no better. Let us follow his lead and devote ourselves wholeheartedly to a life of prayer and fasting.

Dear Lord, you showed through your own life the immense need that we have for prayer. Give me the grace to persevere in prayer, even when it is difficult. Watch over me and protect me from the snares of the enemy!

The Spirit of Power

Lisa Lickona

"Our gospel did not come to you in word alone, but also in power and in the holy Spirit and [with] much conviction."
(1 Thes 1: 5)

Saint Paul is so insistent when he reminds the Thessalonians that the Gospel comes to them not as mere words, but "also in power and the Holy Spirit." In a mechanized society we are accustomed to imagining power as that which pushes and pulls, like the action of the pistons on the crankshaft or the explosive force of a jet engine. But the power of the Spirit is infinitely more subtle and more interior than that of any human invention. Just as the Holy Spirit made the words that the apostles spoke on the day of Pentecost perfectly comprehensible to each man present, no matter what their native tongue, so does he in our own day interpret the Gospel to each and every heart. When the Holy Spirit is involved, the Word of God is something personal and personalized, a living Word that touches us intimately. In his encyclical on the Holy Spirit, Pope John Paul II made a point of reminding our world that the Holy Spirit is the person of the Blessed Trinity who "convinces the world concerning sin." And this activity is no mere "guilt-trip," it involves no arm-twisting. Indeed, the "convincing" that goes on in the depths of our hearts is perhaps the deepest personalization of God's Word. When we become "convinced" concerning sin, the Spirit acts in his gentlest way, touching our very depths. We sense how deeply we are known, how he has always known us and loved us, even in our darkest moments. In this way our confession is not something God wrings out of us, but a moment of self-knowledge that is true freedom. This is not the raw power of an explosion or a violent revolution, but God's creative power that renews the face of the earth.

Come, Holy Spirit, with your power! Help me acknowledge my sin and lead me to a life of true freedom.

Gift of Self

Lisa Lickona

"We were gentle among you, as a nursing mother cares for her children. With such affection for you, we were determined to share with you not only the gospel of God, but our very selves as well, so dearly beloved had you become to us." (1 Thes 2: 7-8)

My sister recently had her first baby – and what a baby she is! Mara has grown at an incredible rate, pushing past the ninety-ninth percentile for weight at every doctor's visit. Christie often calls to report: "Mara has been nursing all day! She is going through another growth spurt!" Sometimes she calls to commiserate; she is just plain exhausted from nursing this one little baby and wonders how long it will last. We talk and reflect on what we see around us – a culture of distance between mothers and babies. It is so easy for baby to go from crib to bouncer to car seat with only a few brief stops in someone's arms for a meal. "There is no love without self-sacrifice," my sister and I agree. And, indeed, this tender time between mother and child – when the mother nourishes her child with her own body, delights the child with her own smile, rocks the child to sleep with the rhythms of her own body – all of it amounts to the child's first experience of love as self-sacrifice. And thus it is the child's first experience of divine Love. In sacred art we sometimes see the stunning parallel of the crucified Lord with the blood and water flowing from his side, and the Mother Mary nursing the infant Jesus at the breast: her self-sacrifice anticipating his, his self-sacrifice making hers possible. Paul paints a similar picture of his work among the Thessalonians, "gentle… as a nursing mother cares for her children." In this beautiful Marian image he teaches us that the Gospel enters the world, not as mere words, but as a gift of person and presence, flesh and blood. So it is for all of us who seek to bring the Gospel to others – as loving mother, compassionate father, faithful friend. The word must become flesh!

Dear Jesus, in your bodily self-gift you held nothing back. Pour out your grace upon me that I may never hold back the gift of my own body for the sake of the Gospel!

More than Words

Lisa Lickona

"For this reason we too give thanks to God unceasingly, that, in receiving the word of God from hearing us, you received not a human word but, as it truly is, the word of God, which is now at work in you who believe." (1 Thes 2: 13)

Not long ago my husband and I were at a dinner party with an old friend. During the evening my husband was asked to explain a particular doctrine of the Church. For some reason, the way Mark answered the question annoyed me, and when we got home I let him have it. I was deeply angry. We fought – for he rightfully defended himself! Finally, things settled down, we kissed, made up, and went to bed. But I could not sleep. I could still feel the force of my emotions, the sting of the words that I had hurled against my dear husband. Where did it all come from? Somehow I knew that something he had said at the party had touched a very deep nerve in me, one that ran all the way into the distant past. How, I wondered, could anyone "get to the bottom" of that nerve? How could the source of this anger – perhaps deep in my childhood – be discovered and rooted out? I felt that no amount of talking, of pouring out my life story with a therapist, could address this wound, could find it and cure it. And that night, as I prayed to God for forgiveness, I felt waves of gratitude wash over me. For our God, in his mercy, has not left us with simple human words and gestures, as heartfelt and well-meant as they may be. He has spoken to us in his Son, whose human words manifest the divine power – the power that knit me in my mother's womb. Truly he knows all of me – the best and the worst, inside and out. He can explain me to myself better than anyone else. And in this saving Word we can have a great hope, a hope of conquering sin and being made new.

Almighty Lord, thank you for the power of your Word, which can speak to the depths of my heart!

More than I Want to Be

Lisa Lickona

"May the Lord make you increase and abound in love for one another and for all, just as we have for you, so as to strengthen your hearts, to be blameless in holiness before our God and Father at the coming of our Lord Jesus with all his holy ones. [Amen.]" (1 Thes 3: 12-13)

Good Friday 1994 found me nine months pregnant with my first child. And as I followed the gestures of the Way of the Cross, hoisting my heavy body repeatedly from a standing position to a kneeling position and back up again, I was suddenly struck by the words of the psalmist: "By your stripes we are healed." Of course, the stripes which the psalmist foretold were the bloody marks that covered the back of Jesus as he was scourged. But, preoccupied as I was in that moment with my own body, they spoke to me of the stripes that had recently appeared all along my abdomen – the dreaded stretch marks. Like every other woman, I had prayed to be spared. But my skin did not have the required elasticity. I was not spared and I was not happy. But in this moment, when the Lord permitted me to make a comparison between his infinite suffering and my tiny self-sacrifice, I saw motherhood for what it really is: letting myself be more than I thought I could be, more even than I wanted to be! With directness and simplicity, Saint Paul gave this recipe for holiness: "May the Lord make you increase and abound in love for one another and for all…" – for love, if it is true love, can never rest. It must become greater and it must become more. And if our love is to grow, the parts of our selves that we hold most dear must shrink. This happens more or less automatically as a baby grows inside its mother – baby takes up more room, mother's lungs and stomach have less room! But becoming spiritual mothers and fathers is a work of the will. We must will to die to all our selfish little habits, the preoccupations that we treasure, but which we secretly know to be holding us back from those we love. We must become more than we thought we could be.

Lord, by the gift of your suffering and death I am made new. Through your infinite love grant me the grace today to let go of something that is keeping my love for others from increasing.

Pray and Work

Lisa Lickona

"This is the will of God, your holiness: that you refrain from immorality. We urge you [...] to progress even more, and to aspire to live a tranquil life, to mind your own affairs, and to work with your [own] hands, as we instructed you."
(1 Thes 4: 3, 10-11)

Hanging above the entrance to our kitchen is the motto of Saint Benedict: *ora et labora* – "pray and work." I often remind my husband and children that the work to which Benedict referred was the manual labor that the monks had to perform to keep the monastery running: working the fields, caring for the animals, hauling wood for the fire. This motto seemed only appropriate when our family moved to a small farm two years ago. In many ways, life has continued with the same tasks that occupied us before we fled the suburbs: the children's schoolwork, my husband's writing, and my seemingly endless household tasks. But now our days are broken up by new duties, work that occupies both brain and body: splitting wood, building a chicken coop, hauling compost for our burgeoning garden. Both I, a country girl, and my husband, a life-long city dweller, have noticed a new spiritual edge, a clarity that comes from the simplicity of physical labor. All of it bears out Saint Paul's advice to the Thessalonians: "Aspire to live a tranquil life, to mind your own affairs, and to work with your [own] hands..." Perhaps we need this advice in our day more than the Thessalonians did. No doubt Paul was counteracting laziness – we imagine the recalcitrant laborer who idles under the olive tree. In our day, we are more likely than ever to be active – to be driving in traffic, to be text-messaging, e-mailing. Indeed, we are always moving, but so often stressed and distracted. Labor with our hands, on the other hand, can be calming and refreshing. It is, as Paul clearly saw, a way to remain focused on the most important things: honest work can lead us to prayer. Thus, we owe it to ourselves, to our souls, occasionally to turn off the modern gadgets and make some time for honest labor, for the simple work of our hands.

Dear Jesus, you lived the life of a simple laborer. Help me to avoid the stress of life's distractions and to realize the value of the work of my hands.

A Real Fairy Tale

Lisa Lickona

"For if we believe that Jesus died and rose, so too will God, through Jesus, bring with him those who have fallen asleep."
(1 Thes 4: 14)

How gently does Saint Paul address the Thessalonians when he refers to those who have "fallen asleep" in Christ! Like the rest of us in our antiseptic culture, I fear a painful death at the hands of *e coli* or *staphyloccus*. I imagine with horror the kinds of havoc a super-virus, mutated out of control, could inflict upon our world. Even tuberculosis, a malady that brought many saints to their holy deaths, causes me to tremble. Death at the hands of disease, it seems to me, is ghastly and unbearable. But Paul's account challenges me to accept the unlikely truth: that death, in Christ, is closer to fairy tale than medical fact. Death, he proclaims, has been given an entirely different meaning in the light of the resurrection of Christ. This resurrection, as absurd as it seems, is the new center, the new source of meaning. Death is no longer a murderer, no longer a ghastly phantom of the night. Suffering remains, it is true, but now in each suffering moment there is a new opportunity – it is the chance to be one with him, our Savior, our champion. Each malady a little death, each little death another triumph of the cross! This is the sweet truth that is proclaimed in the sometimes gruesome suffering of our saints: that death has been transformed! And death, like the prick of the spindle on the finger of the princess, is not an end, but a new beginning. This is the truth to which I hope to return after another dire prediction of world-wide pandemic has gripped my heart: the truth of a man whose body has conquered the flesh-eating microbes, the truth of the man who stands in all his radiance at the door of the tomb – a "real" fairy tale!

Jesus, your resurrection changed everything! Give me today the faith to live this truth!

Children of the Light

Lisa Lickona

"But you, brothers, are not in darkness, for that day to overtake you like a thief. For all of you are children of the light and children of the day." (1 Thes 5: 4-5)

I once heard the advice of a wise mother on how she limited her children's TV time. Television, she explained to them, is a light. And we only need lights at night or on the darkest, rainiest days. Those are the times when we can turn on the TV. Since hearing this advice I have often thought of that simple premise: television is a light! No wonder we are drawn to the TV when darkness comes. Or perhaps we are drawn to that other light, the computer, with the seemingly infinite glow of the internet. Even our cell phones have lights! The modern age has its own definition of "children of the light": "children of the new media." Unlike the faithful of generations gone by, who ended their day with a prayer for mercy, we so often go to sleep with the lights of Fox News or CNN in the background. It takes a mighty effort to return to the other era, a time when light could not be had with the mere touch of a finger. But return we must! For the nighttime brings with it more than physical darkness. How often does the fatigue of the body bring on the troubles of the soul! Every anxiety of the day resurfaces in the darkness. When we can't sleep with worry, we are tempted to get up and turn on the television – anything to take our minds off our problems. But this light is simply a distraction. The glare of the TV cannot really conquer our darkest fears. Indeed, the darkness of night can only be met with the light of faith. This is the time to reach for the rosary or the Bible or the prayer book. Let us truly become children of the Light!

Heavenly Father, in your light we see light! Help me to recognize the distractions of the world for what they truly are. Help me always to seek your light.

Dress for Success

Lisa Lickona

*"Since we are of the day, let us be sober, putting on
the breastplate of faith and love and the helmet that is
hope for salvation."* (1 Thes 5: 8)

Experts in our culture tell us that those who are successful are those who first decided to "dress for success." Salesmen and women who work out of the home are more likely to have success if they are making their sales calls in a suit than in their pajamas. Even stay-at-home moms are more productive if they get out of their bathrobes and slippers and "get dressed to the shoes." Is it any surprise, therefore, that Saint Paul so often encourages us to get "dressed up" in the faith, to "equip" ourselves with the virtues of faith, hope, and love? It is tempting to conclude that this kind of thinking is quaint, not for the modern person. After all, we have much more interior, psychological ways of expressing our need for spiritual readiness. Faith is all about what is "inside" me, what flows out of me. Who needs a spiritual game of "dress-up"? We do! By deciding to "put on" the faith, we commit ourselves to live on the outside the faith we have on the inside. Every child who has ever played dress-up knows this secret: if you dress like a king, it is easier to act like a king. And certainly, it is one thing to profess our allegiance to a heavenly king and another thing entirely to be kingly toward others. By consciously "putting on" the faith, we recommit ourselves to a life of faith that is expressed in our demeanor and our bearing, in our manners and mannerisms, in the way that we speak and act toward others. Let us, therefore, take to heart Paul's words and today put on the "breastplate of faith and love and the helmet that is the hope for salvation." It is a spiritual way to "dress for success"!

Dear Jesus, king of heaven and earth, equip me this day with the breastplate of faith and love, and the helmet that is the hope for salvation. Let my presence radiate your presence in the world.

Our Heavenly Father

Lisa Lickona

"God did not destine us for wrath, but to gain salvation through our Lord Jesus Christ, who died for us, so that whether we are awake or asleep we may live together with him." (1 Thes 5: 9-10)

It has become almost a cliché to see in a person's image of God the image of their father. If you think God is angry with you, then you must have had an angry father. As common as such pop-psychology is, it speaks to a deep truth. For it is from our parents that we first learn about who God is – for good or for ill. This vulnerability of the child certainly puts an enormous responsibility upon each earthly father and mother to radiate authentically the love of God. But as we enter adulthood, each of us must strive to meet God for who he is, no matter who our parents were. As Saint Paul teaches, "God did not destine us for wrath"! Far from a picture of vengeance and anger, the New Testament presents us with a picture of God's paternity that is loving and life-giving. Consider the scene of the baptism of Jesus, a moment when we hear the actual voice of the Father speaking these words: "This is my beloved Son." This is not a Father who questions his son, accuses him, condemns him. In God, paternity expresses the very depths of the bond between Father and Son, which is, in its essence, love. And it is precisely this relationship that is extended to us through Christ. Thus, the words that the Father speaks to Jesus ought to resound in our own lives, the lives of his baptized children. He longs to speak these words to us, even especially to those of us who have struggled with our earthly fathers. When we are lost, it is the Father who will find us. When we feel alone, it is the Father who will reaffirm, at the deepest level, who we are. When we are unloved, it is the Father who will speak the words we long to hear: "beloved son," "beloved daughter."

Heavenly Father, your Fatherhood is beyond everything that we can imagine. Shower upon me this day your Fatherly love!

The Virtue of Patience

Lisa Lickona

"Encourage one another and build one another up, as indeed you do./ Be at peace among yourselves./ We urge you, brothers, admonish the idle, cheer the fainthearted, support the weak, be patient with all." (1 Thes 5: 11, 13-14)

As a mother of six children I often hear the remark, "You must be a very patient person!" But patience is not one of my virtues. I find myself struggling to have patience with my children in every circumstance. These days I need patience with my eldest daughter Monica, who cannot seem to help correcting her eight-year-old brother Max in the most officious tones. When I overhear their conversation in the other room, I know that I have to break in and remind her to be kind: "Don't nag your brother, Monica!" Again, a few minutes later: "Don't harass your brother, Monica." Finally, a few more minutes later, I blow up: "Please, stop it!" Oh, no, I am not a patient person! What keeps me trying to find new ways to control myself, to be loving and compassionate at all times, is the thought of the divine patience. Who among us has yet to live up to the command to forgive our neighbor seven times seventy? And yet has not our gracious God forgiven our seemingly endless infidelities? Every time we approach the sacrament of reconciliation there is that astounding promise: "Give thanks to the Lord for he is good; his mercy endures for ever." We return over and over, confessing the same sins every time – and every time there is the same promise: "His mercy endures for ever!" Truly we must allow God's mercy to penetrate our lives, to recognize how we owe him everything and yet he holds nothing against us. This transformation can come if we keep turning to him in the sacrament of reconciliation, if we keep coming to him and admit that we have fallen – yes, again! And in this repeated recourse to God's mercy is the best chance for us to begin to cultivate mercy in our own lives. Through the riches of this sacrament we can all hope to develop that precious virtue of patience.

Heavenly Father, thank you for the gift of your mercy in the sacrament of reconciliation. Help me always to have recourse to your mercy!

To Return Good for Evil

Lisa Lickona

"See that no one returns evil for evil; rather, always seek what is good [both] for each other and for all." (1 Thes 5: 15)

Not long ago my husband asked me for the second time whether I had found a babysitter for a concert he wanted to take me to. I had to admit that I hadn't even begun the search. He responded with anger – why did he have to ask again? Could it be that I didn't want to go? I was immediately hurt and snapped back. Standing before me was someone who needed me to be present to his needs. And all I could do was return anger for anger, hurt for hurt, evil for evil. I couldn't enter for a moment into his need to have an evening out, to be alone together for a short time away from the pressing needs of our six children. How infantile is the human heart! Our broken condition leaves us defensive and alone, accusing and accursed. The marital spat that played out for the first time in the garden of Eden ("She did it, blame her… No, he did it!") is played out a thousand times a day. If we are able for a moment to rise above this scenario, to seek the good of the other instead of avenging our hurt, it is only because of a man who has entered our history in an entirely unexpected way. He takes upon himself the curse, he bears in his own body the vengeful wrath of the crowd. He returns good for evil. He transforms the human heart from within. Only his personal presence, the presence of a divine person – not an idea, not an ideal – can enable us really to overcome the sins that we have committed a thousand and one times. In the relationship of love between the soul and Jesus, everything that is low and petty and vengeful can be conquered and transformed.

Dear Jesus, you know my weakness. Come to me this day. Transform me with your love.

Desire and the Will of God

Dino Gerard D'Agata

*Rejoice always. Pray without ceasing. In all circumstances give
thanks, for this is the will of God for you in Christ Jesus.*
(1 Thes 5: 16-18)

For a nine-year-old music lover to destroy his family with debt is no trifle – and this is exactly what my stomach felt the day in 1970 when a shipment of a hundred dollars' worth of albums showed up on our porch because I had looked at the tiny faces of Simon and Garfunkel in a Life magazine Columbia House ad, realized you didn't need a stamp on the form, and dropped it in a mailbox, telling no one. Coming home that day, I saw the box, froze, and bolted. At nine, God was "you can't spend your parents' money on albums" and life was "I like music, why not?" Unbeknownst to me, what I was living was the chief tragedy of the modern era: to perceive of God as a parole officer who has nothing to do with the very things that are most pressing – our needs for happiness, love, beauty (of which Simon and Garfunkel albums may be a very pressing sign). What was it about Jesus that created a passion in Saint Paul that was as immediate as my passion for everything I heard on the radio as a kid? Later, when I finally turned myself in, my mother laughed and pulled me to her; I pressed my face against her waist, and cried with relief that she wasn't going to punish me, cried until I soaked the collar of my corduroy jacket. The Presence that apprehended Saint Paul on the road to Damascus that day, despite his previous stance toward it, is the same human Presence that awaits us each time we enter a confessional, no matter what we've done – an interaction where God meets us in a way that is no more abstract and no less human than the arms of my mother were in 1970. God is here, now, in the humanity of the Church, offering us no less than his mercy. Who could not rejoice always?

Jesus, when we are tempted to hide from you in our sin, as Adam and Eve did in the garden, give us the grace to come before you freely, knowing that you never refuse your own, and that whatever we have done, once we say yes to your mercy, these things no longer exist.

Beethoven and Guinness

Dino Gerard D'Agata

"Do not quench the Spirit. Test everything; retain what is good."
(1 Thes 5: 19, 21)

For a family of Roman Catholic Italians moving from a Philadelphia ghetto to the New Jersey suburbs in the early 1960s, the idea that beer was sinful was one of the many foreign oddities that crept up on us when confronted with neighbors of other Christian denominations. Suffice it to say that this planted a lot of confusion in me until I was well past my teens, past college even, and discovered that to be a Catholic did not mean a systematic suppression of things human; that when Jesus told us that whoever followed him would have life to the fullest, he did not mean life to the "religious" fullest, but life, period. These neighbors always invited my sister and me to their Bible schools in the summer in order to save us, and things came to a head when, one Ash Wednesday, my mother invited one of our companions to join us at church to get ashes. "Oh no, I'm not Catholic," was his six-year-old reply. It was probably from that point on that my mother made us understand that *we were*, and that the tiny white host we would receive in a few years was not a symbol, but the body and blood, soul and divinity, of God himself. It is the truth of the fact that when Jesus gave humanity his body and blood, it became irrevocably privy to the reality that all of the goodness of creation was summed up in him, and had been since before time. So when Saint Paul advises us to test all things and retain what is good, it is to remind us that reality, with its dark and light beers, its symphonies, and playoff games, can be trusted, because the Father's hand is in it at all times; that the only thing for us to fear is our "no" to this.

Jesus, when we are tempted to take skepticism or fear as our starting point in life, show us your action once again in all of the realities of our existence; help us to see the hand of your Father in every aspect of our lives so that, like Saint Paul, we may be free to "test everything," and "retain what is good."

As Sick as Our Secrets

Dino Gerard D'Agata

"May the God of peace himself make you perfectly holy and may you entirely, spirit, soul, and body, be preserved blameless for the coming of our Lord Jesus Christ. The one who calls you is faithful, and he will also accomplish it." (1 Thes 5: 23-24)

When I was in my late twenties, I remember watching friends encounter twelve-step programs to face their addictions. Out of curiosity, I picked up AA's *Big Book* and read the story of Bill W. and how he overcame his alcoholism, although "overcame" is the wrong word to use. Any person who has struggled with an addiction of any type knows that it is not willpower that helps conquer addiction, but rather the surrendering of the will to the power of God. In a certain sense, watching these friends made me jealous. I too wanted to have the kind of human encounter with Christ that so many addicts find present in the fellowship of "the rooms." To me, this was far more dramatic and engaging than the elder, non-prodigal son in Saint Luke's Gospel, who winds up resenting both his father and his younger brother because he presumes he has nothing for which to be forgiven. What I understood over time, however, was that alcoholism is just one manifestation of original sin, and that an encounter with Christ is the way the Father lifts us up to bring us back to himself again once we accept the truth that, whether we're alcoholic or not, our condition is that of having strayed from him. Hence, it is he who will preserve us for the coming of our Lord; and the blamelessness Saint Paul speaks of lies not so much in our being ethically coherent as it does in knowing and accepting that it is his mercy and goodness that sustain us; that what he requires from us is not a resolution to be good, but rather an acceptance of the fact that, when left to ourselves, even our best efforts cannot purify us. Instead, it is his Presence as mercy among us that, on a daily basis, gives us back ourselves.

Lord, when we are tempted to think we've nailed down what you ask us to be, help us to see that what you actually ask is a "yes" like Our Lady's to be totally yours, not calculating and measuring what we are or want to become, but keeping our eyes constantly fixed on you as the source of our life.

Pet Dogs

Dino Gerard D'Agata

"We ought to thank God always for you, brothers, as is fitting, because your faith flourishes ever more, and the love of every one of you for one another grows ever greater." (2 Thes 1: 3)

A highly perceptive priest I recently spoke to pointed out the fact that one reason God gives us vocations is so that the others on our path, be they wives, husbands, confreres, fellow priests or sisters, hold a mirror up to us and allow us to see what we are. Fair enough, I thought at first, thinking of all the ways the people around me remind me of my weak points. But he went on to explain how, through this means, everything we are comes before the Father here in this life, so that after death, we need less purging. I would wager that anybody who has ever had difficulty remaining faithful to a community, or faithful to a spouse and children, might admit – perhaps reluctantly – that the difficulty lies, not so much in the others, but in his own inability to accept what he sees about himself that becomes irrevocably reflected to him in time that is unavoidably spent with these others. Take Chekhov's short story *The Lady with the Pet Dog*, for instance, in which the hero embarks on one more adulterous affair among many, despite the logistical difficulties this particular one presents, and realizes that all of the women he ever loved fell in love not with him but with an image they had of him. I suppose if they had fallen in love with who he actually was, he would have accused them of eliciting the same boredom he claimed he found in his wife. Instead of being like Chekhov's hero, however, when we accept the vocational companionship God places in our life, a third factor emerges, namely, that the stance our families and friends hold toward us in remaining with us is a concrete sign of the love and mercy God has for us, so there is no need to run. And the result, as Saint Paul says, is an ever-flourishing faith, and a love that is ever greater.

Lord, help us to see that when we want to hide from those who love us, we hide from you, and that instead, in giving ourselves over completely to those you have given us, we experience the freedom and liberation you have planned for us.

Whose Action Is It Anyway?

Dino Gerard D'Agata

"We always pray for you, that our God may make you worthy of his calling and powerfully bring to fulfillment every good purpose and every effort of faith, that the name of our Lord Jesus may be glorified in you, and you in him, in accord with the grace of our God and Lord Jesus Christ." (2 Thes 1: 11-12)

A lot of times, when people talk about sanctity, the impression you get is that sanctity is something reserved for the exemplary among us, those who can put aside paying bills and cooking dinner in order to concentrate on "the things of the Spirit." We forget that it was not we who made the decision to be baptized, we who decided to will ourselves into existence. But even more importantly, we forget that in becoming a man, God's intention was to remove the presupposition from us that his concerns for us and for the world did not have anything to do with our credit ratings or our income tax headaches. And we forget that, in order to remain with us for the duration of history, Jesus does not rely on vagueness or philosophical speculation, but on a group of people he has chosen to be his visible presence in the reality of history, a group of people made more and more his own via the efficacy of the Church's sacraments – *his* energy to bring to perfection every good (and even misguided) purpose of ours. The mentality that separates sanctity from life is the same mentality that denies the fact that God's will may be known objectively through the Church. And that raises the issue of whether it's my own knowledge and wisdom that makes Christ present to people, or *my following the point where he remains in history* that more efficiently carries the announcement of his presence in the world. It is the difference between watching a man standing on a street corner with a sign saying "repent" and watching footage of Mother Teresa picking up a dying man on a street in Calcutta. Which moves our heart more? And for Mother Teresa, relating to Christ was not something she did after she cleaned scabies from the body of a sick man, but in and through the very reality of his sores.

Lord, when the details of life seem overwhelming to us, show us that a "yes" to the circumstances at hand is a "yes" to you, and that when we give of ourselves to all of reality, your grace completes both ourselves and our actions in ways we could never have imagined.

Here and Now

Dino Gerard D'Agata

"But we ought to give thanks to God for you always, brothers loved by the Lord, because God chose you as the firstfruits for salvation through sanctification by the Spirit and belief in truth." (2 Thes 2: 13)

Anybody who has ever attempted to teach religion in a high school will probably have learned that to talk to people about quarks is less abstract than talking to them about heaven and hell. The truth is, we perceive eternal realities as something irrelevant to what we can see and touch, and when it comes to believing in God's actions, most of us couch this far more easily in terms of earthquakes and lunar eclipses than in terms of a bunch of desert nomads who crossed a sea without drowning, led by somebody who stuttered (i.e., Moses). And so it is with us when Saint Paul tells us we are the "firstfruits for salvation," since we think of salvation as something akin to a pronounced mechanical punch, like the one the attendance clock makes on our time card at the office, once we tally up our good works as nobly as possible and reach the 5 p.m. of life. Truth is, there is no 5 p.m. of life, or rather, if there is, it's something occurring every hour. Eternity – heaven and hell – are realities we have already begun to live here. Simply put, we're either oriented toward this relationship with our Creator – be this at varying speeds – or we're driving in the opposite lane, thinking the oncoming traffic won't hit us, not wanting to notice him at our backs. This is because, as Christians, he has taken us in baptism as his definitive people, and – just as the ancient Israelites, with all their weaknesses and foibles, their unfaithfulness even, were a sign to the Egyptians that they were dealing with something bigger than a bunch of tentmakers; just as the Romans who put us to death were forced to see that they could not put an end to a historical fact – God insists, by making us his firstfruits, in demonstrating that there is a heaven, and it is present here among us now.

Lord, teach us to enjoy the fact that we are your chosen ones, that we bring your face to the world through the gladness of being sons and daughters who know who they are in the hands of their Father.

Something Is Making Me Now

Dino Gerard D'Agata

"[God] has [also] called you through our gospel to possess the glory of our Lord Jesus Christ." (2 Thes 2: 14)

When I think of the word "glory," it conjures up the image of a noble, towering figure with a sunset in the background and white, puffy clouds floating off into the distance. In my education to be a "good Christian," the word "glory" was something reserved in my consciousness for God alone, and any attempts in life to gain personal "glory" were purported anathema to the humility necessary to follow Christ. Yet on that day by the Sea of Galilee, when Jesus called John and Andrew for the first time and asked them what they were looking for, I would hazard a guess that, given the sum total of human desires he brought out in them, a desire for glory, a dramatic break from the monotonous life of small-town fishermen, might not have been something they would have denied. God himself foresaw this desire in us for recognition, for the knowledge that we are worth something, for the sense that our life and our actions matter to others, and thus, he did not forget this aspect of our humanity when he chose to include us in the glory given to his Son. It is a glory that the world ignores, but one that, before the realities of time and eternity, all "powers and principalities," both Jesus and we, as his Body, possess. True, it isn't the glory of receiving an Oscar for our work, but of knowing we are one with him who conquered everything – most importantly, death – through the act of giving himself over totally to glorify the love of the Father. We may be tempted to think that even these words, *glorify the love of the Father*, are an extraneous burden to us, while Jesus himself knew, and we can know, that glorifying the Father means partaking in an awareness of the One who creates us, along with everything else, in every moment, constructs the intricacies of our individual personalities, and preserves them for eternity.

Lord, when we are tempted to think of the Father as a being who imposes something foreign on us, help us see that it is he who gives us who we are, and rejoices in what he sees.

Purple Quartz and Gray Words

Dino Gerard D'Agata

"Stand firm and hold fast to the traditions that you were taught, either by an oral statement or by a letter of ours." (2 Thes 2: 15)

All the time I hear people, even Christian people, musing about friends or relations who have died, saying things like, "I wonder if there's really a resurrection," or, "Do you think she can see us?" Hardcore atheists will come at you with murky phrases like, "I don't care if there's no afterlife, the point is to live now and be ethical," and in the 1980s, I recall acquaintances in New York who hated organized religion but who put purple crystals under their beds in bad times in order to channel good energy. But in the end, whether we like to admit it or not, certainties about our life and destiny are far more correspondent to our nature as humans than pieces of quartz, which can't say anything back to us when they tell us the biopsy was positive. I remember going to the funeral of a Jewish friend of mine in those years and being surprised to see a rosary between his fingers as he lay in state. His family was nominally religious, but he'd met a Jesuit in his final days and praying to Our Lady was perhaps something he hadn't excluded for himself as a possibility. This was very striking to me because, if you knew this man, you'd know he was the type of person who needed to know he'd wake up tomorrow and find his favorite bakery open. No matter how much we kick and scream in front of destiny, God knew this predicament ahead of time, so he didn't leave the knowledge of himself or our destiny to any guessing; rather, he chose a method – incarnation – that can be historically passed on by witnesses, and guaranteed his Spirit to protect this from distortion. Simple statements; simple witnesses; a man risen from the dead, seen by his friends, passed on unambiguously through two thousand years of history so that we can be sure of our own destinies. This is Christianity.

Lord, when our trust is weak, give us the faith to know that the tradition handed on to us through the communion of the Church can be a living rock of certainty for us.

Our Doubts Make Us Traitors

Dino Gerard D'Agata

"May our Lord Jesus Christ himself and God our Father, who has loved us and given us everlasting encouragement and good hope through his grace, encourage your hearts and strengthen them in every good deed and word." (2 Thes 2: 16-17)

*W*hat you're doing is meaningless, it has no effect. You're only doing what you're doing in order to demonstrate how good you are – were it not for a reward, you'd never do this, and didn't Jesus say not to let your right hand know what your left hand is doing? How many times do we hear this voice when we are in the middle of something that requires sacrifice or costs us something, and how often can it even take the form of something told to us by the Church or directly from the Gospel – that is: How often can we turn Christ, who wants to be a presence we love, into a yardstick for measuring our own worth? This is what happens when we reduce the good news of our salvation, the announcement that he is here, to a set of directives to carry out in order to earn heaven (which is already here, when we look for him here, and now). The wisdom of the saints has always reiterated the idea that the best way for the devil to attack you is if you remain alone – even if you are alone writing in your ledger of good deeds and resolutions. This is why God chose as the locus of salvation a Church, that is, a living community of believers, made up of both saints and sinners alike. It is through this body that we can receive the everlasting encouragement and good hope Saint Paul speaks of here, since, were his love not in the sign of those surrounding us, it would remain a figment of our imagination, and the result would be twofold: either an aberrant self-deprecation that would leave us in contempt for everything we are, or an inflated egotism that would cause us prematurely to canonize ourselves. Instead, this body removes the preoccupation with self-evaluation and draws us by attraction, so that our acts become one love that responds to another.

Lord, render reality transparent for us, so that the love you have offered us first, reaching us now in the circumstances that surround us, become the one criterion for which we do anything.

A Literal Quickening

Dino Gerard D'Agata

"Pray for us, so that the word of the Lord may speed forward and be glorified, as it did among you." (2 Thes 3: 1)

We might take note of the fact that, in the Gospel passage recounting Pentecost, when the people surrounding the apostles understood what was happening, it was not with lengthy explanations that those around them became aware that Jesus was the Messiah and had risen, but the very fact of their presence that transcended all languages and communicated something astounding to those who saw them. To speak of the "word" of the Lord is to speak, not about any verbal message, but about God's Word made flesh, his Son. Praying that this incarnate Word of the Father be glorified means praying that our awareness of this fact be all the more acute in our experience and in the experience that surrounds us. Spreading the "word," therefore, does not mean walking the streets shouting the name of Jesus to the masses, but letting our lives be transformed by a giving ourselves over to how he has met us in reality. Throughout the past century and continuing now, the Holy Spirit has bestowed charisms on the Church that have repeated this work of Pentecost: Communion and Liberation, the Neocatecumenate, Opus Dei, and Jean Vanier's L'Arche communities are but a few of the ways Christ has grasped the Church in the modern world in order to make his presence operatively visible within it. Knowing Jesus happens through a human encounter that is exactly the same as that of John and Andrew, along with a host of other saints whom Christ chose to renew the awareness of who he is for the Church in all centuries. If we are looking for the face of Christ, therefore, we must look for a human relationship that is lived in obedience to and verified by the Church's teaching authority, because nothing less than this can persuade our reason and our affection.

Lord, help us to realize that to imagine you as a figure in the past does not do justice to who you are and how you are here now. Show us your face in whatever way you deem best for us, and give us the grace to follow how the Spirit quickens you, the Word made flesh, in our world.

Blame

Dino Gerard D'Agata

*"The Lord is faithful; he will strengthen you
and guard you from the evil one." (2 Thes 3: 3)*

In childhood, bad dreams take the form of monsters chasing us; in adulthood, the images change to more sophisticated ones that reflect things like fear of flying or anxiety over the relationship we have with our boss. Funny how God teaches us what evil is. As kids, he has us perceive monsters coming to get us; as adults who think they're beyond this whole monster business, we grow blind to the monster's identity and full of guilt at how we've cooperated with its tricks. And it's here where we become trapped: we train ourselves to get used to the discomfort and alienation of evil, since the trick of sin isn't so much the evil itself as much as the self-hatred it engenders, the sense that we are no longer sons of the Father and worthy of facing him, and so we build our lives, build cultures, around the pain of this identity loss. The Puritan poet Anne Bradstreet, in *Upon the Burning of Our House…*, speculates in verse how the fire that destroyed her home in 1666 must have been something she deserved for having placed too much stock in material things – as if we need a type of constant self-recrimination in order to please God. But this is never the case. Christ guards us against the evil one by offering our freedom, which must always assent, the attraction of his love. All he asks for is our sorrow, the acknowledgment that we've gone against the truth of ourselves and reality. This is why we need a concrete, outward act – confession – as a remedy, since the newness of salvation, the unexpected and undeserved contradiction to all this, is that Christ himself never lays blame on us; he offers us not recrimination, but mercy, in every moment – something that no human culture before the call of Abraham had ever heard of.

Lord, when we are tempted to define ourselves by the compromise that sets in when we do evil, by the feelings of guilt and recrimination, lift us with your grace and help us see that our cooperation with evil is the source of this, and that you only stand by, ready to make us new in every instant.

Holding out to the End

Dino Gerard D'Agata

*"May the Lord direct your hearts to the love of God
and to the endurance of Christ." (2 Thes 3: 5)*

There's nothing like a presidential election to help us see what our position is regarding the meaning of existence and the major categories of human problems – work, politics, love, meaning. What we expect from a given candidate – the very fact, even, that we demand that a politician exhaustively resolve human affairs, as if he were God – reflects what we really believe about who's in charge of things. It might surprise us to discover that, in debating to death whether Democrats or Republicans are more capable of solving the world's problems, we seldom confront these things ourselves from the point of view of life's goal, which is eternal happiness, the relationship with the Father. Imagine Jesus, faced with his impending crucifixion, starting from the point of his own immediate ease. Were that the case, the world would be a very different place from what it is. And this is precisely the reason why we need him to direct our hearts to the love of God, and to his own endurance – firstly, because it is this love that knows best how to direct both the world's, and our own, affairs and problems to this ultimate happiness everyone is made for; and secondly, because, had Christ not had the endurance to entrust himself to the ultimate meaning the Father intended from his death, the possibility of this happiness would be for ever closed to us. We can see from Christ's endurance in the face of circumstances that, in the end, in spite of appearances, the Father knew what he was doing. If we allow this trust to be the starting point for anything – a difficult marriage, unemployment, economic slumps – while this may not grant us quick satisfaction, it can help us see in the long run that the Father's hand guides all of our lives and all of reality, and that if we start from this fact, we're far more capable of dealing with these things.

Lord, give us the grace to see that our lives and all of reality are guided by you, even through the evil committed by our freedom, and help us to see how, when everything we do is in relationship to you, it bears far greater fruit than we can imagine.

Omissions
Father John Dominic Corbett, O.P.

"But you, brothers, do not be remiss in doing good."
(2 Thes 3: 13)

Advice comes in different forms and so is helpful in different ways. Sometimes advice is very specific and easy to follow. Someone might say, "If you want to create a good impression on the first day of your new job, arrive one half hour early and dress in a conservative, professional manner." This kind of advice is sometimes dreadfully difficult to follow. A doctor might say, "If you want to beat this sort of cancer, you need both chemotherapy and surgery." But at least you know what the advice means.

Sometimes advice is more generic and consequently more difficult to apply. The Apostle's advice, "Do not be remiss in doing good," is advice of that sort. Taken literally, the advice is impossible to follow. How many good things have you *not* done today? Have you put out a fire lately? Have you devised a plan to relieve hunger in Africa? There is really no way to count up all the good things you haven't done, is there? No matter what good things we have done, there are an infinite number of good things we haven't done. So we are remiss no matter what we do.

But the Apostle is not being a prosecutor hoping to catch us in sins of omission. He is calling to us as family. He is encouraging us to do the good thing we see right in front of us, the dishes that need washing, the spouse that needs listening to, and the paper that needs to be written. It is true that it is sometimes difficult to prioritize and sort out which good things need doing right now. Saint Paul does not in this passage offer any advice about prioritizing, but he does offer the encouragement that we are indeed able to achieve some good this day, that it is well worth the doing, and that it is the Lord who initiates and blesses our efforts.

Lord Jesus, help us to know that you do not call us to do every possible good thing. Help us to see and to want to do the very specific good things you want done today.

Nothing Missing

Father John Dominic Corbett, O.P.

"May the Lord of peace himself give you peace at all times and in every way. The Lord be with all of you." (2 Thes 3: 16)

Sunday afternoons in the fall were my father's favorite time. They were set aside for the Cleveland Browns. In those years, the Browns had Fran Ryan, Paul Warfield, Leroy Kelly, and, of course, the great Jimmy Brown taking care of business. These afternoons were peaceful times for me. Not because there wasn't excitement or suspense or the occasional disappointment. There was plenty of that. But no matter how tight the game became I always knew that between the Browns and my father there was nothing missing. Everything necessary was in place to bring us victory.

Could you compare a Sunday afternoon's football game with the peace of the Lord? Sunday is the Sabbath. It is the day the Lord looked out on the world he had made and said that it was very good. There was nothing missing.

When the Apostle prays that the Lord of peace may give us his peace, he is praying that the Lord who is complete goodness, in whom there is nothing missing, who lacks for nothing, may communicate to us that same security and completion.

This prayer that the Lord may give us peace at all times and in every way can't be granted to us in this life if we mean by peace the actual experience of the invulnerable serenity and infinite perfection that belongs to God as God. But all the same, we know in faith that there is nothing missing. The Lord is with us and so, even if we are hungry or thirsty, if we are in trouble, or even if our favorite football team is losing *again*, or if we face hunger or nakedness or the sword, still there is nothing missing. We have what we need to win eternal life. Everything. The Lord is with us. There is nothing missing.

Lord Jesus, our lives are often full of stress and it is often hard to feel your presence with us. Help us to know that you have given us everything we need to be joyful with you for ever.

Family Trees

Father John Dominic Corbett, O.P.

"I repeat the request I made of you [...] to instruct certain people not to teach false doctrines or to concern themselves with myths and endless genealogies, which promote speculations rather than the plan of God that is to be received by faith." (1 Tm 1: 3-4)

Lots of people are interested in their family trees. One of the reasons that they are so interested is that they are hoping to find an explanation of why they are the way they are. Where did they get their good looks from? Their questionable fashion sense? Their pitch-perfect singing? Their high intelligence? Or their tendency to find and lose jobs quickly? Or their tendency to drink a drop more than is good for them? They look to their family trees for clues.

Now there are a couple of different approaches to family trees. One is a genetic approach. The idea seems to be that we can trace our personal behavior to more impersonal causes. "It's no wonder Uncle Bob was so depressed. Look at his family tree. It was in his genes." This kind of thing can be helpful, but you have to be careful. Explaining is not the same as explaining away.

The other kind of family tree explains not by genetics but by personal stories of personal influence that are handed on for the inspiration or for the hurt of the next generation. Here is explanation by way of story. It explains while retaining the mystery that belongs to human life.

The Bible never explains something by explaining it away. The Bible uses genealogies to show us how the human race was created, how it sinned, how God made for himself a people made of flesh and blood, comprised of sinners and saints, and how God's plan for our salvation was completed in Jesus. It shows how God sent his Son to fulfill this plan by becoming man, by dying on a cross, by rising from the dead, and by sending us the Spirit to make us adopted children of God. This is our family tree. This is our explanation about why we are the way we are. Anything to the contrary is idle speculation.

Father, help us to know that we are included in your own family tree. Help us to venerate our fathers and mothers in the faith, and to have confidence that our lives are graced by their prayer for us even now.

Job Search

Father John Dominic Corbett, O.P.

"I am grateful to him who has strengthened me, Christ Jesus our Lord, because he considered me trustworthy in appointing me to the ministry." (1 Tm 1: 12)

It was Pentecost. On this day it was traditional for the bishop of this diocese to ordain men as priests. The seminary rector called out their names one by one. The bishop asked the traditional question, "Do you judge them to be worthy?" The rector, as always when faced with this question which summarized his whole responsibility before the Church, commended his soul to the Holy Spirit and then said, "We judge them to be worthy."

He had often thought about this question. How do you make someone worthy? There is only so much that can be done. You can verify his theological knowledge. You can, to a degree, teach him the people skills so essential to parish ministry. You can be reasonably certain that he prays. Yet none of this makes a man worthy.

The great favor to receive, the one no human being can give, is to make someone to be competent, deserving, and faithful. Paul is grateful to God that he considered Paul faithful in appointing him to the ministry. This word "considered" deserves some attention. It isn't that God had a job opening called "apostle," and then started looking for the best candidate, then saw Paul, then decided that he was a good match, and then fit him in. No, God's knowledge is not like ours. Our knowledge reflects reality. God's knowledge causes reality.

Paul isn't first of all faithful and then recognized as such by God and then appointed as an apostle. Rather, God first knows Paul as worthy and this knowing of God actually causes Paul to be worthy. Now there was nothing Paul could have done to make that happen. It was all God's gracious choice. This explains why Paul is right to be grateful.

Paul is worthy and faithful because God wanted to know him as worthy and faithful. Let us pray that God wishes to know us in the same way.

Lord Jesus Christ, you are worthy to receive all honor as our High Priest. Please look with mercy on your priests and on your servants who are approaching priesthood. Please know them as your chosen friends and make them worthy of their call.

Mercy and Ignorance

Father John Dominic Corbett, O.P.

"I was once a blasphemer and a persecutor and an arrogant man, but I have been mercifully treated because I acted out of ignorance in my unbelief." (1 Tm 1: 13)

So many enemies of the Gospel are writing books these days! Steven Hawkins' *The God Delusion* and Christopher Hitchens' *God Is Not Great* are just two on the market. It's hard not to see their activity as deliberate and as blasphemous and as arrogant. What they do is deliberate. (These books don't write themselves.) What they do is intended to besmirch the name of God. What they do stems from the conviction of their intellectual and moral superiority. It all looks as if their lives are deliberately attempting to ward off any approach of the God of grace.

Saint Paul was once one such as these. Yet he says that he was mercifully treated because he acted out of ignorance in his unbelief. It seems odd to say that Paul didn't know what he was doing when he persecuted Christians. How could anyone blaspheme and not know it? How could anyone persecute anyone else in ignorance? How could anyone be arrogant and not be arrogant on purpose? Saint Paul isn't saying that he didn't act deliberately. He is saying he acted in ignorance.

There are two points worth considering here. The first is that although Paul was objectively blaspheming by despising the cross of Christ, although he was objectively persecuting Christ in his members, he did not realize this and so all his zealous activity against Christ and his members came from a misguided but well-meaning heart. It is the heart that Christ sees. Many of the enemies of the Gospel are in the same position. God alone knows their hearts. And so he alone is judge.

The second point is this. If God can convert Saul into Paul and turn an energetic persecutor of the Church into a great saint, then no one in the unbelieving world should count himself free from the range of God's grace and mercy. No wonder they are nervous.

Lord, it is sometimes scary to wonder about people who don't believe in you. Sometimes they make me question my own faith. Help me to see that unbelief has its own providential purpose and that you are the Lord in darkness as well as in the light.

Abundance

Father John Dominic Corbett, O.P.

"Indeed, the grace of our Lord has been abundant, along with the faith and love that are in Christ Jesus." (1 Tm 1: 14)

Grace for Saint Paul basically means unmerited favor. The first and most astounding favor had to be his encounter with the risen Christ and his commissioning as apostle. Here he received the grace of forgiveness (indeed, in Saint Paul's life there was much to forgive). Here you have the gift of the outpouring of the Holy Spirit with its blessing of divine adoption enabling Paul to cry out to God as his Father. Here you have the consequent favor of being chosen by Jesus to have a share in Jesus' own relationship of love and deathless fidelity with his Father. Saint Paul received faith and love which means that he received the gift of his mind's own knowing of Jesus and the gift of loving God and God's people, not with his own paltry resources, but with God's own love.

As if that were not enough, Saint Paul was given the privilege and role of an apostle. Here he is one personally sent by Jesus. He is sent as his ambassador and with his full power and authority. Not that Saint Paul reveled in power and glory as the world understands these terms. He only reveled in his following of his master and in the imitation of the sufferings of the cross that this entailed. His only boast was the cross of the Lord. What Saint Paul understood was that it was precisely his following of his Lord in the way of the cross that lent his words the power to change lives. It wasn't human eloquence that mattered. It wasn't learning. It was Christ, the power and wisdom of God, foolishness to those being lost and God's highest wisdom to those foolish enough to believe the Gospel and be saved.

Saint Paul was used by Christ to bring the treasures of grace to the whole pagan world. Which was pretty much everybody. Abundance indeed.

Lord Jesus, you made Saint Paul know your mercy. You made him able to preach your saving cross. You made his words bear your own life within them and you have brought life to the whole world through his Gospel. Glory be to you for ever.

Chosen for the Chosen

Father John Dominic Corbett, O.P.

*"This saying is trustworthy and deserves full acceptance:
Christ Jesus came into the world to save sinners. Of these I am
the foremost. But for that reason I was mercifully treated, so that
in me, as the foremost, Christ Jesus might display all his patience
as an example for those who would come to believe in him
for everlasting life." (1 Tm 1: 15-16)*

We often see people in love with someone we would never have chosen. What does he see in her? What does she see in him? It's not brains, looks, money, cuteness. These things get us started, but at the end of the day we love because we want to.

Why does God love us? It isn't because we are good. God loves us not because we are good but because he is. He loves us because he wants to.

Saint Paul makes that clear. He was arrogant, persecuting, judgmental, wrong. Yet God chose him to be the Apostle to the Nations. Why?

Saint Paul asked that question and found a clue in the very fact that he did not deserve to be chosen. He was the foremost of sinners. For that very reason he was chosen as an example of Christ's patience. He was chosen to make it clear that God's choice to love us and save us has nothing to do with any deserving qualities we have. So Paul the sinner was chosen and loved by God to make it clear that all of us sinners are chosen and loved by God.

This is hard for us to understand. We think that being chosen by God involves privilege, rank, merit. The Bible is clear, however, that whenever God chooses someone, it is not principally for that person's own sake but for the sake of others.

Jesus himself was revealed as God's own beloved Son in the context of his baptism in the river Jordan. The special love and intimacy God has with his Son is revealed in the very moment when his Son is sent to be the Lamb of God, the Suffering Servant, and the Crucified, not for his own sake but for the sake of the world.

We are the chosen of God. But we will only know this if we share in the cross.

Lord Jesus, you were seated at the Father's right hand in glory, and yet out of sheer love for us you were sent into the world for our salvation. Help us to see that you wish to send us into the world as well. Please make us willing to be sent.

Eye Has Not Seen

Father John Dominic Corbett, O.P.

"To the king of ages, incorruptible, invisible, the only God, honor and glory forever and ever. Amen." (1 Tm 1: 17)

Saint Paul cannot contain himself, and so he breaks out into praise. He has just described God's matchless mercy in choosing himself, the chief of sinners, to show God's limitless mercy. Who is Paul praising? It seems clear that he is praising God the Father of Jesus the Lord. He calls him the King of the Ages. He praises God as existing majestically above time, and above change. This is praise that can be given to God and to none other. Everything else exists as surrounded or conditioned or limited or pressed by time. God is not pressed. God isn't in time. Time is in God.

Paul praises God as invisible and incorruptible. He is saying that God who is unseen is more real than anything that can be seen and that he lives with a life that cannot die.

Paul praises God as "deserving" of honor and glory. Praise and worship of God is not worship of mere power. We worship him in his goodness. We worship him in his truthful loyalty to everything he has made, and we worship him in the mercy that makes him still (after all this time and after all our sins) want to be our God.

This God is the Father of Jesus, and the qualities that make the Father adorable are in the Son in ways we would never have guessed. The Timeless One enters time. The Almighty enters the world only with the permission of a teenage girl. The Incorruptible and Immortal One dies on a tree. The One who died in disgrace is risen and lives for ever in all the majesty and honor proper to almighty God. God the Father makes his majesty accessible to us in the glorified humanness of his Son. Eye has not seen this glory. For this we live. At the end of the day nothing else matters. Amen.

We praise you, Father, for your infinite glory and majesty. We praise you for showing us this in the crucified and glorified humanity of your Son Jesus Christ. We beg you to send us the Holy Spirit so that we may be transfigured in him and share in his glory for ever.

The Good War

Father John Dominic Corbett, O.P.

*"Fight a good fight by having faith and a good conscience.
Some, by rejecting conscience, have made a shipwreck of
their faith."* (1 Tm 1: 18-19)

We are used to going to communion when we go to Mass. This wasn't always the case. Good Catholics would go to Mass on Sundays, of course, and on holy days of obligation, and the devout would go more often still. But these same devout people would go to Holy Communion maybe twice a year. Why so rarely?

Part of the reason was the severity of the fasts required. But there was another reason as well. People had the idea that they had to make a good confession every time they received communion if they were to be able to approach communion with a good conscience. Having to go to confession is hard. Many people preferred then and prefer now to avoid it.

What is the relationship between confession and a good conscience? A common view was that one first carefully examined one's conscience to see if there were any mortal sins that had not yet been absolved. Then one confessed them and did one's penance. Then one's conscience was clear and one could go to receive the Eucharist. This was true as far as it went. But it could give the impression that access to God in the Eucharist was "achieved" by the scrupulously honest and therefore painful admission of our sins. This was misleading. Access to God is granted by Jesus, our High Priest who for ever entered the presence of God on our behalf pouring out the blood of his own sacrifice. It is this blood, and not honest introspection, that cleanses our consciences and makes us able to enter the Holy of Holies.

If we know the price paid for our redemption by Christ, we know two things. The first is that God loves us more than we can imagine, and wants us to stand before him. The second thing is that we can therefore afford to admit the truth about our sins, repent in peace, and have a good conscience.

Lord, we are able to approach the Father only because you first entered his presence on our behalf. Help us to have confidence in the power of your glorified humanity to save us. Help us to have no fear of the truth about our lives.

Rendering to Caesar

Father John Dominic Corbett, O.P.

"I ask that supplications, prayers, petitions, and thanksgivings be offered for everyone, for kings and for all in authority, that we may lead a quiet and tranquil life in all devotion and dignity."
(1 Tm 2: 1-2)

We are always paying debts to each other. Some debts are easily calculated. What do I owe for this night's dinner? I can ascertain that I owe the restaurant $34.50 plus 15 to 20% for the tip for the waiter. How much extra time after class do I owe an unwilling and unengaged student? That isn't so easily determined.

Some debts are so huge that we can't ever fully repay them. Our debt to our parents is like that. So is our debt to God. These debts are such that all we can do in repayment is to try to be as worthy of these gifts as we can.

When Saint Paul asks for "supplications, prayers, petitions, and thanksgivings for everyone, for kings and for all in authority," it is hard not to think that he is praying for his country and that this prayer is part of an attempt to repay what can never in the nature of the case be repaid. But he is not praying for his country. He is praying for those in authority in his country. They need his prayers. Those in authority have grave responsibilities. They have the obligation to frame laws that are fair and just. If they don't do this they incur great guilt. They have the obligation to see to the common defense in a way that is both effective and just. They must do this without resorting to propaganda, murder, or any of the other short-cuts so tempting to those in power. They must punish wrongdoers but take care not to implicate the innocent. Our rulers, whoever they are and in whatever form of government in which they operate, owe us this. It is a debt difficult to fulfill and terrible in consequence if it is not fulfilled. So our rulers and those in authority need our prayers for their protection. We must pray for them. We owe them this.

Lord, you are the King of kings and the Lord of lords. You alone know the terrible responsibilities that face those who have charge of the common good. Help them to love justice more than power, mercy more than justice, and help them to fear your name.

God's Will Is Our Salvation

Father John Dominic Corbett, O.P.

"God our savior, who wills everyone to be saved and to come to knowledge of the truth." (1 Tm 2: 3-4)

Paul tells us here that God wills everyone to be saved. But there are many meanings to the phrase "God wills," and so it is important to be as clear as we can be about what Paul means to say.

The basic meaning of "God wills" is "God loves." We can only will what we love. We only will something insofar as it seems good to us. When Paul teaches us that God wills everyone be saved, he is teaching us that God has fallen in love with saving everyone. He regards this as "very good."

How far does this take us? After all, I might be in love with the idea of being twenty pounds lighter. Does it follow that I am willing to do the diet and exercise to achieve this happy state? The millions of discarded diet and exercise books in our dumpsters is sad testimony to the contrary.

But God has not only seen that this end is good. He intends to achieve it. How do we know this? Because he has formulated a plan to save us. The details of this plan are gradually and lovingly confided to us in the collection of inspired writings that we call the Holy Bible. God proved his seriousness when he executed his plan in sending his Son to save us by dying in an act of love on the wood of the cross.

But there is another question. When God says of the creation, "Let it be," there is no chance it won't happen. Does he bring about our salvation in the same automatic way? The answer must be no. God did create us without us, but will not save us without us. He makes us an offer we can, in fact, refuse. Love is only love when it is free and not coerced. The most precious grace is the grace freely to say "yes" to him.

Lord, you have created us out of love and have no other end in view for us than an eternity of joy in your presence. When we are tempted, help us to believe this with all our hearts. Give us joy and freedom in your service.

Mediation

Father John Dominic Corbett, O.P.

"For there is one God./ There is also one mediator between God and the human race,/ Christ Jesus, himself human,/ who gave himself as ransom for all." (1 Tm 2: 5-6)

We tend to assume that a relationship with God is fundamentally like a personal relationship with any other person. But this isn't true. Other persons exist on our level. We can reach them. God doesn't exist in the limited way that we do. So we can't reach him. Not without help. There is an old story about traveling in Ireland. If you ask for directions, say, for a walking tour in Limerick from Gortboy to Garryduff, the guide will try out various routes, but the punch line is always, "Ah sure, you can't get there from here." It's the same with a personal relationship with God. Because God is God and we are not God; when we try our own personal walking tour looking for a personal God we end up with, "Ah sure, you can't get there from here."

If we are to approach him on a personal level we need a go-between. This is the doctrine of mediation, and we find it hard to accept for two reasons. The first obstacle is pride. We want to be able to address God on our own terms. The second obstacle is a kind of fear. After all, if I have to go through another person to talk to my friend, he is probably not happy with me.

This isn't the case with our relationship with God. The fact that God has sent his Son to us as a go-between means that it was he who wasn't satisfied with relating to us as creator. It was he who wanted more. Relating to us through his Son on a human level is what makes it possible for us to relate to him on a divine level as his adopted children. For us it is mediation that makes it possible to have God as a friend.

Jesus, we live in a world which doesn't really see why it needs you. Please send the Holy Spirit into all of our lives so that we can know who you really are and can know why you said, "No one comes to the Father but through me."

Christian Revenge

Father J. M. Sullivan, O.P.

"It is my wish, then, that in every place the men should pray,
lifting up holy hands, without anger or argument."
(1 Tm 2: 8)

Revenge tops the charts when it comes to motives for vicious acts. The theme of revenge is woven throughout the movies we go to, the novels we read, and even the talk shows we watch. Why is it that revenge always sells? What is it about "getting back at" someone that excites us? At the heart of revenge, it has to be admitted, is the need for us to be "in control." When we have been hurt, disrespected, or even abused by someone, it was because we were not "in control" at the time, so by seeking and exacting revenge we are proving to others and ourselves that we are now back "in control." The suffering we cause another in an act of revenge is evidence enough to prove that desired control. Is seeking revenge Christian, though? Are we to be proud of it? The Catechism of the Catholic Church teaches us that the fifth commandment does not only prohibit murder, but that it is also a "proscription of anger, hatred, and vengeance. Going further, Christ asks his disciples to turn the other cheek, to love their enemies" (CCC 2262). Saint Paul tells Timothy that the men of the Church particularly are not to be ruled by anger or argument. They are rather to lift up holy hands in prayer. The way that believers in Christ get "revenge" for the wrongs done to them is by offering those acts of injustice to the Lord. We are not to be bound by anger or to be embraced by argument, especially in our lives of prayer. The true Christian is not one who exacts revenge but rather one who extends forgiveness, thereby revealing who truly is "in control" of everything: the One to whom the "holy hands, without anger or argument" were lifted.

Lord, free my heart from seeking any revenge for the wrongs done to me. As I pray, make my hands holy so that they may be offered to others in forgiveness and peace.

The Only Encounter

Father J. M. Sullivan, O.P.

"Undeniably great is the mystery of devotion,/ Who was manifested in the flesh,/ vindicated in the spirit,/ seen by angels,/ proclaimed to the Gentiles,/ believed in throughout the world,/ taken up in glory." (1 Tm 3: 16)

All too often we can think that our Catholic faith is about some abstract working out of theological presuppositions and moral theorems which have nothing to do with the lives we really lead. The Church, this argument goes, is just out of touch with the real world in which we live. Saint Paul counters this thinking though with his own words of wisdom to Timothy. "Undeniably great is the mystery of devotion," he says, but he is not referring to a mysterious book of theology, or a great pamphlet about the teachings of the pope, or even the undeniable Bible itself. Saint Paul is referring to him who is the Mystery of Devotion, Jesus Christ, who "was manifested in the flesh, vindicated in the spirit, seen by angels, proclaimed to the Gentiles, believed in throughout the world, taken up in glory." All of the teachings of the Church come back to this one starting point: the Person of Jesus Christ, God himself, who was made man for our salvation. By making Christ just an "idea" or an "abstraction" we fall into the trap of distancing ourselves from the intimacy for which we were redeemed. This "undeniably great" mystery of our faith, Jesus Christ, draws us again and again into God's eternal love for us, no matter the type of day that we are having, or even the particular suffering we might be enduring. Only Christ can do this for us. In the opening words of his first encyclical, *Deus Caritas Est*, Pope Benedict XVI wrote: "Being Christian is not the result of an ethical choice or a lofty idea, but the encounter with an event, a person, which gives life a new horizon and a decisive direction." Undeniably great is this mystery of devotion!

Loving Father, you have given us your only Son as our Lord and Savior. Draw us closer to you at each moment of our lives so that everything we do might reveal his greatness to the world around us and convert all peoples to him. Give me a new horizon in Christ.

A Mother's Reminder

Father J. M. Sullivan, O.P.

"Now the Spirit explicitly says that in the last times some will turn away from the faith by paying attention to deceitful spirits and demonic instructions through the hypocrisy of liars with branded consciences." (1 Tm 4: 1-2)

How many times does a mother have to tell her children to wash their hands before they sit down at the dinner table? While the answer might be close to the number "infinity," there is an important lesson to be learned here: sometimes we would forget to do certain things if it were not for the reminders of others. Mothers usually do not explain to their children all the intricate reasons for washing hands before dinner, such as the growth of bacteria or the spread of germs; they just tell them to wash their hands and to make it snappy because dinner is getting cold. The Church, as our spiritual mother, has that same responsibility for reminding each one of us of the teachings of Christ, even if it is a difficult topic for us to hear. Given Saint Paul's clear call to be on guard against "deceitful spirits" and "demonic instructions," it seems all the more imperative that we heed the teachings of the Church today. It is all too easy to fall into the "hypocrisy of liars" who justify all of their actions with their "branded consciences." Of course, the Church also teaches us the reasons why we believe what we do, just as a mother does for her children. The key to understanding Saint Paul's caution is to ask ourselves to whom do we pay attention. Is it the Church guided by the Holy Spirit into all truth, or is it some falsification of the truth that only causes us to turn away from the Holy Spirit? We can read the morning newspaper and watch the evening news, but we are also meant to read the Sacred Scriptures and to spend time before the Blessed Sacrament. The "last times" of which Saint Paul speaks might be a little further away if we do.

Spirit of Truth, teach me the fullness of Truth so that I may never fall away from Christ but rather cling to him all the more. Make me docile in learning the Truth in the teachings of the Church.

Hidden Goodness

Father J. M. Sullivan, O.P.

"Everything created by God is good, and nothing is to be rejected when received with thanksgiving, for it is made holy by the invocation of God in prayer." (1 Tm 4: 4-5)

In the span of the seasons, we are often struck by the goodness of God's creation. There is something uniquely "divine" about a dogwood tree in full bloom in the spring, or an evening walk along the beach during a summer's sunset. A tree covered in ice on a cold winter morning and the burning colors of autumn's leaves both seem to point to something more beautiful yet to be seen. In truth, all of this seasonal beauty is meant to direct to us to God, to bring us closer to him, to him who created it all out of nothing. But is this the creation that was Saint Paul's concern? Isn't the beauty of nature apparent, as the examples above remind us? Saint Paul's words invite us to see another type of goodness, another type of beauty, perhaps a beauty and goodness in places where we would rather not see it. He says that "nothing is to be rejected" and so we might imagine a goodness that was at first not visible, a beauty that was only revealed after thanksgiving had been offered in prayer. The hidden goodness that Saint Paul is referring to, then, can be none other than that of suffering. Suffering in and of itself possesses no goodness or beauty. It does however possess both when it is "made holy by the invocation of God in prayer." Nature's "suffering" has a goodness like this as well. Think of those leaves that fall to the ground making a mess, but also making way for a richer soil for next year. Think of the waves of the ocean that pound the beach sometimes mercilessly but make it smooth and debris-free for taking that walk. It is not possible for us to find this hidden goodness in suffering on our own; we can only find it when we offer that suffering to the Lord in prayer, even in prayer of thanksgiving.

Loving Father, you care for me at every moment of my life. Even in the midst of life's sufferings, help me to see the beauty with which you have surrounded me, and the beauty for which I am made. May I always lift up to you a thankful heart, especially in the midst of my sufferings.

The Age for Catechesis

Father J. M. Sullivan, O.P.

*"You will be [...] nourished on the words of the faith and
of the sound teaching you have followed." (1 Tm 4: 6)*

When was the last time that you read a book about the Catholic faith? Don't say the answer out loud, but think now about the last time you watched a television program. We often don't find ourselves very nourished by the "words of the faith" because we are disconnected from them. The Bible is on the bookshelf, the Catechism of the Catholic Church is that new book we haven't had a chance to pick up yet, and religious programming bores us when it comes on television. Probably the greatest difficulty in living out our Catholic faith, though, is the lack of knowledge we have about our faith. We fall victim to public opinion polls about the Church and her teachings. Most Catholic adults stopped learning about the faith in the eighth grade, and so when faced with a forty or fifty-year-old's questions, the mind of a thirteen-year-old doesn't help all that much. Saint Paul reminds us that our faith is meant to nourish us. The "sound teaching" that we have received we are to follow and be nourished with for the rest of our lives. Pope John Paul II wrote in the Catechism of the Catholic Church: "Catechesis is an *education in the faith* of children, young people, and adults which includes especially the teaching of Christian doctrine imparted, generally speaking, in an organic and systematic way, with a view to initiating the hearers into the fullness of Christian life" (CCC 5). It is this fullness which lies within our grasp as we learn about our faith. Catechesis is for every age, not just for children. Being educated in the faith is not something that stops because of a graduation or a sacrament. Rather, those moments become opportunities for learning even more about the Lord Jesus, and in truth falling more deeply in love with him.

*Lord Jesus Christ, help me to know you more and more each day.
Give my mind an ability to understand better the great mysteries
of our faith, and my heart a greater desire to share in the fullness
of the Christian life.*

Spiritual Training

Father J. M. Sullivan, O.P.

"Train yourself for devotion, for, while physical training is of limited value, devotion is valuable in every respect, since it holds a promise of life both for the present and for the future."
(1 Tm 4: 7-8)

One part of physical training that most people never think about but that all great athletes will attest to is the need for rest. Physical training is certainly about the physical activity that the body can do, but physical training is also about the body getting the rest the body needs so that it can accomplish that physical training. Saint Paul's words to Timothy about spiritual training can be seen in the same way: not in terms of doing things spiritually, but in resting in things spiritually. Training ourselves for devotion, then, means "resting" ourselves in devotion. One of the obligations that we as Catholics have every Sunday is to attend Mass and to observe a holy day of rest. Both are intimately related to the other. This obligation not only keeps the worship of the Lord as a regular practice of our life, but it also reminds us of our obligations in other areas of our lives. The Catechism of the Catholic Church makes the point: "The institution of the Lord's Day helps everyone enjoy adequate rest and leisure to cultivate their familial, cultural, social, and religious lives." While Sunday is always to be devoted to the Lord, it is also dedicated to our families and healthy recreation. Sunday helps us to remember in the simplest of terms that there are other people who matter beyond ourselves. "On Sundays and other holy days of obligation, the faithful are to refrain from engaging in work or activities that hinder the worship owed to God, the joy proper to the Lord's Day, the performance of the works of mercy, and the appropriate relaxation of mind and body" (CCC 2184-2185). It is this relaxation, so essential to true spiritual growth, and this training for devotion which hold a promise of life both for the present and for the future.

Lord of the Sabbath, you give me a day of rest each week to worship and to grow in devotion. Give me a greater desire for the holy life of heaven so that each day of my life here might prepare me for that Eternal Day with you.

The Task of Holiness

Father J. M. Sullivan, O.P.

"For this we toil and struggle, because we have set our hope on the living God, who is the savior of all, especially of those who believe." (1 Tm 4: 10)

Pope John Paul II, in closing the Holy Door of Saint Peter's Basilica, issued an apostolic letter to the Church for the beginning of the third millennium of Christianity. As one door closed, another door opened. One of the points that he made in this letter had to do with the universal call to holiness – an important reminder given to the Church during the Second Vatican Council. Pope John Paul II simply called the Church back to holiness, and said that in the spiritual life we realize that the "gift of holiness" soon becomes a task. In other words, what was at first given to us without any movement on our part soon is only sustained by our responding to God's continued invitation to holy works which build up within us a greater desire for God. Saint Paul mentions "toil and struggle," and these words need not scare us off because they are quickly followed by "hope." The "toil and struggle" of the Christian life is real. When we read about the lives of the saints, we come to appreciate all that they gave up so that they could follow Christ wholeheartedly. What we look forward to as Christians is not the "toil and struggle," which are temporary, but rather the fulfillment of that hope, which is eternal. Hope assures us of God's promises and his power to fulfill them. The "task of holiness" is not so much about a particular work, but rather a life's project of coming to set all of "our hope on the living God" and coming to accept him as our Savior. In this new millennium of Christianity, we pass through the door opened before us, and willingly accept the "toil and struggle" ahead. We hope in God and set to work at the task ahead.

Heavenly Father, in sending us your Son, you gave him as a model of holiness for our own lives. Unite our life with Christ's and fill us with the grace to accept your will. Open before us the door to eternal life.

The Benefit of Youth

Father J. M. Sullivan, O.P.

*"Let no one have contempt for your youth, but set an example
for those who believe, in speech, conduct, love, faith, and purity."*
(1 Tm 4: 12)

Children always seem to capture the attention of all those around them whenever they speak. They tell fascinating stories filled with adventure and excitement, and even on occasion reveal "family facts" best left at home! At other times, though, they ask pointed questions while demanding just as pointed answers in return. It's not easy to fool children because somehow they have an innate sense to know when they are being fooled, and that is precisely why children ask so many questions about the Catholic faith. It doesn't make much sense to them. And they want answers. We, as Catholics, believe in things that we cannot see. We profess things in the Creed that we cannot prove, and we live our life in a way that is different from the rest of the people around us. Children just love to ask why we do all these things. This religious questioning though can, at first, be difficult for Catholic parents. Not all parents might know exactly why we do all the things we do, and the questions can be threatening. Then some parents might see these questions as the child questioning their faith. Children's questions though are beneficial both for the child and the parents. Both will end up learning more about their faith by the answers given. And we have the assurance of the Church that as we hand on our faith to our children we might not always explain things in a "crystal-clear" manner, but we are allowing them to come closer to God. The Catechism of the Catholic Church encourages us to talk about the faith: "Admittedly, in speaking about God like this, our language is using human modes of expression; nevertheless it really does attain us to God himself, though unable to express him in his infinite simplicity" (CCC 43). Our explanations might not capture the fullness of God, but these answers do help us attain it.

Father, your gift of youth makes us free to ask what is most troubling us at all times. Free us from any reservation in learning your truth, and make us more open to understand the great gift of our faith.

Evidence of Christ

Father J. M. Sullivan, O.P.

"Be diligent in these matters, be absorbed in them, so that your progress may be evident to everyone." (1 Tm 4: 15)

We want our progress to be evident to everyone. It seems contrary to our understanding of doing something solely for the glory of God, doesn't it? Why would we care if it were evident to everyone? The best way to understand this might be to consider it from the reverse, namely, our "regress" being evident to everyone. Do we ever think about our sins influencing or affecting other people? Of course, we might be all too aware of how our sins affect us, but what about how they affect our families, our friends, or even those we work with? When we sin "boldly and openly," like bragging about not going to Mass every Sunday or what we have seen on the internet, we are not only hurting ourselves, we are also hurting others. Now, of course, we are not intending necessarily to hurt other people but, in fact, we are. We hurt them by the bad example that we are giving them. We are, in a word, giving them *scandal*. The Catechism of the Catholic Church teaches us that "scandal is an attitude or behavior which leads another to do evil. The person who gives scandal becomes his neighbor's tempter" (CCC 2284). As parents, managers, respected persons, friends, each one of us needs to be aware of how other people, maybe weaker than ourselves, might be led more easily into their own sin because of our poor example. Saint Paul, then, wants our good example to shine before others – not for our sake, but for their sake. Our diligence in the matters of the faith is not done so that we might be rewarded, but that others may be drawn closer to Christ through us. Something of ourselves will always be evident to everyone; may it always be the good that we want them to do as well.

Lord Jesus, make the example of my life one that evidences your grace at work within me. May I never give scandal to anyone, and be always willing to help my neighbor in times of struggle and temptation.

A New Family

Father J. M. Sullivan, O.P.

"Do not rebuke an older man, but appeal to him as a father. Treat younger men as brothers, older women as mothers, and younger women as sisters with complete purity." (1 Tm 5: 1-2)

Flip open to any page of any newspaper, listen to the radio for ten minutes, or watch television for only five minutes and most assuredly you will find the family under attack in some way. Whether it is a headline about a homosexual couple adopting a child, a song glorifying pre-marital sex, or a sitcom mocking marital fidelity, each of them is attacking the family. It is the family, though, that Saint Paul uses as a model for the members of the Church – for how we are to treat each other. Sadly, then, when our families suffer in society, so too does the Church. We forget the bonds of love and forgiveness that are meant to hold us together as family, regardless of the suffering we must endure. As the Catechism of the Catholic Church teaches us, "The Church is nothing other than 'the family of God.' From the beginning, the core of the Church was often constituted by those who had become believers 'together with all [their] household' (cf. Acts 18: 8)" (CCC 1655). The family has always been cherished by the Church because the Church understands clearly the importance of the family and its essential role in passing on the truths of salvation. The early families that converted to Christianity were compared to "islands of Christian life in an unbelieving world" (CCC 1655), and it might feel like this is the same reality we are facing today. Instead of depressing us, though, this realization needs to give us all the more reason to protect our families and to listen to Christ and his Church. It needs to give us all the more reason to ensure that our own "Christian islands" will always be there in this wide ocean of disbelief – offering all who pass by safe refuge along with happiness and holiness. If you were to collect enough of these islands, soon you would have enough to build a continent, or even to rebuild the Church.

Loving Father, make our families holy. Make our parishes more like a loving family, where concern for each other makes our worship of you all the more pleasing. Help all families that are in distress, especially those suffering because of divorce.

The Curse of a BMW

Father J. M. Sullivan, O.P.

"We brought nothing into the world, just as we shall not be able to take anything out of it. If we have food and clothing, we shall be content with that. Those who want to be rich are falling into temptation and into a trap and into many foolish and harmful desires, which plunge them into ruin and destruction."

(1 Tm 6: 7-9)

If someone had told you that they were just given seventeen BMWs (all different models – of course!), do you think that your first response would be: "Gee, what a burden!"? Of course it wouldn't; you would probably say, "That's awesome, can I drive one?" Now… what if someone told you that they had seventeen children? Honestly, would your response be closer to "burden" or "awesome"? Presently we live in a society that very often places material possessions over and against the many wonderful gifts that the Lord gives us. Catholics too can often fall into selfishness and self-centeredness even when thinking about the size of their families. There is no doubt that seventeen BMWs require much less "maintenance" than seventeen children do, but aren't seventeen children much more precious than seventeen BMWs? The Catechism of the Catholic Church assures us: "Sacred Scripture and the Church's traditional practice see in *large families* a sign of God's blessing and the parents' generosity (cf. GS 50 § 2)" (CCC 2373). Large families are due not only to the blessing of the Lord but also to the generosity of the parents – a generosity which is evidenced by their sacrificing the many material possessions they could have had if they had given up the blessing of more children. To see the gift of life as a "burden" *in any way* is a result of sin. This "burdensome" view of life, though, pervades our age and our society. Large families counter this tendency by their very presence. Large families are not only a blessing for the immediate family but also for the rest of society as well. Large families remind us all that *life is a gift from God* – and what a precious gift it is! – much more precious than even seventeen BMWs! "We brought nothing into the world, just as we shall not be able to take anything out of it."

Loving Father, your gift of children reminds us of the preciousness of each human person. May we be sacrificing of all material possessions that would impede our generosity in caring for any person you would give to us. May we truly be rich in the ways of your grace.

In God We Trust

Father J. M. Sullivan, O.P.

"For the love of money is the root of all evils, and some people in their desire for it have strayed from the faith and have pierced themselves with many pains." (1 Tm 6: 10)

It can hardly be blamed on money itself since on every dollar bill in the United States we have the clear reminder: "In God we trust." Why, then, is the love of money the root of all evils? First off, it is easy enough to find this Scripture verse misquoted and misrepresented as "money is the root of all evils." Saint Paul is clearly not saying that, since a major endeavor in his preaching was caring for the poor, and to do that he took up numerous collections. Rather, it is the disordered "love of money" that is clearly the root of all evils. Why is this so? Money for most people represents power of some kind: in healthcare, the power to decide to which doctors I can go; in education, the power to determine with whom my children will be educated; in consumerism, the power to have possessions that other people do not. "In money we trust" becomes often enough the sentiment of our heart even if we do not express it in words. We find ourselves, though, plagued with more worries the more possessions we have. We have to worry about their maintenance and their security. We have to worry about getting new and better ones when the time comes along. We can even become so preoccupied with things that we forget the persons who are all around us. If we truly looked at the dollar bill, though, and followed its advice, we wouldn't hold onto it longer than we needed to – just long enough to hand it on to the next person who needed that lesson as well. "In God we trust" is not just a design for currency; it is a way of life that keeps us strong in the faith and free from many pains.

Lord, free me from all love of money. Keep me faithful to your will in all that I do, and especially in the use of the gifts you have entrusted to my care. May I always help others freely with what you have freely given to me.

Hot Pursuit

Dale O'Leary

"Pursue righteousness, devotion, faith, love, patience, and gentleness." (1 Tm 6: 11)

S aint Paul does not call us to study righteousness, devotion, faith, love, patience, and gentleness, or to think about them or even to pray for them, but to "pursue" them – to run after them. Why? Because they are hard to catch.

Sometimes the English translation doesn't communicate the full weight of the original.

"Righteousness," sometimes translated as justice, refers to the judgment and justice of God.

"Devotion," sometimes translated as piety, is not just ordinary devotion. People can be devoted to things which are not worthy of their respect. Rather, it is devotion to the good – that is, to God. For example, our devotion to the saints should be a devotion that sees through the saints to God who is goodness itself.

"Faith" in the New Testament always refers to faith in God.

The "love" referred to here is not *eros*, sexual desire, or philanthropy, the charitable love of mankind, or the friendship of brotherly love. Rather, it is the love that gives all.

"Patience" is sometimes translated as endurance. This is not human patience or natural strength. Rather, we can wait patiently, we can endure trials, because we know that God is faithful.

"Gentleness" is sometimes translated as meekness. Unfortunately, in English, both of these words imply weakness, but there is nothing weak about what Jesus says of himself: "I am meek and humble of heart." Rather, we are called to pursue the attitude of the martyr, who stands before his persecutors facing death with absolute serenity because he knows that everything is in God's hands. Because of this meekness, the martyr has a power, which those who use mere force cannot overcome.

We are not called to be a little more patient, a little more loving, a little more pious; we are called to be like Christ, and since none of us can ever fully achieve that, we must always be in pursuit of the goal.

Dear Father, let me never be satisfied with my efforts, but always try in every way to imitate more perfectly your beloved Son.

Training for Competition

Dale O'Leary

"Compete well for the faith. Lay hold of eternal life, to which you were called when you made the noble confession in the presence of many witnesses." (1 Tm 6: 12)

Saint Paul calls us to a muscular faith – not wimpy Christianity. Saint Paul wants Saint Timothy to take his spiritual life as seriously as Olympic athletes take their physical training – to compete well.

Today we live in a society which idolizes athletes and admires the dedication with which they train, but rejects even the simplest forms of spiritual training. Dieting to improve your looks or health is treated as a moral imperative, but serious fasting for spiritual reasons is seen as a symptom of mental illness. Young men and women push their bodies beyond healthy limits to win medals, but modern sensibilities are shocked by stories of saints who practiced mortification for spiritual reasons. Women, and even some men, undergo painful surgical procedures to improve their exterior appearance, but are appalled at the idea of undergoing even a small deprivation in the pursuit of interior beauty.

Perhaps we need a little more balance. Mortification that is purposely not satisfying the cravings of the body or enduring some small physical pain has been used for centuries by those seeking holiness.

Of course, like anything, fasting and mortification can be overdone or done for the wrong reason or even become a source of pride. Therefore it is recommended that serious mortifications be discussed with a spiritual director. That said, all of us can benefit from regular, simple disciplines. We can fast from a particular food or from some licit pleasure such as television for a set period of time.

We can extend the fast before communion or return to the practice of abstinence from meat on all Fridays. We could go further and abstain from fish as well, since going out for a lobster dinner on Friday night is hardly a penitential practice.

If we are going to compete, we need to train, so that we will be able to run the race and win the prize.

Dear Father in heaven, help me to overcome the desires of the flesh and thereby grow in holiness.

The Commandment

Dale O'Leary

*"I charge [you] before God, who gives life to all things [...]
to keep the commandment without stain or reproach until
the appearance of our Lord Jesus Christ."* (1 Tm 6: 13-14)

As I read through this verse, I noticed that the word "commandment" was singular. Saint Paul had given Saint Timothy a host of instructions; I wondered to which one commandment he is referring. So I read the rest of the letter.

I should have known. It is the commandment to love – love of God, love of neighbor. My question made me think how often I am so occupied trying to follow the instructions and get everything right, that I forget the most important thing – love.

Some of us are called, as Saint Timothy was, to work within the Church, others work in the world, others within the family, but wherever we are placed, most of us have to deal with other people, and frankly this is often the part of the task that causes the most stress. Sometimes we may feel that things would be easier if only other people would do what we want them to do. If we allow this thought to fester, we can become angry or bitter.

It is easy to be tempted to think that our plans are so good, so wise that everyone should follow them. We may become discouraged because others do not join our organization or come to the event we have worked so hard to plan. We may see our hard work as wasted. We can become so concerned about the success of a particular project that we forget the people involved.

Yes, the tasks matter, but what matters more is love. Have we done everything with love? If one person comes when you expect twenty, will you serve that one person with the same love? If, on the other hand, the event is a great success, will you give the glory to God or keep it for yourself.

If we do everything out of love – love of God and love of neighbor – every project, regardless of the natural outcome, will be supernaturally successful.

Father in heaven, help me to remember that the first commandment is love. Never let me become so consumed with the task that I forget the person.

All Honor and Glory

Dale O'Leary

"The King of kings and Lord of lords, who alone has immortality, who dwells in unapproachable light, and whom no human being has seen or can see. To him be honor and eternal power. Amen." (1 Tm 6: 15-16)

When I read the words "King of kings and Lord of lords," the music of Handel's great work *Messiah*, plays in my mind, and if I am alone I begin to sing "and he shall reign for ever and ever."

The story is told that when Handel finished the Hallelujah Chorus he wept and cried out to his servant, "I did think I did see all heaven before me, and the great God himself." There is no question that the work is inspired. So inspired that when the king of England first heard the Hallelujah Chorus he rose from his seat and, in accordance with protocol, the entire audience stood with him, starting a tradition that lasted two hundred years.

However, a few years ago I attended a performance of *Messiah* at Symphony Hall in Boston, Massachusetts. Before the performance began, the audience was instructed not to rise for the Hallelujah Chorus. It was no longer considered appropriate. We were told that such demonstrations weren't necessary and might disturb the orchestra, singers, and audience.

Saint Paul has no such scruples. Just as the king of England felt compelled to stand to honor the King of kings, Saint Paul cannot help himself; he interrupts his instructions to Saint Timothy to break into praise of God to whom is due all honor and glory.

Are we more considerate than all the audiences of the past or just less interested in giving honor to the one who truly deserves all honor and glory? I suppose the management was right: standing up for the King of kings might make some people uncomfortable, but I personally felt deprived. This great hymn of praise to God – this recapitulation of salvation history – had been reduced to a mere performance. I remember feeling very alone in the packed concert hall, wondering, "Is anyone listening to the words?"

Holy Spirit, fill our hearts with such joy that our mouths cannot cease praising God.

Addicted to Stuff

Dale O'Leary

"Tell the rich in the present age not to be proud and not to rely on so uncertain a thing as wealth but rather on God, who richly provides us with all things for our enjoyment. Tell them to do good, to be rich in good works, to be generous, ready to share, thus accumulating as treasure a good foundation for the future, so as to win the life that is true life." (1 Tm 6: 17-19)

Most of us don't think of ourselves as "rich" but, in comparison with those living in the time of Jesus, the average person living in the industrialized world today has many more possessions, more luxuries, more services, and more entertainment than ancient kings. Open your closet, check your garage, you may find it crammed with stuff you don't need and will never use again. Count the number of devices you own that bring music into your home. Consider the luxury of the ordinary automobile and compare it to an ancient wagon.

But our wealth has its dangers. We are tempted to rely on accumulated objects for security. Bounty can become excess. We can become addicted to stuff. I have listened to people rationalize why they really need one hundred tee shirts or seventy-five pairs of shoes. I have seen closets full of junk their owner was hoarding just in case some day they might need that one thing out of all their accumulated stuff. Of course when that day comes they probably won't have the time to go through the "just-in-case" stuff and will be forced to go out and buy another. Many hold on to trash as though it were gold, frankincense, and myrrh. Their basements, garages, and attics are filled with broken promises – furniture, toys, and appliances in various states of disrepair that they promised to fix but haven't gotten around to. Rather than trusting the Lord, they rationalize and make excuses, convincing themselves that their broken and worn out stuff is a hedge against a future financial disaster.

What is worse, they consider their habit of hoarding a virtue. They do not see how their hoard of stuff steals their time, creates chaos and strife in the family, and is a sign of a lack of trust in God.

Were they to give their excess to the poor, they would pile up treasure in heaven.

Dear heavenly Father, teach me detachment from material objects. Help me to be generous to the poor, and to trust that if I give away my excess, you will supply my needs.

The Antithesis of Wisdom

Dale O'Leary

"Avoid profane babbling and the absurdities of so-called knowledge. By professing it, some people have deviated from the faith./ Grace be with all of you." (1 Tm 6: 20-21)

A priest called and asked if I could help a parishioner who was having problems writing a paper for a course he was taking at a local college. The man brought me the textbook for the course. He said he couldn't make head or tail out of it. The professor was giving him failing grades, and he was getting an ulcer. It took me several days to understand what the author was trying to say; I had to read many of the sections several times. Her sentences were long and confusing. She used words that weren't in the dictionary, which she had apparently made up. It would have been easier if the book had been in Greek. However, after some research I was able to grasp what the author was aiming at, and realized that this book corresponded perfectly to the kind of empty sounds and pseudo-knowledge that Saint Paul warned Saint Timothy about.

In Greek, the word in Saint Paul's letter translated as "absurdities" is *antitheseis*. If a thesis is a logical proposition, then this book perfectly fits this description because it is most definitely anti-logic. The author appeared to be driven by a perverse desire to attack everything that is obviously true about life, family, marriage, motherhood, and what it means to be a man or a woman. According to her, everything we believe to be true and natural is actually nothing but a "social construction" designed to oppress women.

The book mounts a frontal attack on natural law and logic. There was no way to argue with those who embrace these absurdities because they reject logic and natural law, which are the foundation for any reasonable discussion.

Unfortunately, at many universities the professors teach these absurdities, and students should therefore heed Saint Paul's warning and avoid this "profane babbling."

Dear Father in heaven, give us the true knowledge and the courage to stand against what is false and dangerous.

Spiritual Children

Dale O'Leary

"To Timothy, my dear child: grace, mercy, and peace from God the Father and Christ Jesus our Lord." (2 Tm 1: 2)

Saint Paul thought of Timothy as his spiritual child. We should all aspire to become the spiritual mother or father of many children.

How is this to be accomplished?

The conception of faith begins with love. Very often we are drawn to particular people. We see their need and their openness, and we want the best for them. And what is best? The best for every person is that they come into a personal relationship with God.

Bringing forth spiritual children requires prayer. The birth of faith in a human heart is the work of grace. We need to invoke the Holy Spirit. We can also pray to a person's guardian angel.

Faith comes by hearing, and how can they believe if they have not heard? Example is great, but there comes a time when we need to speak boldly, proclaiming the Good News that, through the blood of Jesus Christ shed on the cross, our sins are forgiven. Too often it appears to those outside that the Church is about what we must do for God, when it is first about what God has done for us. Our subsequent actions are only a small inadequate response to his love.

Finally, and for most people this is the hard part, we put the question to our friend: "Will you say 'Yes' to God?"

The Church offers her children multiple opportunities to say "Yes" – adult baptism, confirmation, the Easter affirmation, and the many forms of consecrations – but some people don't get the message. They say the words with their mouths, but not their hearts. No one, not even God, can force faith into a human heart. Each person must decide for himself to say "Yes" to God.

As we wait for their answer, the whole universe holds its breath. If the answer is yes, the angels rejoice.

Lord Jesus, fill my heart with a hunger for souls that I may have the courage to speak the word and have many spiritual children.

Fathers and Mothers in the Faith

Dale O'Leary

"I am grateful to God, whom I worship with a clear conscience as my ancestors did, as I remember you constantly in my prayers, night and day." (2 Tm 1: 3)

I often think how fortunate I am to have been given the gift of faith. I know that I did not deserve this wonderful grace. Why have I been so blessed? Why did I receive the grace to escape out of an arrogant, adolescent atheism into the bosom of Holy Mother Church?

I have no doubt that it was through the prayers of my grandmother, grandfather, and great-aunt Kitty who worried, fretted, but most of all prayed that their beloved grandchild would come to the fullness of faith in Jesus. My aunt would read me Bible stories, and encourage me to memorize the psalms.

They all died before I returned to the faith – died without seeing how God had answered their prayer – but I have no doubt that they continued to intercede for me and are rejoicing in heaven.

Saint Paul sees himself as the heir of all the promises made by God to his ancestors. In the Book of Deuteronomy, God promises the Israelites that he will keep the oath he swore to their fathers: "Understand then, that the Lord, your God, [...] the faithful God who keeps his covenant down to the thousandth generation toward those who love him and keep his commandments."

What a wonderful promise. If this is the promise God made to the Israelites, will he not do as much – if not more – for us, the children of the new covenant? Even if our children stray and wander away from the faith, if we keep the covenant and the commandments, he will not forget them. He will continue to pour out his grace on them even until the last moment of their lives.

I know that my grandparents prayed for their son – my father – and although he wandered, I saw that grace draw him back to the faith in the last year of his life.

Dear Father in heaven, I trust that you will be faithful to your promise and remember my children, and grandchildren, and their children.

Friends For Ever

Dale O'Leary

"I yearn to see you again, recalling your tears, so that I may be filled with joy, as I recall your sincere faith." (2 Tm 1: 4-5)

Saint Paul had ministered in many cities. We can see from his letters that he had built close natural and spiritual relationships, and when he was a prisoner in Rome he remembered those friends. He knew that he would never see most of them again – in this life.

Moving is hard. I have lived in seven different states and sixteen different homes. Each move meant leaving behind dear friends. The parting often was a time for tears. We promise to keep in touch, but then Christmas cards come back unopened, emails returned "recipient unknown," and someone, who touched our lives, who shared our joys and sorrows, was lost to us. We may never see them again – in this life.

When Saint Paul's friends in Caesarea were told by the prophet Agabus that if he went to Jerusalem, he would be arrested and handed over to the Gentiles as a prisoner, they wept and begged him not to go. Saint Paul would not be dissuaded; if this was God's will for him, he would go.

There are times when moving away from family and friends is so difficult that we feel our hearts will break, and yet we have to trust that God knows what is best for us.

I had such an experience. I thought we had found the perfect place – a town, a church, a house, everything I had dreamed of, but most of all wonderful friends. And then my husband took a job in another city – the one place I didn't want to live. I did not want to move. I questioned God's plan, but looking back I see so clearly that the move was God's plan, not just for my husband, but for me, for my work, for each of my children.

My tears have been turned to joy, and I know that one day I will be reunited in heaven with the friends I left behind.

Dear Father, help me to trust that your will for me is all love, even though today I may not be able to see how you will bring blessing out of my tears.

On Fire for the Lord

Dale O'Leary

"I remind you to stir into flame the gift of God that you have."
(2 Tm 1: 6)

We have a house in the country, and behind the garage there is a huge woodpile. At one time we heated our cottage with a wood stove, but then we replaced the cottage with a winterized house with a modern heating system. We had a fireplace, but rarely used it. As the years went by the wood went from dry to rotten. Mushrooms grew in it. Animals lived underneath it. Trees grew out of it. In another decade it will merge with the forest from which the wood came.

The gifts of the Holy Spirit can be compared to that woodpile. They were given to us to burn. We don't have to worry about using up our fuel; as we use what God has given us, he will give us more.

Everyone has gifts, and the Church needs everyone's gifts. At our confirmation the bishop anointed us, and the Holy Spirit was supposed to be stirred into flame within us. We were supposed to take the power we had received and go out and set the world on fire, but many of us let our fire go out.

Have we complained about the coldness of the church we attended, never thinking that we were supposed to be providing the warmth? Have we worried about the world situation, never considering the possibility that we have been given the fuel to light a fire that would be a light to the world? Have we prayed that our children will keep the faith, forgetting that we are supposed to supply the spark that lights their fire?

This isn't about hiding our light under a bushel basket. In too many cases our light is only a tiny spark that couldn't be seen if we put it on a lampstand. We need to pile on the wood and stir the ashes until we burst into flame.

Come, Holy Spirit, let the fire from heaven fall on us as it did on the first apostles.

Home of the Brave

Dale O'Leary

"God did not give us a spirit of cowardice but rather of power and love and self-control." (2 Tm 1: 7)

I am often asked by parents how they can raise their children so that they keep the faith. The best answer to this question came from a friend who was a wonderful example of serene, joyful Christian womanhood. To meet her you would think she hadn't a care in the world, when, in fact, her husband had serious health problems and three of her numerous children had been born with birth defects. She was convinced that parents who give their children an example of courage in the face of difficulties lay a foundation for faith that cannot be shaken.

We are raising children during wartime. The great culture war rages all around us. It is no longer easy to be a Christian. Looking at all the challenges, parents may, in an attempt to protect their children from the ugliness of the battle, try to build a fortress, dig a moat, pull up the drawbridge, and lock the gate. Although it is certainly necessary to keep evil out of our homes, we can unintentionally lock in a spirit of fear. In order to face the challenge posed by a hostile culture, our children need an example of courage.

If your goal is that your children "keep" the faith, teach them how to share their faith with others. Their friends are often struggling, and need to know that God loves them. Children are capable of being evangelists. Nothing builds faith like being the messenger who brings good news. When adolescents begin to witness to friends, they often become motivated to study their faith.

Sometimes parents who sincerely want their children to keep the faith are afraid when they see one of their children with true Christian love reach out to someone in trouble. If parents really believe the faith is worth keeping, then they should rejoice when their children have the courage to reach out to those in need.

Dear Lord Jesus, send the power of your Spirit upon us so that we can raise up courageous young men and women who will be able to overcome the present evils with truth and love.

Prisoners for Christ

Dale O'Leary

"Do not be ashamed of your testimony to our Lord, nor of me, a prisoner for his sake; but bear your share of hardship for the gospel with the strength that comes from God." (2 Tm 1: 8)

Saint Paul was imprisoned because he refused to compromise the truth, even when he could foresee the consequences. We can see in his trial before King Agrippa how Saint Paul's first desire was to win converts, not make enemies. He argued his case calmly and rationally and with real concern for souls, but it was not enough to convince those who wanted him punished. Some of those who opposed him may have sincerely believed that they were defending their established traditions. Some may have feared the Gospel message because they had witnessed the rise of false messiahs who led rebellions that left many dead. The Roman officials did not care about theological controversies. What mattered to them was preserving peace and stability.

We may not be jailed for proclaiming the Gospel, but we do live in a society where many individuals and institutions are hostile to the Gospel message. We may wish that everyone who hears the Good News would embrace it enthusiastically, but we know this is not going to happen. If some of those who heard Jesus in person did not believe, can we expect to do better? If Saint Paul – filled with the Holy Spirit – was not able to convince his opposition, why are we surprised when our arguments fail to change every mind? The very real possibility that we will be rejected, insulted, or even persecuted cannot deter us.

We can prudently wait for an opportune moment, but when that moment comes, we must face our fear of rejection and – trusting in the Holy Spirit – speak the truth with love.

Speaking up can be scary. Even when we feel filled with the Spirit, even when we have prayed, our words may fall like seeds on the path and be trampled underfoot. We must accept such rejection with joy as part of our duty to bear a "share of hardship for the Gospel."

Dear Father in heaven, let me never be ashamed of my faith, calm my fear of rejection, and give me the strength to bring the love, joy, and hope of the Gospel to those around me.

The True Path to a Holy Life

Father Roger J. Landry

"[God] saved us and called us to a holy life, not according to our works but according to his own design and the grace bestowed on us in Christ Jesus before time began." (2 Tm 1: 9)

Our fundamental vocation, Saint Paul tells the young Timothy and us, is to become a saint.

On one level that is fairly obvious: through the salvation Jesus won for us, we are called to heaven, and only saints get to heaven.

But Saint Paul is focused more on the present than on the future. He says that we are called to a holy life now.

Sometimes Catholics can behave as if life is a pass-fail test and that all we need to do is to achieve a *D* with the gift of life. But Christ did not die for us to be mediocre disciples. He gave his all and told us to follow him. He calls us to be holy as he is holy, to be perfect as our heavenly Father is perfect, to love others as Christ loves us.

In order to become holy, we must first adopt the proper means. Today Saint Paul distinguishes for us the right and the wrong means. The false means are "according to our works." No matter how hard we try, we cannot make ourselves saints. Saint Paul recognized this autobiographically. His conversion was not from a wicked life to a good one, but from a false version of a holy life to a true one.

He had thought that one became holy merely by carrying out the religious practices laid down in the Old Testament. After his conversion on the road to Damascus, he saw that one is made holy, rather, by "the grace bestowed on us in Christ Jesus before time began." Holiness, in other words, is not something we achieve, but accept.

From "before time began," God has planned to give us all the help we need to live up to our vocation to be holy in this life and in the next. We receive those graces in the sacraments, in prayer, and in a moral life lived in union with him.

Heavenly Father, you created me for no other reason than to become a saint like Saint Paul. Help me to respond to you like he did, so that your holiness may reign in me now and for ever.

Ministers of the Medicine of Immortality

Father Roger J. Landry

*"Now made manifest through the appearance of our savior
Christ Jesus, who destroyed death and brought life and
immortality to light through the gospel, for which I was
appointed preacher and apostle and teacher." (2 Tm 1: 10-11)*

There's a remedy for malaria, but millions still suffer from it.
There is a cure for leprosy, but still many lepers. How is that
possible? The answer is because no one has yet brought the
proper medicine to those who need and lack it. Multitudes are still
suffering and dying as a result.

We were all born with the worst fatal disease of all, something so
virulent that it kills not just our body but our souls. The Son of
God became one of us in order to save us from this cancer. Before
the Red Cross existed, he gave us his blood. Before there were organ
donation protocols, he gave us his whole body. In short, he became
the vaccine that killed what was killing us and made it possible for
us to live for ever.

Saint Paul tells us today that when Jesus appeared, "he destroyed
death and brought life and immortality to light through the
Gospel." His epiphany led to the epiphany of eternal life. For those
who live in Christ, death is nothing other than a change of address,
to an eternal Versailles.

But just as people still suffer and die from malaria and leprosy,
so people still suffer and may die eternally from the cancer of sin.
The reason is the same: no one has yet brought the proper medicine to those who need and lack it.

Saint Paul, the "doctor of the Gentiles," spent his adult life as a
"doctor without borders," bringing the medicine of immortality,
Christ himself, to the nations. He was first a "preacher," who
announced both the disease and the remedy. He was an "apostle,"
commissioned by the Lord to minister the remedy. He was finally
a "teacher," who educated people how to live in an eternally healthy
way.

By the sacraments of baptism and confirmation, we have not
only been cured but commissioned to bring to others the same
medicine that saved our lives.

*Heavenly Father, thank you for the gift of salvation. Help me to
put my thanks into action by spending my life, as Saint Paul did,
to bring this life-saving remedy to others.*

Loving Trust in the Midst of Suffering

Father Roger J. Landry

"On this account I am suffering these things; but I am not ashamed, for I know him in whom I have believed and am confident that he is able to guard what has been entrusted to me until that day." (2 Tm 1: 12)

Jesus often told us that we would suffer on account of our faith in him. During the Last Supper, he reminded us, "No slave is greater than his master. If they persecuted me, they will also persecute you." He added elsewhere, however, that we should not be afraid, but rejoice when persecuted, "for your reward will be great in heaven; thus they persecuted the prophets who were before you."

Suffering will either make us bitter or better. Suffering on account of the faith will either fill us with shame or with joy. What form our reaction takes depends on whether we see our suffering as separating us or uniting us to Christ. Saint Paul viewed all the persecution he suffered as a means to bring about a greater union with Jesus. Jesus had said that unless we deny ourselves, pick up our cross each day and follow him, we cannot be his disciple. Saint Paul saw in his crosses the path to become a true disciple. He told the Galatians, "May I never boast except in the cross of our Lord Jesus Christ, through which the world has been crucified to me, and I to the world." It was only through that double-death that he could fully share in Christ's life. Being crucified with Christ allowed him truthfully to exclaim that it was no longer he who lived, but Christ who lived in him.

Saint Paul's sufferings brought him into greater union with Jesus because, as he tells us today, "I know him in whom I have believed and am confident that he is able to guard what has been entrusted to me."

Saint Paul didn't merely believe in *ideas*, but in the *person* of Christ, trusting that Jesus would guard his soul from those who sought to harm his body. The same Christ protects us in our sufferings so that we might have with him a similar crucified union.

Heavenly Father, help me, like Saint Paul, never to be ashamed of the sufferings I need to bear out of love for your Son, because it is through them that I become united with him and eternally pleasing to you.

The Christian Rule of Life

Father Roger J. Landry

"Take as your norm the sound words that you heard from me, in the faith and love that are in Christ Jesus." (2 Tm 1: 13)

Travelers have guidebooks, doctors have manuals, students have handbooks, chefs have cookbooks, and gadget owners have how-to guides. The "Dummies" series of books, moreover, is enough to show that, in almost any area of life, those who know little about something are highly dependent on those who know more.

There is a need for guidance, for standards, for a norm, so that a beginner can advance more quickly and assuredly along the path to competence in any discipline. The same guidance is needed in discipleship. Today Saint Paul, a seasoned veteran and expert in the Christian life, urges the young Timothy to take as his norm of conduct the "sound" or "health-giving" words Paul has announced to him. Paul is referring to the words of the Gospel, which he himself received, proclaimed, and adopted as his own standard.

The words of the Gospel are the instruction manual for human life. They indicate how a person is to function properly and achieve the purpose for which he was made. They do this because they show us the life of Jesus, who fully reveals who the human person is and makes clear the supreme goal of human life. But the "letter" of the words is not enough; they must be acted upon. Furthermore, they must be observed with the right spirit. Saint Paul explains that the proper motivation is not mere external conformity with the words, which was what he thought prior to his conversion; rather, it's "in the faith and love that are in Christ Jesus."

We must first believe the words because of our trust in Christ who taught them, and then implement them with love for God and others, for faith without love is dead. Saint Paul did. Saint Timothy, at Paul's urging, did as well.

If we follow the same norm with the same spirit, one day we, too, will share their title.

Father, help me, with faith and love, to adopt as the rule of my life the words and example of your Son, so that I, like Saint Paul, may experience his full saving power.

Eternal Investment Strategy

Father Roger J. Landry

"Guard this rich trust with the help of the holy Spirit that dwells within us." (2 Tm 1: 14)

The greatest treasure we have is the priceless fortune given us by Christ.

Through our baptism, we have become in Christ adopted children of God the Father and joint heirs with Christ of heaven and earth.

As if that were not enough, Christ has bequeathed us as our inheritance in this world the words of eternal life to be our norm, his body and blood to be our food, the Spirit of his Father to be our helper and guide, his earthly Mother to be our loving Mother, too, and all the baptized to be our spiritual siblings.

We are, in fact, the richest people in the history of the world, because we have a wealth that thieves can't steal, moths can't destroy, governments can't tax, and even death can't take away. The only way this patrimony can be lost is by squandering it ourselves, as Adam and Eve and the Prodigal Son taught us.

Saint Paul knows that, like with our first parents, there is an envious, ruthless pillager seeking to get us to throw this endowment away, by convincing us it is of little or no value. That's why the Apostle tells the young Timothy today to "guard this rich trust" he has received.

The question is, how does one guard it?

Jesus gave us an indication in the Gospel in the parable of the talents (Mt 25: 14-30). We protect the treasure we have received not by burying it in the ground, but by investing it. As billionaire investors attest, the best way not to lose a fortune is to continue to try to expand it.

Saint Paul tells Timothy and us that to guard our rich legacy we need the help of "the Holy Spirit that dwells within us." The Holy Spirit is our inner "investment advisor," whom we need to consult and whose counsel we need to follow.

If we do so, we will become even richer still.

Through baptism, Father, I have become your child and your heir. Help me always to remember my dignity and, through your Holy Spirit dwelling within me, fill me with the zeal to invest your gifts and expand your kingdom.

The Most Potent Strength of All

Father Roger J. Landry

"So you, my child, be strong in the grace that is in Christ Jesus."
(2 Tm 2: 1)

Our dominant secularist culture expects, even demands, Christians to compromise. Workers are often let go unless they work on Sundays. Those aspiring to public office are compelled against their consciences to acquiesce to immoral planks of their party's platform. Public school teachers are frequently expected to keep the deepest parts of their being hidden, because politically-correct administrators think that the mere witness of faith may harm students. Emergency room personnel and pharmacists in various states are forced to suppress their compassion for the most innocent and vulnerable human beings and give out abortifacient pills to women who may be pregnant

In short, we are living in an age in which the cultural elites think that the only "good Catholic" is one who "reasonably" allows elite opinions to trump God's law.

The early Christians faced similar pressure, too, from both the Jews and the pagans. The Jews expected them to compromise on the new law of grace and maintain circumcision and the practices of the old covenant. The Romans insisted they burn incense to the pagan deities to show they were good citizens.

Christian courage was needed then and it is needed now.

Today, the elderly Saint Paul, imprisoned for his fidelity to Christ, tells the young Timothy, "Be strong in the grace that is in Christ Jesus." He knew that Timothy would need more than human courage and toughness, for those could easily lead to pride before a fall. Instead, Paul urged him to be strong in grace. He realized from personal experience that it was only when he was humanly weak that he became supernaturally strong and capable of doing all things in him who strengthened him.

God's grace is sufficient for us, just as it was for Paul and Timothy, to toughen us to be faithful to the end.

All-powerful Father, send your Holy Spirit to strengthen me with his gift of courage, so that I, like Paul, Timothy, the apostles, and so many martyrs and saints, may bravely give witness to your Son in good times and in bad.

Christ's Special Forces

Father Roger J. Landry

"Bear your share of hardship along with me like a good soldier of Christ Jesus." (2 Tm 2: 3)

As we see in the life of Jesus, Saint Paul, and the first disciples, the Christian life is not easy.

Jesus wanted his followers to recognize that discipleship costs. In one image he says that we must behave like a general before a battle and calculate what it will take to conquer a larger invading army. The only way we will triumph against the powerful forces set against us, Jesus says, is by making the radical choice to prefer him to all our family members and material possessions, to pick up our cross every day and follow him to crucifixion, and to choose life with him even if it means our death.

Saint Paul enlisted in Christ's army and never quit fighting the good fight of faith. He bore his own share of hardship along with Christ, to make up for what was lacking in Christ's sufferings for the sake of the Church. At the end of his life, he encourages Timothy likewise to do his part as a "good soldier of Christ Jesus."

A good soldier is focused, dutiful, disciplined, obedient, courageous, loyal, and honorable. He functions as a member of a unit, fighting for something greater than himself. He is accustomed to sacrifice and is willing to give his life for others. Every disciple is called to have all these soldierly traits.

Today some balk at this militant imagery as unworthy of the Gospel. Christ came to bring peace, they say, and to make us peacemakers, which they equate with diplomats. Apparently Pontius Pilate and the Sanhedrin did not get that memo in time.

Christ himself stressed, in fact, that he had come to bring not peace but the sword, to lay down his life to save his sheep. Peace comes not from negotiation with the forces of evil, but through conquering evil with love on the battlefield of life.

The war continues, and Christ is still looking for a few good men.

Lord, God of hosts, grant me the courage, with Saints Paul and Timothy, to be a good soldier in your Son's army. Strengthen me to bear my share of hardship for him who bore everything for me.

The Fast World's Slow Path to Wisdom

Father Roger J. Landry

"Reflect on what I am saying, for the Lord will give you understanding in everything." (2 Tm 2: 7)

Today we are bombarded with so much information that few of us have time to process it.

News no longer arrives via the morning paper or three evening television programs, but twenty-four hours a day on continuous cable news stations and hundreds of news websites. We receive more emails, text and instant messages in a day than we can possibly answer. Even when we're away from our computer, the flood does not abate, since almost everything is now available on our high-tech mobile telephones, which vibrate more in an hour than most family phones at home used to ring in a whole day.

While keyboards and universal remotes have put more information at our fingertips than at any time before, probably less than ever passes from our fingertips to our brains. Very little of the information actually forms us.

Because we are stationed in the midst of the information superhighway, with so many facts and figures passing us by at breakneck speeds, Saint Paul's advice today is even more relevant to us than it was to the young Timothy. "Reflect on what I am saying," he tells his junior apostle, "for the Lord will give you understanding in everything."

In order to understand anything, we need to slow down and reflect upon it. This is all the more true in matters of faith, when that reflection takes the form of meditation and prayerful conversation with God. Prayer is the means by which reflective faith seeks understanding and the Lord in his goodness helps us to find it.

As those called to evangelize the cyberspatial areopagus from within, we need this "old-fashioned" prayerful reflection and divinely-aided understanding now more than ever.

In the midst of the noise of modern life, help me to slow down, unchanging Father, and to reflect on the advice Saint Paul has given me, so that I may grow in the understanding of the faith and bring the fruits of that deeper understanding to others.

Saint Paul's Gospel… and Mine

Father Roger J. Landry

"Remember Jesus Christ, raised from the dead, a descendant of David: such is my gospel, for which I am suffering, even to the point of chains, like a criminal. But the word of God is not chained." (2 Tm 2: 8-9)

There are 138,020 words in the New Testament. In this passage, Saint Paul – after three decades of preaching – reduces them to three: "Remember Jesus Christ." This, he said, was "my Gospel," the one he proclaimed, and the one for which lived, suffered, and died.

The Good News wasn't always so simple for him. In his early preaching to the Jews, he used to trace in detail all of salvation history before arriving at its climax, Jesus Christ (see Acts 13: 14-52). Later, when he turned to the Gentiles in Athens and elsewhere, he employed sweeping rhetorical flourishes to establish how Christ was the fulfillment of every honest search for God (see Acts 17: 19-34). Both approaches, however, bore relatively little fruit. So he resolved to simplify his message and preach nothing but "Christ, and Christ crucified" (see 1 Cor 1: 23; 2: 2), the Gospel's essential core. Christ on the cross, he announced, is the incarnate synthesis of God's wisdom and power.

At the end of his life, he unchained the Word of God from any of these wordier formulations and simply said, "Remember Jesus Christ." He retained only two characteristics, which he deemed the most important to recall about Jesus.

The first was as "a descendant of David." Jesus, in other words, was the long-awaited messiah-king that the Jewish prophets foretold. As David's heir, he was also fully human like us. He bore our temptations and triumphed over them, giving us hope in all our trials.

The other was as "raised from the dead," which constituted the most powerful testimony of Jesus' divinity. Christ was not just crucified, but risen, alive, and very much present.

To remember this Jesus and live with him in the present is the uncomplicated nucleus of the Christian faith. It is meant to be not just Paul's Gospel, but ours, too.

Loving Father, send your Holy Spirit to unfetter for me your Word so that I may embrace your Son in the present, make this Gospel my own, and, like Saint Paul, live it, proclaim it, and be willing to suffer for it.

God's List

Father Roger J. Landry

"I bear with everything for the sake of those who are chosen, so that they too may obtain the salvation that is in Christ Jesus, together with eternal glory." (2 Tm 2: 10)

Oskar Schindler was a greedy businessman and womanizer who, when he discovered the Nazis were shipping thousands of Jews to death in concentration camps, negotiated with them to buy some for slave labor in his factories.

After befriending, however, a brilliant Jew who became his manager, and falling for the young Jewish woman who became his housekeeper, he realized that those being herded to death camps were not insects to be industrially incinerated, but human beings just like him. He had a deep conversion – chronicled in the 1993 Oscar-winning film *Schindler's List* – and resolved to use all his resources to buy Jews, no longer to make him profit, but to save them from this fate. He liquidated all his business and personal assets until he didn't have another penny to save another life.

Altogether thirteen hundred people made it onto Schindler's list, the catalog of those Jews he redeemed. That number might seem miniscule in comparison to the six million Jews who perished during the Holocaust. But at the end of the movie, those whose lives Schindler saved and their descendants placed rocks on his Jerusalem grave and said, "If you save one, you save a nation." The numbers of those whose lives are owed to Schindler's sacrifices has multiplied with each generation.

Each of us is called to be a spiritual Oskar Schindler, to spend all our resources to save the precious and irreplaceable lives of others from someone more evil than Hitler and a fate worse than concentration camps.

In today's passage, Saint Paul shows how seriously he took this rescue mission. He bore so much suffering "for the sake of those who are chosen, so that they may obtain the salvation that is in Christ Jesus." He tried to get as many as he could onto God's list. That rescue mission is now ours.

Heavenly Father, too often the pursuit of pleasure has blinded me to the eternal stakes, for me and others, that hinge on my cooperation with your saving plan. Help me, like Saint Paul, to bear everything for the sake of others, that they may obtain salvation in your Son.

The All-Important, Ever-Present Choice

Father Roger J. Landry

"This saying is trustworthy:/ If we have died with him,/ we shall also live with him;/ if we persevere/ we shall also reign with him./ But if we deny him/ he will deny us./ If we are unfaithful,/ he remains faithful,/ for he cannot deny himself." (2 Tm 2: 11-13)

Some Christians falsely believe that salvation is once-and-for-all, that if one accepts Jesus as his personal Lord and Savior, then his salvation is for ever assured, regardless of his later choices. Catholics, too, can sometimes be guilty of thinking past acts of faith suffice for the present as well. Adults who haven't been to church in years suggest they are qualified to be godparents because they graduated from parochial school decades ago. Politicians think that having served as altar boys excuses them from failing to uphold the faith today.

Today Saint Paul, using the lyrics of a short, ancient baptismal hymn, tells the young Timothy that past fidelity is not enough. The most important decision he or any Christian faces is to persevere in the faith or to deny it, to endure or to quit, to renew one's choice for Christ or to betray him.

By this point, Timothy had long been faithful. He had heroically allowed Paul to circumcise him as a grown boy, had been a missionary with him, was imprisoned with him, and ordained by him bishop of Ephesus. Yet, like Paul, Timothy needed to persevere.

The hymn teaches that the Christian life is one in tandem with the Lord: we die with him, we live with him, we reign with him. Christ will never break off that communion, the hymn declares, because he is faithful; if we break it off by denying Christ, however, he has no choice but to deny us, because he cannot affirm there's communion between us when we've chosen unilaterally to end it. But his fidelity also shows itself in his mercy, if we repent, come to receive it, and resolve again to live in loving tandem.

Timothy and Paul were faithful in choosing Christ to the end. They now reign with Christ, where they intercede for us, so that we'll persevere in faith and one day join them.

Faithful Father, in baptism I died in Christ and began to live in him and he in me. Help me to persevere in this loving communion, so that I may come to share fully, as your beloved child, in your eternal kingdom.

The Path to Christian Maturity

Father Roger J. Landry

"Be eager to present yourself as acceptable to God, a workman who causes no disgrace, imparting the word of truth without deviation." (2 Tm 2: 15)

Youth is a time when the young search for a cause to which to devote themselves, their talents, enthusiasm, and relentless energies. So much of their own future, and that of the Church and the world, hinges on how and where they choose to dedicate the gift of themselves.

Today Saint Paul tries to guide the young Timothy about how best to channel his youthful vivacity. Whereas most young people seek to please their parents, peers, teachers, bosses, boyfriends, or girlfriends, Saint Paul urges Timothy to be fervent to please God alone.

Timothy was a young bishop in Ephesus and many likely thought he was too inexperienced for the office. Like anyone in his position, Timothy would have been tempted to try to prove himself and win others' admiration.

Knowing this, Saint Paul counsels him rather, "Be eager to present yourself as acceptable to God." He then describes how to be found acceptable.

The first criterion is to be a "workman." Jesus asked us to pray to the Harvest Master to send, not *bodies*, but *laborers* into his vineyard. Christ needs hardworking men and women who know that the fields are ripe for the harvest and work with a steady, diligent urgency.

The second condition was "who causes no disgrace." It's crucial that representatives of God be occasions of grace instead of disgrace, of sanctity, not scandal.

"Imparting the word of truth without deviation" is the final quality. One of the supreme disgraces is to alter the word of God as false teachers do, either by watering it down as if it's not Good News that will set us free, or by abusing one's authority and adding to it.

Timothy followed Saint Paul's advice and was indeed found acceptable. May we act on that word as eagerly, so that we might find the same divine approval!

Beloved Father, help me to follow Saint Paul's advice and as faithfully as the young Timothy did, so that I, like them, may be pleasing and acceptable to you and, through proclaiming and living your Word, give you glory.

Talking Less

Jack Sacco

*"Avoid profane, idle talk, for such people will become more
and more godless, and their teaching will spread like gangrene."*
(2 Tm 2: 16-17)

The good Benedictine sisters who taught me back in grade school used to say that God had given us two eyes, two ears, and one mouth so that we would see more, listen more, and talk less. Some could reasonably argue that this was their way of getting us to remain quiet for the duration of class. But as the years have progressed, I've found their words to contain more and more wisdom.

We live in a society that is obsessed with talking. We even have professional "talking heads" on every television station. And all they do is talk, talk, talk. It seems not to matter what they actually say, as long as they keep talking. In fact, the more scandalous their words, the bigger platform they are given, and the quicker their message spreads.

It's been written that people with brilliant minds talk about ideas, people with average minds talk about things, and people with dulled minds talk about other people. And the truth is that when we spend too much time idly talking about other people, we quickly run out of good things to say. It therefore becomes easy to slip into gossip and talk of scandal.

It's easy to become enamored with the sound of one's own voice and the assumed profundity of one's own words. But often, the quietest person in the room learns the most.

There's an old saying in the legal profession that if you give a man enough rope, he'll hang himself. That's why defense attorneys generally don't like for their clients to take the stand... the prosecutor will do everything in his power to let the defendant talk so much that his own words will convict him.

So the question isn't "What do I say?" but "What does what I say, say about me?"

*Father, help me to listen more, to see more, and to talk less so that
I may learn of you and your will, that I may understand others,
and that I appreciate the wonder and majesty of your creation.*

The Standard of Christ

Jack Sacco

"God's solid foundation stands, bearing this inscription, 'The Lord knows those who are his'; and, 'Let everyone who calls upon the name of the Lord avoid evil.'" (2 Tm 2: 19)

Nothing on earth is more glaringly obvious than hypocrisy. Even a child can spot it in a crowd of adults. I'm sure we've all come across people who were hypocrites, who were willing to go on and on about their holiness, only to conduct their lives in a completely different way. And, to some extent, I'd be willing to bet that we've all done it from time to time.

But if we can't fool a child, then how do we think we could ever fool God? The truth is that the only person on earth we ever really fool is ourselves.

It's easy to get caught up in the "holier-than-thou" game, where one claims to be pious but doesn't have the strength of character actually to live out one's words.

The international media will gleefully cover the fall from grace of someone who claims holiness on one hand while engaging in illicit behavior on the other. Very few things sell like scandal. Unfortunately, they have plenty examples, whether it be clergy, televangelists, or politicians.

But these are just the public hypocrites. What about the ones the media will never know (or care) about? What about you and me?

The measure of a man isn't so much about what he says, but how he conducts his life. Jesus' own account of the last judgment didn't include any mention about who could make the best speech. Instead, he said, "I was hungry, and you gave me food. I was thirsty, and you gave me drink."

We're called to live our lives to a certain standard, and that standard was fixed by Christ two millennia ago. The lives of the saints serve as further examples about how to live our lives in a manner that will be acceptable to God and our neighbor.

Jesus, may your example – and the examples set by your saints – show each of us how to live in accord with your teachings, so that we may avoid all evil, and thus truly be yours.

Cleaning the Hard Drive

Jack Sacco

"If anyone cleanses himself of these things, he will be a vessel for lofty use, dedicated, beneficial to the master of the house, ready for every good work." (2 Tm 2: 21)

I once had a computer that was, when I originally bought it, state-of-the-art. Over a period of years, I purchased and installed a number of different operating systems that promised to upgrade the unit's performance. One day, just after I had installed the latest, greatest operating system, my computer crashed. Despite my engineering training, I couldn't figure out what had gone wrong. I therefore packed up the CPU and took it to an expert. When I explained what had happened, the repairman asked if I had deleted the former operating systems off my computer's hard drive before I'd installed the new one. "No," I told him. "I've just been installing new ones on top of old ones for years."

"Then that's your problem," he informed me. "Your computer has so many confusing instructions telling it how to operate that it doesn't know what to do. So it shut down." He proceeded to go in and delete all former operating systems from the hard drive, then he reinstalled the latest one. And the computer worked like a charm.

From that experience, I learned that we are sometimes required to clean up not only the hard drives of our computers, but, and perhaps more importantly, the hard drives of our lives. Lots of old instructions can get locked away inside of us, causing us to react inappropriately or even to shut down altogether.

In today's world, where we have so many voices competing for our attention, it's vital to take stock of the forces that propel us along, as well as the baggage we insist on carrying on the journey, and then to eliminate what is not beneficial. Then and only then can we live up to our potential, beneficial to the master, and ready for every good work.

Father, help me to look honestly at my life and my beliefs, so that I may eliminate all that prevents me from performing the work you have designed for me.

The Red Ball

Jack Sacco

"Turn from youthful desires and pursue righteousness, faith, love, and peace, along with those who call on the Lord with purity of heart." (2 Tm 2: 22)

"I want that ball," I informed my father, a man known for his generosity. "The red one."

He looked at the shiny new ball on the top shelf of our family-owned grocery story. Then he said a word I'd never heard him utter. "No."

"What?" I asked.

"No," he repeated.

I couldn't believe my ears. It was summer, I was eight, I wanted to play in the backyard, and my old ball was in shreds. I needed a new ball. And I wanted that red one right there.

"But the ball only costs a nickel," I implored. (I didn't know how much it cost.)

"You can't have it," he said firmly.

Hmmm… I had asked nicely, I had used logic, now I had only one more arrow in my quiver. A tantrum.

After several seconds of watching me humiliate myself, my father took the ball from the shelf and handed it to me.

I stopped my antics and took it from him. I looked at it for several long seconds. Then, I suddenly realized that I'd been willing to publicly dishonor my father in order to get what I wanted. I'd been willing to throw a tantrum for the sake of a red rubber ball. And I realized that the price I was willing to pay was far too high for such a toy. I couldn't accept it.

I handed it back to him.

"What?" he asked. "You don't want it now."

I looked at it a bit longer. "No," I said.

Somehow – and I didn't exactly know how at the time – my father had given me a far greater gift that day than I had sought. He had taught me that my own selfish desires are sometimes eclipsed by the needs of others. And he taught me always to consider the price I was willing to pay for the fleeting happiness of getting what I wanted.

Father, give us the wisdom to turn away from our youthful desires so that we may more fully comprehend and enjoy the true fullness of life you wish for us to have.

The Art of the Argument

Jack Sacco

"Avoid foolish and ignorant debates, for you know that they breed quarrels." (2 Tm 2: 23)

Arguing is an art form, not simply an opportunity to hurl insults at one's opponent. True argument can be instructive, constructive, and even entertaining. But we don't hear much in the way of good arguments these days. What we hear – and what we're inclined to engage in – are destructive yelling matches that are rooted in neither logic nor restraint.

We've all been part of a disagreement that spiraled out of control. It's an easy thing to do. The other person insults you in some way, you insult him back, and you're off to the races. Before you know it, the "conversation" has nothing to do with the original subject matter... it's simply a collection of personal attacks that have as their only intention to hurt the other person.

This is often the case in public discourse, where policy talking points inevitably trump rationality or civility. It's also true in private exchanges between friends and family members, where a minor disagreement or misunderstanding can erupt into a full-fledged, emotional attack.

We all run across people who simply love to debate every point, no matter what. When it comes to religion, these people are legion. Some want to engage in a reasonable exchange. Others simply want to tell you that you're wrong.

Growing up in the South, I encountered many people who were eager to inform me that all Catholics and Jews were going to hell. The temptation was to become upset and to engage each one of them in a debate. But, as Saint Paul implies, not all debates are created equal. Some are foolish and ignorant. The trick is to be able to discern the difference between the ones that will lead to some higher good and the ones that will lead to a meaningless quarrel.

Holy Spirit, give us the wisdom to choose our battles wisely, so that we do not fall victim to the temptation of foolish and ignorant debates. Help us to know when to debate, and when simply to walk away.

Speaking Gently

Jack Sacco

"A slave of the Lord should not quarrel, but should be gentle with everyone, able to teach, tolerant, correcting opponents with kindness. It may be that God will grant them repentance that leads to knowledge of the truth, and that they may return to their senses out of the devil's snare, where they are entrapped by him, for his will." (2 Tm 2: 24-26)

My sister has the remarkable ability to engage in debate without taking things personally. Unlike most people, she can stick to the subject at hand, while calmly and rationally seeking a solution, even if her emotions and feelings become involved. She knows that by detaching her emotions from the discussion, she can remain on point and arrive at a solution that may otherwise be elusive.

But that doesn't mean she's a doormat when it comes to debating. She states her case, she listens carefully to different opinions, and then she's able to agree or disagree with those opinions without sacrificing her core beliefs and without reacting to perceived personal insults.

Name-calling is easy. It's also fun. But it's rather ineffective, especially if you're trying to sway someone's opinion. But Saint Paul isn't talking about letting others run roughshod over you or about distancing yourself when you see the error of someone's ways.

There's an old saying, "Evil triumphs when good remains silent." As Christians, we are called to speak out when we see suffering and evil. But how we speak, especially to those with whom we disagree, is vital. To speak as Saint Paul recommends, with gentleness and kindness, while not always easy, does give our words the best chance of taking root.

The proper planting of the seeds of truth can yield a great harvest, but it is often a harvest that God must nurture and grow within the heart of those who hear the message. By doling out insults, we render ineffective whatever nuggets of truth may exist within our words. Our job, therefore, is to speak the truth with genuine kindness, and then efficiently to step out of the way so that the value of our words can take root and grow.

Holy Spirit, give us the rationality and presence of mind we need so that we may always show appropriate respect for those with whom we disagree.

God Is the Solution

Jack Sacco

"You have followed my teaching, way of life, purpose, faith, patience, love, endurance, persecutions, and sufferings [...] persecutions that I endured. Yet from all these things the Lord delivered me. In fact, all who want to live religiously in Christ Jesus will be persecuted." (2 Tm 3: 10-12)

This passage doesn't exactly make you want to run out and be a Christian, does it? After all, why would you want to follow someone who promises to make you suffer?

But is this what Saint Paul is really saying? Could it be possible that there's a deeper meaning to his words?

I've run across many well-intentioned people who feel that God's greatest desire is to cause unbearable pain and suffering to the faithful. They seem convinced that you can't be a good Christian unless you're miserable. So they're miserable. And they're not happy unless everyone around them is miserable as well.

But look closer at Paul's words. He doesn't say that the Lord *brought about* his sufferings... he says that the Lord *delivered* him from his sufferings. In other words, God isn't the problem, he's the Solution. There's a big difference.

I'll go out on a limb and say that God gets no joy out of our misery, as many pseudo-theologians would have you believe. In fact, I'll take it a step further and state that he actively desires to deliver us from our tribulations, much like he delivered Saint Paul.

Is the road to joy and resurrection filled with obstacles and hardships? Yes. And do those hardships bring about sadness, anxiety, and tears? Of course. The persecutions, the difficulties, the sufferings... these are all inevitable. But the fact is that God desires us to travel *through* the difficult times, *through* the hardships, *through* the misery of the Good Fridays of our lives in order to reach the resurrections for which he has designed us.

Saint Paul holds out his own life as an example of how God can and will help each of us find the solutions to life's unavoidable difficulties.

Lord, help us to understand the mystical balance between suffering and joy. Enlighten us so that we do not blame you as the cause of our sufferings, but that we appreciate you as the Solution to all the inevitable difficulties of life.

The Direction You're Looking

Jack Sacco

"But wicked people and charlatans will go from bad to worse, deceivers and deceived. But you, remain faithful to what you have learned and believed, because you know from whom you learned it, and that from infancy you have known [the] sacred scriptures, which are capable of giving you wisdom for salvation through faith in Christ Jesus." (2 Tm 3: 13-15)

I once went horseback riding in an indoor arena. Now, it must be pointed out that I know nothing about riding horses. Fortunately, there was an instructor who guided me through the process and gave me much-needed pointers.

"One more thing," he added after I mounted. "Don't let the horse walk into the wall."

"Huh?"

"He'll try to scrape against the wall and push you off of him," he advised me. "Don't let him do that."

"Well, how do I prevent him from walking toward the wall?" I asked.

"Just look in the direction you want the horse to go," he answered calmly.

"But how will he know where I'm looking?"

"He'll know," he replied.

As we rounded the first turn, the powerful animal began veering toward the wall.

"What's the horse doing?" the instructor asked me.

"He's going into the wall!" I answered.

"What are you looking at?" he asked.

"The wall!"

"Well, just look in the direction you want the horse to go," he advised.

I really had no choice. I looked away from the wall and toward the pathway. Remarkably, the horse gently turned and followed my line of sight. I realized that when I looked in the direction I preferred, I naturally leaned, pulled on the reins, and did everything that sent the correct signals to the horse. And he responded. The lesson I learned that day is that you go in the direction you're looking. If you're looking at the wall, you'll crash into it. If you keep your eye on your ultimate goal, you'll find a way to reach it. As I read Saint Paul's words, I'm reminded that we are constantly moving – either from bad to worse or from good to better – and that our direction is determined by which way we choose to look.

Father, help us to trust Christ and always to look in his direction so that we may move closer to him.

The Ultimate Self-Help Book

Jack Sacco

"All scripture is inspired by God and is useful for teaching, for refutation, for correction, and for training in righteousness, so that one who belongs to God may be competent, equipped for every good work." (2 Tm 3: 16-17)

We live in an age of self-help gurus. Everywhere you look, there are self-proclaimed life coaches, mentors, experts, and pundits.

All claim they can help us reach our potential while not-so-subtly implying they will show us the easy road toward wealth and fame. Each has a website. Each has a book. Each has an abundance of tapes and CDs for sale. Each has a seminar that you must attend. And each promises that, for just a few hundred dollars, they can reveal to you the secrets to true happiness and incredible riches.

The trouble is that the information they contain is generally rehashed babble lifted directly from previous self-help books. Most are conglomerations of doublespeak and nonsense with the singular intention of making the guru, not the student, wealthy and happy.

Taking advantage of an emerging spirituality and the marketing thereof, self-help books in recent years have included more and more spiritual overtones. They speak of God, sometimes referring to him as a "higher power" so as not to offend potential buyers. The problem is that they willingly preach a new and unauthorized gospel to people who are too enamored with the potential payout to recognize or even be concerned with the dangers.

This isn't to say that most motivational books don't contain some elements of truth in them. Even a stopped clock is correct twice a day.

But the Sacred Scripture doesn't simply contain "elements" of truth. It *is* Truth. And it is the Truth against which all other truths should be measured. We don't need to seek the advice of a plethora of competing self-help gurus when we have the inspired word of God to light our way. That Word, that Truth, will provide each of us with the information we need to become competent and equipped for every good work.

Father, inspire us to read and understand your word, so that we may grow in goodness and be better equipped to do your will. May the Scripture provide us with the inspiration we need to live a life of happiness and contentment.

The Message We Live

Jack Sacco

"I charge you in the presence of God and of Christ Jesus, who will judge the living and the dead, and by his appearing and his kingly power: proclaim the word; be persistent whether it is convenient or inconvenient; convince, reprimand, encourage through all patience and teaching." (2 Tm 4: 1-2)

Proclaiming the word, convincing, and reprimanding... these are much easier to say than actually to do. This is especially true in that most lay Catholics can't be expected to know the intricacies of every single teaching included in the deposit of faith.

Unlike theologians who study Church teaching on a full-time basis, most of us have jobs and families that require most of our attention during the day, leaving us little time to explore the depths of our Catholic faith. Fortunately, there are a number of books – including the Catechism of the Catholic Church – that are helpful in answering questions and in explaining our faith.

At the same time, one could have all the knowledge on earth and still be unable to perform the task that Saint Paul charges us with in this passage. The message that is proclaimed the loudest is the one we live, not the one we preach. I'm sure we all know of specific examples of "intellectually holy" people who are anything but holy, kind, or patient in the course of their everyday dealings with people. Their words, no matter how brilliant, will always be drowned out by their actions.

There are others who possess very little theological prowess at all, but whose lives emanate holiness and therefore provide for each of us a clear example of what it means to be a Christian. So perhaps more important than intellectual knowledge or one's ability to debate is how one chooses to live one's life.

I'm reminded of a story told by Mother Teresa of Calcutta. She was offering comfort to a dying man when he asked her the following question: "This Jesus you speak of... is he like you?"

Mother Teresa smiled. "Well, I try to be like him," she responded.

"Then I want to be his follower," the man said before he died.

Heavenly Father, help us to follow the example of your Son, so that others may come to know him through our words and our actions.

The Most Powerful Ability

Jack Sacco

"The time will come when people will not tolerate sound doctrine but, following their own desires and insatiable curiosity, will accumulate teachers and will stop listening to the truth and will be diverted to myths." (2 Tm 4: 3-4)

I've come to the conclusion that the most powerful ability of mankind might just be the ability to miss the point of anything. Have you ever had a conversation with somebody only to later discover that they had completely misunderstood what you were talking about? It can be disheartening, especially when the subject matter is one that's important to you. I sometimes find myself wanting to ask, "Did you hear a word I said?"

Indeed, it seems as if some people are intent on missing the point, no matter what you say or how you say it.

No doubt that miscommunication sometimes plays a role, but often it's a matter of one or more parties simply not wanting to understand what's being said to them. This is especially true when a certain teaching is difficult to follow.

In that case, it becomes easier to choose to discount sound doctrine, and to yield to our own desires, accumulating only those teachers along the way who say what it is we want to hear.

Sometimes it's easier to believe nonsense – no matter how non-sensical or irrational it may be. Purposefully missing the point becomes especially easy when we have ulterior motives. We've all done it from time to time. But to do so is to set oneself on a slippery slope on which we justify the disposal of sound doctrine in favor of what might seem most convenient at that particular moment.

The main casualty of this method of selective hearing is the truth. And, as Saint Paul points out, when we stop listening to the truth because it is inconvenient, we tend to be diverted to myths, which, while fleetingly attractive, will have long-term effects that might not be so pleasant.

Holy Spirit, give us the wisdom to understand the teachings contained in the Scripture and the courage to follow those teachings. Guide us so that we may not simply know what Scripture says but what it truly means.

A Math Lesson for Life

Jack Sacco

*"But you, be self-possessed in all circumstances; put up
with hardship; perform the work of an evangelist;
fulfill your ministry." (2 Tm 4: 5)*

I f there's one thing I've learned, it's that no matter what you're trying to accomplish, frustration will be part of the process. If you let the frustration frustrate you even more, then you'll never perform the work you set out to do.

So many times in life, we focus more on the difficulty than the solution. This can be especially true when it comes to matters of faith.

But Jesus' life teaches us how God can guide us through every difficulty, every persecution, and every frustration. His instructions are that we pick up our crosses and follow him. He didn't say, "Lie on the ground and be crushed under the weight of your cross."

Picking it up is a sign of strength. Following him is a guarantee of victory.

Sure, there will be circumstances and people who get in our way and impede our progress. But the self-possessed person is one who understands their beliefs and goals in a way that prevents them from abandoning their mission, even when someone else discourages or disappoints them.

Perhaps nothing is more disheartening and frustrating – and nothing has caused more people to abandon their faith – than the proverbial wolves in sheep's clothing.

When I was a boy, my mother warned my brother and sisters and me that, at some point in our lives, an assumed "holy" person, perhaps even a priest or a nun, would do or say something that would sorely disappoint us. "But always remember this," she added. "You might not like the math teacher, but two plus two still equals four."

And with those words, she spoke an eternal truth.

It is vital that we have a balanced knowledge of who we are and of what's important so that we are able to separate the truths from the frustrations of life. Only then can we perform the work God has for us.

Jesus, send us your Holy Spirit, so that we may be self-possessed in the best possible way. Thus may we overcome all adversity and fulfill the great mission you have for us.

God Only Knows

Sister Mary Thomas Noble, O.P.

"For I am already being poured out like a libation, and the time of my departure is at hand. I have competed well; I have finished the race; I have kept the faith. From now on the crown of righteousness awaits me, which the Lord, the just judge, will award to me on that day, and not only to me, but to all who have longed for his appearance." (2 Tm 4: 6-8)

The race is over. Maybe I won, maybe I lost. Who knows? I don't know, my friends don't know, my critics don't know, only God knows, really. Of course the records are there for anyone to see, in the media. But the race is over, with all the sound and fury, the plans, the dreams, the competition, the stress, the strife. They are all beginning to fade out, as something else is beginning to move in: old age. Diminishment has come to live with me now, in all sorts of mocking forms. My winter coat hung just a bit long on me this morning, when my wife got it out of the closet smelling of moth balls. And there's one shelf in the pantry I can't quite reach any more, though no one has noticed yet. Worse still, and this I don't intend to talk about: there's a mix-up in the jostling crowd of memories of things both good and bad that have happened to me over the years. Funny, the good things stand out quite clearly sometimes, and I can laugh and reminisce over them and gild them over, too, while I tend to forget the details of my failures. I have fought hard in life, I have kept the faith, I have always counted on God… In this dusk I can no longer read, nor care to. My dog, my Ben, stays by me, loyal at my feet. His chin keeps my ankles warm against the chill. The little day of my life runs out. But wait! My Lord comes, the one I most long to see. He said he would bring his reward with him. Reward? All I want is himself. I'm glad you stopped by, my friend. You know, your time will come too, sooner than you think… but – I must go!

My Lord and my God, I will have thyself!

Another Way Out

Sister Mary Thomas Noble, O.P.

"At my first defense no one appeared on my behalf, but everyone deserted me. May it not be held against them! But the Lord stood by me and gave me strength, so that through me the proclamation might be completed and all the Gentiles might hear it." (2 Tm 4: 16-17)

Ephemeral... the promises of men. "Though they all fall away because of you, I will never fall away," Peter insisted. "Even if I must die with you, I will not deny you." Of course he meant it. But when it came to the crunch, he fled. Peter fled. How can Paul protest? How can I? How can any of us protest the mystery of our own fickleness? It is something we hold in common. A boy gets blamed for the broken classroom window. The whole class knows who did it. It wasn't that boy. But there's dead silence. The room is fetid with fear. You can almost hear it breathe, like a sick whimper. The ball sits in the corner, out of sight. Slivers of broken glass sparkle as if taunting him. The boy starts up in protest. Silence. Feet squirm under desks. Cheeks redden. Yes, this is the human condition. We have our progenitors – Adam, Eve, Peter. But this is not the whole story. We have others – Christ, Stephen, Paul. *Father, forgive them!... Lord, do not hold this sin against them!... May it not be held against them!* We're free to choose our model. Which will it be? "The Lord stood by me and gave me strength." Suppose I have been wronged. My friends know. Still, they say nothing. They are afraid. My whole soul revolts at the injustice. Must I endure this? Not succumb to bitterness, rage? The struggle can be unto death. He stands by. When all seems lost and I am on the point of surrender, he gives me grace. I need not succumb. There is another way out. I can forgive. Through me, the proclamation can be completed, for all the Gentiles to hear. What proclamation? Love's power to forgive. In the strength of the Lord who stands by me I can proclaim it to the ends of the earth.

Lord Christ, in the face of injustice, stand by me, and grant me your strength to love and to forgive, even as you have loved and forgiven me.

A Lion in a Den Full of Daniels

Sister Mary Thomas Noble, O.P.

"I was rescued from the lion's mouth. The Lord will rescue me from every evil threat and will bring me safe to his heavenly kingdom. To him be glory forever and ever. Amen."
(2 Tm 4: 17-18)

Paul faced death in Antioch, Iconium, and Lystra. Angry people pursued him in the temple, on the streets, even in prison. He would be right at home in Iraq or the United States. He knew the look of a lion's mouth opening upon him, the sound of a lion's roar ripping his ears. But again and again, the Lord rescued him. Do I have lions in my life? Are they inside me, or on the outside? Are they mostly other people, or am I myself my greatest threat? Could I be a lion? A lioness? Lions are relatively innocent, compared to human beings. Saint Ignatius of Antioch would have made friends with the lions awaiting him in the Colosseum, whereas he referred to the Roman guards on the ship carrying him to Rome as beasts. Whether I *am* a lion or I must face one, I know that the Lord will rescue me. In the first case, the rescue may take the form of a transformation. Nothing within me, or without, is too much for God's loving ingenuity, that is, his mercy. Nothing outside, past, present, or future, can rival the power of his love for me. When King Darius, hungry from his fast and having tossed in sleeplessness throughout the night, stole down to the lions' den at break of dawn to see what had happened to Daniel, he cried out in dread and anguish, "O Daniel! Has your God been able to deliver you?"

We know the outcome. In the blackness of that terrible night God sent his angel to shut the lions' mouths. No hurtful thing happened to Daniel because he trusted in God. In the light of this story, we can let the lions come on in all their fury. Fear falls away, hope slips in with the new day. To quote that valiant author, Russell Ford, the tables are turned, and "I feel like a lion in a whole den full of Daniels."

Lord, grant me the gift of a trust in you that no terror can daunt, no threat can shake.

A Sacred Entrustment

Sister Mary Thomas Noble, O.P.

"Paul, a slave of God and apostle of Jesus Christ for the sake of the faith of God's chosen ones and the recognition of religious truth, in the hope of eternal life that God, who does not lie, promised before time began, who indeed at the proper time revealed his word in the proclamation with which I was entrusted by the command of God our savior." (Ti 1: 1-3)

Dave, a professed agnostic in whose home religion was never discussed, switched on the microphone in the nursery's intercom above the baby's crib. He kissed his two-year-old daughter on the head and slipped quietly into the living room to join his wife. Why, he and Pat had wondered, had Julie begged so insistently to be alone with the baby this first day home from the hospital? "Is it jealousy?" they asked each other in puzzled anxiety. "What is Julie up to?" "But give her a chance," they decided – "let's just see." That evening the two listened intently at the monitor in their bedroom, hearing every sound from the nursery: *"Tell me about God,"* they heard Julie whisper, *"I'm beginning to forget."* They looked at one another, speechless with sudden enlightenment and self-reproach. One child, seeking the truth from the other. One child, passing the truth on to the other. Struck down on his way to Damascus by the command of Jesus, whom he had persecuted, Paul was entrusted with the proclamation of his word. On the instant he became an apostle, not simply for his own sake, but for the faith of God's chosen ones and the recognition of religious truth. I too am designed to be and to do something special for others. We all run the risk of being stopped short in mid-journey and being given a message to pass on. It will be a very personal thing, unique, one that only we can deliver. Every little child, fresh from the creative hand of God, has a Word to proclaim, and will carry out its mission faithfully if we have ears to hear. Another little child may be the first to hear it. It is a matter of entrustment. This is God's preferred way with us. He prefers to entrust his plans to us for their fulfillment rather than "go it alone." From him, we learn entrustment.

O God, teach me to learn from each one of my brothers and sisters, eager to receive and pass on the message you have entrusted to them for me, so that we may all delight together in the Truth that you are.

Washed Clean

Sister Mary Thomas Noble, O.P.

"To the clean all things are clean, but to those who are defiled and unbelieving nothing is clean; in fact, both their minds and their consciences are tainted. They claim to know God, but by their deeds they deny him. They are vile and disobedient and unqualified for any good deed." (Ti 1: 15-16)

"Do you want to hold her?" Jeff stiffened, stepped back involuntarily, terrified. His sister held the baby out to him confidently. He looked into the deep, shining, unfocused eyes, fixed upon him unblinkingly. How could he do it? How could he hold this child in his rough, crude hands, hold her in safety against his treacherous heart? His sister didn't understand. He didn't want her to understand. All he wanted was to get away... The baby stirred in her arms and stretched out a tiny hand toward him. Against its innocence, he suddenly saw himself in all the ugly reality of the past two years. He had been so far from home. He had lost his faith in the goodness of life, he was tainted in mind and heart, utterly defiled. There was no place here for him now. "No, no," he murmured. Then his sister laughed. She kissed the soft down on the baby's head and whispered, "Go to your Uncle Jeff, little one." His arms jerked out, trembling. Deftly she placed the baby in them, and he felt the light, warm weight slide down against his body. The baby wriggled, fitted herself against his ribs, and sighed in utter content. It was as if the two of them melted into one. Something like union, only much more. It was communion. There are times for us all, and these are good times, when we see ourselves through the eyes of another human being. Against their trusting love we realize how vile we are, detestable, unqualified for any good deed. But the other, a stranger, a brother, a child, may look back at us out of the depths of their innocence, and a miracle happens. We are bathed in their love, washed clean. To the clean, all things are clean. Because they have been cleansed in the flood waters of Christ's purity, there is hope for us.

Lord of all purity, when you come to me in communion tomorrow, make me clean!

You'd Better Believe It

Sister Mary Thomas Noble, O.P.

"As for yourself, you must say what is consistent with sound doctrine." (Ti 2: 1)

Growth, development, change – are they all the same thing? At first glance it would seem so. But wait! Poring over our family album, from the faded nineteenth-century daguerreotypes with their stiff brownish corners, that my grandfather pasted in so carefully, all the way up to my niece's wedding shots from last April, I muse on this. Gramp grew and developed. He changed from the small boy with long curls and the knickers of long ago into the handsome white-haired patriarch we all revere today. Quite a difference! Yet in another sense he hasn't changed essentially. He's the same person – grown to manhood, fully developed, but still the same. The changes from eight to eighty haven't touched the essence of Gramp. "I'm still and always me," he would say with a twinkle in his eye, "and you'd better believe it!" I think this is what Paul is saying to Titus. Sound doctrine doesn't change into some new doctrine. Over the centuries it may grow and develop. But essentially it doesn't change. How could it? It is the expression in human language of eternal Truth, another name for God. Truth cannot change, "and you'd better believe it" as Gramp would say to his relativist grandson. Titus must make sure that what he says to his congregation is consistent with sound doctrine. He must be sure he is not confusing growth and development with some basic change in the essential meaning of sound doctrine. Gramp was endowed with a sturdy pair of legs that have served him well for a lifetime. In the interests of speed and efficiency, would you want to attach two more legs, or a dozen? Hardly helpful, not at all consistent. In fact, monstrous! Nor would Paul have Titus adulterate Truth with essential changes, however expedient or appealing to his age, or ours.

Lord Jesus Christ, grant that I may cleave to the teachings of your Church with the same absolute faith and love with which I cleave to you, who said, "I am the Truth."

It Will Be Glorious

Sister Mary Thomas Noble, O.P.

"Showing yourself as a model of good deeds in every respect, with integrity in your teaching, dignity, and sound speech that cannot be criticized, so that the opponent will be put to shame without anything bad to say about us." (Ti 2: 7-8)

The life of a role model can be arduous. The qualities Paul asks Titus to demonstrate for the benefit of the Cretans are no small matter. He is to amend what is defective in this recent foundation on the island of Crete, continuing Paul's apostolic mission among a people described by one of themselves as "liars, beasts, and lazy gluttons." Titus must stir up the flames of that Pentecostal fire once cast upon some of these same Cretans in Jerusalem, when the apostles were gathered in the Upper Room after Christ's Ascension. He must rekindle their fervor, illustrating in the concrete for them the kind of life they have been called to. Paul has wanted for some time to return to Crete. He has not forgotten his earlier shipwreck on the island, and after two years in a Roman prison he is eager to revisit these people who have been left on their own too long. So he sails there with Titus, and leaves him to cultivate the seeds of faith planted earlier. Titus' assignment is twofold. On the principle that one picture is worth a thousand words, Titus is not only to maintain integrity in his teaching, faithfully recalling to the erring Cretans all that Paul had taught them; he is also to be "a model of good deeds in every respect." We of the third millennium have this same call, this same assignment. We are to teach the truths of faith *with integrity* wherever in our private, personal world we encounter a listening ear or an inquiring mind. It may be a family member, fellow employee, classmate, someone in the market place, the barber shop, on the baseball field, in the theater, the public square, the bar. This is our apostolate in the twenty-first century. And whatever form our verbal witness may take, we are to illustrate it with good deeds. This can be arduous. It will be glorious.

O God, I thank you for the gift of faith. Grant that I may share it with all whom you arrange for me to meet, and that my words may ring true because they are accompanied by the good deeds you have prepared for me to do.

Moment of Grace

Sister Mary Thomas Noble, O.P.

"For the grace of God has appeared, saving all and training us to reject godless ways and worldly desires and to live temperately, justly, and devoutly in this age." (Ti 2: 11-12)

There is a lyrical loveliness in the cadences of this sentence of Paul that surprises and intrigues. Perhaps for you as for me, the words evoke like no other words the hushed excitement, the anticipation of Christmas Eve in childhood: you with your family, packed in homely solidarity into a shadowy pew in your small, pine-scented church, boots dripping and fingers thawing out just enough to turn the pages of your missal. Why, I wonder each year, was this text chosen for Christmas Eve and Midnight Mass? "To live temperately, justly, and devoutly in this age" suggests a quiet, innocuous, almost boring way of life. What does it have to do with Christmas? Or as an earlier translation has it, the words "live sober, upright, and godly lives" might be a truculent injunction blown in off New England's rock-bound coast with the Pilgrim Fathers, an order not to be trifled with. But contrariwise, the words fall gently on the ear at Midnight Mass, mostly unnoticed for their simplicity. Then comes "… the grace of God has appeared." This is specifically for us. God has appeared, he and none other. He is with us. He brings peace. In the darkness we are given the vision of a Babe; in cold, the warmth of small, outstretched hands. Into our silence, his cry drops mercifully light, musical. In this moment of grace we can turn away from ourselves and how we have lived – temperately, justly, and devoutly, or the opposite. Are we sober? upright? godly? Not really. But no matter. *The grace of God has appeared.* It is precisely for us, the unregenerate, the intemperate, unfair, ungodly ones, that he has come. "There is one among you whom you do not recognize," says John the Baptist, our Advent saint. It is true. We hardly know our Brother. We stare up at his Mother with baby-blind eyes. No matter. He has come to save us.

Child of Mary, Christmas Child, you come to save us from ourselves. In you the grace of God, his graciousness, has appeared. It is good for us to be here. Let us stay and feast for ever on the sight of you.

O Blessed Hope!

Sister Mary Thomas Noble, O.P.

"We await the blessed hope, the appearance of the glory of the great God and of our savior Jesus Christ, who gave himself for us to deliver us from all lawlessness and to cleanse for himself a people as his own, eager to do what is good." (Ti 2: 13-14)

What part does hope play in my life? Do I hope mainly for things or for people? Or do I hope for events? As a child I once hoped for a rubber ball with all my heart. It was exactly the size I wanted and had swirls of colors on it, all the right colors. I showed it to my mother in the store. It cost twenty-five cents. She pointed out to me several bigger, better balls, but I couldn't have cared less. I knew what I wanted. No other ball would do. When I tore the wrappings off that little rubber ball on the morning of my eighth birthday and tossed them on the breakfast table, I knew an unadulterated and absolute content such as I have rarely experienced since. I dashed outdoors with my sister before school and threw it, threw it, threw it back and forth across our front lawn in a kind of ecstasy. Hope fulfilled! Such a small hope, just my size. God would like to stretch our longing hearts to hold much more, even himself. Will we let him do it? "We await the blessed hope..." Do we? "... the appearance of the glory of the great God, and of our Savior Jesus Christ..." How high do we set our sights? Do we have hopes to match God's hopes for us? His is a radiant hope. There is glory ahead for us, there is deliverance, there is an indescribable purity to be achieved only through his blood. Each one of us would be totally, uniquely his, were he to have his hopes fulfilled. Our sights would be set on doing "what is good" beyond all our wildest imaginings, empowered as we should be as "his people." His hopes for us will lift us to the blessed vision of himself, where he will hold us, and we shall not fall.

O God, stretch my heart wide with blessed hope, to hold the all that you would give me – your very self!

The Shock of Correction

Sister Mary Thomas Noble, O.P.

"Exhort and correct with all authority.
Let no one look down on you." (Ti 2: 15)

Would that this straightforward direction of Paul to Titus had been carved in stone over the entrance to our third millennium. There is no room for equivocation in Paul's words. Titus must keep the lines of communication ever open between himself and his priests and deacons and the holy women who serve the Churches he has founded. There must be no equivocation, no side-stepping the duty of exhortation and correction. Paul never minces words in his speech or his letters. As with Christ, so with Paul, it is always yes or no. Now Titus must follow his example. Exhortation and correction, conceived as duties, have lost face in our times. Their value has notably deteriorated. For all our concern to be politically correct, who honestly wants to be corrected? Because correction is given so seldom, it usually comes as a shock. Still more unlikely has it become that a person in a highly valued position of authority will courageously offer correction where it is needed. We have witnessed the disastrous consequences of this kind of situation in the Church today, and have grieved over the terrible loss to souls. The pattern is repeated in family life across the world, with obviously disastrous results. Is there anything I, as an individual, can do to counteract the universal yen to stand correct but uncorrected? What part does correction play in my life, in my attitude to myself and to others? Do I have the courage to accept the suggestion of a friend that perhaps my life is not going in the right direction? Am I willing to change course? To make that one change, costly beyond all others? When I see in my children, my friends, or my fellow employees tendencies leading them subtly astray, do I tell them, and help them to redirect their energies before it is too late? Do I love them that much?

Lord Christ, grant me to love my family, friends, and all whom you have placed in my care, with the love you have for them, so that I may discern the dangers in their lives and point them to true growth and change when it is still not too late.

Grace Is Everything

Sister Mary Thomas Noble, O.P.

"Be obedient, [...] be open to every good enterprise."
(Ti 3: 1)

Novitiates can be lively places. Here at the monastery we have a variegated mix of wannabe contemplatives at their freest and frankest, fresh from our twenty-first century culture. Paul would have made a great addition. He tells Titus that his newest disciples, the Cretans, are lazy, liars, and gluttons. Transposing the communication to feminine mode, at the novices' recreation a postulant offers a plan for saving time – work time of course – in favor of "holy leisure," for which read hiding in a nook with a book. Postulant Sister Candida's suggestion is rapidly dissected with a frankness and acumen that leaves it, and her, a bit disheveled. But she rallies with a punch line she garnered yesterday from Saint Francis de Sales: "You can catch more flies with honey than vinegar." Shoots back the senior novice, Sister Candida's classmate from Grade One and best friend: "Who wants you, fly?" Yes, Paul would fit in well here, with his "Cretans are always liars, evil beasts, lazy gluttons... detestable, disobedient, unfit for any good deed." This, no less, is the Church in Crete, his latest foundation, the newest born of all his children. "Rebuke them sharply," he urges Titus, "teach them to be obedient, to be ready for any honest work." Paul can speak this way, for he has already dubbed himself "the foremost of sinners, the least of the apostles, unfit to be called an apostle... But by the grace of God I am what I am," he adds, "and his grace toward me was not in vain" (cf. 1 Cor 15: 9-10). So there is hope for the Cretans, for you, for me, for all of us, in the grace of God. We can tell it like it is, regardless of the lazy, lying Cretans. Indeed, they may be peering over my shoulder at this moment and murmuring, "Paul was right – he always had the last word. Yes, God's grace toward us was not in vain."

Please, Lord, never let not your grace and mercy be in vain for me.

The Way to Green Pastures

Sister Mary Thomas Noble, O.P.

"They are to slander no one, to be peaceable, considerate, exercising all graciousness toward everyone." (Ti 3: 2)

P aul is speaking to Titus about the Church recently founded in Crete and how he is to direct the new converts to the faith – "older men, older women, younger women and their husbands and children, younger men, slaves, rulers, and authorities, *those who have believed in God*." Surely we all fit somewhere in this motley crowd of Cretans, and can take these words as the Word of God for ourselves as well. Paul suggests one really bad thing to avoid, and some very good things to do, almost like a rule of life. The first topic, slander, is particularly contemporaneous. Checking it out in the Catechism of the Catholic Church (2477) we find a number of sub-topics under the discussion of our duty to respect the reputation of persons. Outstanding is detraction, or reporting something damaging (but true) about another. Calumny, on the other hand, is telling injurious lies about another. These noxious weeds, clogging the landscape as we move from morning news to late night shows, must be avoided like poison. We cannot, must not absorb them into our minds and memories, our hearts or our very souls. Not only must we avoid slandering anyone ourselves, we must beware of tacit approval or idle curiosity when someone else's reputation is held up for grabs in the public square or dragged in the mud of the media. On the positive side are the good things to do – things that will build up our Church and feed our souls. "My meat is to do the will of him who sent me," Christ says. And our food? "I am the bread of life," says Christ, "If anyone eats of this bread he will live for ever." To be peaceable, considerate, to exercise all graciousness toward everyone here is our life, our sweetness, our hope.

O Lord, in your sacred word we read that you will ordain peace for us and that you have wrought for us all our works. Lead us into the works you have prepared for us. Let us feed in your pastures and rest by your life-giving waters.

The Heart We Offer

Monsignor Gregory E.S. Malovetz

"We ourselves were once foolish, disobedient, deluded, slaves to various desires and pleasures, living in malice and envy, hateful ourselves and hating one another." (Ti 3: 3)

It happens just about every time. The congregation rises and they turn toward the back of the church. In that moment dozens of flash bulbs create a kind of dance that sweeps over the entire room. All eyes are fixed intently as the bride pauses before beginning the most important walk of her life.

Someone may turn toward the altar and take a quick picture of the groom. But the attention returns quickly to the back. From where I stand, I study the face of the groom. Previous to this moment he was nervous and talkative. Now he is quiet with glistening eyes. I watch him because it is a vision that few actually notice. His face is transfixed as he sees the one to whom he has given his heart – the one who is his future – walking toward him.

There is a great temptation, even for the follower of Christ, to look backward. We hold on to old grudges and disappointments. We may have long forgotten the argument, but the bitterness remains. We remember a bad choice we made and delude ourselves, thinking a new beginning is not possible. So we continue to make the same out-of-focus decisions or hold on to a past that should have long ago been forgotten. It is not flash bulbs that blind us, but our foolish thought that we cannot change.

It is in those moments that Jesus comes walking toward us. If we look up and look ahead, we see that he offers us a future where we are not the sum total of every bad choice. He walks toward us with a grace that says a new beginning is possible for you. Not next week or next year. Jesus offers it to us now. First we have to give him our heart.

Lord, in this time and in this place, I ask that you open my heart. Let me know your presence and turn toward you.

The Wonder of Love

Monsignor Gregory E.S. Malovetz

"But when the kindness and generous love/ of God our savior appeared,/ not because of any righteous deeds we had done/ but because of his mercy,/ he saved us through the bath of rebirth/ and renewal by the holy Spirit,/ whom he richly poured out on us/ through Jesus Christ our savior." (Ti 3: 4-6)

I can still see it happening. It seemed like slow motion. The bottle of olive oil, about to be used for a recipe in progress, slipped out of my hands as I reached for it. It seemed to do several somersaults before it crashed on the tile floor. Oil poured over the floor, under the stove and refrigerator. It got into the cracks in the baseboard and the grout of the tile. I had only needed a small bit of oil for my cooking; it was now generously and completely spread over my kitchen.

At one point or another in our life, we have all been hurt. Maybe it was a small disappointment that created a time of inconvenience. Maybe it was a hope or dream that slipped beyond our grasp and came crashing down around us. We put on a brave face. We say it doesn't matter. But the wound to our heart can run deep.

God desires to heal us. Jesus appears throughout the Gospel standing with the unloved, the sinner, and with those who have seen happiness slip through their fingers. He appears to them and offers them generous love. They do not need to show faith by doing a good deed. No litany of prayers is to be said as a requirement for the love. It is freely given. We are told that God's love is so generous and it is so big, that it is poured out. Not in small doses. Not in a carefully measured cup. It is poured out so that it may reach those wounds of our heart – the ones that no one else can see – and fill them completely.

On my knees I cleaned my floor. I ended up with more oil on me then on the rags. On our knees we call out for mercy. Jesus appears. In that moment we end up with more love then we could ever imagine.

Lord, you know the inner hurts and wounds of my life. Richly pour out your mercy upon me.

The Big Picture

Monsignor Gregory E.S. Malovetz

"[Jesus Christ saved us] so that we might be justified by his grace and become heirs in hope of eternal life." (Ti 3: 7)

Racing to the subway, I cut through Rockefeller Plaza. Moving quickly with the crowd, I pause to look at the Christmas tree. It's then that I notice a family of tourists convincing a passerby to take their picture. They are standing and smiling near the tree. The evening rush hour is beginning, so the crowd swells and is moving fast. It will not be easy to take this picture. The mom, unfazed by the hectic pace around her, keeps encouraging her volunteer photographer to step back. She wants him to get as much of the tree in the picture as possible. He keeps moving backward, dodging commuters, while she continues to shout above the noise, "I hope you are getting most of the tree." The man snaps the picture and hands her the camera. "Lady," he says, "I'd have to be standing in Brooklyn to get most of the tree."

There was something admirable about that woman standing in the plaza. All around her were busy, hectic lives, looking inward, not outward. She encountered a man who insisted that what she wanted was not possible. Yet there she stood – a kind of heir in hope – believing a bigger picture was possible.

Discipleship involves that kind of vision. All around us the world is moving fast. People race from one thing to the next, without noticing life around them. A malaise sets in; a kind of hopelessness.

In the midst of it all, the follower of Jesus must become an heir in hope. The disciple must be that one who says running around, going everywhere but arriving nowhere is not my true self. That picture is too small. The big picture calls me to stop and look around, and discover that Christ is here in this moment.

Lord, let me see beyond myself, beyond this moment, so that I may become a sign of hope to all.

The Sign They Need

Monsignor Gregory E.S. Malovetz

*"This saying is trustworthy. I want you to insist on these points,
that those who have believed in God be careful to devote
themselves to good works; these are excellent and
beneficial to others." (Ti 3: 8)*

"Hey Steve, I'd like a two dollar bag." As a teenager I worked in my grandfather's store. I would often hear the request for one of those bags. My grandfather would bend down and open one of the refrigerated showcases, taking out a brown grocery bag. It contained small cuts of poultry and beef, and bits of cheese and luncheon meats. They were pieces too small to sell individually, and too big to be thrown away. Together these bits and pieces could provide nourishment for the working poor whose wages were spent on rent and bills.

My grandfather did not have a high school diploma and never read a social encyclical. But he knew people. He understood that the hopes and dreams of the person on the other side of the counter were like his own, even if the person was of a different race or ethnicity. For him, those who believed in God could not confine faith to church on Sunday morning. Faith had to be lived in the butcher's shop.

We sometimes think our faith in Christ has to be lived in some big way. So we admire the efforts of saints from centuries ago, or parishioners who are extraordinary in their service. However, the good works that are often most beneficial are those that seem as ordinary as scraps of cold cuts. Within all of us are those bits and pieces, seemingly insignificant gifts which, with the grace of God, have the power to nourish others. We need to let Christ bend down, reach in, and draw them out of us.

There was no sign above the counter indicating the two dollar bags were available. Those who needed them knew they were there. The man who offered them this kindness – so beneficial to their lives – was all the sign they needed.

Lord, take the gifts you have given me, no matter how small, and use them so that I may be an example of love.

371

Letting It Go

Monsignor Gregory E.S. Malovetz

"Avoid foolish arguments, genealogies, rivalries, and quarrels about the law, for they are useless and futile." (Ti 3: 9)

It begins innocently. You start to rummage through a drawer. You go down into the basement to look for something. You go to get the luggage out of a closet. Maybe you find what you are looking for; maybe not. You look around that drawer, that basement, or that closet. You look at stuff you had forgotten you had. You find things you weren't looking for. It is all interesting at first, but then comes the question, "Why am I holding on to this stuff?"

I recently experienced that moment. The question led to a massive cleanup and purging of old college papers, birthday cards, sweaters unworn in years, and books I thought I would one day read. Sorted and bagged, they awaited the city of their final destination: a local charity or the dumpster.

Periodically we need to do that kind of looking and cleaning of our interior lives. We do it through the sacrament of reconciliation or through our observance of Lent. The truth is that every day provides the chance for me to ask, "Why am I holding on to this stuff?" Sometimes it is an old bitterness or misunderstanding. Other times it is an attitude of entitlement. How many quarrels or arguments have led us to a place of needing to be right?

We'll think about it tomorrow, we insist. There is no time today. The psalmist prays that we would know our life's shortness and live in the present moment. Jesus comes and begs, "Let go." Let go today of those things that keep your hands clenched in anger instead of open for service. Let go of the past that cannot be changed, so that you may embrace – with the Spirit's help – a future waiting to be lived.

Lord, guide me this day in letting go of all that is useless and futile. I open my hands so that I can make room for your Spirit.

The Work That Is Everything

Monsignor Gregory E.S. Malovetz

*"Let our people, too, learn to devote themselves to good works
to supply urgent needs, so that they may not be unproductive."*
(Ti 3: 14)

They stand there after every Mass. I see them as the procession leaves the sanctuary and we move to greet people at the door. They are of all different ages and sizes. They smile and say hello, but they take their work seriously. They always try to include me in their work. Even though I have seen it already, I am handed a bulletin by one of the young people as I exit to greet the congregation.

The young people who hand out the bulletins after Mass seem to appear magically. I am sure that there is some method or procedure as to how they get chosen. I guess I have forgotten what it is. Each week there are different faces, but always the same enthusiasm and seriousness for the task at hand.

In the life of a parish, one might think an eight-year-old handing out a bulletin is cute, but not essential. Some might think we could just leave them on a table and let parishioners help themselves. Their work is hardly urgent. But it is their faces I remember each week, more than even the contents of the bulletin they try to hand me. Their simple task becomes an important witness to the Gospel message: everyone has some gift that can benefit the community of believers.

We live in a culture that values people for what they do and how much they get done. When asked, "What did you do today?" we are embarrassed to answer, "Nothing." Discipleship is measured not by what you do. It is measured by who you are. There is an urgent need in our society for friendliness, for compassion, and for the willingness to stand with people in a time of need. An urgent need to stand and do nothing but be there. Jesus calls us to a life where the simple task of standing and greeting people is everything.

*Lord, give me the grace I need this day, that I may extend my hands
in friendship and peace.*

The One Who Stands Near

Monsignor Gregory E.S. Malovetz

"I give thanks to my God always, remembering you in my prayers, as I hear of the love and the faith you have in the Lord Jesus and for all the holy ones." (Phlm 1: 4-5)

The cantor invited the congregation to sing while the ushers, armed with baskets, took up the weekly offering. A lovely family came forward bearing the bread and wine for the Eucharist. The altar servers, prompt and attentive, brought the gifts to the altar. While the singing continued, I softly began the preparation prayers. I turned to the altar server, giving her the water cruet to be returned to a side table. Continuing with the prayers, I was aware that she was still standing there, and in low voice she asked, "What?" I indicated everything was fine and returned to pray softly. She held her ground and asked one more time, "What?" I looked at her and asked if something was wrong. Having heard me softly pray, she responded, "I thought you were talking to me." "No," I told her, "I was talking to God."

A life of prayer includes a lot of words. Words that come in the form of requests, worry, concern, questions, and even the occasional complaint make their way into our prayers. It is all part of talking to God. In the talking, we discover the love and the faith that are ours in the Lord Jesus.

Prayer also involves remembering. It is remembering that we do not stand alone. All around us there are people hoping to be noticed and to be heard. Sometimes we are distracted, and do not see they are there in our lives. Sometimes we choose not to see them, fearing their *"what?"* might require more than our prayers.

I was grateful for that young altar server listening to me so carefully, concerned that she might have missed *what* I was saying. She was one of the holy ones, challenging me to listen more carefully so that I do not miss the *who* standing near.

Lord, open my eyes, that I may see your presence in the needs of those who stand near.

The Good in You

Monsignor Gregory E.S. Malovetz

"Your partnership in the faith may become effective in recognizing every good thing there is in us that leads to Christ."
(Phlm 1: 6)

The items traveled easily on the conveyor belt. Seven items in the "twelve items or less" lane. The cashier quickly scanned them while I bagged. She looked confused as she announced the total. Clearly the items were small and not expensive, but my total came to nearly a hundred dollars. We looked at the register tape. A deli sandwich came up as almost fifty dollars. It continued to scan at that price, so she called the manager. I looked at the cashier and joked, "That must be quite a delicious sandwich." She winked at me and replied, "I've eaten this sandwich, and trust me, it's not that good."

It's hard to know sometimes what is really good, what is really important, or what really matters. Our supermarkets are filled with products, and our television has hundreds of channels. All around us there are people who seem smarter, more spiritual, or better looking. In the midst of it all, we may not feel very significant or important.

It is Jesus who says that your life matters. It is easy to focus on the success of others and on our own failures. Jesus sees the gift that is in each of us. He desires that we use that gift to lead others to him. The key to a spiritual life is discovering that there is something unique about you that is a part of God's plan.

Yes, there are people who are holier and more spiritual than we. But you are not an insignificant player in the story of faith. In your life – your relationships, the situations you encounter each day – you have the opportunity to lead someone to Christ. It may be a word, a gesture, or some choice. You may insist someone else can do it better. Jesus wants you to be that someone because he believes you are that good.

Lord, help me to appreciate my goodness. Let my life lead others to Jesus.

A Heart Refreshed

Monsignor Gregory E.S. Malovetz

"I have experienced much joy and encouragement from your love, because the hearts of the holy ones have been refreshed by you." (Phlm 1: 7)

It was a wonderful staff luncheon to celebrate the coming feast of Christmas. The food was delicious, the conversation warm, and the toasts funny and generous. But as the bill was being paid, there was one matter left undecided. The matter of the gift exchange.

Like other offices, our staff members pull a name from a bowl, and then buy a Christmas gift for that colleague. We agree on a price limit, and exchange the gifts before the lunch. The passage of years brought with it the wisdom that none of us needs another gift. We decided to pool our money and give it to a charity. As we finished coffee and dessert, with the money in the center of the table, we suggested different charities. Each seemed worthy of the over three hundred dollars sitting on the table, but none put the money where we wanted it: in the hands of someone in need.

Unable to decide, we called the manager over and inquired about the restaurant's dishwashers. The manager was confused when we asked him to split the money among them. Once he understood, he took the money to the men cleaning our dishes. No one came up to thank us; and none of us wanted or expected it. It was the reaction of our waitress that meant everything. Her eyes were wide; her heart seemed refreshed. As she refilled our coffee, she whispered, "I really like what you all did."

Jesus wanted his disciples to imitate him, not admire him. Jesus loved in a big way, but not in a way that seemed impossible. His disciples could observe the choices he made, and be encouraged that they could live and love the same way.

A waitress served a meal, but received more than a nice tip. I hold fast to the hope that she was encouraged by the love at our table, and is now refreshing another heart made joyful with her love.

Lord, let the gift of my life refresh and strengthen the hearts of all who encounter me this day.

An Urgent Voice

Monsignor Gregory E.S. Malovetz

*"Although I have the full right in Christ to order you to do what
is proper, I rather urge you out of love, being as I am, Paul,
an old man, and now also a prisoner for Christ Jesus."*
(Phlm 1: 8-9)

I remember the first time it happened. I called the home of a family who had experienced a death about a month before. The phone rang several times and then the familiar click, indicating the answering machine was taking over. It was the voice that startled me. It was the voice of the person who had died weeks before. "We can't come to the phone, but if you leave a message and the time you called, we'll get back to you. Have a nice day." It was surprising and comforting at the same time. I left no message.

The voice of Saint Paul surprised and comforted the early Christian churches. Some had met him; some only heard his voice through his letters or his companions. Even in his darkest hour, he raised his voice in gratitude for the nearness of Jesus. Long after he died, right up until today, it is his voice that urges us, out of love, to live for Christ.

A life of faith is never lived in isolation. We need the support and guidance of those who are making the journey of faith. We need the voice of the community that challenges. We need the voice of the community that comforts and supports. We need the voice of the community that says all we do must be a work of love. As part of that community we realize there is power in our voices. We can imprison others with our petty and critical words. We can free them with our words of peace and love.

And then, there are the other voices; the ones who have gone home to the Lord. The uncle who went to daily Mass. The neighbor who constantly thought of others. The grandmother who prayed us through the tough times. We can still hear those voices that urge us to love.

*Lord, in gratitude I recall the memory of the voices that have loved
me and deepened my faith.*

The Gospel That Is Heard

Monsignor Gregory E.S. Malovetz

*"I did not want to do anything without your consent,
so that the good you do might not be forced but voluntary."*
(Phlm 1: 14)

I t seemed like a fascinating but ambitious project. It would rely on the good will and the kindness of individuals to do their part. When my niece was in elementary school, she participated in a project that involved her stuffed bear named Goldie. She sent the bear, equipped with a journal and bag, to someone she knew. They were asked to take the bear with them wherever they went, recording their adventures and including photos in the journal. After a certain period of time they were to send the bear to someone else. There was a date by which the bear was to be returned to my niece. I worried that she might not see the bear again.

The bear did return on the appropriate date. The bear traveled from New York to Montana to California with numerous stops in between. The journal recorded the bear's visit to Germany, France, and Tuscany. The bear had been passed on by the good will of strangers.

The Gospel of Christ has been placed in our hands, as it was placed in the hands of the early Church. Like those early disciples we have set before us a choice. We can allow the Gospel to stay in our homes, unobserved and unheard. Or we can take the Gospel wherever we go. It's not a door-to-door mission with Bible in hand. Rather it is the loving choices, the respectful silences, and the words of hope we offer at a supermarket, on the soccer field, in the board room.

Through the centuries, the spread of the Gospel depended on the willingness of Christians to take the Good News wherever they went. They were not forced; they were empowered by love. The future stands before us. What if the spread of the Gospel depended solely on you?

Lord, wherever my journey takes me this day, let the Gospel be seen in me.

The Heart That Belongs to Christ

Monsignor Gregory E.S. Malovetz

"Yes, brother, may I profit from you in the Lord.
Refresh my heart in Christ." (Phlm 1: 20)

It was a beautiful autumn day when I went to pick her up. I found her in the kennel, barking at everything and nothing. Her honey-colored coat glistened in the morning sun, and soon I found others standing and watching the little retriever. I laughed as I waited for the kennel staff to complete the adoption papers. A woman also amused by the dog's sweetness turned to me and asked, "Excuse me, but are you thinking about getting that little dog?" I smiled and felt my heart expand. "I'm sorry," I replied, "but that *is* my dog."

We can never truly understand how immense the heart of Christ truly is. Throughout the pages of Scripture we see his tenderness and compassion toward others. No one is excluded from the love of his heart. That is the truth of the Gospel. Centuries pass, and Jesus still knows by name every person who comes to him. We belong to him and he delights in our lives.

Sometimes we don't believe that. We are tempted to think that Jesus only observes us when we have sinned or failed. There are some who may even believe they have wandered so far that Jesus has forgotten them. The thrilling truth is this: his heart is open to each of us. He sees our goodness and our sweetness, and he delights in it.

Some find it hard to believe in Christ's love because they have not experienced that kind of love in their own lives. If we are to be his disciples and evangelize the world, then we must expand our hearts. Whose heart could be refreshed this day because you pointed out their goodness? That is the role of the disciple who looks out into the world, with an expanding heart, and says "that is *my* brother; that is *my* sister."

Lord, I believe that your love has made me your own. Send me your Spirit that I may refresh one heart this day.

Brief Biographies of Contributors

Father Lawrence Boadt, C.S.P., is president and publisher of Paulist Press in Mahwah, NJ, professor emeritus of Scripture studies at Washington Theological Union in Washington, DC, and author of *Reading the Old Testament: An Introduction.*

Douglas Bushman is director of the Institute for Pastoral Theology at Ave Maria University. He received his S.T.L. degree from the University of Fribourg, Switzerland.

Father Peter John Cameron, O.P., is the editor-in-chief of MAGNIFICAT and the author of *Jesus, Present Before Me: Meditations for Eucharistic Adoration.*

Father Gary Caster is a priest of the Diocese of Peoria, IL. He is the Catholic chaplain of Williams College in Massachusetts and the author of *Mary, in Her Own Words: The Mother of God in Scripture.*

Father Romanus Cessario, O.P., serves as senior editor for MAGNIFICAT, and teaches theology at Saint John's Seminary in Boston, MA.

Rebecca Vitz Cherico lives near Philadelphia with her husband and three daughters. She teaches at Villanova University and leads the local community of Communion and Liberation.

Father John Dominic Corbett, O.P., teaches classes in fundamental moral theology in the Dominican House of Studies in Washington, DC. He also preaches retreats for laity and religious.

Father Harry Cronin, C.S.C., is a priest of the Congregation of Holy Cross. He is currently professor in residence at the Graduate Theological Union in Berkeley, CA. He is a professional playwright, winner of two Los Angeles Drama-logue awards, and has been produced in both the US and abroad.

Dino Gerard D'Agata is a poet, fiction writer, and translator. He teaches English at Saint John's College High School in Washington, DC.

Father Raymond J. de Souza is the chaplain of the Newman Center at Queen's University in Kingston, Ontario, and pastor of Sacred Heart of Mary Parish in Wolfe Island, Ontario.

Father J. Augustine Di Noia, O.P., is a Dominican priest who works for the Holy See as undersecretary of the Congregation for the Doctrine of the Faith.

Anthony Esolen is a professor of English at Providence College, and a senior editor of *Touchstone Magazine*. He is the translator and editor of *Dante's Divine Comedy*, and the author of *Ironies of Faith*.

Father Peter M. Girard, O.P., is currently chaplain to the Monastery of the Mother of God and professor of homiletics at Holy Apostles Seminary in Cromwell, CT.

Sister Genevieve Glen, O.S.B., serves as prioress of the contemplative Benedictine Abbey of Saint Walburga and as the editor for daily offices for MAGNIFICAT.

Father Donald Haggerty, a priest of the Archdiocese of New York, teaches moral theology and is a spiritual director at Saint Joseph's Seminary in Yonkers, NY.

Father Andrew Hofer, O.P., is studying at the University of Notre Dame for a Ph.D. in theology, specializing in the Fathers of the Church.

John Janaro is associate professor of theology at Christendom College in Front Royal, VA.

Father William M. Joensen teaches philosophy and is a spiritual director to seminarians at Loras College, and is chaplain at Clarke College, all in Dubuque, IA.

Father Joseph Koterski, S.J., is a member of the philosophy department at Fordham University, Bronx, NY, and the editor of *International Philosophical Quarterly*.

Father Roger J. Landry is pastor of Saint Anthony of Padua Parish in New Bedford, MA, and executive editor of *The Anchor*, the weekly newspaper of the Diocese of Fall River.

Lisa Lickona is a home schooling mother of seven. She writes and farms with her husband in McGraw, NY.

Father Joseph T. Lienhard, S.J., teaches patristics in the department of theology at Fordham University and at St. Joseph's Seminary, Dunwoodie; he is translating Saint Augustine's commentaries on the Old Testament.

Monsignor Gregory E.S. Malovetz, a priest of the Diocese of Metuchen, is the pastor of Saint Charles Borromeo Church in Montgomery Township, NJ.

Father Francis Martin is a professor of New Testament at the Dominican House of Studies in Washington, DC, and chaplain of the Mother of God Community in the same archdiocese.

Father James Martin, S.J., is a Jesuit priest and the author of several books, including *Becoming Who You Are* and *My Life with the Saints*.

Sharon Mollerus is an involved grandmother of three living in Minnesota, formerly a college English instructor. She enjoys literature, blogging, and photography.

James Monti is the author of *The Week of Salvation: History and Traditions of Holy Week* and *The King's Good Servant but God's First: The Life and Writings of Saint Thomas More*.

Father Vincent Nagle, F.S.C.B., is a priest in the Priestly Fraternity of the Missionaries of Saint Charles Borromeo and is currently working as a parish priest in Houson, Jordan.

Sister Mary Thomas Noble, O.P., († 2008) was a cloistered nun at the Dominican Monastery of Our Lady of the Rosary in Buffalo, NY.

Dale O'Leary, a mother and grandmother, lives with her husband in Avon Park, FL. She is a freelance writer and author of *One Man, One Woman: A Catholic's Guide to Defending Marriage* and *The Gender Agenda: Redefining Equality*.

Holly Peterson is an educator at Christian Brothers High School in Sacramento, CA, and also an adjunct professor at the University of San Francisco.

Jack Sacco, a graduate of the University of Notre Dame, is an award-winning author living in Los Angeles. His book *Where the Birds Never Sing* was nominated for the Pulitzer Prize.

Father J. M. Sullivan, O.P., is pastor of Saint Dominic's Church and prior of the Dominican Community in Youngstown, OH.

Monsignor James Turro teaches Scripture at Saint Joseph's Seminary in New York and Holy Apostles Seminary in Cromwell, CT. He writes the *Your Word is a Lamp* column in MAGNIFICAT.

Father Richard Veras teaches religion at Archbishop Stepinac High School in White Plains, NY, and is a member of Communion and Liberation. He is the author of *Jesus of Israel: Finding Christ in the Old Testament* and a regular contributor to MAGNIFICAT.

Publisher: **Pierre-Marie Dumont**
Editor-in-Chief: **Peter John Cameron,** O.P.
Senior Editor: **Romanus Cessario,** O.P.
Assistant to the Editor: **Catherine Kolpak**
Administrative Assistant: **Jeanne Shanahan**
Managing Editor: **Frédérique Chatain**
Assistant: **Diaga Seck**
Iconography: **Isabelle Mascaras**
Cover Design: **Anaïs Acker**
Proofreaders: **Sr. Mary Paul Thomas Maertz,** O.P., **Janet Chevrier,** et al.
Production: **Annie-Laurie Clément**

Contributors: **Father Lawrence Boadt,** C.S.P.,
Douglas Bushman, Father Gary Caster, Rebecca Vitz Cherico,
Father John Dominic Corbett, O.P., **Father Harry Cronin,** C.S.C.,
Dino Gerard D'Agata, Father Raymond J. de Souza,
Father J. Augustine Di Noia, O.P., **Anthony Esolen,**
Father Peter M. Girard, O.P., **Sister Genevieve Glen,** O.S.B.,
Father Donald Haggerty, Father Andrew Hofer, O.P.,
John Janaro, Father William M. Joensen, Father Joseph Koterski, S.J.,
Father Roger J. Landry, Lisa Lickona, Father Joseph T. Lienhard, S.J.,
Monsignor Gregory E.S. Malovetz, Father Francis Martin,
Father James Martin, S.J., **Sharon Mollerus, James Monti,**
Father Vincent Nagle, F.S.C.B., **Sister Mary Thomas Noble,** O.P.,
Dale O'Leary, Holly Peterson, Jack Sacco, Father J. M. Sullivan, O.P.,
Monsignor James Turro, Father Richard Veras.

MAGNIFICAT®

THE BEST BUDDHIST WRITING 2009